*Miracles and Extraordinary
Experience in Northern Kenya*

CONTEMPORARY ETHNOGRAPHY
Kirin Narayan and Paul Stoller, Series Editors

A complete list of books in the series is available from the publisher

Miracles and Extraordinary Experience in Northern Kenya

BILINDA STRAIGHT

PENN

University of Pennsylvania Press

Philadelphia

10 9 8 7 6 5 4 3 2 1

Published by
University of Pennsylvania Press
Philadelphia, Pennsylvania 19104-4112

Library of Congress Cataloging-in-Publication Data

Straight, Bilinda, 1964–
    Miracles and extraordinary experience in northern Kenya / Bilinda Straight.
        p   cm.—(Contemporary ethnography)
    ISBN-13: 978-0-8122-3964-5 (alk. paper)
    ISBN-10: 0-8122-3964-4 (alk. paper)
    Includes bibliographical references (p.   ) and index.
    1. Samburu (African people)—Religion.   2. Miracles—Kenya—Samburu District.
3. Death—Religious aspects.   4. Resurrection.   I. Title.   II. Series
BL2480.S235 S73   2007
299.6'85 22—dc22   2006042182

For Paul Adler, who put philosophy and poetry into the mind of a ten-year-old, Homeric Greek into the hands of a fifteen-year-old, and the entire world of being into the heart of the child who became a woman who became a lifelong friend.

And in Memory of Roy Rappaport, who inspired me from the very beginning of graduate school, told me what he thought, taught me that anthropology could ask the hard, human questions, and encouraged me with wonderful earnestness and kindness. Kind words go a long way.

Contents

Author's Note   ix

Part One: Framing Extraordinary Experience: Roving Agencies   1

1. Experience   3

2. Signs   14

3. Nkai   37

Part Two: Fragile Borders

4. Latukuny   69

5. Ŋoki   94

6. Death   115

7. Resurrection   129

8. Loip   153

Conclusion: Immediacies   177

Appendix 1. From the Derridean Gap to Theorizations of   195
Consciousness and Forgetting

Appendix 2. The "I" Verb Stem   215

Notes   219

Glossary   247

Bibliography   253

Index   271

Author's Note

What you are about to read is an extended meditation on human experi-ence that is simultaneously philosophical and ethnographic. I wrote most of this book's early chapter drafts during a second extended (one-year) field stay in 2001–2002. At that time, in the midst of partaking of Samburu experiences, I found myself meeting Samburu philosophical reflections with my own. And I returned, in my mind, to my earlier fieldwork (two years, from 1992 to 1994), when I first became over-whelmed by the daily grittiness, joys, and profound sufferings of others. Thus, those earlier experiences were seeping into these later ones, and my earlier thoughts, readings, and writings were as well. My first response in 2001, then, to being utterly surrounded and profoundly—as in, at the core of my being—affected by my Samburu friends' way of being in the world, was to return to my 1993 musings on magical realism and a dream:

I first discovered Borges in Kenya in 1993. In "The Aleph" Borges compressed the uni-verse into a single point; in "The Book of Sand" he pressed infinity between the pages of an ancient book. In "The Writing of the God" he summed up the universe in forty syllables.[1]

I understood these parables in a particular way because at the age of sixteen I had an oft-recurring dream in which the universe revealed itself to me. Omniscient, omnipresent, it told me everything at once. Afraid that I would lose the revelation upon waking, I had repeated the secret over and over, but all of a sudden it had gotten away before I'd realized. At first, it seemed retrievable, like it was on the tip of my tongue, as if I could reconjure it with a word. But no, it had slipped away like a living thing, leaving just some fantastic feeling in its place.

Then, much later, the universe returned, this time in a dream of my own passing. I dreamed me in several places and times—one in the Middle Ages—and the near and dis-tant in time and place converged in a single death. I dreamed the pain, the receding vision, the voices disappearing around me. And then, I dreamed myself moving toward a total becoming that I knew was total completion. I felt myself dissolving into each individual atom simultaneously, infinite particles carried somewhere, joining with every other in the universe. And in that joining I awoke, knowing that in that death, I would remember nothing and everything.

What I understood by 1993 was that, for my friends in the lowlands in particular, life was often experienced as being at risk of slipping away, and an understanding of the relationship between the living and the dead was at once necessary and occasionally horrifying. At the same time, I recognized what my dreams were telling me: that writing about Samburu experiences, or anyone's experiences including my own, was also about a slipping away, about conjuring something that had just been on the tip of my tongue. So I wrote most of this book in the field, putting stories in as soon as they happened, letting myself be driven along by the many points of wisdom of my Samburu friends as they revealed them to me. And this animal of a book grew. As soon as I started it, though, I knew that I could not separate myself from their experiences, nor could I separate my thoughts from theirs. My thought as a scholar began to mature during those first two years of fieldwork, and there was no going back to a time when I could distinguish my Euro-American ideas from those of my Samburu friends. Do we ever start fieldwork with a clean philosophical and political slate? I do not believe so. What I have written here is a textual culmination of a joint project of illumination.

And that means I have many people to thank, beginning with my Samburu friends. I cannot thank you all enough, and I cannot name every one of you as individuals. I am indebted to everyone in Samburu District I have known from 1992 to the present. In particular, I would like to thank Musa Letuaa for being more than a friend and always my philosophical challenger. I simply cannot praise you enough, Musa. Our 2001 reunion embrace expressed our friendship better than these words, but these words are for you anyway: Thank you. I would also like to thank Timothy Loishopoko and Augustine Lengerded for likewise extending me very warm friendships and for pushing my understandings of Samburu philosophy and experience in profound ways. In addition, I am grateful to Joy, John Letiwa, Jonathan and Paul Lepoora, and John Lesepe for research assistance. I also cherish the memories of Lydia Lemelita, my first research assistant, and Damaris Lalampaa, my research assistant and friend, whose cheerful personality and sweet generosity I shall always miss. Also in Samburu District I would like to thank Adamson Lanyasunya for transcription assistance in the 1990s and for the many kinds of hospitality and assistance he has extended since then. In addition, Barnabas Lanyasunya has been wonderful (as has Lengerded) in transcribing interviews, and Sammy Letoole has just been a joy to interact with.

My hosts also deserve appreciation, and thus my thanks go out to Lekeren (in the highlands) and the members of his family who have made me feel welcome since 2001, including his wives Meruni and Alenii, his sister Yaniko, who has also been very helpful as a research assistant since 2004, and his brother Stimu. As Lekeren has often said, we are one family. My gratitude also goes to Lkonten Lemarash (in the lowlands) and his family—my family—who adopted me as their own in 1992 and have kept me ever since. I cannot name you all, but I want to thank Naliapu (Ɗoto Ropili) Lemarash for her kindness and friendship, including taking care of me and my sons when we were ill: I have felt like a daughter, and I will always remember that night you cared for my son Jen when we were both very concerned and help was a full day away. I want to also thank Namaita (Ɗoto Tampia) Lemarash for hospitality and humor, Naismari Lemarash for putting up with my video camera, Tampia and Narimu for being sweet younger sisters to me, Ropili for lasting friendship with Jesse, Kokoso for being fun, funny, and always trying to be helpful, and yes, Nolwara, I thank you for being the incredible, warm friend that you are. I love you. I would like also to name Lekanapan and his wife for extraordinary hospitality and friendship over the years, and the same goes for Lopeleu Lekupano and his wives. And a special thanks to Lopeleu's father for being a philosopher king. The Lesirayon family also deserve thanks, and Mepukori Lesirayon deserves particular gratitude for carrying the log that became my big calabash that time. A huge thank-you goes to Josephine Nokorod for caring for and loving my children from 1992 to the present and keeping the house together while I did research. In short, I thank you all, including all of you I cannot take more space to name. Then I want to thank Father Francis Viotto for kindly storing my research vehicle, and Father Marco Prastaro for warm conversations and many kindnesses. Finally, although by no means last in my thoughts, I would like to express my gratitude to Carolyn and Lolkitari Lesorogol for endless hospitality and logistical help over the years, including overseeing the building of a house! My thanks to Carolyn as well for a friendship that has meant a lot and for support as a colleague.

I am grateful to the government of Kenya and the Ministry of Education for allowing me to do this research and to the University of Nairobi's Institute of African Studies for affiliation. My 1992–1994 research was conducted thanks to a Fulbright IIE and money from Rackham Graduate School and the University of Michigan Center for Afro-American and African Studies/Ford Foundation. My subsequent research has been funded by the National Science Foundation and Western Michigan University's Department of Anthropology and the

FRACASF fund. I would like to thank my chair, Robert Ulin, for patience with me and the time off I needed to do this research.

In the United States, I have many people to thank; my apologies to anyone I do not name. For very important encouragement at different points along the way, including nudging me to tread water some more just when I thought I'd be swept away by the current, I would like to thank (in alphabetical order) Ruth Behar, Jean and John Comaroff, Judith Farquhar, Kathleen Stewart, and Edith Turner (as well as Edie and Katie for reading parts of the manuscript). Bruce Mannheim and Gracia Clark have also continued to be supportive over the years, and I cannot thank them enough. I am grateful to Neil Whitehead and Akhil Gupta for their helpful comments on material that morphed into Chapter 8, and to Vigdis Broch-Due and her colleagues at the University of Bergen for kind and insightful responses to Chapter 7. Finally, I would like to thank Paul Stoller and two anonymous reviewers for encouraging and helpful comments on the manuscript. I am tremendously grateful to Paul Stoller, Peter Agree, and Penn's Editorial Board for their support of this project, which meant a lot, to Peter Agree for being a great editor, and for the kind and valuable assistance of Laura Young (promotions manager), Carol Ehrlich (copyeditor), and Alison Anderson (project editor).

Everyone needs friends to get a book written, and I have been blessed by them. So in addition to those I have already named, I thank Christopher Sweetapple for being an incredible student as well as a friend of great humor and playfulness, and for reading this manuscript early on. I am also grateful to my student Cleo Gill for the enormous labor of love she put into the images that this book contains. I would have been lost without her. I would like to express appreciation to Sarah Hill for reading parts of this manuscript and for being a good colleague and friend, and to my colleague Laurie Spielvogel for advice and encouragement. Special thanks go to Charles Hilton and Rosario (Charo) Montoya for very warm friendships, support, encouragement, and for commenting on parts of the manuscript. And I am indebted to Jon Holtzman for always being willing to read my work over the years with a critical eye and for doing the real job of co-parenting that has allowed me to write. And yes, I thank my children, all of whom have been a part of the experiences contained in this book, and without whom life and writing would have been quite a bit duller: Thank you, Jesse, Jen, Clare, and William. And to Paul Adler I extend gratitude without end for being my philosopher-friend, my mentor since childhood, and my most trusted critic.

For the sake of those who would like to get on with it, Chapter 1 includes a fairly brief introduction to the philosophical ideas I engage with in this book. For those of you who would like a more detailed expo-

sition of my theoretical project, I have included an essay in Appendix 1.
I hope that many of you read it, and I apologize to anyone who feels I
have buried my theoretical ideas at the back of this book. These ideas
are no afterthought. Consider them dessert.

A Note on Transcription and Pseudonyms

The Samburu language, northern Maa, does not yet have codified transcription or spelling forms. I have followed some fairly standard spell-
ings in many instances and have followed the dialectical pronunciations
of my Samburu friends and acquaintances in others. It is difficult to
reflect the tonal variety of the language in standard written text. One
thing I have done is to use the velar ŋ (uppercase Ŋ) for the sound of
"n" in English "tongue" throughout because I personally find n'g to be
less than pleasing to the eye and confusing.

I have used pseudonyms throughout this book with two exceptions:
my research assistants and famous or well-known Samburu prophets.

Part I
Framing Extraordinary Experience

. . . The leaves,
pressed against the dank
window of November
soil, remain unwelcome
till transformed, parts
of a puzzle unsolvable
till the edges give a bit
and soften. See how
then the picture becomes clear,
the mind entering the ground
more easily in pieces,
and all the richer for it.

—Jorie Graham

Chapter 1

Experience

Death is never experienced as such, is it—it is never real. Man is only ever afraid of an imaginary fear.

—*Jacques Lacan*

July 10, 2003 Reflecting Back. It was December 1993, and we were returning through Swari to our Wamba home. The nurse at the little Swari clinic stopped our vehicle emphatically, asking me to come and see this patient of his, although maybe it was too late. I went inside, past the waiting room, into the simple interior with its plain table. She was there, a tiny girl, maybe eight years old, struggling for breath while her father squeezed a bellows furiously to pump more air into her fragile throat. No oxygen, just a bellows, like fueling a fire. No, perhaps it is too late, the nurse thought now—now that I was staring helplessly at this little father's darling, her mother outside, holding her breath in the comforting arms of kinswomen. No, I said, it can't be too late. Wamba Catholic Mission Hospital was forty minutes away, she had to hold on that long.

The nurse accompanied us outside, his head demonstrating his uncertainty. We seated the father in the rear driver's side seat with his little girl on his lap. Now my four-passenger Suzuki was more than full, with two of my research assistants, one of my sons, myself, and this man with his daughter. Yet a trip to Wamba from here was broadly enticing, and people tried to crowd in as I sat in disbelief—couldn't they see that this little girl was dying, that she needed space, that we needed to get away? No, they couldn't, they crowded in noisily, while the little girl's mother stood by, also wanting to get in though her husband refused her. The moment was loud, terrible, insane, and I wanted to drive away with the door open. I wanted to get away from all those pleading hands.

At last we drove away. We managed a thousand feet, I guess, and then someone told me to stop the car. As soon as the car stopped I could hear the screams and ululations of the little girl's mother and kinswomen down the road. They knew what stopping meant before I did. I turned in my seat to look. The father was still squeezing that pathetic bellows furiously. And the little girl, she was struggling for her breath like some animal was chasing her, and then she began to reach toward me with long gestures. She stretched her arms and squeezed her palms, her eyes asking for something. I couldn't move. She wasn't looking at me, I could see that, and I was absolutely terrified. She kept reaching, grabbing for something for what seemed like hours until finally she got the breath she was working for—one last breath, the loudest breath I had ever heard, an alto growl. And immediately the smell of death was upon us. I never knew until that moment that death had a smell. I cried, I wanted to join the screaming, but I had to act. I had to get out and let the man out of the car—he was on my side. I had to let him escape with his tragic burden. He walked with her to a nearby tree and slumped down, cradling her in his arms. Other men joined him. And the women continued to scream.

December 5, 1993 Original Field Notes.[1] On the way home from Lorok Onyukie on Wednesday a child died in my car. I don't know how to write it except that bluntly. We were stopped in Swari by the government health worker, asking us to carry a dying girl to Wamba Hospital. When I saw her, I thought he was right—that she couldn't make it. But I didn't really *believe*, and I had to try. Her father had taken over the nurse's job of pumping air into her nose and mouth with a little pump (no real oxygen). He held her on the seat behind me, frantically pumping. I started to drive very fast—there was a lot of noise and confusion as we were leaving—Musa actually pushed some people out of the car, and the mother was screaming on my side of the car as we left. We had not gotten far when Musa told me to stop. I watched as her little hands and arms stiffened several times. I knew she was dying. Then she stared, and her father kept pumping. He finally gave up and slowly carried her from the car. I could hear the mother still screaming at the dispensary. The nurse was the first to the car, and it was he who opened the door, saying, "There is no alternative." The father sat with her under a nearby tree and was joined by a group of elders (about ten). Joy walked a bit from the car. I leaned my head against the top of my door frame and cried while Jesse [my son] grabbed me, sobbing out loud (Jen [my other son] was in Wamba) . . . Even now I see her little hands, fingers, eyes, face. Unnecessary (death), and terrible.

The 1980s and '90s were a crystallizing moment in the humanities and social sciences, solidifying the "literary turn," redrawing the terrain of feminist theory/ies, and luring us into an exciting, critically engaging postmodernism that profoundly shook the ground beneath us. Although perhaps most prominent in feminist and cultural studies, the Lacanian Real played a key role in this process that is not always noted, though the current renaissance of material cultural studies is reinvoking it both explicitly and obliquely. Consistent with philosophical assertions that we cannot "know" reality, Lacan's Real seems to offer a space for theorizing the excessive interplay of signs in the unconscious. In the shorthand of use, the Real becomes a convenient placeholder for the multitude of signs that apparently are *all* the world is for us—a multitude of signs open to fictional moves and playful transformations. In contemporary anthropology, the Real—by whatever name—goes without saying because we have conceded that memory is fragile and experience always mediated by signs (even sensuous ones). In contrast, I have not always been satisfied with the Lacanian Real nor with Derrida's play of signs. Likewise, while I have been delighted with the "sensory turn," I have nevertheless been impatient with the tendency to treat the body as a text or else to let sensuousness thumb its nose at theory altogether. How can we take account of experience? How can we recognize the limits of texts and yet read their significance backward—not as traces of loss but as tracks whose permutations are composed of definite shape, soil, and even loose strands of hair? How, in other words, can we stand imagination on its head, reading it as the latest incarnation of sensuous encounter?

In 1994 a close Samburu friend told me the story of a divine encounter: A Samburu *loiboni* (diviner/healer) had reputedly witnessed Nkai (divinity) punishing a woman. Other stories preceded and followed this, of people witnessing divine retribution and even of people seeing Nkai in the flesh. Returning to the field in 2001, I continued hearing these stories, but now I sometimes knew the people who fell into madness, lost family members to freak accidents, and so on—I knew the people involved well enough to know what was happening to them. As I followed these stories more closely I soon understood the subtleties I had missed before.

In a world hanging precariously at the edge, Samburu in the twenty-first century experience death all too often. Yet my concern here is not only with Samburu ways of explaining death; it is about experiencing the passing of people before your very eyes. How do we think it? Where in me has that little girl traveled? What if *I* were to see her again?

While this little girl has not (to my profound sadness) returned, my experience of her death puts the roundest exclamation on reports that *some* dead Samburu children have indeed returned, tugging their burial shrouds behind them, back inside the houses of their mothers. I have spoken with some of these formerly dead and cannot but ask—how do

I describe the miraculous when there are so many witnesses? Is this a trick of memory, of the fantastic imaginary, the play of signs?

For the Samburu I know, death is both terrifying and ordinary. It is a hyena to be chased, a contagion to be cleansed. And yet, as undeniable as death is for those who have been its unwilling witnesses, it has occasionally reversed itself. No wonder that people and divinity wander here and there, moving bodily between heaven and earth, between death and life.

Anthropology is, if nothing else, all about experience—including the seeming incommensurability of experience, although how we make sense of other people's experience has long been a very contentious and complex issue. On this point, some of our anthropological past bears constant repeating—I am thinking of the rationality debates for example, which were by no means resolved with finality, even if we proceed, however tentatively and contradictorily, as if they were.[2] Thus, while every anthropology graduate student learns to examine "truths in context" while recognizing different "cultural logics," the scientific method—itself the product of a lengthy "local" tradition—remains the fulcrum of the anthropological method in both fieldwork and writing.[3] Yet the scientific method itself hinges on a wondrous paradox borne out of the Cartesian cogito: The experience of a scientist is the authority upon which we judge the experiences of others.

As it turns out, then, the importance of the *witness* underlies anthropology as it does both jurisprudence and born-again Christianity. The more reliable the witness the better, the greater number of witnesses the better. Nevertheless, judgments concerning "truth" rely always upon the experience of another, even though the experience of another is always withheld from us, concealed by a veil that the most incredible technologies have not yet succeeded in lifting. We can see within the brain, but we cannot experience the experiences of another. This is a miracle too often examined in other terms. It is for this that so many have searched for the perfect language, that philosophers have lamented the gap, the loss, the subtle trace. In the first decade of the twenty-first century, this likewise remains the Heideggerean Being that ever recedes, the one possession of an/other that cannot be commodified because it cannot be found, and simultaneously the one thing that those who seek justice need to demonstrate: What does it mean to suffer? How does your suffering differ from mine?[4]

This book, like many others, bears witness to the experiences of others here in the first decade of the twenty-first century—the century that is so far heralding a bitter return to enormous inequities between rich and poor even as the privileged are succeeding as never before in segregating themselves from the disenfranchised (see also Comaroff and Comaroff 2000). This book, like many others, also bears witness to experiences that those schooled in the Euro-American tradition often find difficult to understand. And yet, in focusing on Samburu miracles and other extraordinary experiences, I am making a few departures. Although I take note of Samburu engagements with colonialism, postcoloniality, and Christian conversion where they demand attention, I do so with respect to how these forces are sometimes crucial but often beside the point (see also Holtzman 2004). Thus, when Samburu literally and bodily return from the dead—a miracle, not a terrifying occurrence— the Christian tradition is important for placing Samburu presentist understandings even as it bears on Euro-Americans' cultural baggage associated with "resurrection." Nevertheless, even as Christianity has folded itself into resurrection (*apiu*) as Samburu sign, it is important to engage with apiu *as* Samburu sign as fully as possible, and this requires a look away from the features of postcoloniality and global capitalism. Similarly, when I visit and relate the experiences of children claiming to have been bodily taken to the home of divinity and back, the issues of colonial and postcolonial whiteness force themselves upon my consciousness while simultaneously another way of engaging with these Samburu experiences captures my imagination as well.

There are multiple and necessary tellings here (see Morris 2000) along a single theme of extraordinary experiences. These multiple tellings are unified not only by theme, however, but also by an emphasis on experience itself. As I have suggested, experience is an ultimate paradox, *the* ultimate paradox underpinning the scientific method generally and anthropology more peculiarly. Based on her own cultural, biographical, and scholarly experiences, the anthropologist organizes her experiences of the experiences and claims of her interlocutors in an attempt to translate and/or to make a point through them. In beginning this book with my experience of a tragic death, I have already begun to make my point: The miraculous occurs out of the midst of the mundane, and mundane experience is itself miraculous. My understandings of Samburu extraordinary experiences follow in important ways from unbearable, mundane memories of death, beginning with one little girl's. Yet the most mundane of experiences are already miracles to the understanding. Can you feel what I feel, see how I see? Can you see that little girl's death in all of its significance for me—do you remember her last moments because I describe them for you?

We anthropologists write death all the time—whether we experientially witness those deaths or not, whether our readers are moved by them or not. We write our own hauntings, the hauntings of others; we write within the spaces of loss not merely because of the specter of death but because of our belief in the singular inability to transcend ourselves, cross the experiential gap, and experience the experiences of another. And yet, there are some traditions that claim to cross precisely that gap—to reincarnate, to inhabit, to possess, to *be* another. While the very elusiveness of experience once again prevents us from doing other than recounting, analyzing, or poetically engaging these claims, my witnessing of Samburu claims of the extraordinary has sent me on a metaphorical path to understanding experience as being precisely about reincarnation—as one incarnation of experience becomes another. Thus, I engage the extraordinary through an approach to understanding experience and engage experience through the extraordinary.

The experience of another is always numinous, original, and True. Thus, writing against several grains, my claim is that every experience is an origin, an undeniable Truth, an ephemeral choice en route to other possibilities or choices.[5] In working from these claims, I write within the limits of text and sign while pointing beyond them. At the same time, pointing beyond signs, I simultaneously reposition them to move in the direction that semiotics has been heading if it radicalizes itself enough. I offer the term "expansive experience" to overcome the textual and signifying limits of phenomenological experience—limits I will elaborate in the Conclusion. Expansive experience as I define it is experience in all aspects of Being and Becoming—it takes into account not only experience as laid down in memory and enacted through prelinguistic as well as linguistic signs; it takes into account as well the most ephemeral aspects and moments of experience as a process that includes unrealized possibility.

I will borrow a term from the philosopher/logician Charles Sanders Peirce to think through the process of expansive experience to which I am referring. Peirce referred to "prescissing" (and related term prescind) as the "cutting off" that occurs in the act of experiencing a sign. I extend Peirce's arguments to suggest that prescissing occurs all over experience, beginning with the cutting off that necessarily occurs by virtue of our very physiology. Bodies are not texts here, although we reflect upon them as if they were. Likewise, experience is never simply reducible to physiology, and yet the prescissing that occurs by way of our physiology is crucial to experience and the imagination—and these are simultaneous and multidirectional processes. For example, when we see, processes occur within our own retinas that eliminate "noise" in the visual field. This is one way we prescis by way of our physiology, one way we cut off elements of seemingly infinite information. And yet, our prior experiences (including evolutionary ones) shape the retina itself and the cutting off, delimiting the choices it makes. Vision as an experiential process is already cultural. The prescissive cuttings of experience happen all over us and through us, from our cutting reality by way of our physiology to our "choice" to focus on one aspect of a dialogue, to interpret a text or a moment in one way or set of ways rather than another.

This is a technical explanation for the enculturating aspects of experience we anthropologists take for granted, but it has more radical implications. I argue that in prescissing we reduce a seemingly infinite world—meeting world by way of an *acculturated physiology*—before exploding it in a potentially infinite world of signs of our own making. In that process, our expansive experiences of the world may not even be laid down in verbalizable memory, and yet in them we touch world and it touches us in ways that do not utterly disappear. Instead, those experiences become like phantasms, haunting our brain's architecture with the molecular tracks of a smell that merges with a feeling, moving literally through us, reincarnating from the infinitude of world to the imaginary of signs. Those signs, I suggest, whether verbal or mere hints of feeling, bear tangible signatures of their experiential processes of becoming. To remember a face is to conjure a shape that can be "seen" in the firings of neurons lighting up an MRI—we cannot see what another person sees, but we can witness a vision of a spectral presence that contains some aspect of the very form of that face.[6] This is radical intersubjectivity. These are strange hauntings within the mundane. And moreover, these are invitations to consider that the imagination is *real* in crucial ways.

The experience of the death of little girls haunts many of us. The smell of death tangles up our neurons in ways both scientific and profound—bringing the dead within us. This is my way of making sense of extraordinary claims that are yet believable to my Samburu interlocutors. This is how I understand death as a contagion, visions of the dead in the flesh as authentic experience. And resurrection? I have spoken to the resurrected. That experience is again its own undeniable proof. Writing text about what is beyond text, writing possibility against impossibility, writing tradition within this particular historically dynamic moment, I touch my fingers to keyboard with fingers that have touched Samburu friends and place my words in a here that is nowhere and anywhere.

The Book's Organization

The book is written in two segments. Part One, "Framing Extraordinary Experience," continues from this introductory chapter to Chapter 2, which weaves a detailed ethnographic introduction with a continuing engagement with the theoretical issues at stake. Chapter 3 introduces Nkai, Samburu divinity, a crucial agentive force in everyday Samburu lives and source of recurring miracles. Part Two, "Fragile Borders," begins with two chapters (4 and 5) that examine the extraordinary in the mundane through cannibal persons, cannibalized commodities, and profoundly intersubjective occurrences. Chapter 6 sets the ethnographic stage for the blurring of the boundaries of life/death that Chapters 7 and 8 describe—as some people bodily resurrect, returning from death to resume their lives, while in their turn the dead sometimes make visits to the living. Chapter 9, the book's Conclusion, continues the dialogue concerning experience as about reincarnated, transubstantiated overcoming, and the experience of another as always extraordinary.

In this first chapter I have begun to develop a notion of what I am calling "expansive experience," framed from within a single child's death. In describing expansive experience I am, on the one hand, considering experience itself as a mundane miracle to our understanding that demands constant and renewed philosophical contemplation while, on the other hand, offering Samburu miracles and extraordinary experiences as examples that illuminate a very real, cross-cultural need to understand the inexplicable. In seeking answers to the most strange and difficult dimensions of human experience, we travel the length of a paradox together: Experience, whether mundane or extraordinary, is always simultaneously culturally specific "all the way down" and yet "grounded" in shared aspects of our humanity that resist our attempts to pin them down. Human experience is at once obvious and mundane, elusive and extraordinary.

Chapter 2 begins the book's ethnography by weaving between descriptive vignettes about the interanimated world of Samburu and Samburu daily life in the twenty-first century more broadly, examined through a continuing dialogue concerning signs, text, and experience. In this context I discuss the Samburu concept of *aduŋ* ("cutting"), which recurs in Samburu collective understandings of life's rhythms even as it surfaces in the metaphors of experience I draw upon in this book. For the Samburu, aduŋ is an act of creation *within* creation. It does not impose Kantian order on chaos, but neither does it merely organize unruly sense data. Like Peircean prescissing, Samburu cutting simultaneously divides what already exists and creates something more in the process. "Cutting" will continue to surface implicitly and explicitly in the book's dialogic encounters between Samburu twenty-first-century experiential realities and anthropology's twenty-first century understandings of experiences as viewed by one anthropologist.

Having now gained some understanding of Samburu cultural logic, in Chapter 3 readers travel with me to my meeting with a Samburu child prophet whom many Samburu believe to have bodily visited Nkai's (divinity) home. I place her claims, as she narrated them to me and to other Samburu, in the context of other Samburu children like her and against colonial and postcolonial racial and gendered Euro-American understandings of African divinities like Nkai. Likewise, I introduce here a notion of the "in-between of the in-between," of matter (and divinities) more than "out of place," in keeping with the book's evolving engagement with a reincarnating, experiential reality that involves not only "cutting" but also unruly movement, as it jumps about elusively before being pinned down in the signs of thought.

Having introduced some of the logic of cutting underpinning interanimated, extraordinary occurrences in Chapter 2, and the recurring miraculous appearances of Nkai in the context of modernity in various of its forms in Chapter 3, Part 1 closes. Part 2 begins with Chapter 4's focus on unspeakable thefts of sticks, calabashes, and other objects that behave as persons. Following the logic of theft, I invoke a discourse about loss that tends to surface in discussions about global commodities but that in this case attends on objects meant to circulate only in carefully prescribed and noncommodified ways. When these objects are put into illicit circulation, more is at stake than what those objects might signify to Euro-American understandings: The sale of objects that are both things and persons is a form of cannibalized destruction that entails not only transformations between persons but the overtaking of one person by another, affirming a radical intersubjectivity that the Samburu experience as extraordinary and yet possible.

Chapter 5 continues an examination of radical intersubjectivity, examining Samburu *ŋoki*—something like a living entity and unpropitious state, created out of the wrongs humans inflict on one another. In trying to pin down and understand—from my Euro-American perspective—this changeling butterfly that metamorphoses ceaselessly as it cleverly devours humans and animals, I recall discussions I began in this chapter and in Chapter 2 about the relationship between word and world and between reality, experience, and subjectivity. Through vignettes about ŋoki's occurrences and a famous Samburu cannibal story used to explain it, I describe the ways in which ŋoki eludes all grasp, as it cleverly animates but also *becomes* creatures and objects, serving as a metaphor for wrongdoing while simultaneously enacting suffering in the world. Every occurrence of ŋoki is both fantastic and abject, a unique and perfect example of the paradox of experience as a cannibal that both swallows and partly becomes its own past.

In Chapter 6 I describe Samburu understandings of death, beginning with the description of a troubling murder. Here, ŋoki and death come together, and in exploring this incident I describe as well Samburu experiences of death as moments that require heightened attention to aduŋ ("cutting"). In suggesting that cutting death apart from life is the ultimate cut, the poignant division that haunts Samburu as they move through the process of living, I also assert that death is not easily cut. It has its own contagion and a stench that proliferates in recognizable ways—so that, in Samburu experience, death is most horrifying in that it *spreads*.

Having explained the rules for separating death from life and the dead from the living, in Chapter 7 I relate first- and second-hand accounts of people who have defied that separation by bodily returning to life. Setting these experiences in the context of Samburu engagements with the doctrine of Christian resurrection, as well as practices relating to European vampire beliefs and contemporary anthropological treatments of organ donation, I suggest that Samburu resurrection invites a reexamination of both Samburu understandings of death and Euro-American ones. While many contemporary Muslims and Christians continue to debate whether resurrection will be bodily as well as spiritual, medieval European understandings of resurrection as well as fears of the undead turned on notions of matter and spirit that contradicted Cartesian dualist logic. Contemporary debates on the subject of organ donation also trouble clean dichotomies about what American death is, and I suggest that Samburu experiences of miraculous resurrection provide a rich comparative field at the same time that they upset the clean divisions that would ideally characterize Samburu life. Here, it is the overwhelming undeniability of extraordinary experiences that forces Samburu to explain the in-between of the in-between.

Chapter 8 examines a set of unruly postdeath phenomena Samburu refer to as *loip*, as well as narratives about visiting the dead as told by Samburu near or back from death. In attending to these wanderings across life and death, I conclude this final ethnographic chapter with accounts exemplifying the fragile borders between life and death as Samburu (and others) experience them, in keeping with experience itself as a process that does more than define itself by its margins: It overtakes them in the continual (re)forging of subjectivity.

In the Conclusion I reintegrate crucial points about experience, subjectivity, and life generally as lived through its transubstantiating, reincarnating edges. While embracing the popular notion of ethnography as a process of translation, and phenomenological ethnographies as descriptively beautiful and evocative accounts of experience, here at the end I gently nudge phenomenological and sensory approaches, disagreeing, for example, that some narratives are closer to "prelinguistic" experience than others. I take both prelinguistic and linguistic signs to be *metaphors* of the process of experience, a process I characterize as fundamentally about blurred edges and reincarnation between different kinds of experience. Yet, while experience and memory are as elusive as Samburu "souls," I argue for the ethical importance of affirming experience and its memories as partaking of Truth, even if experience transubstantiates into signs in what has been called the Lacanian (imaginary) Real. I argue that this is a crucial affirmation in an era of "anything goes" flexible accumulation, when the insurmountable act of teasing event from imagination, significance from triviality, can sometimes allow suffering to be lost amid the play of interpretations and signs. Imagination can be liberatory or it can tighten the hegemonic grasp that privileges privilege in the discourses that circulate. In this respect, my book is an introduction rather than a completed argument, offering an alternative trope to the flexible play of signs and commodities. From here, a focus on mundane experience—as already extraordinary—is needed after the celebration of miracles and enchantment. For that reason, I end as I began, with the death of a little girl who died needlessly, because in the end, most Samburu do not resurrect.

Chapter 2
Signs

Let me catch you unaware like a clairvoyant dream that appears in quiet languages. The gazelles shake their heads, shake them this way and again—and you know something. The cows shuffle in the rose-gray light of dawn—and you know something. Even the birds have ways you recognize. And the beetles chirrup a signifying rhythm as you lie sleeping, just preparing to dream. This is the way of Nkai (divinity). This is one way of sensing the life of the universe.

The Language of Nkai

November 9, 2001. I am with Rereita Lemeteki, a prominent Samburu loiboni.[1] I am awed by him, by his ability to read Nkai's words everywhere, in everything around him. It was only recently that I have learned that some Samburu can understand the language of particular animals. I know that some understand birds, others cows, and some even understand hyenas. One Lkileku man I know recalled a man of the Lterito generation who knew the language of hyenas.[2] "And the hyena is saying, it is saying I am going to eat that one [person]" (Lentiwas interview 2001). The hyena's is a dreadful language, announcing impending death. The words of other animals, though, like birds, cows, and crickets, can predict good things as well as terrible ones. It is quite common for Samburu to understand the language of animals. Yet no one before Rereita Lemeteki has been able to understand the language of every animal. His *naibon* ("loibon ability") is great—and increasing—because his ancestors used their naibon to help but never to harm. This is Lemeteki's own explanation, but it is one also corroborated by everyone with whom I have discussed the subject.

Lemeteki lies awake at night, listening to the crickets chirping in the house, and he knows what Nkai is saying to him. On a path as he walks, he meets gazelles and jokes with them.

So I even ask a Thompson's Gazelle, can you let me come closer? And it tells me I cannot "because you are a nuisance." Finally, it does agree, so it just talks to me while it is there. And it doesn't agree for me to come closer to it, because I say, "Do you agree if I come and touch you?" "No, no, you will bother me. It is a mistake if you come near me." Finally, I just love and leave it, because it is true that if I come near it like that, it is a mistake. So as such, it is just the truth. It is Nkai who is in all those things, it is Nkai who talks. (Lemeteki interview, November 9, 2001)

When people come to ask for his professional advice, Lemeteki sometimes asks his own goats for the diagnosis and solution to the problem before him. He does not use an *nkidoŋ*, a gourd calabash with stones and other divination tools inside, like many loibonok. He is a *loibon le nkwe*, a loibon of the head. Nkai speaks to him through the particular turning of a goat's head, the way it scratches its leg, through the sounds of the crickets, and so many other things. He does not need to divine by throwing objects. He simply knows what Nkai is expressing through Nkai's own creation.

Divine Representations

While Lemeteki's reading of goats and crickets might typically, in Euro-American terms, be relegated to the "mystical," Samburu do not divide experience in this way. Rather, Lemeteki's ability to read the turning of a goat's head belongs to practical experience, in this case an inherited skill and also one given by Nkai in a world in which everything both proceeds from Nkai and simultaneously operates according to "obvious" (for Samburu) principles. To continue the metaphor I introduced in Chapter 1, these (to me) extraordinary communications between humans and Nkai via the natural world are an everyday part of how Samburu precissively experience.

In Chapter 1 I mentioned prescissing as a conceptual tool for considering expansive experience simultaneously within and beyond the limits of signs and textuality. *Prescissing is the process by way of which we reduce the potentially infinite we are in contact with in world to the cognizably finite, the ground of those potentially infinite experiences in brute and thoughtful being in the world.* This is not a Kantian constitutive process whereby we use our a priori categories (or neuronal structures) to form associations, imposing form on an inchoate world. Rather, the process of prescissing is a reduction by way of our human physiology in combination with a lifetime of previous, culturally inflected experiences. That the world is unmanageably vast or so far incomprehensibly mysterious does not make it inchoate—we do not impose logos on chaos. Our signifying understandings are based—at some point in their biography—in the real world of which we are a part, with its own dynamism.

As it touches on signs, my approach bears on that of Webb Keane

(1997) (another admirer of Peirce) in his *Signs of Recognition*. My use of Peirce is a bit different from Keane's, however, particularly as it concerns experience. For example, Keane highlights Peirce's requirements that objects must have qualities independent of their meaning and that representations (one could say representamen here) must have real causal connections to their objects. He does so in order to argue that representations are "entities with their own, particular, formal properties . . . and as kinds of practice, [are] distinct and yet inseparable from the full range of people's projects and everyday activities" (8). He continues, suggesting that his book "works at the unstable boundary at which the 'symbolic' and the 'material' meet, reinforcing or undermining one another." While I agree with Keane that representations are inseparable from daily life, I disagree that object-signs have formal properties clearly distinguishable, except heuristically. I think that in some ways Peirce got it wrong, or at least his intentions are less than clear. To the extent that anything has formal properties of its own, we are dealing with an improbable essence rather than a reality that is more elusive than that, and one that changes from moment to moment. This is the case whether we are referring to the reality outside our so-called human boundaries or the reality of our world of thoughts.

There is not merely an unstable boundary. Instead, everything is unstable, transubstantiating from moment to moment, from tree now to tree with its leaves blown by a passing breeze and seen by me and differently by you, and so on. In that respect, there is no formal or original at all—I can agree with Derrida here. Yet, contra Derrida, there are also no copies. There is an infinite world of little paradoxes moving along and changing with respect to themselves and one another. And those little paradoxes are real. There is no infinite play here (see Appendix 1). And again, there is no symbolic and no material, except in the language of Euro-American folk and academic theory, where it often gives us an approximation of something, though perhaps not always of the thing we are after.

This is perhaps what Keane himself (as well as others writing in this genre) is after in highlighting "materiality," in arguing, for example, that "objects are not sign-vehicles alone" (66). Yet this materiality is not captured by Peircean object-signs but rather at the horizon of our experience of a world of things we suppose to exist independently of "the vagaries of me and you" (Peirce 1958: 69) and the *process* of signification that Peirce describes. On the one hand, the objects Keane describes are already signs, even if they can also serve—in a transformed state—as objects in other signs (see Appendix 1). On the other hand, whether as representamen-signs, object-signs, or signs of signs, these signs include a history of contact with world—and that history should not be minimized. It has efficacy. I am reminded of E. Valentine Daniel's attempts to deal with signs in violence, signs that trigger, allow, and re-cognize violence, a context in which the reductive process of prescissing has poignant meaning. Contact with world here can be brutal, and the selecting/forgetting process can be pointed: "—the most effective metaphors are lean and can be mean. Metaphors wrench words from their context. Metaphors and mimicry employ the iconic function only to index, to point, to throw into clear relief" (1996: 102).

Returning to Keane's thoughtful discussion, allow me to continue to push his position a bit farther. Recall his important point that representations are "inseparable from the full range of people's projects and everyday activities" (8). Signs are, indeed, always inseparable. To be more precise, as objects (object-signs), signs potentially contain within themselves the history of everything—every little prescissing, thoughtful, and intersubjective experience that brought them into being.[3] Signs in their triadic fullness are an act of communion that cannot be separated from intersubjective practice insofar as the interpretant—whether in neurons, thoughts, or dialogic encounters with texts, divinity, and world—is irreducibly part of that sign. We are contact with world, we make world as it is for us through our being in it, and we share world. In that sharing, we make world again and again, such that translation—as a making of world—is possible (see Daniel 1984; Mannheim and Tedlock 1995; Straight 2006 for another formulation of making worlds through encounter).

Like Keane (as well as a number of anthropologists grappling recently with the challenge of describing worlds of experience),[4] and admiring the elegance and nearness of Keane's elucidations of Anakalangese fragile "representations," I am attempting to capture the *ephemeral, excessive character of being in the world that signs simultaneously succeed and fail in conveying*. Moreover, while Keane is correct to "avoid privileging words or things or performances a priori" (21), I disagree with his decision to focus on representations to accomplish this because they cannot, by definition, go far enough to describe what I am referring to as the transubstantiations of experience. Signs in the Peircean sense I am using them are neither exclusively linguistic, nor gestural, nor even exclusively communicative in the narrow sense. *They are the tool and the action by which we move through and make sense of world.* They do not present world in another form but rather *are* an aspect (an aspect in Peircean Thirdness) of our being in the world at another moment, at every moment. Thus, the storied signs of experience are *not* fiction but, rather, complex, multilayered signs containing their own history within them, and that history includes contact with world.[5] Even if we cannot remember the moment of contact, the notion of expansive experience acquiesces in its occurrence and in its efficacy as it transubstantiates into and through every experiential moment, leaving its traces in the signs we can and do hold. I will return to expand upon my arguments here, but first let me offer up more of my understandings of how Samburu meet world.

Powerful Genealogies

A gray dove was flying through the Mombasa air where a Samburu man was temporarily living, and although it had a particular purpose, as it turns out, this was probably not apparent to observers at first. When it flew into a pub and landed on a table where several Samburu men were drinking their beer, however, it became obvious to some people that the dove had come for a reason. A prescient man who stood nearby shouted at the table's occupants to get away from the bird, don't touch it, just get up and move away quickly. Most of the men did so immediately, but one drunken man by the name of Leŋwesi picked up the dove and threw it against the wall. The gray bird slid down the wall into unconsciousness. Nevertheless, it had accomplished the desires of the unscrupulous professional (probably a practitioner similar to a loiboni but from another ethnic group) who had sent it. Leŋwesi was soon informed of his error and of the fact that there was no remedy. He would either die or become insane so that someone's client would be cleansed of a wrongdoing or helped with whatever had motivated him or her to seek out this special service. As it turned out, Leŋwesi was involved in a car accident the same day, and he was the sole survivor. Rather than negating the professional's project, however, Leŋwesi's survival may even have helped bring it to fruition. A number of Samburu link his subsequent and continuing insanity to that event in Mombasa, and although he has visited several loibonok, none so far have found a cure.

As I mentioned earlier in this chapter, Lemeteki told me (and others confirm) that he only uses his skills to heal, never to harm. As he and many others have likewise told me, however, there are many other loibonok who do not mind killing another Samburu if it will save the life of the client who is compensating them in money or livestock.[6] Such loibonok may send people with deadly little bundles to sneak into the possession of the person whose death or insanity (social death) will save their own lives, or may have them ask for something belonging to the person that they can use for the job. Alternatively, as in the case of Leŋwesi, many non-Samburu practitioners (whom Samburu may consult) may send other creatures to do the job. Often, they send the creatures one would least expect—little things like flies or medium-size ones like doves. Part of their gift as healing practitioners is that they can communicate with some of these creatures, instructing them to go here or there. Like most Samburu with special skills, loibonok who kill by "remote control" (as some of my educated Samburu friends phrase it) demonstrate the duality of their office. They can heal, but they can also harm. And in harming, in fact, they will also be attempting to heal—by simultaneously augmenting one life with another and sending away one death with another. In so doing, the loiboni will have acted appropriately to separate death from life, but he will also have sacrificed another life in the process.

Samburu society is organized along several axes, of which the ageset system (which I discuss below) is dominant but not exclusive. Marriage, clan, and maternal and paternal kinship ties cross-cut one another to guarantee one's place and shape one's behavior. Membership in each category or status is further expressed by, and performed through, specific clothing and adornment patterns, food prescriptions and taboos (on food see Holtzman 1996, 2001, 2002, 2003), and a seemingly limitless array of ritual observances and inherited skills unique to each family. Thus, there are specific clans and lineages known for producing naibon—an inherited set of skills variously expressed in the form of communicating with Nkai (the Samburu understanding of divinity), prophesying, predicting outcomes of livestock raids, and divinatory healing. Like Lemeteki, men who have naibon are referred to as *loibonok* (plural).[7] Occasionally, a woman also has naibon and might be referred to as an *nkoiboni* (singular), as a woman loiboni, or simply as a woman who communicates with Nkai.

There are also *laisi*, families with a powerful gift for blessing and cursing. Samburu tend to have an ambivalent attitude toward laisi, as they also do toward loibonok. In both cases, the fact that the members of such families can harm people as well as help them has something to do with this ambivalence. However, in the case of laisi, the matter is complicated further by the dangers attendant on marrying laisi. If laisi are at times despised as well as respected (or despised for the same reason as they are respected) they are also highly sought when particular blessings are needed, just as loibonok are sought when their special skills are required.

Loibonok and laisi are not the only Samburu with special, two-edged skills. With the exception of *lairupok* (masculine noun) and *nkairupok* (feminine noun), who cause misfortune by clandestine or mysterious means solely in order to harm, almost every family has some sort of gift. They may have, for example, a gift for communicating with particular animals, for healing or harming people with sticks or fire, and so on. Depending on the skill they possess, members of various families can be specifically sought out if there is a problem that their unique abilities will remedy, but if provoked they can use the same means to injure or even kill. Some families "have fire," for example, and likewise can protect or hurt by means of it. More than protecting, they can even speed the healing of a burn victim. Families "with elephants" can communicate with these great and powerful creatures, beckoning them to kill someone or asking them instead to move benevolently out of the way. Several Samburu I know (including educated ones) say they have themselves seen people talk to elephants in the Samburu language, and the elephants respond (through action). It is difficult to think of something that someone cannot somehow communicate with, from sticks and fire to flies and ticks or goats and elephants. In some cases, as with Lemeteki, people can actually discern the language of an animal, while in many other instances, people use various methods to cajole an animal or command an object to act.

Variations in inherited skill and ritual observance are telling indications of a paradox of Samburu identity. In the 1980s, a number of scholars of East African pastoralists suggested on the one hand, that movement between ethnic groups had been fluid prior to the colonial period (Sobania 1991), while, on the other, pastoralists like the Samburu tended to define themselves in categorical contradistinction to their nonpastoral "others" (Galaty 1982, 1986; Waller 1985). Noting contemporary continuities in these trends, Galaty and Waller concluded that pastoralist identities are fluid and context-dependent but that nonpastoralists are understood against an idealized (pastoralist) self.

While accurate in many respects, this notion is complicated by the fact that scholars have also recognized a variety of groups that inhabit an in-between location at the edge of pastoralism rather than at its center (see Herren 1991; Kratz 1994). Samburu Ltorrobo for example, are hunter-gatherers, many of whom have acquired livestock and sometimes intermarried with Samburu. Likewise, Samburu Lkunono are a blacksmith caste whom other Samburu consider to be inferior while still regarding them as Samburu. Moreover, these marginal statuses have proliferated with the advent of formal schooling, Christianity, and town life (Straight 1997a, b). Samburu place each of these groups at varying degrees of Samburu "purity" while still conceding their identity as Samburu. Thus it would seem that, rather than defining themselves against their others while moving fluidly between ethnic groups, pastoralists like the Samburu inhabit fairly fixed positions within overlapping circles of "cultural purity."[8]

However, cultural purity is not determined solely by blood, or rather, not by blood in the Euro-American understanding of the term. It is determined by one's status as a member of a Samburu family—a status that can be acquired by living with and marrying "pure" Samburu.

(Through such actions, their blood mixes—see Straight 2005b.) Thus a "pure" Turkana married by a Samburu or adopted by a Samburu family becomes a Samburu by living, eating, and performing ritual observances with their Samburu family. And although an adopted Samburu cannot hold leadership positions, nine agesets (approximately four generations) staying with Samburu erases even those limitations. Thus, a pure Samburu is not simply born but made through daily practice and residence over time.

This distinction is important in understanding the variety of practices and skills particular Samburu families perform. In most if not all cases, distinctive skills and ritual observances are recognized as stemming from a family's ancestry in other ethnic groups (thus dividing them from other families), but this in no way diminishes one's claims to being a pure Samburu. Most laisi for example, are of Rendille origin, and other Samburu hold a certain ambivalence toward them even as they acknowledge their purity.[9] Samburu do not necessarily regard nonlaisi families of Rendille origin with the same uneasiness, however. There are families who practice a ceremony called *sorio*, and though of Rendille origin, many of these families are considered to be the oldest and purest Samburu. Additionally, some of the most prominent loibonok families originate from Maasai and Laikipiak clans, which again in no way diminishes their status as pure Samburu.

Thus, variations in inherited skill, adornment style, and ritual observance serve to unify families, even as such distinctions continually remind Samburu that people, like cows, are strongest when they are multicolored. Thus, adoption and intermarriage do not reduce purity—insofar as purity is acquired over time—but often strengthen it instead.

The genealogical distinctions that separate individual families, lineages, subclans, and clans from one another are consistent with a broader and conceptually significant logic structuring Samburu experience—a logic of division that has shaped my own thought in important ways. Thus, even as I theorize expansive experience using Euro-American scholarly metaphors, I likewise slip in and out of the theories by which Samburu organize experience.[10] If we limit the world by way of our physiological, neuronal, and symbolic forgettings, Samburu for their part nod to the reality of cuttings, creating their social and symbolic worlds through division. Samburu "cuts" are crucial to health and life itself—as in cutting girls apart from women (a "cut" made through clitoridectomy but also through beads, clothing, and behavior);[11] cutting every age, gender, and generation class apart from every other; and above all, cutting death apart from life. In an incisive discussion of Maasai beadwork, Corinne Kratz and Donna Pido have eloquently summed up the crucial importance of cutting (referring to it as a "cultural attitude") in ways that largely pertain to the Samburu as well:

> Maasai associate cuts in an ornament with natural and cultural phenomena like slashes in a piece of roasting meat, breaks in a line of cattle or people, or the short interruption when a Maasai woman fills a cup by pouring a little milk, stopping, and then pouring again to fill it up. A general cultural attitude unites these different "cuts": nothing should be continuous and unbroken. Maasai deliberately "cut" beadwork patterns and activities such as pouring, because to create pure color fields or a continuous milk flow would seem to claim the purity and power attributed only to God. (Kratz and Pido 2000: 53)

In their own references to cutting (aduŋ), the Samburu emphasis is not on the act of cutting itself but on the vital divisions (separations) and shared categories of persons or things it creates. Samburu aduŋ can be a radical creative act—creating men out of boys, women out of girls, and the dead out of and apart from the living. In the midst of this enactment of subjectivity, however, crossings between both things and persons can occur—including terrifying or wondrous crossings between the dead and the living.

A Theory of Miracles

During a second major field season spanning twelve months in 2001 and 2002 (and returns in the summers of 2003, 2004, and 2005) I attempted to learn as much about Samburu ethnophilosophy as I could, including engaging in extended discussions about what, if anything, Samburu believe happens after death. In one of those unexpected moments of ethnographic epiphany, one woman abruptly asserted that she had died once and come back to life. My attention was, of course, immediately captured. As she related her fantastic story, she made it pointedly clear that Nkai was responsible for her *apiu*—revival, resurrection, return from death. Was this a near-death experience? Spontaneous resuscitation? As far as she was concerned—and this proved to be a Samburu trope—this was an amazing/astonishing occurrence (*nkiŋasia*), possible because Nkai enacted it.

   Academics in the twenty-first century are out of the habit of reporting on resurrections.[12] Zombies, witchcraft, charismatic healings, even reincarnation, yes, but resurrection from the dead? That term lost its currency in the transition to the modern period, as I will discuss in Chapter 7. Yet the claim that Nkai raises people from death is a common one, and even if the occurrence itself is relatively rare, I have managed to fill several notebooks about it narrated by those who experienced or witnessed it as well as by those who got the story second- or third-hand. I have not chosen to write an entire monograph on this phenomenon, however, but rather to include it as one of many aspects of experience that Samburu themselves perceive as both extraordinary and possible. For the Samburu, the movement between the mundane and the extraordinary is continuous and seamless, because the majority of Samburu continue to experience the world as one enacted by and through Nkai.[13]

As Jean and John Comaroff have clarified with precision and intriguing detail (1991, 1997), the Christian message European missionaries brought to Africa was inseparable from a suite of insidious cultural assumptions. Those cultural assumptions included an acceptance of science as true in ways that impinged on indigenous explanations of experience, and in this Samburu were no exception, as both Catholic and Anglican missionaries frequently challenged Samburu explanations of Nkai's presence on empirical grounds while offering an equally fantastic alternative. Nevertheless, Samburu have continually and actively engaged in repartee with Catholic, Anglican, and various secular European forms of knowledge, sometimes in ways that, ironically, would make sense to one theologian in particular whose influence on European Christian thought has endured. In an intriguing book on medieval miracles, Benedicta Ward argues that "For Augustine, the mechanics of miracles were clear. They were wonderful acts of God shown as events in this world, not in opposition to nature but as drawing out of the hidden workings of God within a nature that was all potentially miraculous" (Ward 1987: 3). In a footnote, Ward offers this direct quote from Augustine: "For how can an event be contrary to nature when it happens by the will of God, since the will of the great creator assuredly is the nature of every created thing? A portent therefore does not occur contrary to nature but contrary to what is known of nature" (Augustine *de Civitate Dei*, 21.8, quoted in Ward 222 n 5).

While most Euro-American academics, including me, feel uneasy at the thought that people are returning from the dead while lying under a tree far from medical intervention, and we contemplate what logical or empirical error has been committed, Samburu experience apiu, like other unusual events, as taken-for-granted evidence of Nkai's presence. Rather than attempting to reconcile these points of view or explain what indeed I cannot explain without a medical team stationed for up to four days at the scene of every Samburu mortuary ritual, I have chosen instead to read both the Euro-American and the Samburu mundane by way of the miraculous. I have chosen, that is, to take several extraordinary phenomena as thought experiments for considering the continuing possibility of experience itself as something worthy of wonder. The extraordinary phenomena I consider include not only resurrection, not only substantive transformations between people and between people and things, but the apparently mundane witnessing of others' lives, particularly instances of suffering and death that have profoundly affected my thought. I self-consciously (and no doubt unconsciously) move between Samburu and Euro-American ways of knowing, and in that movement, this book is an intimate portrait of my field experiences, as I have become the medium in ways that are typical of anthropologists though not always transparent.

Let me consider for a moment the sort of medium I am. Judith Farquhar (2002) has lamented that "most anthropologists have continued to write (or at least teach) as if bodies and texts were two quite separate levels of being." To the contrary, she writes, "Meaning is not dualistic, it does not refer to a deeper ideal stratum of forms; rather, significance is intrinsic to material life" (8). Unfortunately, "one cannot recover in ethnographic prose the phenomenal fullness of any bodily act" (9), and thus Farquhar will leave aside the "illusory" and direct her project about mundane bodily experience to an embodied reader in order to create a "shared pretext of bodies" (10). As should be clear by now, I share many perspectives with Farquhar even as I have taken a route through the unexpected rather than the mundane. At the same time, I am putting experience under a microscope in order to pick the illusory/elusory back up, to affirm that although we indeed cannot recover expansive experience in its totality, *the signs of textuality are expansive experience's reincarnated traces.*

Picture the molecules of a smell, aromatic particles wafting on the air current and into your nose where they initiate a chain reaction of what we can include under the category of signing. That chain reaction may have exponential results, including changing your mood owing to an event in childhood you no longer consciously remember. Yet for all of the signals moving, the neurons firing, new connections being made, by the time you consider the smell in the signs of conscious thought, if you consider it at all, it may be a very simple thought that occurs to you. Yet that simple thought will be a sign at one possible end (or middle) of a process begun in a sensuous encounter that literally brought the world into you. Moreover, the shape of your thought will have depended on a complex history of other experiential moments both of sensuous encounter and of imaginative thought (and the two are simultaneous, overlapping, and conjoined). Even your lies contain histories of encounter.

Farquhar is exactly right that bodies and texts are not two separate levels of being. Thus, when we share stories, we share experience itself—and thus, in Farquhar's own conversation with an imagined embodied reader, new experiences have emerged in imaginary encounters with efficacious entailments. Ours is, as I have already said, an acculturated physiology, by way of which we simultaneously touch, presciss, and create worlds that include ourselves.

As I sit here in a little house in northern Kenya constructed of cedar posts and a tin roof, I am experiencing in ways you can imagine but cannot experience in precisely the same way. My cuttings are not yours. You are experiencing in ways incommensurable to mine, but while I have nothing from you, you are reading what I have typed into this keyboard sitting on my lap on a bed covered in the red tartan blankets Samburu elders like to wear. Moreover, you are trying to picture the red tartan blankets, you have already tried to picture the cedar posts and tin roof, and now if I tell you that it has not rained in a couple of months, so the land is very dry, with dust blowing wherever one walks and acacia thorn trees and shrubs dotting rolling hills all around me, you will begin to imagine the trees, the dust, and the hills. Unless you have been here, you will not imagine them as I see them, but there will doubtless be something shared—however elusive—in your imagining and my memory. We have connected. We cannot say how, we cannot experience one another's experience (at least if we limit ourselves to the empirical), but something of my experience has made it into yours—*into* yours. And insofar as imagination is a part of our bodily being, there is no division there but rather a series of transformations from one dimension of experience to another and from one experiential moment to another.

Consider these crossings when you read about movements between Nkai, people, animals, and things. Consider that Samburu presciss in significantly different ways—experientially reading events as divine or extraordinary and yet possible, "natural" encounters. Yet, though risky—and I do take textual risks here—a connection can be made without resorting to "context-dependent" explanations. Different prescissive cuts can be made in between what we suppose possible.

I have two precise aims in this book, then. The first is to take a route through experience in ways that expand phenomenological anthropology's attempts to recover lives from the morass of abstraction. Countering the literary turn's continuing legacy of conceding that we can only have access to partial truths, I suggest that there are not merely "better" interpretations (see Ahearn 2001; Eco 1999)[14] but a partially recoverable foundation. We do not merely tell partial stories in contrast to complete ones, we tell partial stories in contrast to absolutely baseless ones. Suffering, joy, and meaning are recoverable, and in my claims about experience as at once extraordinary and characterized by real crossings I offer a philosophical basis for that contention.

Second, en route through descriptions of the Samburu extraordinary within the mundane, besides elucidating the problem of experience philosophically and by way of Samburu experience particularly, I also weave through several scholarly literatures and at times an unorthodox plethora of sources to carry through a self-consciously comparative project reading Samburu experiences through the Euro-American practices and cultural assumptions touching them since prior to the colonial period and likewise taking the opportunity to read Euro-American traditions of knowing through Samburu ones. In this more than dialogic encounter—because I am the medium entangling the already entangled—I make transparent that strand of the anthropological project that has long been concerned with broad understanding of what it means to be human, here not through a facile West/rest dichotomy but rather by way of elucidating a dynamic, fragile, and at times violent exchange.[15]

Now I will devote the remainder of this chapter to a brief descriptive background of the Samburu.

The Samburu of Northern Kenya in the First Decade of the New Millennium

The Samburu are herders occupying parts of Kenya's semiarid lands stretching from Mount Diro (below the southern tip of Lake Turkana) in the north to the Uaso Diro River in the south and beyond. Although a number of Samburu have migrated to towns like Nairobi, Mombasa, and Nakuru, and a good number have long lived in Marsabit District (before it was a "district"), the majority of Samburu live in Samburu District. Samburu District occupies approximately 20,000 square kilometers of north central Kenya and is divided into four political divisions: Leroghi, Wamba, Baragoi, and Uaso. The region is ecologically diverse, ranging in altitude from 1,000 feet (in a couple of places) to over 8,000 feet. Rainfall varies from less than 400 millimeters per year in some of the lowland areas to over 1,250 millimeters per year in the mountains (Range Management Handbook 1992). Climate variations follow patterns of rainfall, with cooler temperatures in the highlands; the heat in the lowlands becomes oppressive during the driest months of the year.

The Samburu pursue a livestock economy centered on the rearing of cattle, small stock, and camels (if they can afford them), which is supplemented to varying degrees by livestock trading, wage employment, and other means of generating cash income. The Samburu have been under tremendous and increasing strain since the Independence period owing primarily to the intertwining factors of land pressure and livestock depletion coupled with population increases. Policies initiated in both the colonial and the post-Independence periods have produced land pressures, as land has been allocated to parks, national forests, European settlement, and private plots. Particularly devastating has been the fact that most of the acreage alienated from communal grazing has been

Figure 1. Map of Kenya.

the land with highest rainfall potential—in other words, dry-season grazing (see Fratkin 1991; Holtzman 1996, 2004; Lesorogol 1991, 2002,
2003; Straight 1997b). This, together with livestock disease and periodic
severe droughts, has depleted Samburu livestock, a situation that is particularly devastating to families who are already poor.

The result has been economic diversification with varying levels of
success and an increasing reliance on relief foods donated by wealthy
nations like the United States. Whereas only a couple of decades ago
school was considered a desirable option only for poor families and less
intelligent children, in the new millennium, most families send at least
one child to be educated, and often more (Straight 1997b). Even if children only attend a few primary grades, getting some basic competence
in Kiswahili assists young men in getting employment as watchmen or
casual laborers.[16] Completing secondary school is even more lucrative,

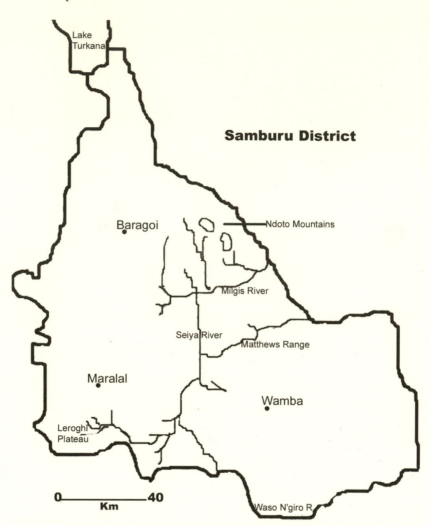

Figure 2. Map of Samburu District.

since competence in English and the Form IV Certificate make better jobs possible, although even Form IV graduates usually have difficulty finding employment. Thus they may turn to livestock trading if they can get start-up capital or try their hand at other businesses.

The education of Samburu girls lags far behind that of boys. It is expected that girls will get married, not become employed (unless they live near towns), hopefully to men who have a herd that can support the family. Young men who have at least a Form IV education themselves, however, will often choose to educate their daughters, and educated young men often prefer to marry women who have at least some formal schooling. Christian conversion also plays a role, particularly in the case of Protestants, who are most likely to have smaller families and educate all of their children. Although Protestants have often chosen monogamy as a demonstration of devotion to their faith, a new trend has developed just at the turn of the twenty-first century, and some Protestants are starting to marry second wives.

Except for the wealthiest Samburu elite and the most destitute, the economic pressures that have increased and become widespread in the past few decades have not meant the end of herding as the most viable means of subsistence. Most families have at least a couple of animals, though they may rely heavily on relief foods and foods purchased through sale of animal products like milk and hides, wage labor, and begging. In a few areas of the highlands where rainfall allows it (and sporadically in the lowlands), some families have also been augmenting their resources through farming. Their primary goal in farming is often subsistence, but with an aim to sell any surplus they are lucky enough to generate. Most families manage to scrape by, either through having sufficient animals or through a variety of strategies. And there are still a substantial number of families that are wealthy in livestock.

The AgeSet Organization

A dominant feature of Samburu social organization and indeed daily life continues to be the ageset system, whereby a group of young men is set apart from the rest of society, forming a collective (of *lmurran*) for the purposes of warfare and defense. Men in the ageset system are divided into the age-grades of boy, unmarried young man (lmurran), junior elder, firestick elder (*lpiroi*), and senior elder.[17] Lpiroi (firestick) elders supervise the ageset two generations younger than themselves, while a lmurrani's father should be at least three generations older than he is. These age-grades are stages through which every Samburu man must pass, thus forming a cyclical periodicity. In contrast, a new ageset is formed approximately every fourteen years, and membership in a particular ageset is lifelong, so that agesets comprise temporally linear generations. The new ageset is given a name and is comprised of the newly initiated unmarried young men (see Table 1 for a timeline of Samburu agesets). Thus, for example, in 2002 *Lkishili* were the lpiroi for *Lmooli* (the current lmurran), *Lkiroro* were young elders, and *Lkimaniki* were the fathers of Lmooli. At any given time, lpiroi and older generations assume the greatest leadership roles, while the oldest living generations are retired elders.

Figure 3. Lmurran (warriors) with a girlfriend in 2001.

In spite of Spencer's assertions (1965) that the British administration had rendered the military function of the lmurran largely obsolete, the Samburu lmurran I knew in 1992–94, and again from 2001 to the present (2006), continued to protect herds from neighboring groups like the Turkana and Somali and from predators like lions. During my fieldwork in 1992–94, the Samburu were experiencing increasing hostilities with the Somali and Pokot, and Samburu lmurran organized retaliatory expeditions against Somali who had stolen Samburu cattle.[18] Although many lmurran who lived in towns departed from a number of the practices associated with their status, lmurran-hood was alive and well in Samburu District as of 2006. The majority of lmurran continued to follow the dietary restrictions required of young men of their status— such as not eating food in front of women. (However, lmurran living in town often abbreviated these, and there were notable changes surrounding food preparation and eating locus (see Holtzman 1996, 2001, 2002, 2003). Lmurran living in rural areas also continued to *look like* lmurran—conforming to the visual image that has been popularized in cof-

TABLE 1. SAMBURU AGESETS

Date	Ageset Name
16??	Circumcision of Lkipilash
17??	Circumcision of Lwantaro
17??	Circumcision of Lchiŋeo
c.1739	Circumcision of Lsalkanya[1]
c.1753	Circumcision of Lŋerejon
c.1767	Circumcision of Lpepeet
c.1781	Circumcision of Lmeishopo
c.1795	Circumcision of Lkurukua
c.1809	Circumcision of Lpetaa
c.1823	Circumcision of Lkipayang
c.1837	Circumcision of Lkipiku
c.1851	Circumcision of Lkiteku
c.1865	Circumcision of Ltarigirig
c.1880	Circumcision of Lmarinkon
1893	Circumcision of Lterito
1912	Circumcision of Lmirisho
1923	Circumcision of Lkileku
1936	Circumcision of Lmekuri
1948	Circumcision of Lkimaniki
1961	Circumcision of Likshili
1976	Circumcision of Lkiroro
1990	Circumcision of Lmooli

[1]Beginning of Samburu Lminoŋ (food prohibitions for lmurran)

fee-table books and in the international media. Thus, the majority of rural lmurran adorned themselves with lavish beads and red ochre, wore brightly patterned cloth wraps (*shuka* or *kikoi*), and grew their hair long—braiding it into "pigtails" (*lmasi*), which they also covered with red ochre. Finally, although men of older agesets have been criticizing the current, Lmooli, generation of lmurran for not engaging in the practice enough, many of them continued to "bead" their girlfriends—a practice whereby an lmurrani demonstrates commitment to one girl-friend by giving her enormous quantities of beads.

The ageset system also has implications for women. Just as men are divided into agegrades based on the ageset system, women can be divided based on marriage and the age of their sons. Thus, a woman's status rises from girl (*ntito*)[19] to married woman (*ntomonok*) to mother of lmurran sons (and married daughters) to mother of sons who are all lmurran or older.[20] If a girl reaches the age of seventeen (approximately) without marrying or is attending school as a teenager, her parents will usually have her initiated ("circumcised"/clitoridectomized—*emurati*), and the unmarried initiated girl/woman is referred to as a *surmolei*, particularly if she stays too long without marrying.[21]

Figure 4. Lowland Samburu settlement in 2002. A thorn fence encloses the settlement; livestock are at the left; on the right, two women's houses flank a goat enclosure.

Since the majority of women still typically marry between the ages of fifteen and seventeen, however, they frequently have their first son initiated (emurati) while still in their thirties, and their status rises. This rise in status is both social and practical because of the close relationship they have with their sons and the shared economic interests between them. As a Samburu woman's son moves through the Samburu age-grades, he exerts increasing control over the portion of her allocated herd that he will eventually inherit. Additionally, many young Samburu men have been entering the wage labor force, and they often remit money home to their mothers (see also Holtzman 1996, 2003; see Ensminger 1987 on Oromo). Even if her eldest son is not yet initiated, there will often be a second wife by the time one or more of her sons are lmurran, and this too, increases a Samburu woman's status (particularly because younger wives may take over some of the more tedious or physically taxing chores). By age fifty-five or sixty, it is possible that all of a woman's sons will have been initiated, and about ten or more years later, she will be considered so old that all her needs should be met by children and grandchildren.

The Daily Rhythms of Samburu Life

Samburu settlements are usually dispersed, although density is higher in the highlands and in and around towns. Most settlements contain between one and ten houses, although one house is unusual and special large settlements of even one hundred houses (*lorora*) are constructed when new generations of young men are being initiated. Typically, more than one family occupies a settlement together, especially to share herding responsibilities. Frequently, a family with few animals lives with a family wealthy in livestock—the latter share animals and the former assist with herding. If disagreements become frequent, however, families may separate, usually believing it better to move apart rather than spoil a friendship.

Samburu continue to be nomadic or seminomadic in many areas, although near towns, small centers, and in some areas of Leroghi Plateau, for example, some families have built permanent houses and fenced in large plots. In the last decade, some husbands have financed the building of a "modern" house, constructed of vertical timber posts, stone, or cement block, with a corrugated tin ("mabati") roof. These mabati houses vary in size from one to several rooms, and there is frequently an outdoor latrine (also a sign of "development" or "modernity")[22] built at the same time. Such houses belong to the husband, except in women-headed households in which women have raised the capital to build the house. Most of the time women avoid sleeping in these mabati houses except when summoned by their husbands. A number of Samburu women have explained this avoidance to me by complaining that these houses are too cold for children because they lack a fire, but this doesn't seem to deter the women with the means to finance the building of such a house themselves, as a few have done in towns.[23]

The typical house pattern, followed even if the husband is flaunting a mabati house, is for women to build and own their own houses. Women's houses vary in construction depending on region, season, family size, and women's preferences. In the hottest part of the lowlands, where families move frequently, houses are small and very temporary. Women construct the frame with several strong poles and many smooth branches. Leaves are placed on the floor to support the sleeping skins and to make them fragrant. Hides are placed up against the walls, and woven fiber mats (*suuti*) cover the roof to keep out the rain. The woman's fire, composed of at least three large stones (though there may be a few smaller ones added), is at the center of the house, always positioned near her sleeping area.

This basic design has many variations. Some women build shelves inside their houses, for example, or elevate their sleeping areas more

Figure 5. Lowland Samburu house interior in 1994. The woman's cooking fire (three large stones) is in the left foreground; a shelf behind the fire holds sacks of U.S. famine relief food; various belongings are on walls and floor.

than other women do. Some women have almost completely neglected their suuti roof mats in favor of any scrap cloth they have plus a generous covering of vinyl sheeting. In addition, it has become increasingly popular to flatten metal cans, sew them together with leather or nylon string, and lay them against the wall instead of hides. This is particularly useful if the family is poor in animals, but some women wealthy in animals also use the tin wall. Besides these variations, houses increase in size if families do not move often, and houses are generally very large in the highlands. In lowland areas where families stay in place longer, women cover the walls with a mixture of cow dung and mud. These houses are quite different from the less permanent structures. Highland houses are in even greater contrast, constructed with heavy poles; leaves, branches, and mud and cow dung at the walls; and poles, leaves, and mud for roofs.

When a family is preparing to move—usually to follow pasture, but there are other reasons as well, including the death of a family member—the husband and eldest sons travel to the new location first in order to build the new settlement's fence. Although this continues to be the typical pattern, in some areas wealthy families have started hiring others to build the fence. Whether the husbands build it or hire out the work, women only travel to the new area to build their new houses after the fence is complete. In the case of highly nomadic lowland families, the entire family moves once the fence is complete. Women pack the main support posts for the house and all of their belongings onto donkeys and build their new homes within a day upon arrival. In highland areas where wood is more plentiful, women cut new posts and travel daily to work on their new houses until they are complete. Only then does the family move.

While men are responsible for fencing, digging wells, watering livestock, and overall management of the family herd, women and children are responsible for most other tasks pertaining to the daily operation of the home. Children and young people do virtually all of the herding, though women assist in herding animals close to home. Women and children milk the livestock, fetch water and firewood, and prepare meals. Women are not only responsible for preparing food but are entrusted with all decisions regarding its allocation (see Holtzman 1996, 2001, 2002). Although it may seem that the burden on women is great, based on the time-allocation surveys I conducted from 1992 to 1994, I found that the gender division of labor was most balanced in areas where families depended almost exclusively on their herds. Women in transitional economies, where livestock responsibilities were combined with loss of children's labor to school and additional responsibilities related to alternative income-generating activities, were the most unevenly burdened vis-à-vis men (Straight 1997a, 1997b, 2000; see also Fratkin 1989 on the Samburu and Ariaal; Hodgson 2001 and Talle 1988 for the Maasai).

Unfortunately in some respects for already burdened wives, school attendance and the need to engage in alternative economic strategies have been on the rise. Thus, in 2002, some Samburu women were being called upon to farm, travel away from home to sell hides, milk, or other products, and so on. At the same time, men were seeking employment as often as possible, and if the employment was close to home, they were the ones finding themselves burdened. Thus, a watchman working near his home might need to check on the children herding, water the animals, and even search for missing animals (a frequent occurrence) before coming to work in the evening. Since animals do not come home until dusk, checking on the herds and following up on lost animals would inevitably occur just as the man needed to run to his job.

On the face of things then the lifestyles of most Samburu in the first years of the new millennium continue to be shaped by livestock rearing. Women rise before dawn to milk their animals, children not attending school spend the day following the animals and playing while they graze, and men carefully manage their herds' overall movements and health.

In between, women sell milk, other animal products they control, or various sundries; men look for other ways to earn cash and resort to selling animals when necessary for school fees, veterinary medicines, family illnesses, and so on; children attend school; and entire families eagerly collect famine relief foods. More ominously, a substantial number of women brew liquor, and some men—and increasingly, women—drink to the point of neglecting their families.[24] This mixed economy is visible and is accompanied by a variety of other changes—seen particularly in a proliferation of clothing and adornment styles. All of these changes, from dietary to clothing, are highly marked for the Samburu and find expression in casual commentary, stories, songs, and daily experiences. Changes are most subtle, however, in prayer, in routine practices related to prayer, and in the major ceremonies that punctuate daily life. Yet even here, important transformations are visible, as will become apparent as I turn to examine Samburu experiences of Nkai, divinity.

Chapter 3

Nkai

Remeta

For most Samburu, Nkai (divinity) continues to be present in the world, occasionally appearing to people in various shapes, including human.[1] Sometimes, these appearances take on a more fantastic dimension, as children and young people disappear for hours or days and return to describe one of Nkai's own dwelling places. Hearing of a somewhat recent example—of a child prophet whose family had no clear lineage connection to naibon[2]—in May 2002 I paid a personal visit to the home of a young girl named Remeta.

Remeta was herding goats far from her settlement, so we wandered across the plain looking for the goats her kinsman would recognize. We walked slowly, casually, noticing how many settlements there were in this part of Laikipia. And the wind came, bringing the smell of something mildly sweet, a scent I had often picked up in the lowlands. It had been so overwhelming at times that I felt like just following the breeze wherever it took me, just to keep that smell coming into me. It wasn't sweet like honeysuckle, more like sweet grass, but even milder. How can you describe a smell? "This is *suchiai*," Timothy said.[3] He picked it up and crushed it. "It has a little smell when you do this." Even crushed, it had very little smell. Nkai still likes it for many ceremonies because it is always green, always growing even in the driest times. And it is everywhere. Like *reteti* trees. They too, are always green, even in the worst drought.[4] They have a pleasant gum people like to chew in a leisurely way. And more important, they have edible fruit that can nourish hungry people. That is why the reteti tree is the tree Nkai asists people with—*aret*, to help—reteti. Later we would learn that when she visited Nkai, Remeta had disappeared at a reteti tree, then found herself in Nkai's home. Trees can be dense signs—for Samburu, trees are signs partaking of salvation amid starvation, signs that are meeting places for Nkai.

We continued walking, slowly, trying different plants to see if they brought the smell that was hypnotizing me. "I think this is it," Timothy said, picking up some little green spikes close to the ground. "*Lodua mporo.*" I thought he had said blood blood (*lodo* mporo).[5] "No, lodua, bitter. If cows eat it, it makes their milk bitter." A sweet yet bitter scent. Maybe it was the paradox that attracted my nostrils. It is used medicinally, as a cure for malaria, for example, and girls like to wear it around their necks as perfume. Yet it has no ritual purpose, as I had hoped it might. Smells are also little points of infinity. For Samburu as for many people, particular smells can conjure any number of things, from the coming of rain to the presence of particular animals or even a sick person in the house. Like reteti trees, though, smell has associations outsiders might not expect. Thus, burnt offerings to Nkai need to have a good smell, just as a person wants to die with a good smell, as I will describe in Chapter 4.

Timothy and I continued walking, past other people's goats, across the site of the 1997 Samburu-Kikuyu clashes where so many Kikuyu had been killed. Timothy told me a Samburu version of what had happened there, of Kikuyu who were no match for Samburu, of Samburu shouting not to use bullets because these were merely women they were fighting, of Samburu calling to their fellows to "grab one for me because I have not yet killed." Although my anthropological sympathies were usually with Timothy and my other Samburu friends, an image burst upon me of a young Kikuyu man living his last moments held forcefully by Samburu men just so that one young man could say that he, too, had killed that day.[6] I marveled that there were no signs of this violence, less than a decade old. Noticing a number of large, very white mushrooms growing randomly around where we walked, I began to imagine they were purposely springing from the ground to mark the site of every fallen Kikuyu. It was just in this area of mushrooms and third-hand memories that we found Remeta's goats. Even when one of their fellows is being slaughtered, goats show no surprise or alarm. These were quietly munching grass just next to Kikuyu burial mounds. And here and there there were more soul-white mushrooms.

Remeta herself was near these graves (did she know, did she think about those deaths?). Her brothers exclaimed when they saw me, the little one telling the older, "Maybe this is Remeta's Nkai coming to see us!" Remeta herself thought at first that I might be Nkai, but as we talked under a tree, she saw that my Samburu was not as perfect as Nkai's had been, and soon decided that I was a human woman.

A few years before, while Remeta was in her settlement, an Nkai child came and spoke to her. Remeta was afraid, and after a few moments the child disappeared. A day or so later, an Nkai woman came to her, and this time Remeta was very comfortable. After a few minutes, the Nkai woman also disappeared.[7] Again, one or a few days passed, and now an

Nkai lmurrani appeared to her. Again, she was not at all afraid. He led her to the nearby reteti tree where women usually poured offerings and sang prayers to Nkai. Suddenly Remeta was in Nkai's settlement, but she has no memory of how she got there from Nkai's reteti tree, nor how she later got back to the tree from Nkai's settlement. Her siblings report seeing her vanishing, and her mother goes so far as to exaggerate the duration of her disappearance. What happened? Is this complete fabrication? Where did little Remeta, about six years old at the time, disappear to? Her answer is that she was literally swept to the home of divinity.

According to Remeta, the settlement was very large, and all of the houses were mabati—the "modern" house of timber or block with a corrugated tin roof that elders (and occasionally women) have started to build in recent decades if they can afford it. When we asked her what Nkai had looked like, Remeta told Timothy and me that the Nkai women had looked like me. Even their hair was like mine, but closely cropped like Samburu women's. They wore white cloths and nice beads. All the Nkai people wore white cloths, in fact—the Nkai husband, wives, lmurran, even children—while the beads they all wore were the appropriate ones for their age, gender, and social status.

The woman invited Remeta inside a house and gave her milk to drink. There were many calabashes in the house, and *ruati*—permanent beds built on a platform, the typical style for non-mabati highland houses. She drank that sweet milk until she was full, and then came outside to leave. The Nkai husband was sitting nearby but spoke only greetings. The lmurran, the woman, and the child however, all gave her messages to take back to her family and others. As a child (a little girl), Nkai said, She did not like the bright orange cloths that had become fashionable for Samburu women and lmurran. She said that when she flashed— making lightning to bring rain—women and lmurran wearing such bright colors also flashed, as if they were competing with Nkai. (Lmurran have stopped wearing them since Remeta's experience, and women have started covering theirs with blue cloth capes.) As an lmurrani, Nkai wanted boys to wear their *lmanchewin* (shaved heads with a little tuft on top), children to stop drinking tea, and women to sing prayers and always to use calabashes but never plastic containers for milking. As a woman, Nkai gave instructions for Remeta's mother specifically to stop drinking *chaŋaa* (a home-distilled liquor, a bit weaker than rum). Remeta took the messages back, but her father's brother soon told her to stop talking about visiting Nkai. It is a common thing for fathers to say—they are the ones, after all, who may be forced to slaughter animals when visitors come. And a child like Remeta will draw many visitors, even light-haired, blue-eyed anthropologists like me.

When we went to Remeta's settlement after leaving her with her goats, we understood why Nkai did not want her mother drinking. Remeta's mother was waiting for us and was thoroughly intoxicated, so much so that she kissed me on the mouth repeatedly as drunk Samburu women invariably seem to do when all of their inhibitions have left them. (They should kiss on the cheek or hand if they are happy to see someone they do not know well.) As I entered her house, I found the most untidy, disorganized Samburu house I had ever seen. Her older daughter (about twelve years old) and another boy of the settlement came into the house and tried to rein her in. They sent her out for firewood, they sent her out to milk goats—she came inside and poured exactly one drop of milk into the pot as if she had done precisely the job she had been asked to do. She waved her arms dramatically as she spoke, telling me that her husband had gone and become a *malaika* (Kiswahili for angel) and that her daughter Remeta was a malaika of Nkai. Did I visit her Remeta? Yes? Good! Yes, she doesn't tell lies. She tells the truth. She really disappeared—for four days! Remeta herself had said she had only been gone a few hours, and her older sister now contradicted their mother to say it had been three hours. Her mother continued loudly— she had disappeared for four days and she told the truth. She had gone to Nkai's settlement. I wondered why Remeta's message forbidding hard liquor had escaped her mother's attention.

"My husband went and became a malaika. My daughter is a Malaika of Nkai." She continued even after Remeta had returned with the goats. Remeta hid behind her mother and sister as we talked. Timothy thought of questions he wanted to ask, but she continued hiding, a timid little nine-year-old creature. I asked her to come and sit by me; she stood immediately, left her drunken mother, and came to sit behind me, taking my hair into her hands to play with as we talked. Shyness had all but left her now as she turned and twisted my hair over and over again in her hands. I sat with the pleasure of it and felt like I didn't want to leave her. And I was sure she felt the same way, whether it was just her memory of Nkai or simply the deliciousness of holding my long hair in her fingers and palm. Children often play with my hair, but this experience was different. I had to drag myself away—I wanted so much to stay. Yet the hour was getting late and I had left my three-year-old son a few hours' walk and drive away.

Had Remeta disappeared and visited the home of a light-skinned Nkai family? Everyone I spoke to afterward, Timothy included, believed she had. My then sixteen-year-old son (Jen), the great skeptic, said, "Yeah, right, white Nkai in mabati houses." What whiteness was this? Surely it was not the whiteness of Cuna figurines Taussig (1993) has famously examined.[8] I suspect that this was a Samburu whiteness that mixed cultural critique aimed at some aspects of Samburu daily life with prevailing

Samburu stereotypes that often idealize Euro-American habitus—even when they simultaneously castigate colonial actions. Put simply, if Nkai chose to appear to a little girl, why not appear in the shape of what the child regarded as perfection? A Samburu settlement with "modern" houses and a light-skinned Nkai family because Nkai is indeed wealthy, powerful, and organized—the qualities Samburu stereotypically associate with Europeans. Mabati houses and light skin, but a *Samburu* settlement with a proper assortment of calabashes, the right beads, mporo marriage necklaces hanging on the wall, and beautiful, fat livestock munching on grass in a place that was entirely, eternally, green.

There are multiple approaches possible here for understanding Nkai, each of which I will examine in due course. In examining Nkai and the messages Nkai conveyed to Remeta and to other Samburu whom Nkai has taken Home, it is possible to view Nkai as a continually transforming divinity Who, like the Samburu, is grappling with the issues entailed by colonialism, Christianity, and postcolonialism. Alongside this view, it is also possible to examine changing gendered and racial understandings of Nkai in previous scholarship, where possible, and in the stories about Nkai's appearance themselves. Embedded in all of these approaches is an understanding of Nkai as active in the Samburu world and central to Samburu subjectivity, as making frequent appearances to everyday people as well as communicating to professional healers/diviners/prophets like Lemeteki and other Samburu loibonok.

Before proceeding, I will take up the issue of gender and ontology, particularly as it relates to the embodiment of Nkai, with some conclusions that I will transpose to a discussion of race in a later section.

Prescissing Gender

Gender remains a contentious issue and object of Western scholarly debates, one that has long moved between the poles of essentialism and constructionism even as a number of scholars have recently, in their different ways, attempted to resolve this dichotomy. I do not intend to do justice here to a rich and detailed debate that has been widely covered in innumerable writings.[9] Rather, with particular respect to Nkai, my intention in discussing gender here is to trouble the Eurocentric dualistic ontology that has tended to underwrite both missionary and scholarly understandings of Nkai—understandings that insidiously presume that Samburu and Judeo-Christian divinities each have a "body" (even if an "imagined" one) in the Western sense (opposed to and separate from "mind"), and a male one in particular. More broadly, and for the purpose of understanding Samburu processes of experience and subjectivity in the chapters that follow, my arguments here are meant to disturb clear notions of bodies and minds, including divine ones.

For Western feminists, given new reproductive technologies and rapidly increasing global poverty, the body has never been more urgent or its risks greater and more salient. One of the critical conundrums posed in these debates is that if we cannot call the (European) sensuous body by name, how can we set the theoretical parameters (with policy implications) by which marginalized populations can take control of their bodies? If, however, we do call the body by name—as a sensuous reality and not merely a discursive surface—how can we be sure that the Truth created does not work toward further marginalization? Thus, while so-called constructionists have walked politely or gingerly around the eating, fucking, birthing, defecating body by treating it as a signifying object, the claims of so-called essentialists that bodies "matter" (Fuss 1991) have been decried quickly or else weakened by necessary ambiguity when their arguments are supple and complex. This is not least because when careful and sustained attention is given to the arguments of the proponents of these two poles, it often becomes apparent that each is attempting to overcome dualism itself either by somehow encapsulating one side within the other or by working in the interstices.[10]

Judith Butler's theory of gender is among the best known and most supple, indeed pathbreaking, approaches meant to overcome dualism:

If sex does not limit gender, then perhaps there are genders, ways of culturally interpreting the sexed body, which are in no way restricted by the apparent duality of sex. Consider the further consequence that if gender is something that one becomes—but can never be—then gender is itself a kind of becoming or activity, and that gender ought not to be conceived as a noun or a substantial thing or a static cultural marker, but rather as an incessant and repeated action of some sort. (Butler 1990: 112)

Thus, gender is performed and enacted in the repeated actions of the techniques of the body that Bourdieu (1977) expresses in terms of the habitus and Connerton (1989) describes similarly, though with more sustained attention to the problematics of memory. Further, while arguing that gender is performative, Butler obviates the sex-gender distinction by suggesting a sort of Derridean play on a sex that, as historical artifact, is itself an effect of language: "As both discursive and perceptual, 'sex' denotes an historically contingent epistemic regime, a language that forms perception by forcibly shaping the interrelationships through which physical bodies are perceived" (114). Sex here collapses into another space of cultural (re)production, such that the sex-gender dichotomy is overcome at the same time that its usefulness is maintained because of the claim that sex and gender are each produced by a different set of grand narratives.

Elizabeth Grosz (1994) operates in the interstices in ways similar to Butler's, as her self-inclusion in the category of "sexual difference" theorists would suggest. However, where Butler's play is in the performance of gender and the historical narrativizing of sex, Grosz is concerned specifically with the play or flexibility of physiology. Grosz describes recent theoretical developments in medicine and neurobiology to demonstrate that "matter" is not fixed but neither is it a tabula rasa. Rather, what we take to be psychical can effect changes in what we take to be physical (and I use "what we take" advisedly to remind us that we are still discussing Western ontological understandings here): "Our ideas and attitudes seep into the functioning of the body itself, making up the realm of its possibilities or impossibilities" (Grosz 1994: 190). As attractive as I find Grosz's Möbius strip model in which mind and body twist one into the other—and write myself within it in many instances—it is perhaps her lack of familiarity with cultural difference that limits her to one ontology, one sort of difference.[11] Thus, she concludes her book with the categories that shaped her thought: "The infinite pliability of the *body* that I have suggested throughout implies that a host of other models may, for other purposes and in other contexts, prove just as useful. The task ahead . . . involves not a death of man or of *God* but the generation of a new productivity between and of the *two sexes*" (210, emphases added).

All of these theorists leave us, then, with a sexed body, even if sex itself is pliable and gender enacted through performative practice. We continue to be mired, that is, in the slippage between body and sex defined as the "stuff" from which cultural understandings are created or as "always-already" live-in categories whose ground dissolves into deconstructive air (Broch-Due 1993).[12] Essentialist or materialist approaches to gender ultimately cannot work—not because there is no reality (or what European scholars have referred to as the "material")—but because we have a tendency to forget "matter out of place" to such a degree that the unruly objects of Mary Douglas's discourse are already very *clean* anomalies. Through the reductive process of prescissing we arrive at categories of the in-between that are every bit as clear as those of the correct and proper—the in-between of the in-between is, like so much of experience, left out of memory making (see Straight 2005b). This has broad implications for cross-cultural ontologies, for sex that is not necessarily one or two or three, for sex and gender that may not exist in tandem or opposition to one another, for configurations we have not yet allowed ourselves to imagine. And imagination is crucial.

Thus, there are two issues that confound attempts to adequately theorize sex and gender, mind and body. One is that theorists continue to privilege Western ontologies and to employ Western binary categories as the starting point, even if these authors are attempting to overcome them or write in their interstices. Categories like body and mind, sex and gender, are so embedded in Western thought that it is difficult to imagine that they do not have some sort of basis—even if that basis turns out to be discursive, with different narratives producing each side of the binary.[13] Again, imagining a different ontology means imagining the possibility that there is no body and no mind as Westerners configure them, even if dualisms are apparent that we find ourselves (wrongly or simplistically) translating as body and mind.[14] That is, in grappling with the slippage and paradoxes between the two sides of these Western dichotomies, theorists have a tendency to substitute a Western ontology in the place of an adequate (even if necessarily limited) theorization of experience. Thus, the essentialists founder on, the constructionists avoid, and the sexual difference theorists attempt to work in-between the apparent paradoxes of a material reality underlying an "immaterial" one. In all instances, a Western ontology prefigures a Western notion of reality, and while it may not be possible to obviate this difficulty completely, a notion of the process of prescissing as I have discussed beginning in Chapter 1 allows us to discuss sex and gender as Western reductions of some aspect of the reality we share, even as what we share may be so elusive that other ontologies have all the appearance of being utterly particular and different. Yet (1) we do prescissively experience in some similar ways; (2) the fact of reality (as continually transforming with and without us) means that experiences and the stories from them are real *and* that there are grounds for translation; and, finally, (3) while we cannot assume that what Westerners presciss as biological sex is precisely the same aspect of reality that is prescinded cross-culturally (a crucial point),[15] there is *some* aspect of human experiential reality that is so compelling that it instantiates itself cross-culturally—however differently configured ontologically. This is what leads us to assume that bodies are everywhere, even though they are not—particularly insofar as the contemporary Western body presupposes a mind to oppose it, and that in a particular way.

For this chapter—because specificity remains important—and in the case of divinity as I am discussing it here, I want to suggest that two very different ontologies have been competing with one another. It is not (in any definitive way) that a masculine view of divinity has overcome a feminine (or, as I shall argue, a plural) one. Nor is it that a white Nkai is replacing a Samburu one. It is that the apparent similarities between two ontologies (Samburu and European) have obfuscated their differences, and, moreover, a Western preoccupation with gender and race has occluded other, possibly more important for the Samburu, dimensions of divinity. Now, I will turn to examine different genderings of divinity in Western scholarship as it pertains to Western and Samburu understandings—a task I cannot accomplish in the case of race, since this has not figured into scholarship on Maasai and Samburu divinity. Then I will turn to both gender and race in the context of Nkai's dynamic qualities as these relate to Samburu engagements with so-called modernity.

Christian Masculinities

Protestant Christianity arrived in Samburu District in 1934 in the shape of Mr. and Mrs. Charles Scudder and their assistant, Miss Grindley—Anglican missionaries of the Bible Churchmen's Missionary Society (BCMS). In the first decade of the new century, many of the most devoted Samburu Christians were descendants of the Scudders' first converts. Catholicism came to Samburu District in 1947 but did not become firmly established until the 1950s and especially the 1960s. Their late start notwithstanding, with their much larger financial base the Catholics have reached many more Samburu with their message, either directly or indirectly. While there are substantial differences between Protestants and Catholics in the implications of conversion for everyday cultural practices (post-Vatican II Catholics have been more prepared to accept rather than reject Samburu practices), they share a masculine God. This is surprising, given the Marian roots of the Consolata Catholics who have been working in Samburu District (see Straight 1997b), but often true in practice nevertheless.

In spite of the distance the Catholics in particular have covered in bringing their message to the "nomads," as of 2005 the majority of Samburu living in the district were only rudimentarily familiar with the Christian message, while regular churchgoers lived predominantly in and adjacent to towns. Thus, Nkai enjoyed continuing vitality, on the one hand, while clearly making appearances to Samburu in ways that acknowledged Christianity's presence, on the other. Contestation about the gender and shape of Nkai was, for me, one of the more obvious signs of an increasing familiarity with Christianity as a cultural form, although not the only one. Thus, Samburu Christians tended to assert unswervingly that Nkai and God are the same and that Nkai/God is male. Those near town and educated in schools from a young age often appeared to have no conscious awareness that Nkai/God could be anything else. This was in spite of overwhelming evidence to the contrary, to which I will soon turn. It was also in spite of the fact that many Samburu living close to towns and churches and all or nearly all Samburu in rural areas accessible only by very poor roads (or on foot) asserted something quite different. This means that a substantial portion of the population were not thinking of Nkai as male, even as a growing number—particularly nearest towns—thought just that.

Interestingly, their very different contentions are both based on actual sightings of God or of Nkai, like Remeta's. If feminine Christian divinity has continued to appear in the person of Mary in recent decades or centuries, these sightings are often controversial in comparison to masculine biblical appearances. Thus, in the experiences endorsed by Christians en masse—Samburu Christians in particular—God is invariably male. Moses saw the back of God and presumably heard a masculine voice.[16] If there is ambiguity on the latter point, the biblical translation presents God as unequivocally male. Notice how close Moses came to God, speaking with Him "face to face."

And the Lord spake unto Moses face to face, as a man speaketh unto his friend. And he turned again into the camp: but his servant Joshua, the son of Nun, a young man, departed not out of the tabernacle. (Exodus 33: 11)

Yet perhaps we are to suppose that Moses did not actually see God's face in this encounter, since just a few verses later God claims to have a *deadly* face:

And He said, Thou canst not see my face: for there shall no man see me, and live. [21] And the Lord said, Behold, there is a place by me, and thou shalt stand upon a rock: [22] And it shall come to pass, while my glory passeth by, that I will put thee in a clift of the rock, and will cover thee with my hand while I pass by: [23] And I will take away mine hand, and thou shalt see my back parts: but my face shall not be seen. (Exodus 33: 20–23)

And it came to pass, when Moses came down from Mount Sinai with the two tables of testimony in Moses' hand, when he came down from the mount, that Moses wist not that the skin of his face shone while he talked with him. (Exodus 34: 29)

Seeing the back of God was a transfiguring experience, His divine brilliance impressing itself onto the face of His prophet, Moses. And just in case the common people doubted (and they did doubt), God appeared in the shape of thunder, rain, and fire to the entire congregation of Israel:

And it came to pass on the third day in the morning, that there were thunders and lightnings, and a thick cloud upon the mount, and the voice of the trumpet exceeding loud; so that all the people that was in the camp trembled. [17] And Moses brought forth the people out of the camp to meet with God; and they stood at the nether part of the mount. [18] And Mount Sinai was altogether on a smoke, because the Lord descended upon it in fire: and the smoke thereof ascended as the smoke of a furnace, and the whole mount quaked greatly. (Exodus 19: 16–18)

God made appearances—frequent ones—to the people who passed down in oral traditions the stories that later became the Old Testament. Perhaps more dramatically, even as Moses, Abraham, Jacob, and other chosen people saw what has come to be their masculine God in brief appearances,[17] according to Christians, Jesus *was* God—God in the shape of His Son. The New Testament likewise, then, contains accounts of many who claimed to have seen God—in the shape of His Son, Jesus, who referred to God as His Father.

These claims of seeing God in both the Old and the New Testament are important to Samburu Christians, but, they are even meaningful and convincing to Samburu who have been exposed to elements of the Christian message without having converted. In contrast to Remeta's experience of a polygynous divine family, there are many accounts of Nkai's appearances to the Samburu that bear striking similarity to these biblical accounts. Such appearances of Nkai to the Samburu appear not only in "legendary" time; Nkai has appeared to Samburu of specific generations, generations that predate the British colonial presence at the end of the nineteenth century, as well as more recent and even current generations. Prior to the British presence, for example, Nkai is said to have appeared in thunder and rain, as well as in the shape of large snakes in particular caves—and, as of 2002, Nkai was still appearing in these forms. As one woman told me in 1994, "We ask Nkai to spare us when there are thunder storms. We spill milk because when it thunders we say Nkai is speaking" (Elizabeth Lolwamba interview, 1994).

From the 1870s to the 1890s, Nkai brought widespread destruction on the Samburu because of the pride of the previous (1860s) generation—particularly that generation's girls (see Straight 2005a). There are overlapping stories relating to this history. In one, Nkai brought a flood to destroy all of the proud girls, burying them in their houses. In another, Nkai appeared as an impoverished person who turned people to stone statues when they laughed at Him: "People came to a wedding celebration and the song started, and a certain thing with rags [ragged clothing] dropped and joined the song. You see when He just dropped into the song they were amused, laughing. Yesterday He had warned them not to laugh. My child, you see those people, they became statues. Up to now, the tourists normally go and take pictures [of the statues]" (Lelesimoi interview, February 2002). And in yet another story, the Samburu were punished because young people were bathing in milk out of excessive pride in their wealth and carelessness about its source in Nkai. All of these recollections merge as different occurrences of pride and disrespect in the 1860s, which resulted in Nkai "finishing" all of the Samburu with the "Disaster" (*Mutai*)—a series of wars, disease, and drought from the 1870s to the 1890s.[18]

Later, in the 1950s or 1960s (and in the context of the colonial government), Nkai covered a woman of the Lesootia family and her home with a rain of fire and water because she refused to give people water for their animals. "And water came down like this from the mountain, and they [the family] were downhill on the slopes of the mountain. That water just came and flooded everyone, it was just death. It burned people like fire—it was boiling where they had those cows. It buried the cows in their enclosure" (Rebecca Lolwamba interview, 1994). As of 2003, Nkai was still appearing as They/It did to the Lesootia family in the 1950s. Thus, in March 2002, as I was conducting fieldwork, Nkai used thunder and rain to destroy a woman's mother, child, and sibling, reportedly because she had run away after having an incestuous affair.[19] Nkai can also bring good things with rain however, and thus, Nkai's hand (shaped like an elephant's trunk) appeared during rains (a good sign) with some regularity during all of my fieldwork periods (1992–94 as well as periods from 2001 to 2005).

In view of these stories of Nkai, the willingness of many Samburu to believe that God appeared to the Israelites is perhaps not a cause for surprise. Indeed, the similarity between such accounts of Nkai's appearances and stories of God's appearances in the Old Testament is noted both by Samburu Christians and by non-Christians who are familiar with some of the biblical stories. Moreover, many Samburu experience the Old Testament as being particularly compatible with Samburu understandings of Nkai's presence because the Israelites were pastoralists like the Samburu—and, also like the Samburu, observed numerous food taboos and made offerings to God that included sacrificed livestock, blood, animal fat, honey, and incense. The similarities between God and Nkai in these particular appearances are highlighted further in terms of gender—a crucial point for Samburu Christians, who have accepted an apparently Western masculine view of divinity. To support their argument in Samburu terms, they draw upon stories of Nkai's appearance like those I have just described in which Nkai has no obvious gender or even takes the genderless shape of thunder, rain, or fire-rain. Moreover, the general assumption is that, in the story of Nkai changing people to stone, Nkai appeared as a man, probably an lmurran (warrior). Man or woman, however, a point worthy of highlighting is that unconverted Samburu and Samburu Christians all agree on one thing: Nkai continues to be miraculously present in the world.

Scholarship on East African Pastoralists: From Masculinities to Femininities

The tendency for Samburu Christians to assert that God is the same as Nkai, who is in any case male, is echoed in scholarship on the Samburu as well as on other Maa-speaking pastoralists like the Maasai. Notably, the fact that Samburu pronouns do not show gender makes it challenging to argue definitively whether a subject is male or female—or, conversely, makes it relatively simple to argue in favor of either one. Names and nouns do show gender, however, and gender agreement follows the words modifying the noun. Indeed, this is the closest that Samburu come to what Westerners would characterize as an assumption of sexual difference, though there is no sex-gender configuration.[20] Thus, the name Nkai itself betrays that it is feminine, but this does not settle the matter, either for scholars or for many Samburu. Nor does the fact that large items are usually marked as masculine, small ones as feminine, and yet Nkai (which Samburu presume to be a very large and important "thing") is a feminine noun, seem to resolve the situation.

Thus, a masculine Enkai can and does appear in the works of prominent theological scholars such as Hillman (1989), Mol (1978, 1981), and Priest (1990),[21] who also have a tendency to universalize Maa understandings of Enkai by making Enkai over in Christian terms. Enkai becomes masculine, omniscient, omnipresent, immanent, and transcendant—and, moreover, a set of Eurocentric Judeo-Christian understandings informs the meanings of these terms. In his exhaustive Maa dictionary, for example, Mol (1978) includes terms for Enkai that belong uniquely to the Christian context, such as *Enkai Papa* ("God the Father"), and he has given general terms like *olaitajeunoni* (person who provides protection), which are only occasionally used for Enkai, a Christian nuance (75). Moreover, Mol has given an explicitly masculine Christian gloss for feminine or neutral terms used frequently by Maa speakers to mean something quite different.[22] A notable example is his *Enkerai e Nkai* (child of Nkai), which he translates as the Son of God. Typically, Maasai and Samburu refer to children (*Nkera*) rather than a single child of E/Nkai, and these E/Nkera e Nkai are girls as well as boys, as Remeta herself experienced. Making similar arguments on these points, theologian and Maasai specialist Jan Voshaar suggests that through these missionary interpretations and biblical translations into Maasai, "Enkai becomes a configuration in which a number of particular and conflicting Jewish, Greek, Roman, German and Christian concepts are combined via a universally conceived of concept of God" (1998: 132).

Christian missionaries and theologians are not unique in masculinizing East African pastoralist societies however. In his famous studies of the Nuer, for example, Evans-Pritchard (1940, 1951, 1956) seems to go to great lengths to preserve a singularly masculine view of Nuer cultural understandings, even in the face of overwhelming evidence to the contrary.[23] This masculine bias has been particularly insidious in anthropological scholarship insofar as scholars have often neglected to examine the cultural particularities of divinity but have opted to assume a masculine divinity instead. Thus, in the case of the Samburu specifically, Paul Spencer (1965) repeated missionary assumptions in assuming Nkai to be male, translating Nkai unreflectingly as God: "God is the supreme arbiter who decides whether the curse is justified or not and who brings misfortune to the wrong doer. It is he who confers a potent curse on certain persons such as mother's brothers, firestick elders, bond brothers, etc." (186). In not scrutinizing Samburu understandings of Nkai, Spencer's failure was not merely subject to the 1970s feminist critique of "ignoring" women. He also failed to understand the peculiarities of Samburu notions of divinity and cosmos, including those that might have pertained to his own subject matter.[24]

Recently, a number of scholars of East African pastoralists have attempted to take a more gender nuanced and balanced view of pastoral understandings of divinity—in both anthropological (Broch-Due 1993; Burton 1991; Hodgson 2001, 2005)[25] and theological studies (Voshaar 1998). Within anthropology, John W. Burton (1991) has examined Nilotic groups comparatively, finding a preponderance of feminine themes in stories about creation, which he links, in turn, to metaphors these groups draw upon in their understandings of everyday social existence.[26] Creation as a feminine birthing experience that includes a "rope" to divinity that becomes severed as a result of human action is a recurring theme across the Shilluk, Anuak, Dinka, Nuer, and Atuot he examines. In these stories, human life begins at the same moment as human death, through the severing of the rope that connects humans with divinity.

These particular stories bear remarkable resemblance, in fact, to a creation story Maasai and Samburu share, which focuses on a strap that gave humans access to E/Nkai. Although the Maasai and Samburu stories locate the strap at different sites, they are virtually identical in other respects. In the Maasai account, Enkai has a leather strap—*enkeene*—that drops to Earth (see Kipury 1983).[27] I have heard a number of Samburu versions of the story, but none that specify the type of nkeene Nkai used, although some speculate that it could be the long strap Samburu women use to carry firewood with. Whatever type of leather strap it was, Nkai dropped the nkeene to Earth and gave gifts of livestock to Samburu. Moreover, people moved freely up and down the strap, asking for whatever they desired. Some Samburu women have told me that they could even receive beads from Nkai during that time. Unfortunately, an impatient Ltorrobo (hunter-gatherer group that lives alongside Samburu) named Lesuyai cut the strap when Nkai delayed in giving him his livestock gift. Notably, he cut the strap after visiting Nkai four times—the same number of times a Samburu midwife asks a new mother if she should cut the umbilical cord.[28] The first three times the midwife asks, the mother says "No, don't cut." After the fourth time, the mother keeps quiet and the midwife cuts. Then the mother must always tell her new baby to take care of his/her heart (*ltau*—used metaphorically for life in this context) and she'll take care of hers. If the mother and child both die before the umbilical cord is cut and these words spoken, they will be buried together.[29] Otherwise, they will always be buried separately.

When Lesuyai cut Nkai's nkeene, half of it went to Nkai and half went to Earth. The half that fell to earth dropped many things, including an *nkeene e nkosheke* (stomach belt). A stomach belt is a leather strap often embellished with cowrie shells, which is worn by postpartum women until they wean their babies. The skin a newborn child sleeps on (*ndadap*) also fell out, along with beads and cowries (the latter strongly associated with women). Furthermore, a spring arose immediately from the dry ground. While the Maasai and Samburu stories thus seem similar to those Burton describes as birthing metaphors, I have not heard uterine interpretations of the Samburu version. Thus, even as it appears to *me* (a North American) very much like an account of the birthing experience—complete with the cutting of the umbilical cord and even the presence of the afterbirth (the spring)—I cannot say definitively that this is the Samburu understanding, but merely suggest the parallels. Moreover, a comparison with Godfrey Lienhardt's (1961) description of Dinka versions of the story illuminates the story's multivalence. According to Lienhardt, the divinity at work in the Dinka stories is the male, yet the procreative principles are clear, and, as in the Adam and Eve story, birth and death arrive together. In the Dinka and Samburu versions, this intertwining of birth and death is through a somewhat violent (umbilical cordlike) cut. As Lienhardt insightfully points out for the Dinka, this cut of separation reflects a logic of division running through Dinka thought, and the parallels to Samburu cuts of separation are striking here.

There are many other feminine metaphors relating to Nkai that are more explicit than the creation story. Jan Voshaar (1998) finds a number of them in a very detailed, insightful study of Maasai divinity. On this basis he argues in favor of a preponderantly feminine Maasai Enkai. Voshaar points out as I have that Enkai is a feminine noun, a realization that I used as a basis for one line of questioning during my 1992–94 fieldwork.[30] Aside from this obvious grammatical fact, Voshaar argues that the majority of metaphorical references to Enkai are feminine. For example, Enkai can be called " 'Noonkipa' [Enkai] of the fertile womb" (137). (Samburu sometimes use this appellation also.) Voshaar also mentions that "when the sky shows lighter coloured clouds, the divine may be referred to as 'Empush Oshoke,' Grey of Womb or 'Parmuain,' the Multi-faceted one" (137).[31] Through these and other references to Enkai, Voshaar argues for a shift from the masculine scholarly interpretations that have predominated to an understanding that includes both masculine and feminine—but with a much heavier emphasis on the feminine aspect in songs, prayers, and daily speech. Importantly, Voshaar suggests that we need to abandon a personified notion of Enkai based in Western notions of the individual and person that do not exist for the Maasai (or Samburu). In this sense, Voshaar argues that "divine gender is not an issue" (136). Rather, Maasai use metaphors for Enkai that reflect their own human understandings of a divine reality.

While Voshaar is undoubedly correct in many ways, and some of his insights are repeated, moreover, in interpretations of Nkai a number of Samburu have offered me, there is more at stake here in this process of divining divine gender and attributing metaphor. European missionaries gave Nkai a unitary, unequivocally masculine gender based in a sexed body—complete with pictures—*and* a uniquely Judeo-Christian theology and purpose. And these characteristics are not metaphorical in any straightforward sense. If this fact has escaped the attention of some Samburu, it has not escaped the attention of many others, nor of Nkai Itself.

Gendering Divinity, Shaping Nkai

From the collection of stories and interviews I have, it has become apparent to me that both Nkai's appearances and messages to the Samburu have been transforming over time, and, moreover, they have been doing so with such complexity that I cannot do justice to all of their features here. I would like to state explicitly at the outset what some readers might already take for granted concerning the temporality of these phenomena. The age of a story does not make it a clear window onto the Samburu past. That is, even if a story of Nkai's appearance is reputed to be seventy or a hundred years old, the telling of that story has been transforming over time with its telling. In this sense, historical transformation makes the Samburu "strangers to [them]selves" (Kristeva 1991) in their own presentist recollections of their past. All I can hope for (and this may be a grand assumption) is that some features of old stories— particularly those that clearly differ from contemporary stories—have been more or less invariant. Using the nearness of contemporary divine appearances as my primary focus here, I am thus writing from within the space of absence and forgetting—taking the absence, simplicity, or unmarked nature of some features of older stories as telling in comparison to their presence in contemporary stories.[32]

During my 1990s fieldwork, my impression was that Samburu were agnostic concerning Nkai's shape and gender, or that perhaps a masculine Christian God was merging with a feminine Nkai. Not surprisingly, Samburu Christians asserted that Nkai, like God, was singular and male. Yet it seemed to me that the unconverted majority was equivocating about Nkai's gender, since they occasionally chose a masculine or feminine attribution at my prompting but more often said that Nkai had both masculine and feminine aspects or was even both and more. In one interview, my educated Samburu research assistant—a descendant of BCMS converts—argued strenuously with a Samburu woman friend of mine on just this topic. While my friend Naliapu said matter-of-factly that Samburu believe that Nkai is both masculine and feminine, my research assistant objected that Nkai could only be one—much to my amusement at the time:

We normally say there are two. [There is only one Nkai. (Laughter from me.)] Aren't they two? [There aren't.] You see then, the Samburu just say there are two, there is a postpartum woman one and there is a masculine one. You see, all those people I heard talking, they just say it is a postpartum [fecund] woman. Because I heard another one saying that Nkai took [a person to Her/Their home] and opened [a cow pen] and removed a black cow with an *arus* calf [calf with black and white at the neck]. And there was a fecund woman [Nkai] with mporo [a marriage necklace] and two calabashes, one She has [is] an *nkoitiŋ* [long and slender shaped gourd]. And [She] put them near a calves' pen and took an *nkilip* [long but not slender gourd] and milked a cow with it and finished. And [She] took that nkoitiŋ and milked a cow with it and finished. She turned the mporo to face that side [out of her way while working], and She [Nkai] had *lmasi* [matted hair] like those ones of postpartum women.[33] And She had a stomach belt with cowrie shells and so when then why shouldn't we say that that the Nkai who had been seen is a Fecund Woman?" (Naliapu interview, 1994)

While I found the idea of Samburu agnosticism appealing then, Naliapu's statements indicated otherwise, and a less equivocal story emerged quite clearly late in my 1992–94 fieldwork as I began to approach the issue resolutely and from many perspectives. Thus, as attractive as a feminine Nkai or even agnosticism might be to a feminist scholar, the contradictions I saw in 1992–94 and again in 2001–2 concerning Nkai were not evidence of agnosticism. Indeed, Naliapu seemed quite certain about her information. As I questioned Christian Samburu more closely, I found that many of them conceded that "traditional" understandings were that Nkai was precisely what the majority had been telling me—*both* masculine and feminine. Moreover, Nkai was not even merely masculine *and* feminine; in keeping with a *Samburu* sense of "gender," Nkai was always particularized, as an lmurran, for example, or a post-partum woman (Ntomononi). Like Samburu persons, Nkai could not be imagined with an abstract sexed body—Nkai's human shapes presupposed specific social roles within which gender was thoroughly entangled. Not simply "male" or "female," when human, Nkai appeared as a specific kind of moral person, an exemplar a Samburu could relate to.

As I became more attuned to the Nkai talk around me, I began to understand that Nkai gave evidence of Their nature all of the time. Indeed, cases of people being taken to Nkai's home were not rare events but fairly frequent occurrences. And a number of things recounted in these experiences recurred frequently—among them, that *Nkai was also neither singular nor dual but an entire polygynous family.* Even on Mount Diro, perhaps Samburu's most sacred place,[34] Nkai regularly appears in ways that imply a family with livestock. A woman I met in 2002 said that she herself had experienced Nkai while climbing Mount Diro, where she used to live. There is a large stone at the top, which is said to tremble frequently for no apparent reason, and there are often thunder, mist, and rain. Moreover, according to my acquaintance, many other women frequently heard or saw what she saw, even while walking in groups.

Nkai is in that stone. . . . And in the morning, you see Their sheep coming out because they [the sheep] are how many? [Three] You just hear a Child [Nkai] saying, "Hey, Twala [the name of the sheep], hey Twala!" [Mm] It is like a picture [Mm]. In just a little while they [Nkai's sheep] disappear. (Kurungu interview January 2002)

With regard to experiences of actually going away to Nkai's home (presumed to be somewhere in the sky, from which Mount Diro is perhaps an excellent meeting point, joining Earth and sky), children are the most frequent visitors. I have heard numerous accounts of such children—like Remeta—disappearing for hours or even days, returning to tell wonderful stories about Nkai or Nkai's home. Sometimes, the children do not note other people in Nkai's home—or else this piece of information gets lost in frequent tellings. Even in the less detailed stories, however, children remember being taken home by an Nkai wife who had enough calabashes and livestock to imply a large family. I recall one story in particular of a little girl who returned after being missing for a few days saying that a nicely clothed Nkai fecund woman had taken her home. The latter was wearing a large, beautiful mporo (marriage necklace) and full (two-piece) leather dress as only brides wear these days. Nkai's livestock were healthy and fat, and the Nkai fecund woman gave her a lot of milk and meat to eat and a very clean cowhide to sleep on in the house. After a few days, Nkai led the child in the direction of home and people found her, looking healthy and well fed.

Many of the stories I have heard of children visiting or speaking with Nkai are only months, years, or a decade or two old, but some stories are much older. My friend Naliapu told me a story of a child whom Nkai spoke to during the Lmekuri ageset (1940s), for example. Naliapu herself had been playing with other children near a cave. A goat came out, and they followed it inside, in the direction from which it had come. Then, a wind came suddenly and blew the children out of the cave. One of the little girls fell and cracked her skull. After she was brought home and her father went to get a goat to slaughter to help her heal, Nkai called her, asking what her father had gone to bring. Following the little girl's response, Nkai said to her, "Tell your father not to give you oil [from the goat]. Instead, tell him to give you blood from a gray cow." The little girl's head was open with blood pouring from the wound, yet Naliapu maintains that she survived to give her father these instructions, and she survived the following day, and the next, eventually healing (Naliapu interview, 1994).

My research assistant, Timothy, told me that his grandfather's sister, Turaso, had disappeared for a few days late in the Lmarinkon ageset (probably late 1880s or early 1890s) and was discovered in a cave saying that she had been to Nkai's home. Nkai had given her honey to eat and a message to bring back to her home. Although she appeared healthy, the family and community were concerned about what had transpired in the cave on that hill. Thus, they "changed the color of," as in ceremonially cleansing, the entire hill.[35] Then they moved from there and the little girl continually begged her father to move from the new place as well, but he refused. It is said that as he was dying he told the elders that he was dying for refusing to listen to his daughter, who had clearly prophesied his death if he remained. The little girl was so furious with Nkai for taking her father that she stopped prophesying after that, and eventually she married someone of the Lorokushu clan and moved to Marsabit (Naado and Ntegis interviews, 2002). Timothy told me that her grandchildren are still there.

It is not only children who literally travel to "Heaven" (Nkai's home) and back or speak to Nkai, however. Lmurran or even young elders also disappear sometimes and return recounting experiences of visiting Nkai. I suspect that this is the context in which Naomi Kipury's (1983) Maasai story about the lmurran who visited "God's country" should be placed, despite the fact that she includes it with a group of stories she implies are simple fiction. Unlike Kipury's story, which appears as if it is a unique piece of timeless folklore, as I have been arguing, Samburu visits to Nkai's home are regular, if unusual, occurrences. I heard two stories in 2002 of young men visiting Nkai's home. In both of these stories, as with Remeta's and other stories I have heard, Nkai had a large settlement with a Nkai husband, Nkai wives, Nkai children and Imurran, and Nkai livestock. It would seem from everyday Samburu stories of visiting Nkai that Nkai is not masculine or feminine but both and more. Moreover, Nkai is many—a polygynous family with many livestock.

In considering these divine appearances I want to strenuously argue that Nkai's varying and multiple incarnations are not metaphorical, at least not in any simple sense. For Remeta, Nkai simply was a family, and moreover, an ideal family to emulate. That Nkai can choose to appear in many forms, from large snake to stone to polygynous family, does not suggest that Nkai is not all of those things in a real sense. Nkai does have livestock—and thus is in a position to give them freely as gifts or to take them in compensation if people err. The cows Samburu women milk each morning to feed their families are not metaphors. And, as I first heard from a famous woman loibon, Doto Malapen, in 1993, "Nkai is a Fecund Woman." Nkai literally gives birth—to Her own Children and to every living thing. Later, in 2002, Doto Malapen described one of her visions of Nkai to me in detail, a vision in which there were two Nkai postpartum/fecund women. "She told the Other, 'Come, let us take turns with my child. You will carry and I will also carry, so that we'll go and seek a person who will understand our language.' " (The two Nkai found Doto Malapen to tell their message to.) Moreover, Nkai is a Imurran, especially when He has bad news to tell, as Doto Malapen also told me in 2002. Recall that one of Remeta's Nkai was also an Imurran, and she was not afraid of him, although I have heard that one of the Imurran's messages was negative—an implicit warning. More frequently, though, as Voshaar noted for the Maasai, Nkai is feminine. She is a fecund woman who rains urine and leaves fecund postpartum moisture; She is the sky, and the clouds belong to Her. All of these features of Nkai are obvious and everywhere, real and metaphorical simultaneously, as I heard eloquently from the old father of a good friend in Ndikir Nanyukie as he spoke to my research assistant and me.

You see usually when it thunders, they [Samburu] pray saying, "Oh my Nkai, give us your urine. Save our cattle, have mercy on us . . . There is no mountain that Nkai is not in, because this air is Nkai and She is the one who brings it . . . There is no mountain without Nkai because when it rains She puts down Her little cloth [clouds], that white *morole* [fecund moisture] of Hers. Why should She put it down? After raining—giving us this sweet water of Hers. And this is Her frost on top of the mountains . . . You see now this soil we are sitting on. Elder people say it is the Nkai of Samburu we are stepping on . . . And isn't that Nkai of the mountains that comes to rain, just that one that we don't see, just that one we pray to. You see that one attached to the mountains, we just pray to that one, that one that is cut off [isolated]. And these Europeans who go on planes [Mm], and the clouds, don't they go beyond? [They go beyond.] Can they go through the black one?[36] [M-m (No).] What? [M-m (No).] That is how it is, my boy, these are just like the birth membrane. [Yes.] You see this cloud, it is the one that brings Her leather dress again, cutting it [separating lighter clouds from rain clouds], putting a shadow over us [a shadow portending fertile rain, and a shadow generally is assumed to protect from the harshness of the sun, from death-bringing drought]. (Leropili interview, March 2002)

As I did when Nkai was thought to be an lmurrani in the story of destroying the Samburu in the 1870s to '90s, I have attributed "sex-gender" to Nkai in this quote. This time, however, following the images and Samburu advice, I have used the feminine pronoun. Yet I am translating through Western categories here—Nkai is always a feminine noun even as the descriptive features of particular stories about Them/It lend themselves to masculine, feminine, or a sexless, genderless rendering in Western (and here, English) translation. For the Samburu, Nkai is a multisexed/gendered/aged/wedded, and so on, descriptively dense sign because of Nkai's profundity, but crucially, this does not make Nkai's attributes metaphorical any more than the world Nkai creates and the rain Nkai gives are metaphorical. When Remeta visited Nkai, she visited an instantiation of Nkai that is very real to many Samburu. And if the attribution of gender here (or multiple ages and genders) appears trivial, we would do well to consider the strength of many Christians' insistence worldwide that God is He, in counterpoint to feminist Christians who assert something else (as in Johnson 1993).[37] Moreover, we would also do well to consider why it is Nkai insists on appearing to lmurran, women, and children as fecund women, as children, or as an entire family. I will leave that question for now, however, as I turn to another dimension of Remeta's Nkai—Their color.

Racing Nkai

On the basis of Remeta's account of her visit to Nkai's home, I was immediately struck with a thought that I found immensely disturbing: Nkai is becoming white. Part of my eventual conclusion was that such an assumption already presumed a North American racialized view in which race could be a category of its own, and that it could be defined by a single surface feature (skin color). Yet my initial and gut reaction was to identify with a particularly facile view of a many-sided historical, and historically complex, debate. As Gordon and Newfield (1995) have so astutely pointed out, in attending to the complexities of race and racial identity, we should not "simply assert a principle of reason to rule all domains in the same way" (400). Race, like gender, has complicated and multiple histories—for the Samburu, race (or rather here, the marked category of "Europeanness") has become a dense sign that must be understood with respect to the process of colonialism that was its crucible (see Stoler 1989 for a path-breaking discussion of colonialism, race, and gender). Yet, as in the case of "gender," we cannot assume that "race" (for which there is no Samburu term, borrowed or otherwise) is ontologically the same for the Samburu as it is for North American scholars any more than we should homogenize understandings of race within North America generally or elsewhere. What should I do, then, with my experience of Remeta's brothers exclaiming, upon seeing me, that perhaps I was Remeta's Nkai? Let me continue, first, with my description of what I did at the time.

Following my experience with Remeta, I cast about for possible explanations of Nkai's whiteness, and, simultaneously, I began to focus intensely in subsequent interviews on Samburu descriptions of Nkai particularly, as those pertained to "color." I focused on the fact that the term Remeta used in referring to an Nkai that looked like me was neither "white" (naibor) nor "European" (mzungui or l/mshumpa), but, rather, "red" (nyokie). Checking transcriptions of previous interviews and noting the terms carefully in subsequent interviews, I soon realized that Nkai was/were frequently described as being "red": "He asked, 'My Turaso,' 'Father.' 'What has taken you?' She said, 'a certain woman with a black [leather] cloth carrying a baby.' [What color was Nkai?] She said a certain red" (Naado interview, 2002).[38] Was redness synonymous with whiteness? It took a great deal of discussion and many interviews to surmise that "color" was a fairly flexible attribute through which ethnicity could sometimes be presumed (though not with certainty), as in very "black" Turkana and "white" Europeans, while "red" could refer to almost anyone whether white European or Samburu. Thus, one of my friends put the matter to rest this way: "It [Nkai] is just a black person, it is just red [and it is just brown] and it is just brown. And she mentioned the calabashes, because she is saying, 'I saw the calabashes, they also have nchongoro [a calabash] that are like copper and they have calabashes just like ours'" (Naliapu interview, 2002).

For Naliapu, what was crucial in defining Nkai as Samburu rather than European was the presence of calabashes and, moreover, the specific calabashes that Samburu women milk with. Even if Remeta and her brothers thought at first that I was Nkai, Remeta also described Nkai as having calabashes, Samburu beds, and Samburu ornaments. Also, as I have pointed out elsewhere (Straight 1997a, b), Samburu refer to African Americans and even educated Samburu as mzungui-narok (black "Europeans").[39] If "color" is metonymic for race in North America, such is not the case for the Samburu. Indeed, what North American academics might refer to as racialized discourse belies a North American racial ontology.[40] Yet this is not to deny that something significant is transpiring when little girls and their older brothers can mistake white Americans in Samburu cloth and beads as Nkai.[41]

Samburu descriptions of colonial administrators, their employees, and missionaries suggest an ambivalent relationship moving between hatred for policies and practices that clearly oppressed (and even killed) them and admiration for some of those practices and things. The stuff of colonialism has often been greatly admired, as is apparent from the mabati ("modern") houses that have been springing up on the landscape for decades and the popularity of hats, shorts, radios, tape players, flashlights, books, and so on. Certainly, Samburu have adopted these things in their own ways, but at the same time they are quite clear that mzungus brought these "clever" things. Moreover, modernity—with its capitalist entrepreneurial ethic and consumer goods (Straight 2000)—is a concept and a set of practices that the overwhelming majority of Samburu admire even if they criticize some of its entailments. To be in the midst of "developing," to be on the way to "modernity," has become a feature of Samburu identity even as the precise terms of development and modernity are debated.

Thus, while I would argue that the question of whether Nkai is becoming white is a problematic one at the outset, Samburu understandings of their own modernity *are* at stake here. On the one hand, in mistaking me for Nkai Remeta was reacting to my sudden appearance on the horizon as a cause for disorientation—the sort of disorientation I believe happens just before those ah-ha moments of fieldwork, when we are jolted into recognizing at once the profundity of our difference and the possibility of partially overcoming it through shared experience with our interlocutors. On the other hand, the character of that disorientation, of a difference crossed by troubling, unequal encounter, embraces the contradictory possibilities I have been describing—possibilities of ontology, embodiment, gender, race, and identity. Nkai is at once an echo of Samburu predicaments and choices and an astute elder—measuring, observing, measuring again, and cutting. Thus, what is problematic about looking to race, gender, or possibilities for embodiment for understanding Nkai is not that these issues are meaningless for the Samburu but that Samburu engagements with Euro-American practices and assumptions follow different priorities. What is of concern to the Samburu who follow the messages of Nkai transmitted through Remeta and many others is what Nkai is saying about what it means to be a proper Samburu. Amid a globalizing "modernity"—for Samburu, a trope of gadget seeking, Euro-American commodity fetishizing, cash-centered "development"—being a proper Samburu is a sign whose transubstantiations are continually and problematically unstable.

There is a third way of approaching stories about Nkai's appearances, one involving the problematics of this subjectivity, Nkai's deft movements, and at least nodding to Euro-American conceptions of race and gender while enacting and reenacting a Samburu subjectivity. The attributes that I ascribe to Nkai along the way are not singularly located or determined but rather are moving and indeterminate—roaming across the landscape from one hill to another in one shape or another just as people and cattle move across the horizon or as children like Remeta move between "Heaven" and "Earth." Thus, they are at once well suited to a roaming Samburu subjectivity and to what will be my attempt to juxtapose a notion of indeterminate, transubstantiating *Being* with Samburu philosophical understandings impinging on the person.

Prescissing Nkai

When it happens, Nkai's appearance is always strange, disorienting, and worthy of comment. And this should come as no surprise—the appearance of divinity is, for Samburu as it is for Euro-Americans, a wonder, a miracle. Most commonly, Nkai appears in the sky (as rain clouds) in the shape of an elephant's trunk or in the shape of extraordinarily large snakes in caves and on hills.[42] Less commonly and more amazingly, Nkai also sometimes appears in human form—as unexpected for a girl like Remeta as the sudden appearance of a white, North American anthropologist.

There is some consistency to Nkai's intervention in human affairs, however. From a presentist Samburu perspective, Nkai continually gives birth to and nourishes the world and as such is a target of supplication and a source of joy. Nkai also, however, presents Itself/Themselves as a perfect model for moral Samburu personhood, and in this respect Nkai's presence is double-edged. Nkai's appearances can incarnate moral perfection to emulate, but Nkai can, as well, offer warnings and even bring harm as exemplary punishment for wrongdoing. I have touched on Nkai's appearance as a punishment or warning against adultery, particularly incest, as when a woman has affairs with lmurran (warriors) though her husband belongs to an ageset that is categorically the fathers of current lmurran. I have also described the prescriptions Nkai gave to Remeta and other children who have visited or communicated with Nkai. Nkai has seemingly innumerable reasons for appearing. I will discuss just a few of them here, in an attempt to elucidate what they might mean to the Samburu who experience or carefully heed them.

I will start with Nkai's warnings against selfishness, which appear in the reputedly oldest stories of Nkai's appearances. I mentioned a couple of these narratives earlier in this chapter. The selfishness and arrogance of young people, particularly girls, is widely blamed for the Mutai Disas-

ter—a series of wars, diseases, drought, and famine—of the 1870s to
'90s. Thus, in one series of stories, the girlfriends of the Ltarigirig generation of lmurran, known as the Leisa, were too proud of their beautiful
ornaments and were consequently selfish, withholding milk from hungry kin and neighbors. Some Samburu suggest the Leisa also lacked
respect—intimating that they may have been guilty of "standing too
close" to their elders, perhaps to the point of having affairs with them.
On the one hand, the potential implications of abundant commodities—beads and other baubles—is clear. On the other hand, Nkai did
not take offense at girls' ostentatious ornaments but rather at behavior
that upset clear moral boundaries (see Straight 2005a). Similarly, in
another narrative cycle, sometimes also attributed to the period of Mutai
but frequently attributed to an older period, young people demon-
strated lack of respect and restraint by bathing in milk. Nkai brought
famine as a result, whether it was in the 1870s or earlier.

Selfishness, with its attendant lack of respect, has figured consistently
and prominently in Nkai's appearances over time. Thus, as I also mentioned earlier, beginning in 1992 I heard of how Nkai had brought a
deluge of fire and water to the Lesootia family in the 1950s when the
wife of that family refused to share water from a source the colonial government had given her husband authority over (see Straight 1997b). In
2002 I heard of a greedy and selfish local (male) shopkeeper whom Nkai
had killed within the past year while he slept—agreement that it was
indeed Nkai was fairly widespread, even among many Christians.
Indeed, stories of Nkai's killing individuals for selfishness or particularly
grievous acts of adultery (as in incest) are too many to recount. More
notable, perhaps, especially in their details, are the stories of Nkai's
appearing to people and issuing general warnings against selfishness.[43]

I recall a story I heard in 2002 of a young man taken by Nkai—a young
Lkiroro named Lolosuli of the Lkirina subclan of Lorokushu. After
nourishing him until he was full, Nkai gave him several warnings to
bring back to people.

He was told . . . tell [child-bearing] women to sing and pray to me[44] . . . tell
children to pray to me [Yes] because all of these problems that have come
[Mm], it is Me who brought them. There is no more milk [Mhmm]. It is Me who
took it [Mm]. And I took animals—I came with that drought [Mm]. It/They say,
what brought these problems [Mhmm]? You. You, these curses [Mm]. You curse
children and you curse women [Mm] and you even curse adults [Mhmm]. And
you are no longer pitying one another. And you are no longer pitying one
another [Yes]. And you are no longer pitying one another that whoever has food
can share with another [Mhmm]. Everyone just wants to live all by themselves
and they don't want to share food when they have it [Mhmm]. And so that is
the thing [Mhmm]. And so I took milk, because of these curses . . . And so that
is what you do to the Samburu [Yes]. It is your people who have and don't have

[Mm]. So a hyena said it is you all [Yes]. I will equalize you all. (Lelesimoi interview, 2002)

There are several things worthy of note in this story. This is a timely indictment of the Samburu, occurring in the midst of droughts that were particularly disastrous in the mid-1980s (when the Lkiroro were finishing their time of being lmurran) and into the early and late 1990s—the effects of which are still being felt. Many people point to the warnings in Remeta's own message, noting that during one of her experiences the Nkai lmurrani had shown her the results of Samburu wrongdoing. Pointing to a great white stone with black spots on it he asked, "Do you see this stone, Remeta?" "Yes," she replied. "The black spots on this stone are all the terrible things Samburu do to one another. And we are dropping them back down, one by one. That is your wars, diseases, and other disasters." It is a timely indictment, but apparently a consistent one as well—it would seem that whenever Nkai visits widespread destruction on the Samburu It/They appear to explain the reasons. Selfishness and pride (and to a lesser extent, certain forms of adultery) upset the Samburu moral universe dramatically and, as such, cannot be tolerated. Moreover, even in times of scarcity, Samburu must share according to the norms of their own society—the agreements they themselves have held over time.

If Nkai is periodically vexed by collective selfishness, there are other things that seem to have vexed Nkai only recently, and these are worth investigating further. I want to touch on two here—adornment and calabashes. As another young Lkiroro noted after his visit to Nkai's settlement, everyone was wearing leather clothes and the appropriate beaded ornaments for their age/gender/marital status, and the married women were wearing the sort of very large mporo necklaces I used to see in the lowlands in 1992 but that are increasingly scarce and hidden from daily sight (for fear of theft—see Straight 2002a). One among the Nkai family asked the lmurran if people dressed this way in his place. When he responded that they didn't, Nkai said that they should.

I recall a paper (unpublished) I wrote in graduate school, based particularly on media research and a handful of interviews I conducted with Maasai in Tanzania. I was intrigued by the different ways that Christian missions and the Kenyan and Tanzanian colonial and postindependence governments had dealt with Maasai "traditional" dress, as well as how Maasai themselves had responded. Clothing and missions have certainly received a lot of scholarly attention in the past decade. For the Maasai, the struggle over clothing that began with missions (and is echoed in the Samburu case—Straight 1997b) reached a strange climax when the Tanzanian government ordered pastoralist men and women to wear trousers and dresses. The government order was notable enough to be picked up in the American media, where the latter focused its attention on Maasai lmurran, though the government order was clearly aimed at both men and women. As *Time* magazine reported, the police were ready to "herd" lmurran "into mass baths, burn their ceremonial garb in public and shave off their ochred hair" (1967: 40). The Kenyan government did not take so drastic a position, though in 1985 it did attempt (as the colonial government had attempted well prior) to ban the lmurran age-grade and its adornment accouterments—ironically at the same time that the media was lamenting Kenya's lack of a "national dress" (Straight 1991; Talle 1988).

I will not take the space here to elaborate further on this intriguing debate over clothing, but suffice it to say that Nkai has taken due note of these contestations. In the Tanzanian Maasai case, in 1989 I was intrigued to learn from an American Catholic missionary and several other individuals—several Maasai among them—that women had had visions instructing them to take off their cloths and put on their leather clothing (Fr. Kohler and others, personal communication, 1989). In my 1991 paper, I examined this debate as a struggle over ethnic and national identity (see also Ole Saibull and Carr 1981), a position that is no doubt an appropriate one, though it is not the only one. Why would pastoralist women experience this debate in the form of visions from Nkai telling them to wear leather clothing? In the Samburu case specifically, why has Nkai been telling men and women to wear leather and beads? Why also has Nkai appeared so notably—even in older stories from the 1950s—with the calabashes Samburu recognize as their own? Recall that Nkai told Remeta specifically that women should use calabashes, not plastic jugs, when milking—a prescription I took very seriously in 2002 when a couple of my neighbors started using plastic jugs while milking. Although they usually poured the milk into calabashes afterward, I expressed surprise that they were using plastic at all, after what Remeta had said, and they were amused that I was being "holier than" they. (My concern here in fact was that Nkai may have also had a public health reason for banning plastic—calabashes are purified with fire, while plastic may be washed with water of dubious quality.)

It is tempting to suggest that Nkai's pronouncements about beads, clothing, and calabashes are moments of Samburu resistance to capitalist commodities or things Western and/or assertions of their right to an ethnic as well as a national identity, just as it is equally tempting to consider that Nkai may be becoming white and male. (Eventually, the latter will be an empirical issue.) I am not willing to yield these conclusions quite so fast, nor do I think Nkai is. In the case of race and gender, I have already made my points. With respect to beads, clothing, and cala-

Figure 6. A girl milks livestock with her beads and other ornaments on. The author's son Jen is milking in the left foreground at age eight, 1994.

bashes, to suggest resistance is to reassert an overly simplified pastoralists-as-conservative assumption. Indeed, I think there is more at stake here than a simple Samburu-versus-outsider dichotomy. Nkai and the Samburu who follow Nkai's pronouncements are undoubtedly asserting their identity as Samburu, but they are not doing so in any straightforward or uniform way.

I have elaborated in some detail elsewhere that Samburu beaded ornaments are not timeless but rather have a history, and, moreover, that Samburu are well aware and proud that Samburu fashions—in beads and songs—change (Straight 2002a, 2005a). Samburu are not ignorant of the fact that their beads come as commodities from abroad. They are known to grumble about the prices and have even devised a process for manufacturing some beads of their own (Straight 2000), but in principle they are not in the least disturbed by the commodity origins of their ornaments. Regardless of origin, the ornaments Samburu fashion are their own, and these fashions change—both within and especially across ageset generations. They are aware, likewise, that the red beads used in mporo necklaces came from abroad, though they simultaneously assert that the necklaces have "always" been there.

Regardless of origins or change, mporo and other beaded ornaments are a critical marker of Samburu identity, and differences in ornaments and clothing (especially leather, but cloth as well) importantly distinguish gender, age, marital status, and generations. Moreover, with respect to women, ornaments are critical markers of personhood. As my dear friend Nolsintani tearfully exclaimed in referring to my importance as bead giver when she had taken refuge in my home after disputing with her husband, "Bilinda made me a person!" A woman without beads is not only *not* a person, she signals her ill health or invites disease. As women have repeatedly told me, an abundance of beads is a sign of health—of health that accompanies wealth in a society for which abundant animals mean abundant food. Conversely, women who are very sick remove their beads—they are not well enough to dress fully and engage in their routine tasks. Old women reduce their number of beads as they near the end of life but keep at least a few until they die. Upon death, a person is stripped of all ornaments—thus it is said that only a dead person has no ornaments.

That Nkai, like the Samburu, is not simply refusing things Western is clear from Samburu interpretations of Nkai's prescriptions that it is appropriate to remove beads when entering the space of commerce, formal schooling, and wage labor. Women—and men likewise—who work outside a Samburu home are expected to wear Western forms of attire in that context. However, if they are staying at home for any length of time and especially if they are milking livestock, they need to dress appropriately Samburu. To live as a Samburu in a Samburu home, milking Samburu livestock, it is not only appropriate but expedient to dress as a Samburu. To remove one's ornaments before milking a cow is to invite disaster—it is to suggest that one is terribly sick or dead already, not a very propitious way to request a cow's fecundity. And this is precisely the reason for banning plastic jugs in milking as well. As I will elucidate in detail in Chapter 4, calabashes are thoroughly entangled in Samburu personhood. Indeed, in some instances, they *are* Samburu persons. To approach a Samburu cow with a plastic container is to mix what cannot properly mix—outside and propitious inside. An animal's vital substance should not be poured into a foreign container but rather should mix with what fundamentally belongs to its Samburu family.

Certainly, the task of maintaining important boundaries is a difficult one in the context of capitalist commodification, wage labor, and so on. Nkai recognizes this, and like the Samburu themselves, has been engaging in a delicate negotiation, on the one hand affirming the aesthetics of sharing that continue to be crucial while simultaneously lamenting new assaults on the sharing ethic; and on the other hand tolerating many changes (like mabati houses) while endlessly (re)positioning the line that should not be crossed. Ultimately, Nkai seems to be engaged in affirming what is most presumed, what everyone already knows. As I have suggested and according to everyone I have talked to, Nkai does not render judgment on those wearing Western clothes in contexts like wage labor. Rather, Nkai calls attention to Samburu who forget the most mundane and crucial markers of their own personhood; indeed, Nkai is engaged in the all-important and delicate task of *redefining* Samburu personhood in the new millennium. Thus, for example, while they are in Samburu settlements milking their cows, Samburu women must remember themselves and their families with beads on their necks and calabashes in their hands.

In conclusion, then, while it is tempting to suggest that the features of Nkai's recent appearances reflect a deep concern with issues impinging on Samburu modernity like race and gender, I think that as a summation this is woefully inadequate. It reflects a Eurocentric preoccupation with Otherness and the Other's engagement with Us. Instead, I would suggest that in some ways Nkai has ignored Christianity and what many Samburu as well as Western academics term modernity. Or, to put it another way, Nkai has observed modernity only insofar as it impinges on the business of instructing Samburu about the practices that affirm Samburu personhood in ways that pragmatically bring propitious results to themselves and their families. This is consistent with the Samburu's own preoccupation with a so-called Otherness both fundamentally distinct from and more subtle than West/rest.[45] It is a Samburu preoccupation that contains within it an understanding of simultaneity, of both mixing and dividing in multiple ways and in multiple spheres. For now, and in keeping with Nkai's profundity, then, I will leave this chapter with the suggestion that Nkai both comments on and ignores modernity, both rewards and punishes, and—as Lemeteki said (Chapter 2)—that Nkai echoes human words and makes them powerful.

Part II
Fragile Borders

. . . Therefore this
          is what I
must ask you
          to imagine: wind;
the moment
          when the wind

drops; and grapes,
          which are nothing,
which break
          in your hands

—*Jorie Graham*

Chapter 4

Latukuny

At first I gave birth to a girl. I gave birth late, because it was in the evening that I gave birth. Then this *mporoi* was removed and roasted, it was roasted completely.[1] [Yes] Then a woman just came and removed that mporoi [Yes] and took it, because she took it that way [Yes] and dug into the ground and put it in, the whole thing [Yes]. Then another woman, an old Maasai woman, came and said, "Cow friend, cow friend just come because it has been taken long ago. Do you know this woman who was brought here, she has come and taken away the mporoi and done to it what she did. So just come, tell Lekurtut [Ŋoto Malapen's husband] to come." Then my late husband came and said, "These cows now, these ones of my herding efforts, a person will now die. The one who took the mporoi for this baby" [cursing the offender by his cows]. (Ŋoto Malapen interview, 1993)

In stealing the mporoi (clotted blood) associated with the birth of Ŋoto Malapen's daughter, a transient woman nearly succeeded in killing both this child and all of Ŋoto Malapen's future children.[2] Luckily for Ŋoto Malapen, a close friend (one with whom she had exchanged cow gifts) intervened. Her husband publicly cursed the woman for this grave offense, and by this act prompted her to exhume the mporoi and return it. After it had been blessed with curdled milk and fragrant incense, Ŋoto Malapen's daughter, Malapen, lived and Ŋoto Malapen herself succeeded in becoming pregnant again. However, this was not the end of the matter. Ŋoto Malapen, one of the most famous Samburu prophetesses of the twentieth century, was the victim of theft after the birth of her son as well. And while his mporoi was likewise safely returned, she was not so lucky after her third child:

That same woman took it again. Then she took that away and people asked where it was without success. I think she had said, "I won't exhume it this time, I'll die with it. I won't give it back." So those two children are the only ones I got [Yes]. So that child passed away, as did the others that I would have gotten. So I remained without giving birth any more. (Ŋoto Malapen interview, 1993)

In this chapter I will move from the miraculous to the improbable, from children who bodily wander in and out of Heaven to unremarkable babies whose lives are contained in calabashes and goat bones. In so

doing, I will point to Samburu prescissive cuttings whereby the boundaries between objects and persons flow in between the taken-for-granted
limits of Euro-American subjectivity. This would seem a commonplace
comparison between secure Euro-American empiricism and the "mystical" beliefs of others for an anthropologist, and yet, why do the terrors
of metaphysical assault excite imagination and resurface in experience?
Why, particularly in the context of capitalism, do we persist in interro-
gating the vulnerabilities associated with materiality and the meaning of
loss?

Objects That Do Not Return

In "Marx's Coat" (1998) Peter Stallybrass argues that "only if an object
is stripped of its particularity and history can it again become a commodity and an exchange value" (195). Stallybrass writes here of clothing
pawned for potential resale, a capitalist context in which customers
desired what was least worn—that is, what showed the least evidence of
being on the backs of other human beings. Let us take note of what
Amariglio and Callari (1993) have so cogently persuaded, that "the construction of value relations presumes and exemplifies a conception of
the relationship" between circulation and subjectivity (193). In cases
like Marx's pawned coat, that relationship includes consumers' desires
to dissociate previous wearers from the coat they now possess, to imagine
the coat as if it lacks the shape of another human being. Yet for Marx,
as for many others in his impoverished circumstances, to pawn a possession was to be haunted by its loss, by precisely the memories that the
new owner wanted to forget, as Stallybrass informs us:

> If their things were sometimes animated by their loves, their histories, their han-
> dlings, they were often animated by the workings of a marketplace that took
> back those things and stripped them of their loves and their histories, devalued
> them because they had been handled. (199)

Patricia Spyer (1998) likewise offers a version of this process of reciprocal remembering and forgetting. Writing of the colonization of the
Aru in what is contemporary eastern Indonesia, Spyer treats us to a view
of a clothing market quite different from the one Stallybrass describes.
Looking on while Aru islanders joyfully experimented with and transformed European clothing and adornment fashions, the Dutch were
utterly scandalized. If pawnshop consumers could teach themselves to
forget that their (presumably) fellow Europeans had once worn or
owned their "new" possessions, the Dutch could not bring themselves
even close to forgetting that their fellow Europeans ordinarily inhabited
clothing now draped in *wrong* fashion across their racial "inferiors":

One of the problems must have been that the islanders—made over in some-thing akin to metropole mode—seemed to stand before the Europeans as an unsettling, slightly skewed copy of themselves as well as of the "civilization" they had come to convey through clothes. I suspect that the sheer materiality of this "meeting ground"—the mere physical fact of being confronted with native bod-ies contained in one's own colonizer clothes—is one aspect of the discomfort that seems to filter through the writings of these Europeans. (Spyer 1998: 163–64)

Spyer contends, moreover, that through this vision of "native bodies" in one's "own" clothes the Aruese became figures of "uncanny" doubling, alarming these Dutch colonizers by presenting them with something "close to home," yet slightly "askew" (165).

In an apparent reversal of this theme, I have elsewhere discussed North American women's desires for Samburu mporo (marriage beads) as linked to the fact that these objects *have* been fondled and worn pre-viously by African women (Straight 2002a). Here, North American women often only vaguely know the context of the beads' previous use but fill in with imagination what they cannot provide in ethnographic detail, creating what I have called a fictitious inalienability. This exam-ple—of desiring objects because of their association with their former context even as these objects have been alienated from it—is the crucial complement to Stallybrass's and Spyer's examples and is particularly pal-pable in Marx's early writings. For the early Marx particularly (and as I have discussed elsewhere—2002a), alienation entailed an irretrievable loss, as a person was at once parted from the objects that should have been inseparably connected to his or her personhood yet admitted into a covetous relationship with others on the basis of an illicit desire that could only feebly substitute for one's lost autonomy and wholeness. In other theorists' hands, this combination would become a theory of a (Euro-American) subjectivity always already predicated on loss.[3]

Let me pause on the threshold of these various nonreturning, decon-textualized objects and consider their foil. For if there are objects desired for their newness as well as those desired for real or fictitious associations—all turning on a similar premise of alienation and loss—there are as well objects that do what Marx would want, remaining with or returning to their owners. Is there loss here as well? What sort of bond connects both the nonreturning and the returning to those who hold them? Is there a comparison possible here that allows us to consider pos-session without eliding Samburu prescissive priorities?

Personhood and the Stickiness of Objects

While Marx drew attention to various nuances of alienation and nonre-turning objects, Marcel Mauss famously posed the question of what makes things return to their givers—that is, to their earlier possessors (Mauss 1967 [1925]). Mauss was of course, not describing capitalist exchange, although capitalism's exploitative tendencies troubled him. Mauss identified the "*hau*" as the glue that bound objects to their original owners and likewise bound givers and receivers in socially contextualized cycles of exchange. If Marx was troubled by objects that simply do not return, moving in a cycle of impersonal and alienating production and exchange, Mauss was fascinated by what he saw as a somewhat idyllic counterpoint of inalienability and social connection. Although Mauss examined possession and reciprocity in so-called primitive contexts, Marx saw clearly how objects strongly signify possession for both "givers" and "receivers" in capitalist contexts as well. However, *how* they signify possession may differ—particularly at the opposite poles of exchange.

A number of scholars have attended to personhood and one or both sides of the process of exchange, whether inside or outside of the context of the market (for example, Appadurai 1986, 1996; Hoskins 1998; Keane 1997; Miller 1994, 1995; Riesman 1977; Strathern 1988; Weiner 1992). When they embark on a careful reexamination of the relationship between persons and objects, these authors seemingly attempt to express the inexpressible—to name the "hau"—insofar as desires for and attachments to objects (linked to conceptions of value) appear to form at an enormously complicated nexus of prestige, profit, culturally shaped aesthetic impulses, and features of personal biographies (recall again Amariglio and Callari 1993).

Many authors have also been increasingly cautious about assuming a clear division between capitalist, noncapitalist, and edge-of-capitalism objects and exchange forms (see, for example, Carrier 1995; Hoskins 1998; Thomas 1991). However, notions of attachment connected to "loss" are typically reserved for capitalist examples like Stallybrass's discussion of Marx's coat or my example of Samburu mporo reentering the capitalist market. That is, it is usually only in examples like these that scholars characterize the circulation of objects as marked by reluctant "givers"—one might even say "losers"—who continue to be affected by the loss of their objects.[4] This is in spite of Weiner's insightful illumination that the value of noncirculating objects is maintained by their opposition to objects that do circulate. Moreover, Keane (1997) has reminded us of the "vicissitudes of objects," of the fact that inalienable keepsakes are often not only dangerous but in danger.[5] That is, they are vulnerable to loss through fire, theft, and sale (223). Again, though, Keane directs most of his attention to loss by sale as objects become commodified or recommodified.

The examples I offered at the beginning of this chapter similarly turn on losses relating to the capitalist market. Stallybrass refers to the specter of losing objects to capitalist exchange that mark and contain (or are metonymic containers for) one's memories. At the other side of the exchange, European used-clothing consumers seemed to have preferred clothing they could forget had been worn, while in Spyer's example the Aruese recut and refashioned European styles to suit themselves. At the same time however, Dutch colonizers—imaginary givers, in this case, since they had not worn the clothing they were so discomfited by— were unnerved by seeing these transformations of familiar fashions. In the case of North American women newly possessing Samburu marriage beads, I offer a notion of imagined loss and imagined connection (2002a). While I do not describe Samburu responses (since they have not typically been afforded the opportunity of witnessing North American women wearing their beads), I do offer a strong suggestion in the form of Samburu women's uneasiness about selling objects that contain their *latukuny*. (For now, let me gloss latukuny as bodily effluence in the form of sweat, blood, hair, and so forth.)

What sort of "hau" is it that seems to haunt all these examples, whether sellers or buyers, Europeans or Aruese or Africans? Although I do not suggest collapsing important distinctions, it would appear that there is something "sticky" here, something adhering to all of these objects—and it is so excessive in its signifying that neither "memory" nor "imagination" can account for it.

Latukuny

When we women of the U.S. are raped,
what is it we wash from our bodies,
as we scrub flesh until it is raw and sore
until we can safely imagine that not even
a thumbprint remains?

And when my father died in 1964, what
was it that turned my mother's grief
to insanity as she held the clothes he wore the day before,
feeling, smelling, breathing him in
against every inch of her face?

Would there be a way to separate this sweat,
this smell, this imperceptible indentation
on the surface of people and things
from the person who touched and felt and lived?

Nkima ("Fire")

Every morning at dawn, a Samburu woman—as long as her family has even just a few animals—wakes up and goes out to milk her livestock. If she is observant of Nkai's desires, she puts on at least some of her beads before going, so that Nkai does not see her with an empty neck—as if she is inviting illness. Only a sick or dead person wears no beads.[6] If she wakes early enough and the cows, goats, or sheep will not be wandering far that day, she might reignite her fire before going out. If she rushes out to milk while her fire is still just smoldering from the previous night, she must be sure to reignite it immediately after milking before doing anything else. A woman is intimately connected with her "fire" (*nkima*)—even her ability to have children is referred to as her nkima. She got it soon after marriage, at her *nkaji naibor* (white house)—the ceremony of making her a home/at home.

I remember an nkaji naibor I attended early in 2002. Women from the young wife's settlement and neighboring settlements came to build the new house. This particular nkaji naibor was in the highlands, but the new house was still made in the temporary, lowland style. Slim poles were erected vertically for the walls, and others were curved over and across these to form the roof. In the lowlands, suuti (fiber mats woven as a roof protection) would have been used to cover the roof. Here, the entire house was covered in clear vinyl to give the "white" effect. As usual, new hides were placed inside to cover walls and floor after fresh-smelling green branches had been laid down. In the evening, the groom's brother and other elders of their clan came to kindle the wife's first fire. There, in complete darkness, they held the wooden base (*ntoome*—a feminine noun)[7] with its little depression and swished the kindling stick (*lpiroi*—a masculine noun) back and forth in the depression, back and forth, back and forth, back and forth in the darkness until a tiny spark was seen. An elder bent and blew into the spark gently, and the spark increased a little, then drew back. Soon the spark was seen again, and the elder blew again. This time the spark grew slowly, then suddenly burst into a little flame. The elders continued, coaxing the little flame until it was a robust fire and we were not in darkness anymore. They had succeeded in joining male and female—mimicking the procreative acts the married couple would be exhorted to accomplish in their married life. The elders uttered many blessings for the couple, to encourage and safeguard the family's fertility and general well-being. Now, this new young wife had fire, even as she herself *was* fire because of her life-generating womb. She would never be able to kindle a fire from "nothing"—something only boys and men can do—yet she would be charged with nurturing her fire, keeping it alive as much as possible.[8] If it were to go out, she would need to ask her husband to rekindle it for her, or she would need to borrow some flame from another woman's fire.

From that first fire, the new bride became a part of her husband's own

Figure 7. A girl tends to her mother's cooking fire (three large stones with pot on top at right) in 2005.

ageset, with all the relationships his ageset entails. Thus, children of her husband's entire ageset were now her classificatory children, parents of his ageset were her parents, and so forth.[9] Moreover, one of her husband's own lpiroi elders must have helped to kindle her nkaji naibor fire. That is, one of the elders who had helped to kindle the fire long before, when her husband's ageset was initiated, must have been present at her nkaji naibor to ensure that her fire was linked to that earlier one. Thus, after the nkaji naibor, the woman's own fate became bound up with the fate of her husband's ageset. If his ageset were to be cursed (ldeket), for example, the consequences would pass through her and into her own children.

Yet a woman's fire is not only linked to her husband's ageset. While it entails relationships pertaining to that ageset, its fertile potential is up to her and her own natal family. If a woman comes from one of those families known to "have fire," as in a fertile fire, it is expected that her own fire will also be fertile. And this fecundity extends from her child-bearing potential to the life-giving potentials of her entire home, including the health of her husband, children, and livestock.[10] Yet there are also families whose daughters do not have fire, and it is said that when these women marry they will cause their family's herds to decline, their children's health to be poor if they manage to get children, and they will even be lucky if their husbands do not grow weak and die. Not surprisingly, women from such families can often have a difficult time getting husbands. Sometimes, though, even women from families who do have fire have difficulty getting pregnant and having children for inexplicable reasons, or perhaps their family's livestock or overall health declines. It may be that something has happened to adversely affect the woman's *lorien* ("luck," "fecundity," "good fortune"). Alternatively, it may be the husband's *sobua* (his "luck," "wealth-generating fecundity," "good fortune") or the entire family's lorien that has been compromised.

Lorien 1

This is my lorien
This wood, this firestick, this charcoal purity
I have touched it, held it, grasped it firmly
the day I freed it from the tree
and since, each time I plunged it
into the calabashes
of my children, my husband, myself.

Nkirau, nyatii, nkoiting
holders of milk, keepers of life
our latukuny slips into them
rubs off our curled fingers as we drink
the latukuny of our beloved
cow, sheep, goat.

Yes, this is my lorien
my luck, my fortune, my fond fertility.
This is what I pray for
and what I guard carefully
as it oozes out my pores,
latukuny anyone might steal
as it clings to the firestick
hanging in glistening beads
merging inscrutably with the latukuny of animals,
the bountiful nub of their precious bones.

Lorien 2

March 2002: I am sitting in Lemarei's settlement, playing with my digital video camera. I move to sit near him, pointing the lens at his fourth wife as she cleans her calabashes. He smiles, watching this young wife, whom he likes very much, as she performs a routine task carefully and well. After a few minutes, I walk over and sit directly in front of her, so she can see me filming her. She smiles but continues with her work, cleaning each calabash thoroughly with a piece of burnt lorien, then whisking it inside and out with a cow's tail and, finally, shaking out any residue. I watch as she plunges the lorien down into each calabash, as she whisks, shakes, and sets it aside, taking the next calabash. Finally, she finishes cleaning the last calabash and sets it down with more finality than the others, laughing at me. We laugh together and I turn off the camera to join her. I have captured something from her and we both know it, but I am too close to this family for it to matter.

Fecund "Objects"

Lorien is a tree that tends to grow on hills, high places close to Nkai. It has a good "smell" (*nkuaama*), too.[11] Like the reteti I discussed in Chapter 3, lorien is both associated with Nkai and liked by Nkai. Women make a regular point of going to places where it grows to cut wood from it, and in doing so, they merge their latukuny—their sweat, the substances they constantly exude—with pieces of Nkai's lorien trees. Thus, lorien is a metonym for both this fecundity-producing process and its fertile entailments (of both livestock and children). Similarly, a man has his own masculine form of fecund wealth and the continual potential for producing it. While a woman's lorien is intimately bound up with

Figure 8. My friend finishing up the cleaning of her calabashes in front of my video camera in 2002.

her nkima ("fire")—even as she herself *is* her husband's nkima—a man's fortune (likewise of both livestock and children) is his walking stick (sobua) which, in turn, is linked to his face (*nkomom*). (He is, of course, born with his "face," just as a woman inherits her nkima.) His sobua comes from an *lgweita* tree,[12] and even if he does not cut it himself, his latukuny falls into it as he touches it daily. While a woman uses lorien regularly to clean the calabashes that hold the sustenance of life, a man uses his sobua as he walks among his animals, and he imparts blessings to others through it. In this way, he continually imparts small portions of his wealth-producing fecundity to others as his wife or wives impart theirs in the acts of birthing and food distribution.

As with lorien (women's calabash-cleansing charcoal), then, a sobua as walking, herding, and blessing stick refers metonymically to a man's wealth-producing fecundity, his luck, his fortune, even as it *is* his fortune insofar as it contains it in an inseparable connection.[13] And, just as a woman's lorien depends on the quality of her nkima, a man's sobua depends in large measure on his nkomom—his face. Here, nkomom is a man's face and also his face as luck-generating. Recall that a man does not have his own fire—his wife is his fire, and the quality of her fire impinges on his well-being. Similarly, a woman's nkomom is simply her face, but her husband's nkomom is both his face and a luck-generating potential that always affects her. Lorien and nkima on the one hand, and sobua and nkomom on the other, are both integrally related pairs and intimately bound up with a person/family. "You see, your nkima and this wood (*lshata*) you broke with your hands, they are the ones that have *seerr*" (Nolsilalei interview, 2002).

Seerr is a way of life with all of its necessary prescriptions and habits, all of the required practices that a particular family or clan or entire ethnic group shares. Different *seerri* (plural) set certain families apart from others, clans apart from others, the Samburu apart from others in overlapping circles of cultural (or family) purity (as in Chapter 2).[14] In this case, Nolsilalei uses seerr to mark the division between families in a specific way by calling attention to the need to keep certain things—like lorien and sobua, latukuny and nkuaama—separate between families. She illustrates this well in the case of a woman's lorien, but the example can extend as well to a man's sobua.

You see now, the "smell" [nkuaama] of a person, you see when you clean the calabash like this now—and I put it like this—you just clean like this and don't you finish? [Yes.] Then you bring that whisk [musuti] [mhmm] and you put it in. Then don't you put your hands inside the calabash? [Yes.] You put it deeply in to wipe, just to remove the charcoal so that you'll milk the cows with it. You see then, this nkuaama of yours is now in the calabash. What, then is inside the calabash? [Inside] Inside [mhmm]. There is an nkuaama of cow's milk. And so you don't want to give out this lorien (charcoal/"luck") of yours because it has this nkuaama of yours, it even has that [nkuaama] of the cow's milk. (Nolsilalei interview, 2002)

As in the case of nkima (fire/"fecundity") and lorien (charcoal/"luck") or nkomom (face/"luck") and sobua (stick/"fecundity"), latukuny ("bodily substance") and nkuaama ("smell") are intimately related, though distinct. A family shares latukuny from the day when the husband and wife were shaved and their hair mixed on a stool. Latukuny of husband and wife commingle and drip into their children—indeed, children are sometimes referred to as their latukuny—and their fortunes expand or diminish together. Even if a husband has several wives, the husband's latukuny enters the houses of all. Nevertheless, the latukuny and lorien of individual wives will differ in significant ways according to the distinctness of their own nkima ("fire") and nkuaama. That is, although latukuny is shared to a large extent between husband, wife, and thus children, everyone has their own nkuaama ("smell"), and it is the nkuaama that contains a woman's lorien and a man's sobua. Thus, one's nkuaama (and therefore one's lorien or sobua) is always in one's latukuny, but one's nkuaama can also be separate from latukuny. For clarity—though the gloss is far from adequate—I will put this briefly in English. If you sweat, your smell is in the sweat—and the smell has your luck. Even apart from things that *contain* your smell, however—like your sweat, blood, hair, tears, sperm, and so forth (including your children)—you constantly *exude* a smell. When Nolsilalei cautioned that a woman does not want to give out her lorien (the firestick in this case), she justified this by explaining that the woman's smell (and thus lorien/"fecundity") and her animals' smell are both in that firestick. In other words, her lorien ("luck") is in her lorien (firestick), just as a man's sobua ("luck") is in his sobua (walking stick). And though it first got into that lorien wood when she cut it from the tree, it became more potent in the stick the day she used her hands and the stick to clean a calabash into which her animals' milk had been and would be poured. In that cleaning, she merged the health or fecundity of Nkai, herself, her animals, and her children, making both the calabash and the wood used to clean it, very important objects indeed.[15]

What Is in a Smell?

Although a woman's nkima (fire/"fecundity") is largely inherited, there are ways she can nurture the well-being of her lorien (charcoal/"luck"). In this context it is possible to see that lorien is not merely luck, not merely fecundity, but health as well. Depending on how women or men take care of their nkuaama ("smell"), their health and general well-being will increase or diminish. This is particularly the case for women. "And you see a certain person who doesn't take care of herself—that person doesn't survive. She's just dead so she'll return to the soil [mhmm], becoming thin" (Nasapisho interview, 2002). In contrast, a woman who takes good care of herself will improve herself in several ways. By giving herself (or her child) a "good smell," a woman (or child) becomes healthier—that is, her lorien becomes good. And remember that her lorien is at once her health, her fecundity, and her fortune.

Yes, a person's sesen ["body"] becomes good [yes] and [it] also becomes good for her child because you'll get a *serishoi* root [yes, serishoi][16] and you'll get *silalei* [a gum like frankincense][17] and you'll bring a dry wood. You'll light it by putting it on a plate or a tin. [Mhmm.] You'll remove a cloth and you'll wrap it so that you get that smoke into the sesen [mhmm], and [with] that absorption of smoke into your sesen and your child's, s/he smells good. (Nasapisho interview, 2002)

By doing this regularly, a woman of childbearing age makes herself "smell good"—*kerropil.* Telling is the fact that a man can be typically said to already "smell good," unless he becomes ill, commits a serious wrongdoing, or is generally mean. Likewise, old people (postmenopausal women included) are *ropili* (kerropil—they smell good). Those who need to take special care of themselves are also the ones who are most fragile or vulnerable—women who regularly produce life, babies, newly circumcised boys and girls (*laibartak* and *nkaibartak*—shaved ones), and lmurran who spend a lot of time in *soro* (the bush). Laibartak carry silalei with them everywhere for the month of their liminality, putting it on their arrows, holding it, and burning it to absorb its "smell." Childbearing women, as we have just seen, regularly use silalei and a variety of other important plant and animal products (including fat) to maintain their nkuaama ("smell") and thus their lorien ("fecundity"). Moreover, newly postpartum women (ntomonok) and newly circumcised boys and girls observe similar health and dietary restrictions.

All people in these vulnerable states have to remain unwashed for a prescribed period (approximately one month for laibartak/male initiates, a few days to a month for nkaibartak/female initiates, and four days for ntomonok/postpartum women), during which time they cannot touch the food they eat.[18] They use sticks to eat small pieces of meat that has been cut for them, and they avoid bones altogether (because these must be eaten with the hands). Significantly, if they break these rules, they risk ingesting a very special form of latukuny—*kereet*—composed of a variety of things—including the blood they have shed and specific herbs or animal products that they have used ceremonially.[19] This person who *anya kereet* (eats their kereet) will have a "bad smell" and experience diminished health and fortune. It is a form of autocannibalism—they are literally consuming their own latukuny. This notion of consuming latukuny is crucial to my points, and I will return to it.

Like the Euro-American "body," then, sesen is indeed a sign of enormous density—but as a sign, sesen differs substantially from the Euro-American "body."[20] As Andrew Strathern has noted for Melanesia, Samburu pharmacology treats sesen as the "site of health or sickness" but also as "the site of socially defined and constrained morality" (1996: 64; see also Knauft 1989). Thus, caring for one's sesen includes Eurocentric notions of bodily health as through a combination of Western biomedicine, Samburu herbal remedies, and humoral or tactile treatments.[21] However, the success of these depends on nurturing one's "smell" (nkuaama), and one's nkuaama, in turn, can be affected both by how one takes care of one's sesen and by one's treatment of others (including kindness, meanness, and murder—as we will see in Chapters 5 and 6). There are a number of "cuts" (aduŋ) to be made here—in particular, there are objects to be kept noncirculating and separate in the maintenance of one's nkuaama, lorien, and sesen.

The Vulnerability of Latukuny—Illicit Circulation

The interdependence of people and livestock recurs—seemingly in every domain and dimension of Samburu life. In many cases, this interdependence brings a certain vulnerability, as the most precious elements of personhood, like fecundity and even good health itself, can be stolen by unscrupulous persons. A family's latukuny is constantly intermingling between family members and between people and animals. That sharedness is both inevitable and desirable; and, moreover, the degree to which latukuny and lorien ooze and drip even between people and animals suggests an intersubjective notion of personhood that crosses species as well as so-called individuals. It is not only said of married men that kerropil (they "smell good") but that their animals like (and respond to) their nkuaama ("smell"). If a man dies, in fact, it is said that his animals may begin to get sick, wander off, and generally diminish in health and number, particularly if he had a good nkomom ("face") and sobua ("luck/fecundity"). According to Nolsilalei, this recognition of nkuaama is equally significant in the case of wives. As a number of other women told me as well, a woman's livestock *have* her nkuaama ("smell") if she has "good" urine (*nkula*—related to transmission of nkima), just as the livestock have her husband's nkuaama. And possession of someone's nkuaama is a fact of no small consequence, as is evident if the person dies. Nolsilalei elaborates this in detail, focusing on the implications of a woman's death.

You see, if she is standing [herding] inside the livestock and those livestock get enough of her nkuaama, then it is good [and] the animals multiply, coming up a lot. And if she is no longer there, the livestock go back [decrease] because the owner [the woman] is no longer there. The livestock go back because the owner is no longer standing in the midst of her livestock. They go back, maybe get a certain disease that kills them, finishing them. The livestock go back, they no longer go ahead, even the whole home, they go back. If she had children, then they won't have animals—they are finished . . . They go because the owner who is taking care enough and *even the nkuaama that usually multiplies*, no longer multiplies. They are going back when the husband's house has fallen on him. (Nolsilalei interview 2002)

Here, Nolsilalei suggests that the loss of a woman (and, similarly, of a man) can be of such proportion as to cause the deaths of her livestock by illness and lack of care—even due to lack of her nkuaama. The potential gravity of the situation is rendered all the more transparent by the metaphors invoked when a wife dies. It is said that the husband's fire has gone out or, in this case, that the house has fallen on him. Moreover, in case it might be thought that the danger posed to the livestock is merely from the lack of usual attentiveness during herding, Nolsilalei refers several times to the importance of the woman's nkuaama to her livestock—including the comment that her nkuaama itself multiplies. Another woman I know, Helen, pointed out that many animals will not even allow themselves to be milked by other women because of the strength of nkuaama ("smell") recognition (understandable even from a Western "scientific" viewpoint). More forcefully, Nolsilalei listed among the dangers to the livestock of a deceased woman that they might wander into the bush (soro) to die or be eaten by wild animals. And again, this is not merely due to inattention but to missing her nkuaama and seeking it where her corpse has been laid. "The livestock are consumed in the bush like that because the livestock finish, looking as if they have followed that person who has died" (Nolsilalei interview 2002).

The strength of this interdependence between livestock and the woman who milks them underlies the weightiness of the wife's regular cleaning of her calabash. As a stick for cleaning a calabash, lorien is a tremendously excessive sign—an object that a woman holds in her hand almost daily, joining Nkai's tree to her own and her livestock's lorien ("luck") and nkuaama ("smell"). That is, in its utility, it purifies a container holding livestock's life-giving latukuny (milk is one form of latukuny); in that process, it comes to hold the nkuaama of that fecund life itself. Because of this, lorien is a very special object that must be protected from those who might harm a woman through its misuse: "For the one [lorien] you have used, you refuse [to lend it], saying, 'Oh! I don't have lorien that has not cleansed. I only have lorien that has cleaned a calabash.' So you don't want to give your black mouth [dark from purifying fire], the ones you have cleaned your calabashes with. You don't want to give it to another person to take" (Nolsilalei interview, 2002). The lorien that should meander only within a single home, mingling the fortunes of one woman's family and livestock, can be taken away surreptitiously—and at least some part of her lorien ("fortune") will go with it. A woman's "black mouth" is a very personal and inalienable keepsake, not meant for circulation. That is, in contrast to possessions that are inalienable but do circulate, the circulation of a Samburu woman's black mouth is always illicit. Thus, if another woman steals it, she will never gain just a useful piece of charcoal but, rather, the previous owner's nkuaama and livestock lorien (livestock fecundity).[22] Moreover, in that illicit transaction, what was inalienable becomes thoroughly *alienated* from the rightful owner—she will not retrieve her lost lorien without powerful intervention from a loiboni (ritual/healing specialist).

It is not only women who are in danger of these illicit transactions, however. Recall that at marriage, the groom's hair (containing his latukuny) was mixed with the bride's and that later a fire was kindled that reaffirmed the bride's connection to her natal family as well as creating a new connection with her husband's ageset. Indeed, the kindling of the fire itself was through a joining of male to female. Men and women, like people and livestock, are always interdependent, and both husband and wife have their own wealth that must merge, on the one hand, but be kept separate from that of other families, on the other. While a woman's fecund "wealth" is her lorien—metonymically named for the stick that regularly purifies her calabashes, a man's fecund "wealth" is his sobua— also metonymically named. Like lorien (calabash charcoal), sobua (herding stick) is an inalienable keepsake of great significance—containing his latukuny ("bodily substance"), his nkuaama ("smell"), and his sobua ("wealth").

As he goes through his daily tasks of checking on animals where his children herd them, giving animals water through his own labor, and generally moving through his herd to check on the animals' health, a man may carry a thin branch, ŋudi, in addition to his sobua. A ŋudi can be useful for little tasks—guiding a small animal, for example. Like a woman's lorien, it is not something that he gives to people outside his family; and, in fact, he normally takes care to dispose of it where other people cannot get it—by putting it in the animal pens for them to trample and destroy. He would not want to destroy it by his own hand. If he is careless, though, another man who admires his livestock and family wealth may steal it, and if he does steal the man's ŋudi on repeated occasions, he can successfully alienate that man's wealth. More ominously, an unscrupulous man might attempt to steal a man's sobua (walking stick) itself, particularly when he dies. If a deceased man's sons do not guard their father's sobua carefully, they can lose their birthright. Should a man steal the sobua, he can utter words over it that may be of startling simplicity but of great effect. With a single theft, he will alienate another man's livestock and family wealth (in the broadest sense)—even to the point of taking it from the latter's sons. Like lorien as wealth, sobua as wealth will not return except perhaps (if one is lucky indeed) through the intervention of a proficient specialist.

Lorien and sobua are vulnerable objects containing a family's latukuny, which only circulate within families in carefully prescribed ways. Lorien (charcoal), of course, is ephemeral, used routinely and carefully, surreptitiously discarded so that no one outside a woman's house touches it lest they go with it in the way a person stealing another's blanket might breathe in their smell as well as the smallpox they are dying from. (The difference is that through repeated attempts, a woman can utterly alienate another woman's lorien. Smallpox and smell in the Euro-American sense can be taken and sensed by others but are simultaneously inalienable from their original possessor.) Sobua and a number of other inalienable keepsakes are, if anything, in more danger of theft than lorien because they endure—seen in public in the context of use and/or of inheritance.

I have already discussed some details of the marriage process, including the inheritance of nkima (fire/"fertility") from a daughter's natal family. Nkima is not the only conduit to a woman's fecundity. On the day she is married, a daughter's father and mother both transmit their "wealth" to her through several precious and inalienable objects. As I have discussed elsewhere (Straight 1997b, 2002a), a mother makes her daughter an mporo marriage necklace using beads from her own necklace—thus passing her potent latukuny to her daughter. Even if (in the wake of the bead trade) mporo has to be borrowed for the celebration, a mother will smear the borrowed necklace with fat from her own animals using her own hands. She also gives her daughter a special small calabash (lboliboli) to carry on her back, completely filled with fat.[23] As she walks to her new home, the daughter carries the lboliboli on her back like the child she will one day carry there. This calabash is moist inside with life-signifying animal fat from her groom's herd—her infant will be moist with urine, and she should also have fecund moistness. Through these objects (the mporo necklace and a calabash "inseminated" by her husband), it is expected that a daughter inherits and carries with her the proven child-fertility of her mother. Her father also transmits fecund wealth to her, however, by blessing a sobua (walking stick) with his own saliva and handing it to her as she leaves his settlement with her new husband. Through the sobua, she inherits her father's general potential for lorien—fecundity and health of people and animals.[24]

Sons likewise inherit from each parent. A man's eldest son inherits his sobua—the walking/herding stick with all its signifying sobua ("wealth") and responsibility. In effect, the son becomes the guardian as well as the caretaker of his father's sobua ("wealth") on behalf of all of his brothers. Like his father, the eldest son will use the sobua to "cut" (aduŋ) many things—guiding/dividing children and livestock on the path and bestowing blessings. Similarly, in some families, a woman's youngest son inherits his mother's *lbene* (woven bag) and thus safeguards its precious contents for the whole family.[25] Every wife has her special lbene, into which she puts beads and other precious objects, especially those generated in the performance of certain ceremonies. Thus, these objects and the lbene itself have potent forms of the latukuny of that woman's entire house. All of these objects, then—lorien (charcoal), sobua (walking stick), mporo (marriage necklace), lboliboli (fat-containing calabash), and woman's lbene (bag of special objects)— are precious, inalienable objects, and, moreover, they are keepsakes that should only circulate within families. Yet, like lorien and sobua, all of them can be stolen.

Illicit circulation is not limited to such metonymic objects as charcoal and herding sticks then. Anything containing one's nkuaama ("smell") or latukuny ("bodily substance") is vulnerable to theft, in forms that are no doubt familiar from the literature on "witchcraft" and "magic." However, Euro-American concepts like these obfuscate more than they reveal, here as well as in a number of other cross-cultural contexts.[26] While a Samburu laruponi or nkaruponi (the closest gloss is witch) may use someone's latukuny to accomplish malicious deeds, the mechanism underlying the various harms I am describing is clear and not mysterious. Stealing a person's sobua is not a form of magic or the supernatural (as in witchcraft) and neither is passing one's saliva to it in the process of uttering propitious or unpropitious words. Rather, such acts are normal and predictable consequences of everyday forms of lorien ("luck"/ "wealth") maintenance and transmission. Caring for one's nkuaama, latukuny, and sesen, then, is part of an entire complex of mundane practices for maintaining and sustaining a good life, of which their loss causes the diminution of that very life. As I noted early on in this chapter, the logic of circulation typically depends on some things not circulating (Weiner 1992). In the Samburu case, this becomes all the more transparent if we look at the reasons for and implications of forcibly circulating precisely those inalienable keepsakes that should not circulate, or forcibly circulating inalienable detachables in ways that transgress moral boundaries.[27] Samburu sesen ("body") and moral personhood are so thoroughly entangled that Samburu subjectivities are continually reenacted through the circulation of their inalienable detachables like nkuaama and latukuny. If what should be kept within prescribed kinship boundaries is put into broader, illicit circulation, individuals and even whole families and their livestock may experience a diminution of fecundity and vitality in what approximates a zero-sum game. The severity of the loss is contingent upon what precisely has been alienated as well as the motivations of the thieves themselves, as I will now describe.

The Motivations of Thieves

I have not begun to cover the ways that latukuny can be stolen. Latukuny and nkuaama find their way into many things, from calabashes and walking sticks to shoes and *nkeene e nkosheke*—the leather belts women wear after giving birth. For every object that latukuny drips into, there are ways to protect against the vulnerability to a person's lorien (or sobua) posed by theft. Some objects have more potent forms of latukuny than others, however, and as such, their theft is even more feared and dangerous. This is the case, for example, with blood and other objects associated with birth. I will describe an aspect of the highly charged associations of such objects by way of beginning to differentiate the possible motivations for theft, starting with malice.

After a baby is born, various animals are slaughtered as thanksgiving to the birth attendants, to Nkai, and also for the mother's recovery process. *Lbutan* is one of the animals slaughtered expressly for the mother to eat—this is the goat that the postpartum woman will eat with sticks after it has been cut into tiny pieces for her. *Morr*, in contrast, is a goat slaughtered for the birth attendants and other neighboring girls and women— the mother cannot eat it at all. Lbutan is closely connected to the health of both child and mother in ways that go beyond nutritional replenishment. Morr is of similar significance, but its entanglement is particularly with the life of the child (see Straight 1999). Every part of the morr is accounted for in its distribution or treatment. In its connection to the postpartum mother lies a taboo on any man or boy—even a woman breastfeeding a son—eating it lest he become utterly insane. The meat is a feminine possession, joining the life-giving properties of livestock with the life-giving properties of fertile women. The goat's bones, though, are connected to the life of the child, whether a baby boy or girl. Four bones are hung from the ceiling of the house—iconically demonstrating that the child will be "brought up" (raised in health and behavior) nicely and well. Like a woman's lorien and a man's sobua, the child's bones—bones of a goat that come to stand for the bones of the child, just as the child depends on the animals for life—can be stolen. And here we come to the most dangerous of thefts.

Why would someone wish to steal a child's "bones"? The answer is not to increase the vitality of the thief's own child, nor is it to enable him or her to get a child. The person who steals a child's morr bones commits the worst kind of theft—a theft meant to kill for pure envy and malice. This unscrupulous woman (here it will be a woman who has enviously watched the woman give birth to healthy children while she, presumably, has not) steals the bones in order to put them into the ground. Perhaps one of the most unpropitious actions a person can inflict on another is to send their vitality into an anthill, either by cursing them to go literally to the ground or by, in this case, putting a highly potent form of their latukuny into an anthill. A woman's child-fertility can be sent to the ground similarly, by burying the clotted blood from birthing (mporo—significantly a noun that shares its name with the marriage necklace beads) in an anthill. She can harm the newborn or the mother's fertility in this way—again as with morr—for no reason other than malice or envy.

Stealing the bones of morr or the blood from the afterbirth are not the only malicious thefts possible, of course. I have earlier discussed the potential theft of sobua and lorien—and the potential consequences. In fact, the seriousness of a theft is contingent on the motivation for it. Malice is the worst motive, particularly because it seems to benefit no one but also because it often has the worst consequences for the victim. A poor man can steal another man's sobua because he wants to become wealthy in livestock and/or children—the abundance of which are interdependent. An infertile woman can steal another woman's fertility because she wants to become fertile and she can do this in various ways, including getting some of a fertile woman's latukuny from the mporo (marriage necklace) or other beads she wears. Depending on the method, the thief might be alienating all of another person's fecundity or just a portion of it. A very envious person, however, can utterly destroy another person's lorien ("luck"/"wealth") by burying a potent form of their latukuny in an anthill or by doing some other terrible mischief to the latukuny. While a man or woman who suddenly experiences a reversal of fortunes—of their own fertility or health, or the health or fertility of livestock and children—may suspect that a theft has occurred, it is often only a skilled professional (a loiboni or nkoiboni) who can say for certain. Moreover, in some cases—as with burying the bones of morr in an anthill—death or madness may occur, and the latter may prove as irreversible as death.

If the loss to the person whose latukuny has been stolen for malicious reasons is terrible, the consequences to the thief should be equally terrible. It is expected (and hoped) that such a person will experience a violent or lingering form of death, and there are many Samburu anecdotes attesting to the fact that this often occurs. Petty thieves—who steal latukuny to augment their wealth—are more pitied than despised, and the consequences they face are less severe. It is more likely that the victim of such a theft will not only feel the loss but may even be able to remedy it. Remember that it is only a person with proven fecundity who would be stolen from. Such a person will inevitably notice their loss fairly quickly, when the thief is more likely to be caught. In some cases, unfortunately, the loss is very great—resulting in a woman's reduced fertility or the reduced fertility or health of livestock and/or children. And though many remedies may be tried, none may succeed. Regardless of the repercussions for the victim, however, Samburu assert that although the thief may experience a temporary increase in livestock and/or or child lorien ("luck"/"wealth"/"fecundity"), inevitably this improved lorien will ebb and flow. Eventually, even if it does not occur until old age or later—striking the thief's descendants—the thief's lorien and perhaps even his/her own health will weaken.

Those who steal latukuny in order to *sell* it share with other thieves of latukuny the inevitability of dire consequences. However, by selling latukuny rather than using it to augment their lorien directly, such thieves have put themselves in a special category—they are engaging in the unthinkable. I turn now to examine purchases and thefts that bring latukuny into the marketplace—keeping in view that the same logic of subjectivity and value underlies these illicit exchanges whether in or out of the marketplace. Yet, in many instances, the stakes are quite a bit higher.

Unlawful Acts of Consumption

Putting an inalienable keepsake into circulation outside the family to which it belongs can be tantamount to stealing a person.[28] This has particular clarity if we examine calabashes—which should not circulate outside the family. The lboliboli that a bride carries filled with fat is not only a prayer for fertility, it *is* a child. As such, neither this calabash nor any other should be given outside the family—every calabash is powerfully associated with its owner. So strong is the inclination to protect the life and fecundity entangled in calabashes that old calabashes are normally left in the animal pens so that the animals crush them—a person should never do so. The thief who steals latukuny in order to augment their own lorien, then, is stealing another person's (un)born children or livestock. However, the person who obtains inalienable keepsakes—inevitably imbued with latukuny—in order to *sell* them has done something else again.

To return to the lboliboli calabash example, the bride smears herself with the fat contained in the lboliboli and she may give some to postmenopausal women to smear on themselves—she does not fear that they will steal her child-lorien. No one, including herself, may *eat* this fat however—to do so is to eat her unborn children. Like eating meat without washing (the kereet or latukuny off) one's hands, it is an act of consuming humans, in other words—though in this case it is the more sinister consuming of someone else rather than oneself. Quite clearly, selling and eating are not the same—so why discuss selling in this context? For Samburu, selling implies the act of killing something for consumption, as when livestock are slaughtered and their meat consumed. (This is not so far from the European perspective of commodity consumption.) Whereas consuming livestock is normal and sanctioned, selling inalienable keepsakes containing latukuny is, quite simply, to consume humans. One may as well eat the fat in a bride's lboliboli. Nevertheless, a number of Samburu have been committing various forms of "cannibalism" for decades—consuming both humans and elephants.

Elephants have a status approaching (though not equivalent to) humanness, and there are a number of blessings (*mayian*), curses (*ldeket*), and prohibitions relating to them. As with latukuny, eating taboos figure prominently here. Of animals that Samburu should not eat, elephants rank high on the list. Related to this, Samburu are never supposed to break open the skull of an elephant in order to extract its ivory. This is not a taboo exclusive to the commodity (ivory-selling) context. Samburu lmurran wear ivory plugs in their ears, for example, but they are only supposed to acquire this ivory from dead elephants whose tusks have already fallen off of their skulls. Extracting ivory by breaking open the skull is the same as eating the elephant, with the same unpropitious consequences.

This was not a strong enough deterrent for Lejil (an Lkimaniki), however. As a young man, Lejil was employed by the Kenya Wildlife Service, and he soon learned how to extract and sell ivory. Some Samburu suggest that he may have paid others to actually break the elephants' skulls, but they maintain that this loophole would not actually work. Whether or not he actually broke open the skulls, Lejil was responsible for breaking an enormous number of elephant skulls in the 1960s and '70s, and he became rich this way, buying many cows, sheep, and goats, and much land. However, according to a number of Samburu, bodily weakness and somewhat early dementia have plagued him as a result.

Selling human latukuny is far worse than selling elephant latukuny (ivory), however, though the implication of eating is similar for both. Whereas women and men who steal latukuny in order to increase their own lorien are guilty of committing an unworthy act, their behavior is understandable, as is the eating of a tabooed animal if a person is hungry. The consequences are comparable to selling an elephant's latukuny—a sudden or gradual reversal of fortunes and possibly a gradual weakening of the thief's sesen ("body"). Those who steal latukuny in order to destroy a person face greater consequences, however—if they do not suffer themselves, their descendants surely will. And it appears that selling latukuny is, if anything, worse. Nevertheless, as with ivory poaching, this has not deterred some people.

I have already hinted at women's uneasiness when their mporo marriage beads and necklaces are sold—both elsewhere (2002a) and early in this chapter. Beginning in the 1980s, African Heritage stores in Nairobi commissioned the acquisition of Samburu and Rendille mporo marriage beads. The result was that many women—desperate for food, tobacco, children's school fees, or other goods or services—began to sell the beads they had in the backs of their necklaces or stored in their lbene (special bags). The trend started in the highlands but spread to the lowlands, becoming well entrenched by the 1990s. While many women refused—even becoming violent as the trade intensified—others sold beads a few or many at a time. In some cases, desperate girls trying to leave home for what they believed were better options when they become pregnant and could not find a suitor (Straight 2005b) have sold their entire necklaces—an abomination for non-Christian families who pride themselves on their "purity."

While even Samburu elders running small shops in rural areas became middle-men for the mporo bead trade, young Christian Samburu men were the driving force behind it. As their profits rose and they bought an increasing number of livestock or invested their money in other ways, their tactics became more aggressive and offensive. There were numerous reports in the lowlands—where women were most reluctant to part with their mporo—of young Samburu men daring to touch women's lbene and steal the mporo beads these precious bags contained. These were terrible thefts.

As of 2002, the consequences were palpable and controversial, particularly since some of the main traders from the 1990s had begun to repent their deeds, inaugurating forms of Protestant Christianity that would now be compatible with Samburu "traditional culture"— including the marrying of multiple wives.[29] These young men had now settled down to marry and were acutely aware that mporo marriage necklaces must *still* be found for their weddings, regardless of their scarcity. In the highlands of Leroghi Plateau particularly, it was not uncommon to travel great distances—to the lowlands if necessary—to "borrow" an mporo necklace. And those women who had kept their necklaces were enjoying an unexpected benefit because the borrowers were willing to pay—they were renting the necklaces!

Besides the practical dilemmas posed by the scarcity of mporo, the controversy surrounding their continued sale also turned on the latukuny they contained and what it meant to put it into the hands of strangers. All of the Samburu I talked to perceived the repercussions of selling latukuny to be multiple, complex, and even unpredictable. On the one hand, women continued to feel uneasy that their latukuny was leaving at all, whether they were getting money in exchange or whether the mporo were stolen. This combined with a vague sense that the mporo belonged to them as Samburu and should not be taken. On the other hand, there were concerns about the consequences that those who sold mporo—by theft or "legitimate" purchase—were going to face sooner or later.[30]

In this regard, concerns for these young Samburu men who bought and sold so many of their (classificatory) mothers' mporo were even greater than individual cases of women selling some or all of their beads (or later, renting out necklaces). While the women were eating their own latukuny and thus might expect some diminution of their lorien, the young men had "cannibalized" ("eaten," "consumed") the latukuny of many.[31] They may not have been buying or selling latukuny specifically, yet they were well aware that latukuny was part of the transaction. Indeed, they were even aware that their actions entailed the eating of someone else's latukuny—even if it was for the purposes of enhancing their own wealth rather than destroying others.

The first person known to sell mporo has reportedly already paid the price—and it was a heavy one. From mporo sales alone (in the 1980s and '90s), Lenaudo managed to buy one hundred cows and as many as five hundred goats and sheep. Then, still a young man, he died—from complications relating to tuberculosis (and some suggest, AIDS). Such a death is not at all surprising for one who had "eaten" so many people, an act suggestive of destruction and thus similar to a theft of malice. Yet it is unbearably tragic nonetheless. Indeed, some family members of other young men who sold mporo have now become fearful for their own kin. In describing Samburu fears in this way I am balancing on a slender thread dividing Euro-American empiricism from Samburu ways of knowing that I argue are more than interpretation. The ways in which Samburu presciss—and this is no less true of other individuals or groups—are at once acts of experiencing and of creating reality. Samburu cuts are both diagnostic and efficacious, whether *we* understand the mechanism in the biomedical terms of stress and placebo or as influential or even failed (always a possibility) acts of the imagination, and so on.

Conclusion

In this chapter, I have been elucidating Samburu latukuny as fully as possible in its relation to the value associated with latukuny-containing objects based in the intersubjective leakage between Samburu persons. This has necessarily and appropriately entailed an examination of latukuny's vulnerability—since the maintenance of the precious nkuaama and lorien (or sobua) that latukuny contains is crucial and includes protection against its illicit circulation. My suggestion has been that it is in this very context—of stolen latukuny and motivations that range from envy to greed—that thefts and unpropitious acquisitions of inalienable keepsakes like mporo that contain latukuny must be understood. In this way, I am suggesting along the way that cross-cultural work examining the logic of "witchcraft" and "sorcery" in "traditional" cultural contexts may be fruitfully merged with work on the licit and illicit circulation of objects both within and alongside (or apparently outside of) capitalist exchange.[32] In the Samburu case, latukuny is involved in *every* theft, even if latukuny per se is not what the thief actually wants. And, moreover, because wealth itself is an English gloss for Samburu terms with very specific Samburu associations, the benefit derived from the theft of an object containing latukuny must be understood in more than monetary terms, even when the apparent goal is actually money. Indeed, Samburu themselves are uneasy about exactly what mporo traders are taking and getting.

It is certainly the case that Samburu understandings of wealth are transforming in ways worth examining, as increasing numbers of Samburu acquire a formal education, become converted (or merely exposed) to Christianity, and/or generally engage in market activities. Yet, these understandings are becoming no more homogeneous with Euro-American understandings than the value and understandings attached to the global commodities that Miller and others have explored (Miller 1994; see also Appadurai 1996; Burke 1996; Friedman et al. 1994; Holtzman 2003; Howes et al. 1996; Johnson 1998; Weiss 1996). For Samburu, wealth implies simultaneously an abundance of children and livestock and the health entailed by their propitious and fruitful interdependence. A poor man who steals another man's ŋudi (temporary herding switch) on repeated occasions, or worse, his sobua (walking stick), is not merely seeking to have a lot of money, except insofar as it complements or facilitates the acquisition of livestock. And, notably, money cannot buy fertility for infertile wives nor for livestock—not yet, in any case!

(Certainly, there is no shortage of wealthy American or European couples whose best efforts at expensive fertility treatments do not succeed.)

Thus, lorien ("luck," "wealth," "fortune") is an overdetermined Samburu sign whose value is rooted in a Samburu moral economy that flexibly extends to market transactions insofar as capitalist successes are already intimately linked to features of personhood. Likewise, when certain precious objects enter the capitalist marketplace, the vitality of some persons can itself be at stake, as value is indeed tied to subjectivity and circulation. If contextualized with respect to other things that must be kept separate and noncirculating, it is possible that yet another nuance would be added to our understanding of acts like blood stealing that stir the anthropological imagination.[33] In the Samburu case, at least, it would appear that new forms of illicit wealth or cannibalism have not sprung, fully formed, from the seemingly encompassing maw of capitalism. Rather, the previously unthinkable—that is nevertheless imagined in some form—has become not only conceivable but commonplace.

Moreover, what makes the sale of objects containing latukuny horrifying is a Samburu personhood that challenges Euro-American notions of material/spiritual dualism. In an intriguing variation on Mary Douglas's work on "matter out of place," Samburu subjectivity is continually reconfigured and transformed as latukuny slides from one person to the next in ways that defy dualistic categorization and that can be positive as well as negative. It is not the leakiness of boundaries that is hazardous. Rather, it is the very desire to mix, to share what is most precious about one's unique personhood among those within a "proper" kinship circle (even as kinship ties are not all biologically based), that makes people vulnerable. In the next chapter I will examine the consequences of a variety of wrongful actions in more detail as I describe ŋoki—a monstrous changeling that jumps between persons in ways that blur the borders between them.

Chapter 5
Ŋoki

Because I heard from some other women of the Lenyankume settlement that one of them gave birth to something that looked like a cat. She just gave birth to something that looked like a cat. As soon as she pushed it out—pang!—the women [midwives] took off through the door of the house. She gave birth to how many? [Two] This one is a person. And that one is a cat. It just went, pang! And then a cat just appeared instead. The women said, "Karr!" because something with a huge ear emerged. The women ran away immediately. The women ran off through the door of the house. "Wooi!" the birthing woman said, "Wooi!" Don't leave me! Just then the baby followed. "Woi, don't leave me! Oi, get this one because it is a child." (Nolpesi interview, October 2001)

Understanding how a Samburu woman can give birth to a "cat" will take us to the core of a Samburu personhood that radically includes others, of forms of subjectivity by which the effects of behavior can manifest themselves in potentially startling ways across persons and generations. Certainly, intimations of a critically understood, fragmented self—a self that might even include aspects of divinity—have long been with us. Classical Greek philosophy already suggested a break between certain elements of human subjectivity (material) and others (spiritual). Freud went farther and offered us an inspiring myth to explain a similar duality (and one ultimately related to that classical one), and more recently Jacques Lacan and Julia Kristeva followed Freud's lead, theorizing the separation between mother and child as the genesis of subjectivity itself. In positing her notion of negativity (she relates it to Freud's drive of rejection) Kristeva suggests that there is a prelinguistic moment of separation from the mother's body that simultaneously inaugurates language acquisition and the child's union with social life: "Within this specific space, which is corporeal and biological but already social since it is a link with others, there operates a nonsymbolized negativity that is neither arrested within the terms of judgment, nor predicated as negation in judgment. This negativity—this expenditure—posits an object as separate from the body proper and, at the very moment of separation, fixes it in place as *absent*, as a *sign*" (Kristeva 1984: 123).

Kristeva has used this logic to posit a division and alienation within the subject, opening up a space for critique of the unified "in-dividual" subject.[1] As I will elaborate in the Conclusion, I disagree where it seems that Kristeva posits this as a universal origin of a universal, individual self. Be that as it may, these and other recent theories pertaining to subjectivity (including Bakhtin's and Derrida's) have prompted a radical rethinking of Euro-American notions of the individual self. The work of feminist theorists has been prominent and crucial here, reinvigorating earlier feminist critiques from Simone de Beauvoir onward and fruitfully merging their insights with the theories of Jacques Lacan, Derrida, and others.[2] Likewise, postcolonial critiques of Euro-American feminist theories have enlivened these debates as they pertain to gender, multiple forms of personhood, and intersubjectivity.[3] Moreover, there has been constant cross-fertilization between feminist theories and anthropology,[4] and some of the same theorists (e.g., Bakhtin, Derrida, and Lacan) who have inspired certain strands of feminist critiques have likewise inspired a number of linguistic anthropologists.[5] Meanwhile, a number of cultural anthropologists have reexamined the phenomenology of Husserl, Heidegger, and Merleau-Ponty with similar results.[6] Again, while in my Conclusion I will push the phenomenological turn in anthropology a bit farther, I am largely enthusiastic about the approach and build upon its insights here. In particular, my emphasis in this chapter, continuing from the previous one, is on elucidating cross-cultural alternatives to Euro-American notions of the so-called individual person in ways that also help us to recognize the dividual aspects of *Euro-American* personhood.[7] Michael Jackson (1996) offers us a helpful beginning when he argues that "an emphasis on the transitive and intersubjective does not mean denying the substantive and subjective; rather it implies that these terms denote not contrasted entities, but moments of a dialectic" (Jackson 1996: 28).

Like Euro-Americans, the Samburu do understand persons as having individual integrity and "biographical" histories (not in the sense of the writing of a life but in the sense of one person's corpus of life experiences). At the same time, however, they understand individual persons as inheriting characteristics of their predecessors that include not only appearance and personality but also propitious or unpropitious conditions (as manifested in siring a cat, for example), not only fertility (or infertility) but the relative potential to inspire or nurture fecundity and health in related people and livestock. Thus, we might begin an approximate understanding of Samburu personhood as intersubjective—as including relations between persons and other persons and between persons and things—in the terms Jackson suggests. We have already seen the intimate and embedded character of Samburu relations between persons and things and between persons and other persons in previous chapters, yet we are left with the challenge of adequately radicalizing the intersubjectivity of Samburu personhood. Insofar as Samburu person-hood *contains* a history of persons and objects, it can be difficult to iden-tify anything like an individual that is not already a complicated and shifting bundle of other objects and persons.[8] When we attempt to con-sider this intersubjectivity inherent in Samburu ways of prescissing peronhood, we begin to presciss Euro-American personhood differently as well. We push Kristeva with Samburu.

In previous chapters I have discussed some of the crucial divisions that should be maintained in protecting Samburu persons and families and the potential consequences of their violation. Chapter 4 in particular examined Samburu vulnerability to inauspicious mixing of lorien, latu-kuny, and blood through theft. Not all tragedies or weakened states of health are explicable in the terms of theft, however. Many are due to individual actions that have generational consequences in the form of ŋoki—a dynamic, Samburu unpropitious "state" that Samburu suggest has a certain life, expressing itself from generation to generation in the form of birth defects, violent deaths, and general ill health. There are many paths leading to ŋoki. I will begin with a very common one—ldeket (typically glossed as "curse")—pairing it with its positive complement, mayian (typically glossed as "blessing") before describing ŋoki in more detail.

Ldeket and Mayian

While mayian is imparted to those one loves or genuinely wishes the best for, ldeket is the last and worst resort when social relationships have gone awry. Because of the latukuny they share (in the form of milk or food, as well as forms of latukuny like blood that cross people), the most potent ldeket passes between close relatives.[9] The connection forged through lpiroi ("firestick") elders at ageset initiation likewise generates a potent ldeket, and indeed lpiroi elders can visit this calamitous condi-tion upon the entire ageset for which they kindled nkima ("fire") (see especially Spencer 1965). While people connected in these and other ways have the potential for a particularly potent ldeket, anyone can "curse" another if there is just cause. Justice is a matter for Nkai, just as it is ultimately Nkai who echoes ldeket back, bringing it to fruition. "S/he [Nkai] gives you a certain disease because you have done some-thing wrong there. Who calls for this? It is you who calls for this, and don't you see that it is Nkai who cares for all and S/he Who brings [everything, good or bad]?" (Leropili-Lkimaniki interview, 2001).

Mayian and ldeket have a common origin in the nkosheke ("stom-ach"), although in the case of ldeket, one's eyes may be the first to alert

the nkosheke of another person's wrongdoing. A common cause of ldeket, for example, and the only one Samburu generally cite as forming a
ŋoki that sons can inherit from their mothers, is the withholding of food
from a hungry person.[10] It is a terrible infraction to eat in front of a hungry person or to withhold food from such a person when the latter
knows that food is available (Jon Holtzman, personal communication,
2002). As I heard many times, the hungry person's eyes send a message
to their nkosheke, and ldeket begins to form and be stored there. It
is especially dangerous to deny girls food "because *kedekisho* [they
"curse"]. Yes, and if there is not enough food they are at least given a
little milk in a lid [of a calabash] to whiten their mouths" (Lenkosheke
interview, 2001). Since girls will eventually join their husband's family,
they are considered to be like guests in their parents' home. As such,
they are not expected to understand why they should be denied food,
and will "curse" in their nkosheke. In contrast, it is said (often amid
laughter) that boys will pray for more livestock if they don't receive
enough food.

Even if the cause for anger does not concern food—it might be that
someone cheated another person, stole from them, abused them publicly or secretly, or committed some other unkind act—ldeket will still
form in the nkosheke. Samburu nkosheke is an important site of personality characteristics and some emotions, though not all. Samburu
describe a kind, thoughtful, generous, and responsible person as having
an *nkosheke naibor,* a "white stomach." In contrast, a mean, selfish, or
generally disagreeable person is characterized as having an *nkosheke
narok,* a "black stomach" (somewhat similarly to Euro-American metaphors of good or kind heart and black heart). A mean or hot-tempered
person (or a murderer) might also be said to be *koŋu* (stinky),[11] and a
selfish person might be said to stink up the place in which s/he lives:
ketoŋua.[12] What makes a person have an nkosheke naibor or nkosheke
narok is not entirely clear to people, though those I have asked have
ultimately attributed it to Nkai. It is Nkai who "builds" a child in a woman's womb, and it is likewise Nkai who decides what kind of nkosheke
that child will have. Again, no one knows why Nkai would give some people a mean disposition.

Ldeket ("curse") and mayian ("blessing") always form in the nkosheke, but ldeket may be voiced or not voiced. If voiced, ldeket travels
up to *ltau* ("heart"), the core of a person's life and origin of *nkiyeŋet*
("breath"); from there it can pass with nkiyeŋet and *nkamilak* ("saliva")
into *ltoilo* ("voice") to form the words of the ldeket itself.[13] The role of
nkamilak in both ldeket and mayian is crucial, and thus people with the
most potent ldeket and mayian are said to "have nkamilak" ("saliva")
and are feared for this reason.[14] Like mayian, ldeket in its spoken form

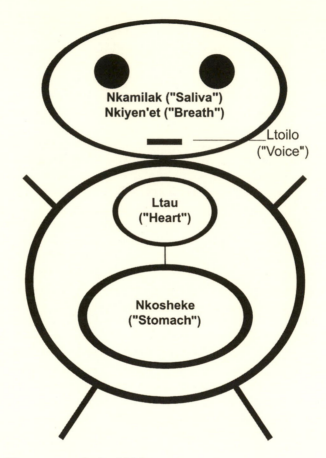

Figure 9. The passage of voiced ldeket.

is invariably accompanied by actions. In the case of mayian, it will typically be a gesture with the man's sobua (walking stick), although it may involve spitting gently on the person also (especially when women perform it). Whatever way the sobua is involved, men often spit on the sobua itself, thus imparting the strength of their nkamilak. In the case of ldeket in contrast, it will be an inauspicious action, from flicking one's finger to the more serious breaking a dry stick and hurling it toward the setting sun. In this way, the power of the ldeket as formed in one person's stomach is rendered more potent by wreaking disaster on the person's latukuny—implicitly, by gesture or explicitly, by burying someone's sobua in an anthill, for example. The result is that the person with ldeket carries *lŋonchoi* (a form of unpropitiousness) around—like ŋoki, this too is like a living thing, and eventually it becomes ŋoki. Thus, *adekisho* ("cursing") is a process whereby the anger that forms in the nkosheke of one person takes on a life of its own and jumps into another person, where it invades every particle of their being, producing a radical and terrible transformation that their descendants can inherit.

The gestures and actions associated with ldeket matter a great deal because they signal the strength of the anger emanating from the person's nkosheke. In this way, each ldeket is somewhat unique—some may have almost immediate and terrible effect, while others may be less predictable. I recall one case in particular that happened very recently, in June 2002. Lemarei's son Ldirinye was ill, and he sought treatment from a healer related to his first wife's family. The treatment was a common but very special one, involving sucking blood (using a tool that prevents blood from entering the healer's mouth) from the painful areas. Unfortunately, Lemarei delayed in making payment. Meanwhile, his first wife, Naliapu, also became ill and the healer was sought once again to perform the same service. The health of both the son and the wife improved, but again Lemarei delayed in making payment. For his part, the healer was becoming increasingly angry, and the anger was building up in his nkosheke. Apparently, his anger was so intense that when Lemarei realized the danger and rushed to pay him, the healer refused to accept the payment. The healer wreaked ldeket upon the family, and his refusal of payment rendered the ldeket even more powerful than it would otherwise have been. Within days, Ldirinye accidentally overturned a boiling soup pot onto his mother, Naliapu, so that her legs were covered in second-degree burns. No transport was available (their settlement is hours from the nearest major road) at the time, and so she suffered terribly for a couple of days while another son walked as fast as he could to the nearest clinic for medicine. This was not the first fire tragedy the Lemarei family had experienced, and some people speculated that there was another ldeket in addition to the healer's that continued to surface from time to time. That there would still be an old ldeket is hard to believe, however, since Lemarei visits loibonok and *laŋeni* frequently to consult on such matters.[15]

The strength of people's anger, which can leave the nkosheke and take shape against others, is an ever-constant cause for vigilance. When I was negotiating with Lemarei about how one of his runaway wives should be returned after my husband and I had taken responsibility for finding and coaxing her to come to our home, we exchanged heated words. In the morning, I discovered a black mamba in my bed, behind my three-year-old son. Many present at the time agreed that it was Lemarei's and my mutual anger that had attracted that deadly poisonous snake. Luckily we had remained respectful toward one another even as we strongly disagreed, and certainly no ldeket had formed or been exchanged. (We remained very close friends.) The snake passed by without harming anyone.[16] Samburu words can be powerfully efficacious indeed, although it is not the words themselves that have potency. Rather, it is a person's nkosheke ("stomach") that is responsible, working cooperatively with ltau ("heart"), nkiyeŋet ("breath"), nkamilak ("saliva"), and ltoilo ("voice"). Because of the potency of nkosheke, every Samburu has the ability to affect others for good or ill, even if some families like laisi have stronger nkamilak than others. Ldeket is an awesome and terrible thing—"the mouth of a person can make a green tree dry up and die" (Lengare interview, 1994).

Webb Keane (1997) suggests that "How people understand their language to function can both reflect their concepts of person and agency and in turn help shape how they act" (98). Keane describes Anakalangese speech as efficacious, with some of its forms having direct physical effects—reminiscent of summoning snakes or causing boys to overturn soup pots. For the Anakalangese, Keane elucidates this in terms of the powerful agency of ancestral speech, which ritual speech attempts to harness. According to Keane, "The agency embodied in ancestral speech, at the limits, is self-sufficient, requires no cooperation with others and no bodily activity other than the action of the voice alone." He continues, suggesting that "What sets the ancestors apart from the living is that for them, there was no gap between word and world." The Anakalangese use ritual speech to capture some of this ancestral power. Thus, ritual speech "iconically reproduces ancestral words and indexically proclaims the speaker's links to ancestral powers" (99).[17]

In this context of "no gap between word and world," we can recall Derrida's "exposure" of the "delusion" of living speech, a delusion that he says contemporary western philosophy inherited from classical Greece. As he says,

If, for Aristotle, for example, "spoken words (*ta en tē phonē*) are the symbols of mental experience (*pathēmata tes psychēs*) and written words are the symbols of spoken words" (*De interpretatione* 116a3) it is because the voice, producer of the first symbols, has a relationship of essential and immediate proximity with the mind. Producer of the first signifier, it is not just a simple signifier among others. It signifies "mental experiences" which themselves reflect or mirror things by natural resemblance. (Derrida 1976: 11)

Living speech unites all human minds because, according to Aristotle's theory, although speech may differ in various languages, spoken words are the direct expression of "mind," which in turn is the direct expression of "things-in-themselves." This is an early manifestation of the correspondence theory of truth. Moreover, it is a Euro-American theory of the power of words. That is, while Derrida's aim is to expose the fictitious basis of speech's preeminence over writing—strengthening his argument that speech is just another form of writing—I would suggest that both Aristotle's and Derrida's are (competing) folk theories of language. Both are theories of the relationship between thought and world, whether expressed through speech or writing, or whether, as for Derrida, all words are forms of writing at some remove from thought—enacting a gap between thought and word and between word and world.

Moreover, following Keane's suggestion, both theories (Aristotle's and Derrida's) have something to tell us about competing contemporary Euro-American theories and popular understandings of person and agency. In positing a "gap" between the so-called signifier and the so-called signified, Derrida has posited a challenge to the supposition that there is any contact between persons and things or persons and other persons at all. And if his is a new articulation of this challenge, it is in itself not new at all but instead preceded by a dynamic history of (Western) ideas, including Hume's skepticism that human consciousness can know reality. Thus, the appearance of "man" (cum Foucault) may have heralded a certain solipsistic individualism, but it simultaneously accompanied a critique of human power and agency. Humans may be able to transform the world, but that is by way of changing something *they perceive to be external and separate from themselves*, something they can never really touch or know as it is. Thus, for many (though not all—hence, the competing understandings) Euro-Americans,[18] the voice, like the pen, may have the power of persuasion, but it has little else. It cannot, as Keane says of Anakalangese true ancestral speech, "summon the lightning and whirlwind" or "tame the wild" with one's "voice alone" (Keane 1997: 99). Nor can human agency part the Red Sea with the help of God.

For the overwhelming majority of Samburu, however, humans are radically in touch with reality; in that connection, human agency has the ability to fundamentally shape persons and things. Yet this is not through the power of words or the voice alone as with the Anakalangese; rather, voice and word are merely proximate causes. It is the stomach and the saliva in particular—aspects of the person—that enact a human will powerful enough to create a living thing that will jump into another person. The Anakalangese, then, grasp fragments of ancestral power by repeating the ancestors' own words—as if ancestral power has attached itself to the words themselves, proliferating and repeating itself every time the words are spoken in ways that duplicate their precise and original form. For the Samburu, it is human rather than ancestral words that have efficacy—even if Nkai ultimately "echoes" human desires back to Earth. Moreover, words are not even necessary—because the power at work here takes shape in a person's nkosheke, assuming a form that can escape even in the absence of speech. And it can get into another person. Thus, people have the ability to make powerful connections with one another and with things in the world, generating transformations in the shape of living, changeable ŋoki that will reproduce for nine agesets (about four birth generations).[19]

Even when people do not voice their ldeket, making it a public and known action, any ldeket that forms in the stomach is bound to escape and affect the wrongdoer. It is very common, in fact, to hear of people getting ldeket from their mothers or grandmothers through unvoiced ldeket. Although mothers and grandmothers in particular (in contrast to fathers and grandfathers) rarely voice ldeket against their own children, if their children mistreat them, the ldeket will be released anyway. There is an old man (Lmekuri ageset) I know who wanders from place to place begging for change or a bit of food. He has no home or wives of his own, and he wanders in apparent mental confusion, though people say that there was a time he was like everyone else. His problems stem from an awful deed he committed as a boy, when his family was moving their settlement a long distance. His father gave him the responsibility of leading his very old, blind grandmother while he (his father) led the livestock, but he tired of the task. The boy told his grandmother to stay in a certain place, waiting while he went to relieve himself.

It is said that he went to a small gulley and "Pio!", he disappeared. He left and went away, and his path was "dry." So he went and said, "I went [to relieve himself] but when I came back I couldn't find her." Men left to go—he told them where he had lost her, and the men left at night and couldn't find her. And they went to sleep and left again in the morning, and then they found where the beasts had eaten her. It is said that it was that [deed] that made him like that—that one of the Lmekuri. Yes, so he will also be helpless. Yes, so he will also become nothing, he will just be moving. (Lenaudo interview, 2001)

Figure 10. Samburu elders perform at blessing with their sobua (walking sticks) at a wedding in 1994.

It will never be known for certain whether the grandmother passed ldeket through words, as she sat in the night waiting for hyenas and lions to attack her, or whether the ldeket escaped from her nkosheke as she died. In most cases, bystanders assume that ldeket formed in the mother's or grandmother's nkosheke and escaped whether they intended to voice it or not. And such ldeketa are powerful.

A person who has kept *rerei* ("words") in his/her nkosheke will not spare you. [That one is stronger?] That one is stronger . . . because the rerei you kept in your nkosheke, so that you have not adekisho ["cursed"] from your mouth, it cannot spare a person. [Mhmm.] Yes. So as to spare you? It just takes [kills] a person, what else? And there is no one who knows that an ldeket was made against you. (Nooltualan Lenaibor, interview, 2002)

The fact that ldeket can escape from the nkosheke of the dying without anyone knowing has important implications for mortuary practices in fact, as I will elaborate in the next chapter.

Many Paths to Doki

The remedy for ldeket is mayian—its opposite—performed by the very person who transmitted the ldeket in the first place. This can be done very informally between the two people or in a more lavish ceremony with a number of elders (including the principal parties) with beer.

It gets to the whole *sesen* ["body"] . . . the one who has ldeket becomes sick, ailing and not dying. And s/he doesn't rise from the ground, s/he is just sleeping, not alive and not dead. [Mhmm] Yes. [How would you know that a person has ldeket?] That person who has ldeket sleeps even while being treated (lies around weakly), s/he is taken to hospitals, is given herbs, and it doesn't heal him or her. "Let's go to the loiboni [mhmm] so as to tell us what has hurt him or her, this person who is just lying." And it is this ldeket that s/he has. When a loiboni plays his shoes, he goes "rra" [sound of pouring the stones]. "Rra." "Hai," he says. "This one has ldeket! Go and bring him or her [the person who transmitted the ldeket] to bless [mayian] him or her." And the whole settlement fills up with the gathering of Samburu. Even in the shady places, beer is brewed to be drunk and livestock are slaughtered to be eaten, whether a goat or cow. And [they] drink and elders bless [*nemayiani*]. "Nkai, Nkai, Nkai, Nkai." (Nooltualan Lenaibor, interview, 2002)

It is incumbent upon a person with ldeket (assuming the cause was just) to seek out the person s/he has wronged and reconcile as soon as possible, hopefully before any effects of the ldeket have been realized. This is all the more crucial because if the wronged person dies before blessing the one s/he "cursed" (*ketedikishe*), the remedies will be more complex and less assured. It may be necessary to visit many laŋeni ("wise people") or loibonok (ritual specialists/healers) before one finally arrives at a solution.

In the event that a person with ldeket (a "curse") does not successfully seek a remedy, or if the wounded person who effected the ldeket dies and all efforts to reverse the ldeket fail, ŋoki will follow. Indeed, ldeket is perhaps the most common way for people to get ŋoki, since ŋoki is the result of one's own wrongdoing, typically committed against people, who then transfer ldeket to the perpetrator. Yet there are other ways to get ŋoki, some of which I have touched on previously. In Chapter 4, for example, I mentioned the consequences of selling human and elephant latukuny. There is an even worse, though related, offense I have heard about. Lendonyio (an Lkimaniki) is another wandering man who exhibits mental confusion.

People who know say that when he was working, he was strong. [Mm.] He was strong. [Mm.] Yet when a young person would die Lendonyio would go and take that person's belongings [beads particularly]. [Mm.] He would take all of that person's things, be they what or what. It is said that he would take them and sew them [repairing or changing them] and sell them to Europeans [tourists]. [Mm.] Isn't he eating that ŋoki? [Mm] Yes. [Taking things from a dead person?!] Yes, taking things from a dead person! (Lenaudo interview, 2001)

This is a form of *itadee*—wrongdoing related to eating prohibited foods—one that, as I related in Chapter 4, has been novel and shocking to people insofar as it involves consuming elephant or worse, human, latukuny. As such, the ŋoki is bound to be serious. There are a variety of older, more common, and often less serious forms of itadee however, like eating tabooed animals such as donkeys, zebras, snakes, lions, rhino, or any animal (including livestock) killed by an elephant.[20] Warthogs are also tabooed, but the consequences are not typically as serious as for eating other forbidden animals. Cleansing should be done for all these cases, including warthogs, to avoid ŋoki. Here, the offense is against animals, except where consuming human latukuny is involved, and the seriousness of the consequences is contingent on the seriousness of the itadee.

Besides ldeket, murder, and itadee, there are *sanyon*—wrongdoing related to wealth and property—that can eventually bring ŋoki upon the person who commits them if left unremedied. As with most causes of ŋoki (though not all, as itadee illustrates), sanyon are offenses between humans that illustrate the radical intersubjectivity of Samburu persons, as one person's wrongdoing jumps the gap between them and eventually invades the offender. Sanyon include *aiŋop suam, akiny ŋoroyeni/nkoiliai*, and *anaŋ sile*. A person commits *aiŋop suam* (hiding animals) if s/he (usually he) lies about how many animals another person's livestock have produced while he herded them for that person. (It is especially bad in the case of cattle, as when the person puts his own brand on someone else's calves and hides them from the owner.) A person commits *akiny ŋoroyeni/nkoiliai* (stealing from women/widows) by depriving a widow of animals or taking away her animals. This can happen to widows who are very young and childless, or those with no sons, or those whose sons are still young.

Finally, *anaŋ sile* means to die before repaying a debt. This includes all debts, however minor they may appear to be. Thus, if a woman borrows water from someone, she must be sure to repay it before the lender dies or moves away. Her only recourse if the person has died or moved away is to pour the equivalent amount of water onto the ground (she can also pour it on the ground if the lender does not need the water back). Dying in credit is comparable to ldeket ("curse")—indeed, one way to "curse" someone is to say, "*Mikitanaŋa sile*" (May you die in credit). Debts should be repaid before one dies or risk poverty for their children, which will become sanyon if their children do not settle them. In the midst of dying, it is a father's responsibility to tell his eldest son all of his debts so that the son will be responsible. It will become ŋoki if the son doesn't agree to pay or if he doesn't pay because he wasn't told. It is a worse ŋoki if he knows and refuses. Dying mothers are obligated to tell their youngest sons of all their debts so that the son can assume responsibility for them. Even in the case of giving birth, if a woman had to borrow the animal she ate after giving birth because the family was poor, the child she gave birth to will be responsible to repay the animal if s/he grows up and the mother still can't pay.

Ŋoki to Nine Generations

I have so far discussed several of the many ways a person can get ŋoki, but I have yet to describe precisely what ŋoki is, beyond being something *like* a living thing. Scholars of Maa-speaking pastoralists like the Maasai and Samburu have glossed ŋoki in a variety of ways. Voshaar (1998) glosses it as related to the "deeds of human failure," noting that ldeket and ŋoki "share the same breast" without detailing the precise relationship between the two. Spencer (1965: 187) describes it as an "unpropitious ritual state"—a description that is fairly accurate, though not exhaustive. Although Spencer mentions consequences befalling one's children, for example, he does not elaborate much farther, and the only path to ŋoki he mentions is ldeket.

Ŋoki is elusive, in fact. It certainly is an unpropitious state that results from someone's wrongdoing, and it can affect one's children. The biblical parallels are worth noting here because Samburu Christians frequently cite them in their efforts to read Samburu practices through biblical ones. Thus, in Exodus 34: 7 God says that He will visit "the iniquity of the fathers upon the children, and upon the children's children, unto the third and to the fourth generation." Ŋoki has a twist, however: It is not merely that Nkai punishes subsequent generations. Samburu are very clear that it is the ŋoki itself that expresses itself in multitudinous ways and that it is somehow a living thing. It gets into a person's sesen ("body") and is transmitted to one's children and onward like elements of the genetic code. Moreover, like genetic traits (particularly recessive ones), its expression is unpredictable—it may take two generations or more to surface. Unlike genes, however, it *will* have a clear and definable end—ŋoki can pass through nine agesets and then it will surely lose its efficacy. Moreover, it is not limited to personality or appearance traits but can take an untold number of forms, some of them even amusing.

There is the story, for example, of the Lkileku who had killed and eaten a warthog while on a raid.[21] When he returned, he neglected to mention precisely what animal he had eaten, claiming in fact that he did not really know. A few years ago, though, warthogs started to wander freely into his settlement as if they belonged there. The Lkileku consulted a loiboni, who said that the man had knowingly eaten a warthog while on that difficult raid and then had not cleansed himself of that itadee. Because of this, warthogs were now claiming his settlement (*nkaŋ*) as home—confusing it with the bush (*soro*). The warthogs must have thought, "If this man can eat warthogs as freely as goats and cows, surely we can stay in his settlement too." With the help of the loiboni, the man performed the appropriate cleansing and the warthogs immediately recognized the clear and crucial distinction between his nkaŋ and soro.

In another case, another Lkileku man killed a disabled Turkana while on a raid. This is a clear offense, preying on weak or defenseless people. Within a generation or two, the man's family began to sire similarly disabled children—it was a very evident instance of ŋoki. Similarly, an Lkishili man living near me is said to have poked out the eyes of seven puppies in his youth, burning them in a fire (why he would do this went unexplained). When he married and his wife gave birth, the children were born blind or with vision problems, one after another, until she had given birth seven times. Only the eighth child and subsequent children could see properly.

The example with which I started this chapter—of the woman who gave birth to a cat—is of course another expression of ŋoki. While it is rare for women to pass their own ŋoki on to their sons (one notable exception being food-related ldeketa, as I have mentioned), as birthgivers, women are invariably the victims of their husband's ŋoki, seeing it manifested in their children. Ŋoki is a sex-linked "trait," patrilineally inherited like many other conditions, features, and skills. Thus, girls cannot inherit their father's ŋoki—they will eventually marry and suffer the consequences of any ŋoki lurking in their husband's lineage. When expressed in this way, ŋoki takes the shape of a variety of birth defects, from missing joints or limbs to severe deformity.[22] In all of these cases, the child itself is referred to as ŋoki, and sometimes—as with the "cat"—is left to die. "[And what is ŋoki?] When you kill things—that becomes a ŋoki. And it goes sometimes and a ŋoki is born, a thing that has no joints, or sometimes it has no ears or eyes" (Lemarei interview, 2001). Ŋoki can also manifest itself in deformed livestock and in a variety of other ways, some of which I have suggested. What all ŋoki have in common is that they will eventually express themselves. "It goes and catches you and you go to the loiboni, and he tells you to go (and do as he instructs), because that is how it is. And that, and so it is the ŋoki that is eating you" (Lemarei interview, 2001).

Explaining ŋoki in the idiom of eating or consuming someone is an archetypical Samburu convention. Indeed, just as powerfully as beaded ornaments and clothing (Straight 2005a, 2005b), food and eating practices are crucial "cuts" organizing Samburu society and consciousness (see Holtzman 1996, 2002). If food sharing is a crucial virtue and hunger a fearful condition, consuming others is a terrible abomination. It is by no coincidence, then, that in imparting the logic, nature, and behavior of ŋoki to their children, Samburu often tell a "cannibal" tale, which I relate here in slightly abbreviated form.[23]

Chudum and the Cannibal

There were once nine lmurran going into the forest to eat an ox they had brought with them to slaughter. They met another lmurrani with beautiful long hair, not realizing that in fact he was a cannibal with two mouths, one normal and one at the nape of his neck. He asked them if they were looking for a place to slaughter their ox, and said he would prepare a nice camp for them. He went back to his cave and swept away the bones of all the people he had eaten, then led them there. They were very pleased and slaughtered their ox and gave some of the meat and blood to the cannibal. The latter took it behind a bush and ate it privately, while his two mouths talked back and forth and threatened to expose him if they did not get enough food to eat. As he ate, one of the nine lmurran, Chudum, approached him secretly, watching him eat. After everyone had finished eating, the cannibal said he was going to look after his cattle. Then Chudum told the others what he had seen and warned them to watch out. They did not listen to him at all, especially because the cannibal was so handsome.

At night, the other eight lmurran spread themselves out to sleep, but Chudum climbed a tree to watch what would happen. Late at night, the cannibal came into the camp, counting the men, "One, two, three, four, five, six, seven, eight. Where is the ninth?" He counted them again and still found that there were eight. He wondered about it, but ate them all. Chudum climbed down the tree very quietly and went back home to report what had happened. Eight lmurran decided to accompany him back to slay the cannibal, while Chudum disguised himself with a black cloth, a limp, and a squinting eye. When they arrived at the previous place in the forest, everything transpired as before. However, this time when the cannibal ate, some of Chudum's companions secretly watched him. And at night, while the cannibal was away, Chudum and his companions rolled logs over to the sleeping place, covering all of them with sheets to look like people sleeping. Then they went and hid. When the cannibal returned in the middle of the night, he counted them and was satisfied that they were all there. Chudum and the other eight lmurran sprang on him then and killed him. As he died, however, he exclaimed that he should have known that Chudum's limp and squinting eye were a disguise. He vowed that one day he would catch Chudum and eat him. At that, one small piece of the cannibal escaped and ran away. As time passed, the cannibal assumed many shapes in an attempt to trick and eat Chudum, but Chudum was too clever every time. The cannibal turned into a log, and Chudum knew better and avoided it. The cannibal metamorphosed into a pretty girl whom the elders tried to force Chudum to marry, but despite all of their attempts Chudum refused. The cannibal even jumped into Chudum's own mother's womb, biding its time until she gave birth to the cannibal. While Chudum's mother was out milking the cows, the baby sang a song that called the utensils and the meat of the ram that had been slaughtered for Chudum's mother to eat. The cannibal ate it all and was satisfied, but Chudum's mother wondered what had become of her meat. Meat continued to disappear and disappear, until at last Chudum spied the cannibal baby in the act. When Chudum told his mother, she would not believe it until she and every member of the family had spied for themselves. Then they slaughtered a very fat ram and gave the cannibal baby the fat. When the baby went to sleep, the family moved the entire settlement far away.

Things continued going like this until finally, one day, the cannibal transformed himself into a large shade tree. All of the elders gathered there, enjoying its shade very much. Then there came a day when they called Chudum to a meeting at that very shade tree. He tried to refuse, knowing that the tree was the cannibal, even trying to reason with them, asking them how they could fail to notice that the tree had never been there before. The elders refused to listen, and eventually it was clear that they were forcing Chudum to attend the meeting under that tree. Chudum relented, but he told everyone that he knew he would never return from the meeting. He carried his neck rest and sleeping skin with him and curled himself up on his right side to go to sleep, knowing that he would not wake up. A single leaf dropped from the tree, falling on his head, and then the entire tree and Chudum vanished into the ground.

Ŋoki is like that cannibal, a living thing that chases people unrelentingly, constantly changing, reincarnating in unpredictable forms, until at last it eats the wrongdoer or the wrongdoer's descendants over and over again until nine agesets pass. When a person wrongs other people or animals, their anger takes shape in their nkosheke, then springs into the sesen ("body") of the wrongdoer. It may be the lŋonchoi (unpropitious condition) from an ldeket ("curse") that the wrongdoer carries for awhile, until—if left unremedied—it transforms into ŋoki (which is worse). It may be *marar* (another unpropitious condition), acquired from beating weaker persons or from a wrongdoing of similar gravity, which takes control of the wrongdoer, causing him or her to commit additional, more serious wrongs—to the point of killing another human being. At this point the person gets *lmogiro* (unpropitiousness associated with killing that can cause more killing) as well, and like marar, that lmogiro will eventually transform into ŋoki.[24]

Samburu describe lnonchoi, marar, lmogiro, and ŋoki as living things, or very like them, that affect behavior, are transferable to other persons, and, in the case of ŋoki in particular, are capable of expressing themselves in every form imaginable, from trees and rivers to lizards and human babies. And yet, as powerful as they are, all are the result of human agency, whether through the spoken or unspoken ldeket resulting from wronging others or through a less precisely named form of anger from people or animals cheated, murdered, or killed by another. Ŋoki is the direct result and manifestation of two beings interacting in powerfully negative ways, just as mayian and its positive consequences exemplify the positive mingling of two or more persons.

The idiom through which we make sense of such transferences and fusions determines that sense making itself. Were we to compare ŋoki to spirits or spirit possession, for example, it might capture something of the lived form that ŋoki and its siblings (marar, and so on) seem to have.

However, it would inaccurately portray these conditions/substances as originating from elsewhere, foreigners like the *orpeko* inhabiting some Maasai women (Hodgson 1997; Johnsen 1997) or the *kiarabu* and *jini* spirits inhabiting some coastal Swahili persons (Giles 1999).[25] Yet ŋoki are not spirits, not foreigners with substance apart from people or animals or inanimate things. They are the changing and tangible expression of negative human interaction—and their effects are observable by non-Samburu as well as Samburu. They make leaves or whole trees fall, stir water into violence, weaken or deform people and animals—and at the same time they *are* those leaves, those trees, those rivers, those babies and cows. Thus, to suggest that they animate creatures and things in the world is not sufficient—they both animate and become. I am reminded here of Pels's (1998) distinction between "the spirit in matter" and "the spirit of matter," and, like reality and Being itself, I cannot finalize ŋoki, marar, lmogiro, or lŋonchoi to be one or the other. Nkai creates them and gives them force as surely as S/he does humans and animals, but Nkai's procreative action in no way diminishes their independent existence. Ɗoki in the shape of a deformed goat, a goat that is a ŋoki, will never cease being both. Ɗoki scatters, jumps about, invades living and nonliving things, but it does not animate them like something that could later withdraw—it proliferates, controlling because (to a partial extent) it becomes.[26]

Dreaming Ɗoki

Immediately after completing the first draft of this chapter and while still in the field, I had a dream that I at once understood as a parable of ŋoki and Being simultaneously—a crossing of my Samburu and Euro-American philosophical understandings:

I was in a shop, as if in Kenya yet also in the United States. I no longer remember why I first entered, but I remember having a motorcycle and needing to buy a seat for it. Like an excellent Kenyan bricoleur, the shopkeeper tried to sell me a bicycle seat for it. I chastised him and he followed me from there to my home, where I was surprised to see that a children's party was taking place. It was dark at first, and my husband, Jon, and I took pictures of one another taking pictures of one another. Soon there were lights, and my youngest children, Clare and William, and other children were there, sitting on a sofa. The motorcycle clerk had now transformed into the party entertainer, dressed in a horse costume, sitting with the children. And the motorcycle sat in a corner, appearing as if it too had transformed into a horse. And there were other pictures to take—of the party entertainer in his costume, of the motorcycle in its horse pose, and then of my mother and children (including Clare) seated on the motorcycle as if it were a horse. The motorcycle clerk turned party entertainer asked to borrow some money for dinner because he said he couldn't get his salary from the shop yet—it felt like the sort of thing that would happen in Kenya and we complied.

Then we were outside, still taking pictures—this time of Clare and my child-hood friend, Renee, and others on a car parked nearby. Jon and I became frustrated then, because of the long time the digital cameras were taking to process between pictures. We wandered into a shop to inquire about increasing the speed, and the party entertainer became a camera shop clerk, and soon he had even become one of the women clerks there. I asked the women if Renee's digital camera was any faster than mine, since mine seemed to take forever. Apparently, though, the women were having their own problems with speed—they only had one phone line for email and credit card approvals. Jon began thinking about how to assist them with this problem, and it seemed they had become anthropology department secretaries. Because he is a professor, he managed to arrange another phone line for them.

Meanwhile, I had wandered into another room that was my own house, to look for the camera's manual. I saw my son Jen's geometry tools scattered on the bed, so I began to put them carefully away. The motorcycle clerk/party entertainer/ camera clerk/department secretary wandered in then and struck up a conversation with me. She pointed to one of the protractors and commented that in her work she uses that solid little one and then she asked why I have all of them. I replied that they used to belong to my son Jen, and now my daughter Clare, uses them. Then I mused that perhaps soon I won't really need to keep the tools, since Jen has finished geometry, although Clare will use them awhile. And then again, my brother still likes to do technical drawing—maybe Jen will too. I mentioned that my brother likes to design and build things like models and sculptures and cars and then blow them up. I looked up at the television to see a video of my brother blowing up a car he had built. The woman remarked that this seems like a very silly thing to do. I said perhaps—but then again, is it so different from other ephemeral things, like the sand mandalas the Tibetan monks make?

And suddenly I was on a patio where a Tibetan monk had just completed a beautiful sand mandala and was about to sweep it all away. A little boy was crying, not wanting to see it destroyed, and then it was a rug with the same pattern, which can be unraveled easily. I showed the little boy how easy and fun it is—the little boy was my boyfriend (and eventual husband), Jon, as a little boy. We folded up the mandala in fragments of yarn and pieces of still-intact rug, together with the laundry. And Jon remarked how easy it is to destroy your girl-friend's rug and sell the yarn back to her.

When I awoke I realized immediately that I had dreamed ŋoki and Being as parables of one another—a dream like the cannibal story, of one thing transforming into another while maintaining the thread of connection from one image to the next. As my own life wound through the transformations, some thread of connection joined each, tying ephemeral mandalas with my brother's alternating constructions and destructions—things that change without losing some aspect of what they were, ready to take a beautiful shape once again, somehow like ŋoki and like reality and our experiential meeting with it in Being.

I read Gananath Obeyesekere's (2002) *Imagining Karma* and considered how ŋoki is karma's inverse in many ways, belonging more properly to Being, to an experiential reality that is in us as well as around us, moving between indeterminate and determined, becoming the very shape our shared ways of prescissing lead us to expect (like a hammer rather than some wood attached to metal, or like a reteti tree with all of the complexity of its signification rather than an apple tree with its own complicated signification, or even like a particle rather than a wave of light, or a chair rather than all of the phenomena of which it and its current boundaries are composed). While karma affects one person, who assumes new shapes from one existence to another according to a predictable ethical logic, ŋoki moves between persons (and even animals and things), affecting the innocent as well as the guilty just as reality reincarnates constantly between and among us, affecting all who share context. Like experiential reality, ŋoki is unpredictable, continually changing without losing some thread of continuity, some means of uncanny recognition.

Ŋoki is a parable and real instantiation of intersubjective Being, of the power of persons to experience reality together in similar ways and in that shared experience to powerfully affect one another—like the woman who dies within a week of her beloved husband, like the sick child who gets well when his mother finally returns from a trip to lay soothing hands upon him, or like Lemarei and myself, who called a snake into our midst with the power of our shared anger. For the Samburu, ŋoki is very real, reincarnating from one generation to the next unpredictably. For me, it is additionally a thought-lesson suggesting that the Derridean gap between word and world (and imagination and reality) is never complete—it is elusive, a symptom of a unique, Euro-American ontology that likewise separates "minds" from "bodies," persons from world, and people from one another.

There are two interrelated points ensconced here—one concerning the efficacy of prescissing and the other, expansive experience's intersubjective aspects. In asserting, as I have throughout this book, that prescissing within expansive experience is profoundly efficacious—a cutting that declares, connects, and becomes—I am pushing the envelope of a classic anthropological trope. The Sapir-Whorf hypothesis suggested that language shapes (human) reality. The consequences of this hypothesis have endured, taking an intriguing "linguistic" and "interpretive" turn in the postmodernism of the 1980s and '90s, although some of us in the first decade of the twenty-first century have registered some caution.[27] Nevertheless, anthropologists continue to suppose that language in some way shapes reality, and this issue relates to another anthropological trope—cultural relativism. Apropos of my discussion of ŋoki and reincarnation, Akhil Gupta, contemplating the seriousness most in India accord reincarnation,[28] suggests "thinking of the way in which categories found in discourse shape experience" (1992: 190). Writing during the heyday of identity politics and critiques of otherizing discourses, Gupta points up the need for a reinvention of categories toward a "genuinely anti-imperialist and non-Eurocentric critical practice" (208). In this way, he maintains the assumption that the categories themselves have efficacy, and I think he is quite right. At the same time, I think he reserves a space for the experiential *reality* of reincarnation, indeed explaining Euro-American understandings of commodities through reincarnation in an attempt to eschew both facile dichotomies of difference and flattening homogenizations.

In a similar vein—as the medium of this ethnography—I am reading in two directions, highlighting the differences and the similarities while finding—in the permeable borders of personhood—the conceptual thread that links Samburu and Euro-American theories of experience. My argument for prescissing's efficaciousness thus challenges body/text dualism, the hegemony of the "word," and the gap they engender. Thus, it partially upsets and reformulates the notion that language and its categories shape reality in the sense anthropologists have tended to suppose, by contending that language is the last in a series of reincarnations in experience.[29] As such, language wants more humility, a recognition that more than language has transpired at the boundaries of prescissing within expansive experience. Moreover, in the reincarnations of experiences, the lizards we expansively experience become the lizards we imagine—intersubjectively passing through us in waves or particles of light or sound or smell or in the rubbings off of direct contact. Whether we use physics, neuroscience, or "mystical" philosophies as our metaphor, experience and its cuttings are simultaneously intersubjective and efficacious, efficacious because intersubjective. As one movement turns into the next—eventuating in thought and language, the actions of others become actions within us, whether negative or positive.

Samburu experience the universe as dynamically interanimated according to a logic whose configuration I have followed here. In thinking Euro-American and Samburu understandings through each other I am attempting to foreground similarities while not eliding differences, coming to the limits of empiricism's rationality without accounting for or explaining the limits themselves. In this, I am according Euro-American and Samburu understandings the same tender respect. Indeed, there are many ideas that run against the grain in the histories of Euro-American thought as well as in Samburu, challenging neat separations like Samburu healthy cuts, Western substantive dualism, or cohesive academic theories. Heretofore, I have tracked the divine appearances that the Samburu find miraculous but somehow expected, as well as the mundane intersubjective crossings that follow a clear Samburu logic, even if observers like me and sometimes Samburu, find them extraordinary. In the final chapters, in contrast, I will draw increasing attention to events that challenge Samburu as well as Euro-American cultural logics—instances when the boundaries that Samburu and Euro-Americans each work hard to maintain become unstable or blurred. Before getting to the transgressive, however, it is necessary to consider the limits, and thus I will pause in the next chapter to consider Samburu understandings of death and the meaningful practices by which Samburu attempt to cut, bind, and separate it.

Chapter 6

Death

Death—like ŋoki—like all aspects of Being (where we experientially meet reality)—is a tangible, slippery changeling, transmuting across cultural and temporal contexts to the point of appearing almost unrecognizable. Almost. Like the death of the little girl I opened this book with, death as more than sign is always extraordinary. Indeed, the witnessing of death is the quintessential occurrence of expansive experience, perhaps because it finally and terrifyingly becomes a conversation with an absent interlocutor, a breach of signifying etiquette, a socially hazardous (non)relation.[1] Not surprisingly, for the Samburu, the break from the living must be handled very carefully—because persons are radically intersubjective, susceptible to the terrors that pop in and out of the lives of others in a world for which the gaps are always filled in.

In this chapter I will describe the ways Samburu make the break, cutting death from life. Yet the cut is ever a tenuous one, death only barely subject to human intervention, and thus this chapter is the imperfect complement to the wanderings across the terrifying border, the strange sutures of the gap, that I will describe in Chapters 7 and 8. For now, in this chapter, body, object, and text are all conjoined in radical forms of intersubjective personhood—personhood a gritty, evanescent sign reincarnating from multitudinous incarnations of expansive experiences, incarnations that for Samburu erupt into objects tinged with aspects of personhood, into conversations that have lives of their own, and into persons whose attributes slip casually into beloved others. Death is always a horrifying intruder. Yet when someone you share latukuny with is stolen wretchedly away or worse, taken deliberately, death itself can be the stuff that fills the gap.

April 25, 2002: An eighteen-year-old uncircumcised "boy" killed a married Lmooli the day before yesterday—within a ten-minute drive of my house. Evidently, the Lmooli had been beating his wife, and she ran into the house where the boy was staying, asking for refuge. The boy came outside, trying to separate the wife and the Lmooli and to ask the Lmooli not to beat her. I don't know exactly what happened then, but somehow the boy stabbed the Lmooli with his knife. My friend Leriten

Lemadero rushed the Lmooli towards the hospital but he died en route. The boy ran away to his home here—between Loltulelei and Lodokejek (just near Timothy Loishopoko's place). Timothy saw him yesterday morning before hearing that he had killed someone, and then heard later.

The boy's family also did not know at first that he had killed anyone. When they found out, they chased him away this morning. They slaughtered a sheep and poured the contents of its stomach and intestines (including feces, the whole called *maiyog*) plus a little unmixed fat and blood around the compound and down the road over the boy's tracks. They cursed as they did so—telling him to leave with his marar and lmogiro. They said: *"Tiriko* [take it with you] *marar, lmogiro lino* [your marar, lmogiro], *iij!"*[2] Iij is an exclamation of absolute refusal. Everyone in the family he had shared food with washed their hands with the feces from the maiyog—a sheep is utterly innocent. They also smeared their hands, faces, and neck ornaments with fat, and poured milk. Elders came to eat the meat and perform mayian ("blessing") for the whole settlement to remove the inauspiciousness of the boy's having come there after killing another Samburu. In fact, the Lmooli was the boy's own mother's brother from the same stomach ("womb"), and the suspicion at first was that the boy was having an incestuous affair with the Lmooli's wife. By having the affair, he would have brought marar upon himself—an unpropitious "thing" that would inevitably cause him to kill or be killed. And in actually killing, he would bring lmogiro upon himself, an even worse unpropitiousness. By itself, even before eventuating into ŋoki, it would cause death to him and to anyone he comes into contact with.

In killing, the boy also brought the *ŋuan* ("stench") of death upon himself, and that ŋuan of death will inevitably attract more death. Everything and everyone he touched will likewise pick up the ŋuan and associated lmogiro, and thus it was necessary for his family to cleanse the entire settlement and adekisho ("curse") the boy in order to chase away the ŋuan of death—and thus chase away death itself. The boy did more than visit his family after the murder, however. He removed his clothes and shoes and stole others, trying to dilute the ŋuan and the lmogiro by passing some of it on to others. In this way, he gave himself time, hopefully long enough to stay in the bush (as a *lowaru*—wild beast) without dying for the requisite six months that must pass before he can be cleansed. Though he can dilute the strength of the ŋuan and the lmogiro, he must be cleansed by another (already cleansed) murderer or a non-Samburu (like a Turkana) before he can return to live with people. It will never again be said, however, that kerropil—he "smells" good/virtuous/sweet.[3] Though cleansed and thus free of the danger of death, perhaps, he will stink (koŋu). And that stink is not the benign unpleasant odor of postpartum women, newly circumcised young people, or sick people. Of them it is said *kelili*—they smell fetid (of urine, blood, fat, of various combinations of things). No, this boy stinks in the way death stinks, and he and his family will always be more or less despised. From the perspective of the murderer, however, the important thing was to take himself out of danger.

In the last chapter, I examined in some detail the eventual consequences of murder in my discussion of ŋoki. This murderous boy may escape death now by transferring some of the immediate combination of stench and unpropitiousness to others, but ŋoki will surely follow. And he may have a very difficult time ridding himself of it. If he sires children through extramarital affairs, his progeny may effectively bring about the deaths of other children (Straight 2005b). Moreover, he and his own children (to nine agesets) will suffer the consequences as well, even if the forms that the suffering takes are unpredictable and varied.

According to Samburu I know, the force of that unpropitiousness has already begun to make itself felt in the intervening months since the murder. Hearing about the murder the day immediately following its occurrence, I shuddered—how many deaths had I already heard about this year? How many bandits had killed people on roads I travel? How many children had died through illness or tragic accident? No, I had no doubt that more suffering would take place in that family, both realized directly in grief and in other ways. And sure enough, several months later, I heard that the murderer's co-mother—the very woman whose house the boy had slept in right after he had killed his uncle, the very woman most in danger of getting some of his "stench," marar, and lmogiro—had begun to behave terribly inappropriately. She had gotten severely drunk, and in her drunken condition she had behaved out of the ordinary for even a drunken person. She had ventured into the bush where lmurran were eating and had verbally abused them. Since the food of lmurran is never supposed to be seen by women, going near them intentionally was infraction enough. Yet she refused to leave despite all their persuasions. She verbally abused and finally fought with them, until one of them hit her on the head with his *rungu* (club). At that, she shook her head violently, flinging her blood in all directions, yelling ldeketa as she did so.

The next morning, in sober condition, she tried to repair some of what she had done. The family was forced to slaughter two rams, one to speed *her* healing and one for the mayian that she had to perform. As the family did after they discovered the murder, the woman had to retrace all of her own path, pouring on her every step the unmixed contents of the ram's stomach and intestines, some unmixed fat, and blood. In this way she lined her entire path and covered every spot where her blood had fallen the previous day. Yet this was only an immediate measure. The family very soon agreed that this wife, this co-mother of a murderer, would have to move away to live with her allocated livestock all by herself in a lonely settlement—keeping her unpropitiousness far away from the people it might hurt. And I wonder whether even this will be enough.

I have described some of the causes, shapes, and signs of ŋoki, and I have also discussed ŋoki in comparison with the "reincarnating" process of prescissive experience. Now I will leave ŋoki in the background as I examine Samburu experiences and understandings of death with respect to the Samburu practice of "cutting" (aduŋ) that generates healthy separations and healthy mixtures. Death (lkiye) is of course the ultimate division, and indeed, this fact is signaled by the Samburu term itself. Lkiye derives from the verb root aya, to take.[4] In other words, people who die are taken away from the living, and they are "thrown" into the bush (soro). Moreover, death is not usually spoken of directly (and neither are the vulnerable conditions of pregnancy and childbirth) but metaphorically. For example, a dead person is one whose heart is "cut" (ltuŋani otuduŋie ltau), one who has slept (kelure), one who has been "laid to rest" (neperr), or one who has been "thrown" (anaŋ, from which lmeneŋai—corpse derives).[5] As a taking away from the living and from the habitations of the living (thrown into soro), lkiye is also an opposing complement to the twin verbs aishu (to be alive) and aisho (to give birth, that is, to give life). When Nkai kills people because of their wrongdoing, women join collectively to sing, asking Nkai to make a cut—cutting that death to spare the yet living: "Neomoni ake Nkai, aajo naake, 'Nkai tuduŋu yoo'" (They just pray to Nkai, just saying, "Nkai, cut [it for] us"— "Spare us") (Lenaudo interview, 2001). As I argue by example in Appendix 2, both aishu and aisho linguistically refer to the process of life giving. In contrast, lkiye and anaŋ refer to the taking or throwing away of life, nkishui (with life understood as the object taken).

The death that is thrown away must also be kept away, and in examining how this is done we come closest to the sort of oppositions Lévi-Straussian structuralism described so well. Indeed, in Samburu understandings lkiye is opposed to nkishui, left to right, female to male—even to the moment of conception when girls enter their mother's wombs from the left, boys from the right. At the same time, women are quintessentially associated with life, and right is not merely propitious in life but also in burial at death, when corpses are laid on their right in a curled sleeping pose. Women—who enter their mother's wombs from the left and who have difficulty attaining the same level of nkanyit (something like respect pertaining to social distance) and *lkiti* (something like reverence/shame combined) as men (at least until they reach venerable age)—yet resemble Nkai more closely in Her/His/Its life-giving and -sustaining capacities. There are no perfect or perfectly consistent oppositions, but there are always crucial cuts, divisions, and mixtures, and these are very context-sensitive. Here, I will examine the cutting that separates lkiye from nkishui in order that nkishui might be kept together and safe. Before that, however, I will discuss the sticky stinkiness of lkiye.

Death Stinks

The care with which Samburu take in burying the dead reflects an understanding of death as something with a "stench" that multiplies unpropitiously, attracting life to itself and, in that process, taking other lives away with it. This is not because death is some mysterious contagion but because people who share milk and latukuny are connected—some aspects of their personhood cross into one another. It is like a fire moving along a fuse connecting every house in the neighborhood—as each house combusts into flame the fire continues along the next fuse to another house, onward and onward until that fuse is cut and the fire extinguished there. Latukuny is the fuse and, predictably, death is the flame that consumes those once-propitious connections now turned tragically against them. Moreover, social status and the circumstances of death determine the shape of the fire. For some, the entailments of personhood must be thoroughly annihilated, while for others—like sweet grandparents—some aspects of personhood can be left to endure. In this regard, objects that behave as persons must be cherished or destroyed, remembered or forgotten, as persons. Thus, calabashes, like children, have uncertain lives. I will come to the significance of this as I follow the trail of crucial cuts.

CUTTING SPACE

As throughout life, the cutting divisions of age and gender determine one's treatment at death, but here they acquire a new significance. As I have said, death is a sticky (and stinky) thing—operating like latukuny (though a hideous inversion) in some respects—and the more unpropitious the circumstances surrounding it, the greater the strength with which it attracts the living. Thus, death is more hazardous at some periods of life than at others, at some places than others, and by some causes than others—its danger increasing when certain propitious cuts of life are violated. Moreover, the degree of danger a particular death poses determines how thoroughly the corpse (with its death clinging and ready to spread) must be separated from the living. Ultimately, what belongs to soro (bush) must be kept in or returned to soro, and what belongs to *nkajijik* and *nkaɲitie* (houses and settlement—life's social spaces) must be kept there.

Once babies are weaned, their lkiye ("death") becomes dangerous— they should have been strong enough to survive in the first place. Thus, dead little boys' and girls' (*nkiyo*) clothes and ornaments are removed,[6] their heads shaved, and their corpses wrapped in an animal hide or blanket, positioned on their right side as if sleeping and placed beneath an uncut, unblemished *ltepes* (Acacia tortilis) tree. Then they are covered with green leaves. This pattern—shaving, right-side position, sleeping skin, unblemished acacia tree, and green leaves—is the propitious basis of all Samburu mortuary ritual, although it will be elaborated and the corpse's final location altered depending on the age/gender status and manner of death. Once a person has children, for example, their mortuary rites will be more elaborate. A sheep or cow will be slaughtered and its fat poured in the dead elder's (*lkimaita*)[7] or mother's (*ntaɲatana*)[8] mouth, together with milk and a bit of tobacco.

As they age and successfully move through the many propitious cuts of life, men and women are brought nearer and nearer to the settlement for burial—the strength of the death that clings to them is becoming increasingly diminished. Marriage brings them closer, siring or giving birth to children brings them closer, having initiated their sons and daughters brings them closer still, and becoming grandparents often brings the dead right into the settlement itself. People at life's vulnerable ends (grandparents and unweaned babies) are so close to Nkai as to defy the usual conventions of division.[9] As such, not only should they die at home (as most people should), but they are the only people whom most Samburu families routinely bury within the settlement, even within the house. Stillborn (*ketetemaka*)[10] or days-old babies (*ketorrorre*)[11] are buried under one of the mother's fire stones or between the fire stones and her bed.[12] Other babies are buried in the calves' enclosure (within the settlement). Grandparents (*lkimatia lorropil* for men and *ntaɲatana norropil* for women ("good/virtuous/sweet-smelling" elders and mothers) are buried in the center of the settlement, and the family avoids moving for (ideally) a period of years. "You even finish how many years for old men? Five years. [Five?] Until the place 'smells' good" (Leropili interview, 2002). Samburu say that they want to wait until their grandmothers or grandfathers have turned completely to bones underneath the ground—and thus their corpse will "smell" as good as their revered lives did. For those closest to Nkai, then, there is no need to preserve the vital distinction between nkaŋ and soro—it is a weak form of lkiye that clings to them.

If infant and grandparents' lkiye are relatively (or even wholly) benign, the "taking away" (lkiye) of lmurran occupies the opposite extreme. In contrast to all other Samburu age and gender categories, lmurran (*laiŋoni*—bulls) and never-married circumcised men (*lmaasha*)[13] must not only be disposed of far from human habitation, they must even die there—and their clothing and ornaments will be left on them rather than being removed. "Lmurran are usually meat of the bush" (Lefuraha interview, 2001). For an lmurran or unmarried man to die in the settlement is so terrible and dangerous that it is only heard of once in a period of many years. And when it does occur, the donkeys are called and packed with the family's belongings immediately and the whole settlement moves, leaving the lmurran where he died. There is no way to get lkiye out of that settlement—anyone who lingers will surely get it on themselves and die. "You see the youth, they are not left to die where? It is said that when they die at home they will finish that family" (Leropili interview, 2002). The girls who sing and engage in romantic trysts with lmurran (*ndorop sesen*—short bodies) are next in the line of unpropitiousness. They should die at home, but like their lmurran boyfriends, they will be disposed of with their clothing and ornaments still on.

Besides unmarried circumcised men, lmurran, and their girlfriends—whose deaths are always highly unpropitious—any death that occurs away from home is unpropitious, particularly if it is the result of violence, accident, or attack by wild animals.[14] The mortuary rituals of such persons are treated differently, with the corpse laid at or near the site of death. People are also more hesitant to *touch* those who have died in these ways, raising the compensation for the elders who assume responsibility for guarding the corpse until burial, preparing it, and placing the corpse under leaves.[15] Finally, in the case of married people (who have children) dying away from home, they will not be smeared with fat or given milk and tobacco as would usually be the case when they are buried. Some manners of death (as with violent or accidental death) are already unpropitious, but for small children or married people to die away from home is unpropitious regardless of the cause. While mortuary location depends on the level of danger according to the age-gender category of the deceased, all people's lives must be taken away from them in the place they belong in life. For almost all this is the settlement (nkaŋ), while for lmurran it is the soro.

FOOLING HYENAS

Yes, they [hyenas] tell. May they eat *themselves*! [Yes.] Yes. [How?] They come barking in a group. [Yes] Mhmm, and it is not good. It is not good. (Lenkosheke interview, 2001)

And the hyena is saying [Mhmm], it is saying I am going to eat that one [person]. (Lentiwas interview, 2001)

With the exception of grandparents (in most families) and unweaned babies, all other Samburu deceased persons in the more rural parts of the lowlands are disposed of ("buried"—*aitibiraa*, prepared/made) by being placed under an ltepes tree. However, in some parts of the lowlands and especially in the highlands, this practice is on the decline owing primarily to increasing exposure to Christianity, knowledge of national legal statutes, and increasing population densities in some areas. When corpses that would have been left exposed to the elements are buried instead, most other mortuary practices—such as removing ornaments, shaving, covering with green leaves—nevertheless continue to be followed. Moreover, where burial has replaced exposure, the important distinction between soro and nkaŋ continues to be maintained because the rules of burial location tend to be followed. However, the hyenas' important role in eating the corpse has been eliminated because elders guard the deceased against scavengers just as they would in preparation for a grandparent burial.

The reason that grandparents can be buried in the settlement is that kerropil (they "smell good/sweet/virtuous") and thus they bring propitiousness rather than death to the living. This "sweetness" is not guaranteed in the case of all other deceased persons, however. For the Samburu, hyenas eating corpses is not inevitable fact—although it is an absolutely necessary outcome for a couple of reasons. Recall that murderers carry the ŋuan ("stench") of death with them. In fact, there is a very subtle distinction between the bad "smell" acquired through murder and the general "smell" of death. While people cannot detect the difference, hyenas can—and they will refuse to eat a corpse that "smells" of serious wrongdoing. "[How does the hyena know that this person is bad so as not to eat him/her?] It *knows* my child" (Nolpesi interview, 2001). Hyenas are special scavengers, with a cleansing function that extends beyond consuming the dead and death. Even when the deceased smells murderous, it is absolutely essential to entice hyenas into eating the corpse, so that they consume unpropitiousness (and its "stench") itself—thereby preventing both death and unpropitiousness from returning to the living.

Thus, Samburu mortuary practices require that elders visit the corpse in the days immediately following disposal, to see if hyenas have fulfilled their obligation by at least nibbling at the deceased. If they have not, danger hangs in the air, and elders will bring a goat to slaughter at the site, leaving its (good) stomach with the corpse.[16] The expectation is that this will both fool and attract the hyenas into taking at least a small bite somewhere.

If the hyenas don't eat him or her after staying overnight, and s/he's not eaten by the hyenas [Mm], tomorrow—the following day—a goat is slaughtered. [Mm.] A goat is killed, just leaving its stomach [mm], waiting until evening [mm] so that the vultures don't eat it. [Mm.] It is killed. [Mm.] The hyenas come. All of that [unpropitiousness] is going to be cleansed because there is nothing that can remain [mm] once this goat is paired with this person. [Mm.] They will eat all of it. [Mhmm.] The whole person will be eaten. [Mhmm.] Once they have eaten at least enough to tear his/her stomach [mm], that person ceases being unpropitious [ntolo] [yes] once a hyena has eaten even a small part of him or her. (Nolpesi interview, 2001)

There are at least two clear disadvantages to burying people who are neither young enough to be free of their own wrongdoing nor old enough to be ropili.[17] First, valuable information is lost that might allow the family of the deceased to seek the cause of the deceased's unpropitious "smell" and remedy it. This is especially crucial if there is ŋoki involved, which will eventually express itself in the most grievous ways. Second, the immediate unpropitiousness that lingers about the corpse is left as it is—it is not possible for hyenas to consume it. Nevertheless, while the Samburu I know who have begun practicing universal burial recognize these dilemmas, they do not seem overly concerned. Instead, they perform mayian and "cleansing" (literally, changing the color of something) as often as appropriate and attend to ŋoki and ntolo when they express themselves.[18]

Almost every aspect of Samburu mortuary practices is designed to successfully cut death off from the living. As a general rule, the deceased are stripped of their ornaments as well as their clothes, except when circumstances are too dangerous to remove them (as with lmurran and their girlfriends, violent deaths, and so forth).[19] Samburu describe this removal of clothes and ornaments as "stealing"—what belonged to them in life is stolen from them just as they, as persons, have been stolen from the living. When children's ornaments are removed, they are disposed of separately from the corpse, together with the child's (or other childless person's) other belongings—since their deaths are always unpropitious, every object associated with them must be separated from the living, annihilated as the child's personhood has been annihilated. Every trace of the youthful dead must be erased, as if they had never been—and indeed, having had no children they have not left a single track that could be followed. They leave nothing for the living.

In contrast, in the case of deceased parents—particularly grandparents—children and grandchildren inherit ornaments and other belongings. Indeed, old women and men begin giving away many of their ornaments and other belongings as they age. Thus, disposal of things follows the logic of nkishui/lkiye ("life/death") and nkaŋ/soro (settlement/bush) separation rather closely. Grandparents, whose sweetness can be the source of continued, posthumous blessings, can be safely and indeed propitiously memorialized through their things. Thus, as we saw in Chapter 4, a father's sobua (walking stick) should be passed to his sons, a mother's mporo marriage necklace should be passed to her daughters, and through them grandparents' fecundity will endure. Even grandparents' calabashes can be kept, while those of deceased children must be destroyed, cutting their latukuny apart even from the livestock that once nourished them.

Following the shaving, "stealing," wrapping, and disposing of the corpse, mortuary attendants must take care not to expose themselves or others to the lkiye they have touched. Likewise, elders carefully wash their hands and feet in water and then smear their hands with fat after a funeral is completed, and all of the implements used for the ritual are cleansed with fat. No death should be allowed to remain. However, even after all of these rites surrounding death and burial are carefully observed, the latukuny of the deceased still clings to those related to him or her. After an appropriate period of mourning, this too must be removed.

Grief and Mourning: Removing "Shock" and Dreadful Latukuny

For approximately one month following a death, no animals are traded in or out of the settlement of the deceased, and no one moves. Everyone closely related to the deceased (and in the case of lmurran this extends to all members of his ageset and clan) is in a period of mourning during that month. If it is a man who has died, his widows remove their copper marriage earrings (only putting them back on if they initiate sons—who are then said to be their "husbands"). If an lmurran has died, the other lmurran and the girls of the clan remove their red ochre and most of their ornaments. Everyone is experiencing a period of grief and mourning. While the degree of grief personally experienced varies a great deal from one person to the next, it is expected that everyone has at least some amount of "shock" (lputukuny) that settles in their nkosheke ("stomach"), turning it "bad." While in this period of mourning, they are still connected to the deceased, but this connection must be broken for the sake of their own healing and also to keep death—even in the shape of the deceased him- or herself—from coming to claim them.

At the end of about a month, then, the family performs a shaving ceremony that marks the end of mourning and likewise breaks all ties with the deceased with finality. This is done in several ways, each with their own significance. Mourning is ended in a couple of ways. First, everyone in the family vomits or is made to vomit.

[Why is a person made to vomit?] Maybe because when someone is screaming because of the lputukuny ["shock"] someone is made to vomit to get rid of the shock in her. (Josephine Leapa interview, 1994)

You see now that waiting, if it was a woman she would fall down hitting the ground, wailing, "Uuiii, uuii," and faint. Maybe the lputukuny would have settled so that it concentrates here [nkosheke] like this. So when you are induced to vomit, it breaks the concentration and the lputukuny in the nkosheke subsides. Yes, that is why a person is made to vomit. (Doris Lolkazi, interview 1994)

Besides vomiting out the lputukuny ("shock") of their grief, everyone (even those outside the family) ceases to say the deceased's first name. Ideally, no one will ever call the name of that person again—to do so risks bringing grief back and also risks calling the dead back to claim the relatives that summoned him or her. I will examine the implications of this in Chapter 8.

Besides vomiting, the most visible component of the shaving ceremony is of course the shaving itself. All members of the family (what Spencer 1965: 74 referred to as the "hair-sharing group"); or in the case of lmurran, one's father, mother, and siblings, together with all lmurran of one's clan, shave their hair. Although Spencer limits his discussion of shaving to deceased men, people shave their hair whether the death is of a girl, boy, woman, or man, and the reasons are the same as those Spencer describes for men. That is, one shaves one's hair because the "contamination of his [deceased's] death infects the hair of his age mates within a certain range of kinship, and in order to rid themselves of this contamination and avert misfortune, they must all shave off their hair soon after death: they are said to 'share their hair' (kong'ar lpapit)" (74).

While Spencer does not venture beyond this, I will relate the shaving practice to understandings of latukuny. It is indeed the latukuny that one shares with the deceased—and all it contains and signifies—that must be cut off. One's hair is a very potent form of concentrated latukuny, and as such is the best site for this cutting separation. While the deceased was shaved in preparation for mortuary placement, it is the family's (as well as ageset companions' in the case of an lmurran) shaving that completes that aspect of the cut. And, as Spencer suggests, it is a crucial part of the mortuary and mourning process. One woman I know described the implications of failing to shave in this way, using the example of a migrant father not appearing for the ceremony following the death of one of his children. "If the man fails to come where that work [shaving] is being done, he becomes an outsider/foreigner. He doesn't get to the home, and if he does come home, he will just remain far [from people]—an outsider. He's like a wild thing/thing from the soro"

(Doris Lolkazi, interview 1994). And, of course, the fact that the unshaved family member joins the deceased in soro has further implications. "[So is it like if you don't shave yourself.] It is bad [So it means you are still carrying those tears?] You leave that alone. See now if someone of yours dies and those lmurran refuse to shave, it will be close enough for you to shave again. [You mean someone else will die?] Yes. It is like they left you with some marar" (Lefuraha interview, 2001). The only way to get rid of the contagious unpropitiousness lkiye ("death") brings is to cut oneself off from the person with whom one once shared the most intimate components of one's being. One must separate whatever parts of one's latukuny are mixed with the latukuny of the person who has been taken away. To fail to do so risks bringing soro—and its life-taking features—right into the center of social life, the nkaŋ. Even for those like lmurran who in many ways belong to the soro, failing to shave risks mixing their lives with the soro more thoroughly than was ever intended.

Having disposed of (or distributed, if the death is of a "sweet-smelling" grandparent) the deceased's belongings, disposed of their corpse, vomited out the lputukuny ("shock") that took shape in each mourner's nkosheke, having ceased calling the deceased's name—and now, having fully separated one's latukuny from the deceased's, one action remains. The last action, the final action, will be to move the settlement itself, even if only a few yards from where it was when the deceased person was alive.[20] The cut will then be completely accomplished—lkiye will be thoroughly separated from the living.

Death Lingers and Hovers

When done properly—and my impression is that they usually are—Samburu mortuary and mourning rites are wonderfully cleansing, superbly affirming the propitious cuts that organize Samburu daily life and consciousness. Yet lkiye seems to be everywhere nevertheless, a continual and awful threat that too often comes to pass. Months after the murder I related in opening this chapter, another astonishingly similar murder took place in one of the remotest parts of the lowlands, far from the first murder. Again, a man was beating his wife in close proximity to her male relatives, and again one of those relatives killed the abusive husband.[21] In this case it was an older (Lkishili) man who killed the married Lmooli son of a man I know well. The Lkishili tried to separate the Lmooli husband and his kinswoman, but—in a drunken condition—he soon resorted to violence with his knife (Jon Holtzman, personal communication, July 2002). This happened in July 2002, soon before my scheduled (August) departure from the field, while my husband was making a brief visit to the area, so my last image before leaving that year of a community I know and love very well was of their absolute shock. And my own sadness—I immediately remembered that I had promised to buy the deceased young man a blanket. Such little things. Why should he be killed? Why should that Lkishili man (whom I don't know) kill? In the case of the boy near my home, the most recent answer I have been given (the incest rumor having been put aside) is that his grandfather also committed murder. So that ŋoki is still following him—despite whatever cleansing ceremonies had no doubt been performed. If it were easy to cleanse or deflect ŋoki, the loibonok would have an easy job—not needing to resort to killing innocent people, as I mentioned in Chapter 2 and will return to in the next chapter.

While my account of Samburu mortuary rituals abstracts them from Samburu experiences of them—a form of conceptual decontextualization (even if unavoidable)—Samburu lkiye is a wrenching, screaming subject—of an experience so horrifying that people often vomit spontaneously in the first hours of their grief and vomit again a month later. And marar, lmogiro, and ŋoki are not benign things that jump about from one person to the next; they are terrible expressions and visible manifestations of the worst wrongs humans can do to one another and the worst they can suffer. And they are accompanied by intense, shrieking pain—or absolute stunned or numb silence. I am thinking of what I have experienced textually—Daniel's (1996) torture accounts, Nancy Scheper-Hughes's (1993) neglected babies and their impoverished mothers, Kathleen Stewart's (2005) powerfully emotive and personal "still lifes," Ruth Behar's (1997) moving stories of vulnerable witness, and so many deaths. I am thinking of my own grief.

Lkiye must be cut off from nkishui. And yet lkiye seems to linger, seems to hover everywhere. When diseases strike—particularly in areas far from access to Western biomedicine—children do not die singly, they die in pairs and triplets. They die in droves, and people rush to treat the ones still clinging to life and simultaneously diagnose what awful thing is following the family. How can Nkai take so many from the same family without a reason? Why would Nkai take anyone at all? As one of my research assistants (Musa) once asked a person in the lpurkel (lowlands), "Can Nkai give life and then take it away again?" The answer was a sighing, "I don't know." And again, another time, he asked, "Where does lkiye come from?" Our friend Lenkosheke said, "It is them [Europeans] who know where it comes from," to which I foolishly, automatically, interjected, "Nkai." Musa followed, obviously doubting my answer, "Does lkiye come from Nkai?" Lenkosheke responded simply, "It is not from Nkai" (Lenkosheke interview, 2001). Yet most Samburu supposed that it *was* Nkai, though they could not understand why that should be, any more than Lenkosheke, Musa, or I could. There are many explanations of how and there are proximate causes, but no definitive and final answers to the ultimate question why. Nevertheless, the how and its consequences remain crucial.

Lacan said that we never experience death "as such," that death "is never real."[22] By this move, Lacan, like Derrida, performs a substantial dualism that is its own (Euro-American) imaginary. Word is out of touch with world, person is out of touch with person, and the witness is struck dumb as experience is misrecognized as mundane. There is no room for intersubjectivity here, except as a play of words that have no real efficacy. And yet, this is not quite the sum of what most Euro-Americans believe, and for the Samburu the inadequacy of such a speech-act is baldly transparent. Cows may have monetary value, commodities may pour in and bring unspeakable, cannibalistic acts into their midst, but so far, the clarity of intersubjective relations continues to inflect Samburu understandings of death and misfortune. "A mouth can make a green tree dry up and die." The wrongdoing of one can infect the children one gives birth to. The death of a child can both point to wrong relations between people and invade a healthy person and cause them to weaken and die. Death is no imaginary here, but a dynamic substance, both particle and wave, that can join the living together in terrifying ways. The witness experiences, and becomes. The witness is bound to the spectacle and to the joys or sufferings of the person witnessed. Those joys and sufferings move dynamically in the shape of blessings or curses, making the line between persons momentarily dissolve and disappear.

Let us suppose that word does not merely meet world, that it is an incarnation of world, an enunciation of transformations that include the neurochemical shapes that world takes as we meet it in a form of witness that is always more than binary separations can describe. This is a supple imaginary, it is the how of things, the explanation that makes the architectures of thought a malleable feast of the emotions and the senses. It shifts the boundaries, opens up possibilities for the in-between of the in-between, affirms anthropology's most radical claims to intersubjectivity, and, in that move, raises the bar of accountability. For the Samburu, the bar of accountability is of course already raised—the actions of one *become* the actions of another.[23] One wrong action, one murder, one death demands others. We are not strangers to ourselves (Kristeva 1991); we are the architects simultaneously of ourselves and our others—to an extent. Yet I will leave the finality of death and its causes here for now, and turn to the utterly miraculous.

Chapter 7
Resurrection

As I sat on a stool with friends and neighbors near my home in the Samburu highlands, two old men engaged in a spirited dialogue, each trying to outdo the other in his knowledge of Samburu recent and historical events. One was my neighbor, Leyielo, while the other was a friend of his visiting from the lowlands. By this time, I had talked formally and informally to dozens of people claiming first- or second-hand knowledge of apiu—resurrection from death.[1] Thus, I was amused that Leyielo was confused when queried about incidences of apiu, while his friend triumphantly took the high ground in this turn of the discussion.[2] He knew of several cases, including one in which a man's cattle nudged him back to existence from where his corpse lay, awaiting the hyenas.

And he was left there laying in mortuary leaves, when the cattle came back in the evening. Some of his cattle went there and started to bellow at him and they [his cattle] took away those leaves. When people went to chase the cattle away from there they found him alive. And he was brought home . . . And he came back to life and he recovered completely, that is, he was completely well. Now he will stay, performing all of his duties. (Friend of Leyielo's, Leyielo interview, 2003)

This incident puts Chapter 4's discussion of latukuny and nkuaama ("smell") in another context, as here a dead man's cattle indeed seem to have "followed" him into the bush—in this case calling him back. Leyielo's friend related another, more recent case—again naming precisely who the person was and whom he eventually married—that must have been even more startling to people, particularly to his mother. "He was taken to soro and he revived [nepiu], and came back home, straight to his mother's house in the evening. And he was carrying the animal hide used for his mortuary rites." At this point in the story, my neighbor Leyielo exclaimed "Unheard of!" to which his friend replied with laughter, "It is not just one person that this happened to!" (Leyielo interview, 2003).

Like most people relating cases of apiu ("resurrection"), Leyielo's friend asserted emphatically that these people are "completely dead"—

They stay there for some time, in death, because they die completely, they don't
even breathe . . . They're not breathing, because people make sure that a person
is not breathing . . . they are taken from home when they have died, they're not
half-dead. (Leyielo interview, 2003)

Through this emphatic assertion that people really are dead, Samburu
affirm that what they are talking about is a miracle.

In her book about death in contemporary inner Mani, Nadia Seremetakis has described the "semiology of death" as a "semiology of the non-
sedentary, of things, people, and tokens in movement: an imagery that
establishes a relation between the here and there, between the then and
now" (1991: 83).[3] Death for the Samburu is likewise about movement
and relation, but in addition, Samburu experiences surrounding death
are about fundamental blurrings of the very boundaries that the mortuary practices described in Chapter 6 would seek to fix. Thus, against
every attempt to "cut" death from life there is the real possibility that
corpses will resurrect, that children will visit the land of the dead and
return unharmed, and that reciprocally, the dead will visit the living.
Death here is an ambivalent affair, capable of devouring whole families
through monstrous ŋoki, yet a state of being with agency that can be
enacted for the benefit, the consolation, or indeed, the harm, of the
living.

I will come to crossings back and forth in Chapter 8. For now, I will
hover nearer the moment of expiration, juxtaposing Samburu resurrection with miracles and strange occurrences in a European tradition that
has long had its own difficulty keeping the edges clean. While Samburu
presciss resurrection in ways that bear similarity to some aspects of the
Christian tradition, both have also engaged in their different ways with
a Euro-American scientific tradition that succeeded in transforming the
terms, though it has yet to *contain* the formidable extraordinary. This is
largely because—whatever the grounds for explaining resurrection—
the most crucial issues its occurrence raises remain ontological, cultural,
and personal. Samburu apiu—"resurrection"—forces itself on the families who experience it, demanding that they accept the amazing. It is no
wonder that the borders must be vigilantly policed, as the apparently
healthy slip into death and the dead occasionally come loping back to
human existence.

The utter astonishment that apiu provokes is readily apparent in the
narration of the apiu of a young girl (warrior's girlfriend) who died during the Lkileku period (c. 1922–1936). The narrator in this case was one
of my neighbors, a woman in her nineties who had been one of the
young girl's own age-mates and a witness to the events as they occurred:

Wasn't she taken away to be disposed of? [Mm.] She was laid. Isn't it that a person is usually laid? [Yes.] She lay there. The hyenas didn't eat her. [Mm.] Her father was not at home—that chief—he was not at home. [Yes.] Her brother, a Lkileku lmurran, got up. [Mm.] Is it not that people are usually checked to see whether hyenas have eaten them? [Yes.] He went, and as he went [mm] he found her just sitting like this, blinking her eyes. [Blinking her eyes?] Blinking her eyes. She just kept her eyes open like mine now. [Mm.] Don't the eyes get dry when a person dies? [Mm.] So she was just blinking her eyes like this. [Mmm.] The lmurrani was shocked. [Mmm.] He went back and called another lmurrani, coming. They came and found her just sitting, staring at people. They went, went to call others. (Nolpesi interview, 2001)

The lmurran reported her resurrection secretly to elders, but not to her own parents and closest relatives lest the shock be too great—or worse, in case she should die again and bring renewed grief. They arranged a *loikar* for her recovery,[4] keeping her away from home until they were certain that she was fully healed. Then they took her father and mother aside, one by one, gently explaining to them that their daughter had returned from the dead. ("*Wooii!*" they exclaimed.) The elders brought her from loikar then, returning her to the living.

An even more remarkable case of "complete death" and "resurrection" (apiu) was of a man who, like the biblical Lazarus, had been dead four days before he woke to rejoin the living.

(Which one? Lmalen?)[5] Yes, that one who is called {What?} Yes, that Lkimaniki. Yes, that tall one. {He died and came back to life?} Yes, he slept how many? {How many?} Four with the day he revived. {There is that one this woman [referring to his wife] is talking about of theirs [from her natal family]}. [Yes.] {He slept four in the grave then he revived.} It is said it was his dog that defended him so that the hyenas wouldn't eat him. Yes, the hyenas came and were chased. [Yes.] The hyenas just came and the dog chased them away. [Mm.] Then he was seen doing what? [Living then, rising.] Moving. {Yes.} [Mm.] Then he was brought back home. (Lenaura interview, 2001)

In noting that a dog intervened, actually defending the corpse against hyenas, Lenaura highlights the important point that when people are laid to rest in the soro (bush), the fact that the hyenas did not eat them is almost as amazing as the fact that they came back to life. In Lmalen's case, it was his dog that is said to have defended him, which was itself highly memorable for people. In most cases, however, as in the Lkileku girl's apiu described earlier, there is no dog (or cattle)—the hyenas simply do not eat the corpse, as if once again, they *know.* As my friend Lenkosheke suggested, maybe hyenas are loibonok—terrible ones—sent from Nkai.

Yet there is another dimension of the hyenas' significance in the process of apiu ("resurrection"), one that reveals the ontological assumptions surrounding it as well as the strange relationship between Nkai and hyenas. Recall from Chapter 6 that hyenas fulfill the important role of eating death and unpropitiousness—helping to keep both away from the living. A person who comes back to life prevents the hyenas from carrying out this necessary function, and, moreover, deprives them of a meal. Thus, when apiu occurs, people invariably slaughter a goat at the burial site. Just as the slaughter of a ram or he-goat fools the hyenas into eating the corpse of a "stinky" person—one who had committed serious wrongs—the slaughter following resurrection is an offering to the hyenas. It is simultaneously a gesture of thanksgiving for the return of life and a request for the hyenas to take the resurrected person's death away completely, so that the hyenas do not come to reclaim him/her or to claim others from the living.

[Why is the goat slaughtered?] So that it eats as if it has eaten that person, and the fact that s/he has come back to life. That is a thank you . . . So that it looks as if that evil [or badness—ntorruno] has finished, [been taken away] from that person. That person has revived. So they [hyenas] eat that goat so that it will appear as if they had eaten that person, and that is over. And that person lives so that s/he doesn't die quickly again. We say that Nkai has risen him/her and that the death is left for the hyenas. (Lenaisho interview, 2001)

In this way, resurrection implies not only that Nkai has intervened to return a life—"Nkai has risen him/her"; it also implies the promise that the resurrected will now enjoy a long life. "And they just say that whoever was taken to leaves [another metaphor for death and burial] and resurrected,[6] that person will live long because a hyena has eaten his/her skin [the mortuary animal hide]" (Leropili interview, 2001). That is, the goat slaughtered for the hyenas has replaced the person wrapped in his/her death shroud. "[And now is it the hyenas who ate that death?] Yes. [Yes.] Yes, it is the hyenas who ate it, and that death shroud/hide" (Lenaisho interview, 2001).

In Samburu understandings, then, there are two processes at work here, one turning on the power of Nkai and the other turning on the power Nkai has invested in hyenas. Nkai miraculously restores life to some dead: As my friend Leropili mused in describing the resurrection of a man whose corpse he had himself seen shaved and placed under the ltepes tree, "I think Nkai just returned his breath back to him" (Leropili interview, 2001). Nkai's is a fragile miracle, however, necessitating human action to solidify it by offering an alternative sacrifice to the hyenas (not to Nkai, it should be noted) so that they will eat that person's death. By that human practice, resurrected persons hopefully gain a longer life, while at the same time and more crucially for the broader human community, the boundary between life and death, which Nkai's miracle blurred, is fixed once again—at least temporarily.

Four Resurrections (and Always a Funeral)

I have translated Samburu apiu as "resurrection," following the lead of educated Samburu friends who are quite conscious of the term's relationship to a very famous resurrection story. Samburu, for their part, are generally familiar with the story of Jesus' resurrection, and their acceptance of it as fact is linked in important ways to the tendency for Nkai to appear to ordinary Samburu, to take mundane shapes such as rain clouds that look like elephant trunks and, indeed, to breathe life back into a corpse. Resurrection is an obvious miracle, as obvious as the presence of dead children returned to their mothers' homes. Moreover, the fact that Jesus' resurrection was written down—recorded in what Samburu take to be a perfect and immutable form of witness—also contributes to its assumed veracity. It is worth noting, however, that as an obvious miracle, many Samburu find the greater miracle in the fact that Jesus sacrificed Himself willingly, an understanding that bears on certain aspects of Samburu prescissing of lkiye ("death"), including ascertaining the ultimate cause. In Jesus' case, that ultimate cause impinges on another Samburu sign—the practice and meaningful entailments of augmenting one life through the destruction of another. For the Samburu who have become familiar with Jesus' resurrection, his actions as a sacrificial lamb are tremendously meaningful, signaling the atonement Samburu typically engage in, substituting the spilling of an animal's innocent life for the tragedies attending human weaknesses. These sacrifices reach their horrifying apex in the practices of unscrupulous loibonok who are willing to "make," or "repair" (aitibir) one human life with another, as I described in Chapter 2.

Even as Samburu—increasingly exposed to the Christian message—accept Jesus' resurrection as fact and link it to their own experiences with both apiu and the logic of sacrifice, there are multiple resurrections at stake here in understanding the reciprocal complexities of Samburu apiu and Euro-American resurrection. Let me make a brief metaphysical tour across the centuries in order to make careful distinctions and raise intriguing questions that bring living and dead bodies and their agentive personhood, medieval Christianity, the rise of empiricism, and commodity capitalism into an unlikely conversation with one another. I will start at the beginning, with the most disputed resurrection.

RESURRECTION NUMBER ONE: JESUS HIMSELF

What kind of resurrection should we attribute to the Jesus story? If we follow the body in the text, we soon come to the crux of the dispute—the fact that, as the text avers, the body *disappears*. That special bodies might in fact vanish seems to have already been taken for granted by the officials involved in the crucifixion. In Matthew, chapter 27, the author relates that the chief priests and Pharisees conspired with Pilate to guard Jesus' tomb against his disciples' theft:

Command therefore that the sepulchre be made sure until the third day, lest his disciples come by night, and steal him away, and say unto the people, He is risen from the dead: so the last error shall be worse than the first. Pilate said unto them, Ye have a watch: go your way, make it as sure as ye can. So they went, and made the sepulchre sure, sealing the stone, and setting a watch. (Matthew 27: 64–66)

The author continues from here, relating a version of the famous story of Jesus' resurrection. In the Matthew version, an angel comes, causing an earthquake, and rolls the stone away at the moment when Mary Magdalene and Mary arrive to visit the body. As they run to tell Jesus' disciples, Jesus Himself appears to them, and they "held Him by the feet, and worshipped Him" (Matthew 28: 9). In the meantime, however, the guards appointed to watch the corpse report to the chief priests the corpse's disappearance, the angelic appearance, or both. And, according to the author, the priests conspire once again.

Now when they were going, behold, some of the watch came into the city, and shewed unto the chief priests all the things that were done. And when they were assembled with the elders, and had taken counsel, they gave large money unto the soldiers, Saying, Say ye, His disciples came by night, and stole him away while we slept. And if this come to the governor's ears, we will persuade him, and secure you. So they took the money, and did as they were taught: and this saying is commonly reported among the Jews until this day. (Matthew 28: 11–15)

The differences between the Matthew account and the one given in the Gospel of John bear noting. As in the story of Matthew, the possibility that Jesus' corpse could be stolen—in contrast to resurrecting—is likewise given voice. Here, however, there is no dramatic earthquake; rather, Mary Magdalene comes alone and discovers that Jesus is missing. She rushes to tell two of Jesus' disciples, who confirm that it is true and then simply go home. (There is no additional comment about this.) Mary remains at the tomb crying, and angels appear to her so unobtrusively that she does not seem to realize what they are. When they ask her the reason for her tears, she tells them that "they" (whoever that might be) have taken away her "Lord."

And when she had thus said, she turned herself back, and saw Jesus standing, and knew not that it was Jesus. Jesus saith unto her, Woman, why weepest thou? whom seekest thou? She, supposing him to be the gardener, saith unto him, Sir, if thou have borne Him hence, tell me where thou hast laid Him, and I will take

Him away. Jesus saith unto her, Mary. She turned herself, and saith unto Him, Rabboni; which is to say, Master. Jesus saith unto her, Touch me not; for I am not yet ascended to my Father: but go to my brethren, and say unto them, I ascend unto my Father, and your Father; and to my God, and your God. (John 20: 14–17)

Both the Matthew and John versions raise the possibility that the corpse could have been merely stolen, but in very different ways. In Matthew, the chief priests and Pharisees conspire with Pilate to prevent the disciples from stealing the corpse and claiming a resurrection, while the author of John suggests that Mary Magdalene herself believed that the corpse had been stolen. Who the thief might be is left unspecified, just as there is no explanation for why the disciples would simply return home after such strange news—as opposed to reporting it to others, as so often occurs in these biblical texts.[7]

In their different ways, the Matthew and John gospels place the resurrection claim in the context of its own doubt—a doubt rooted in a mysteriously vanishing corpse. While Samburu apiu return to resume their social obligations just as Lazarus (John 11: 39–44) and a young girl (Matthew 9: 23–25) did, the body of Jesus was never recovered. Thus, we are left with the competing assertions that Jesus rose from the dead and *momentarily* appeared to people or else that his corpse was stolen, perhaps by the very people who spread the rumor that He had been seen. For Samburu, this would not be a miracle of apiu but rather a scratch-your-head puzzler. As transformed in the gospel texts, however, Jesus' resurrection comes to define resurrection itself. Or does it? The slippage here spans millennia.

RESURRECTION TWO: THE MIRACLES OF SAINTS

Children and adults alike met all manner of unspeakable ends in the fourteenth century. On September 6, 1303, a two-year-old named Roger of Conway fell twenty-eight feet, into the deep stone moat of one of Edward I's castles. Since his parents were at an all-night vigil for a dead neighbor, they did not know of Roger's fall until the next morning, when by all accounts he was quite dead, his body "as stiff as wood and cold as stone" (original text quoted in Finucane 1997: 128).[8] Roger did not remain dead, however, as we know from eyewitness accounts recorded at the time and four years later during the inquisition that determined that a dead bishop, Thomas de Cantilupe, was worthy of sainthood (Finucane 1997). According to those documents, a townsman bent a penny and invoked Thomas de Cantilupe's shrine at Hereford (near the Welsh/English border). Just as the coroner's scribe was beginning to record Roger's death, the same townsman shouted that Roger's tongue had moved. Even so, when the child was brought to his mother, Dionysia, he "seemed dead—Dionysia could sense no breath in him, even though she placed her tongue in his mouth, which was so cold that it pained her" (129). Next, she cut open her blouse and warmed him against her skin, then carried him into the village church where over two hundred witnesses watched him revive. Finucane notes the interesting variability in fourteenth-century conceptions of death, as the toddler is deemed to have miraculously resurrected while still in the moat through invocations to St. Thomas Cantilupe but is declared dead again by his mother and only fully (and officially) resurrected in the church.

A more remarkable case involves the drowning of a little girl—for this case Finucane provides complete translations of several of the witness testimonies taken during the inquisition hearings for St. Thomas's canonization. Those witnesses include the little resurrected girl herself. Again, the case had been documented briefly contemporaneously but in more detail with the examination and cross-examination of witnesses during the canonization hearings. According to all the witnesses, when Joanna was five years old, a playmate pushed her into a fishpond located in a tavern's gardens while their parents were drinking in the tavern. Roughly sixty to a hundred young townspeople were at the tavern, many of whom soon formed a dance line through the garden. During one pass near the fishpond some of the dancers noticed cloth in the pond but continued on. The second time they came closer and realized that the cloth belonged to a drowned child. Because English law could be quite punitive toward those declared to be the official "finders" of corpses, the dancers agreed not to say anything. Eventually, however, Joanna's own playmate alerted her mother and godmother, and the godmother jumped in to pull the child out.

By this time, Joanna had been face-down in the pond from sometime in the early afternoon until just after sunset. The witnesses corroborated one another in saying that her face and body were so badly bloated as to be unrecognizable. Her father, Adam, could not open her mouth and used a knife to pry it open to put her "black and swollen tongue" back into her mouth. Once open, witnesses reported that her mouth would not remain closed except by force. Adam also cut her belt, and when "I had cut her belt and opened her mouth, I and others heard a kind of noise within her body, and one of the bystanders, Walter de Pirebrok, now dead, said, 'If there was any breath of life in the girl, she's completely exhaled it,' whereas others said that through St. Thomas's merits, God had breathed life into her" (Finucane 176–77). All the forty or so people present at the time prayed on their knees for a miracle through St. Thomas. The mother, Cecilia, then carried Joanna into the tavern and everyone present continued to pray until the middle of the night, but there were still no signs of life. Nevertheless, Cecilia carried her little girl home, where she insisted on holding the drowned Joanna in bed with her, next to her skin. Since Cecilia was about eight months pregnant, her husband and bystanders were concerned that she would be harmed by the coldness of Joanna's body, so they moved the bed near to the fire. At dawn, Cecilia felt Joanna move. At sunrise Joanna's parents carried her to the parish church and put her on the altar, the bells were rung, and people gathered to sing a hymn. Then her father took her on horseback to the Hereford cathedral to lay her on the altar there, with about thirty people accompanying him (Finucane 1997).

Numerous such miraculous resurrections were reported during the medieval period, meticulously recorded by local parish clerics and documented in more detail during canonization hearings. Thomas Cantilupe seems to have been a favorite to invoke for this miracle, given the number of resurrections he was deemed responsible for (see Bartlett 2004). Moreover, St. Thomas was a friend to adults as well as children, including the rather amazing case of a Welshman, William Cragh, who apparently revived after being hanged three times. As in Joanna's case, witnesses testified in excruciating detail concerning the state of Cragh's body after he was finally cut down. In his fascinating book, *The Hanged Man*, Robert Bartlett quotes one of the principal witnesses at length:

His whole face was black and in parts bloody or stained with blood. His eyes had come out of their sockets and hung outside the eyelids and the sockets were filled with blood. His mouth, neck, and throat and the parts around them, and also his nostrils, were filled with blood, so that it was impossible in the natural course of things for him to breathe air through his nostrils or through his mouth or through his throat . . . his tongue hung out of his mouth, the length of a man's finger, and it was completely black and swollen and as thick with the blood sticking to it that it seemed the size of a man's two fists together. (Quoted in Bartlett 2004: 6)

Despite this gruesome appearance as reported by witnesses, William Cragh resurrected after various bystanders (most notably the wife of the very nobleman who had sentenced him to be hanged) prayed to Thomas Cantilupe for a miracle on his behalf. Bartlett notes that while many of the miracles surrounding hangings involve ropes breaking and other ways in which the condemned are saved during the execution,[9] William Cragh's was a "true resurrection," occurring only after he had been duly hanged and left swinging for hours.

This, then, is the second resurrection, the revival of persons from the dead and their restoration to the living. These are resurrections that bear a certain resemblance to both Samburu *apiu* and the miracles Jesus performed over Lazarus and a young girl, resurrections that a contemporary biomedical discourse would refer to as premature burial. The very path to that biomedical discourse came, however, by way of these medieval miracles, as the process of inquiry through which resurrections might be declared legitimate and real was an increasingly empirical one. Thus, as Bartlett notes, "By this period scholastic thinking had developed complex positions about which features made events 'natural' or 'supernatural' (the latter term being, as it turns out, an invention of thirteenth-century theologians and philosophers). The inquisitors knew that if the resuscitation had been a natural event it could not have been a miracle and hence could not be used to support Thomas de Cantilupe's canonization" (Bartlett 2004: 110–11).[10] Thus the vividly detailed descriptions of persons drowned, hanged, burned, and so on. I am not suggesting that some medieval persons did not extraordinarily resuscitate, but rather, I am pointing to the rise of empiricism, which would eventually undermine future claims to resurrection.

This turn in European thought and the changes in European burial practices associated with it are what makes Samburu apiu—the idea that some dead are still awakening—catch us by surprise. By the nineteenth century, a series of subtle transformations had transpired that denied saints credit for miraculous resuscitations even while initiating new forms of reanimation that I will come to in due course. First, I will continue on, from saintly resurrection miracles to medieval scholarly wranglings with yet another resurrection—that of the already putrifying and desiccated dead.

Resurrection Number Three: The Problem of Re-Animation

In a provocative article on resurrection, Fernando Vidal (2002) deftly explores transformations in scholarly attention to the Christian conundrum of how exactly God would eventually resurrect the dead. The problem centers specifically on the tendency of early Christianity to contradict dualistic understandings of mind/body and self. As Vidal asserts: "The Christian requirements for an afterlife are just the opposite of metempsychosis. Souls are not persons; life after death necessitates the original body; and death is not the joyful liberation of soul from a prison of flesh but the disruption of the original unity of the human being" (935). For early (and later) Christians, the problem the concept of resurrection posed was how "our resurrected bodies will be spiritual and yet numerically identical (*idem numero*) to the bodies of flesh we possessed during our life on earth" (940). That is, what constitutes identity of the person in such a way that God can restore it precisely as it was? As Vidal suggests, this problem—as it arises beginning with Saint Paul and onward into twentieth-century papal declarations, assumes an identity thoroughly entangled with a particular body: "The person exists only in an embodied form; possession of the same flesh attests to possession of the same self. Such are the basic convictions highlighted by the doctrine of the resurrection" (943; see also Bynum 1991).

Indeed, throughout the medieval period, souls remained fundamentally united with the body, albeit in transforming ways, and what happened to the body had everything to do with the state of the soul. Thus, for example, the holiness of the saintly soul was matched by incorruptible corpses and miracles wrought through every body part (Bynum 1991; Daston and Park 1998; Ward 1987). The disarticulation of saints' bodies and their gift, sale, and theft as relics were notorious forces driving the popularity of the miracle shrines that dotted the European landscape. It was not merely the saints' dismembered bodies but the miracles performed through them that made saints' shrines lucrative. For every case of miraculous resurrection or healing, there were thankful or hopeful families and bystanders making pilgrimages, purchasing candles, making offerings, and thus contributing to the vitality of parish economies by enlivening the market for miracles (see Finucane 1977, 1997; Geary 1986; Ward 1987).[11] This medieval economy of agentive corpses and miraculous resurrections and healings eventually extended to commoners as well. With the disarticulation of common corpses, ossuaries became a crucial part of churches and, as with saints, the proximity of one's remains to the holy spaces of churches was beneficial for the soul. In some cases ossuaries within churches were located "in such a position that the bones could watch the liturgy being celebrated" (Bynum 1995: 204), and the reciprocal relation of "good" (i.e., saintly and later, baptized commoner) human remains and holy location required careful distinctions to be made about who could or could not be interred on church grounds. As Bynum remarks, all of these disarticulating and distributing practices associated with body parts were "an indication—not a denial—that body is integral to person" (204–5).[12]

Given these ontological understandings by which bodies were so conjoined with person as to possess agentive qualities throughout every little fragment of corpse (Bynum 1991), the claim that all the desiccated dead shall rise was a formidable conundrum. The Christian promise of Judgment-Day resurrection suggests that fully decomposed and even cannibalized or animal-devoured bodies (or, one might add, the disarticulated bodies of saints) would not merely have agency but would be restored with full personhood intact. For Christians, this has required understandings of personal identity that not only define the "essence" of the person but link that essentialized personhood to the terms of what became a *scientific* discourse of reanimation.

For Thomas Aquinas in the thirteenth century, the problem was resolved by suggesting, in Aristotelian fashion, that the "soul is the 'form' of a natural body that potentially has life" (Vidal 2002: 945). By rejoining form/soul and matter/body, the full person would be restored. By the seventeenth century, the resurrection conundrum would be resolved quite differently by suggesting an embryo like "stamen" that contains the body in minute form and can be increased in size. This stamen included body and personality together. As the Enlightenment continued, other writers would debate whether memory could be contained in one "organ" or brain area or was dispersed throughout the nervous system—the decentralized view (see also Lock 2002). The decentralized view can be intriguingly paralleled incidentally, with contemporary challenges to mind/body dualism in cognitive neuroscience (see Appendix 1). The stamen or embryological view likewise has contemporary parallels in understandings and uses of DNA that in some ways do indeed seem to mimic reanimation.[13]

Vidal very usefully charts the ideological transformations necessary for coming to terms with a Christian resurrection doctrine that effectively challenged *and transformed* soul/body dualistic understandings. The doctrine of the resurrection went against the grain of specific cultural understandings from at least a.d. 200 and onward through the medieval period. When the stamen theory was suggested, it was in the context of a peculiar debate about how God would achieve an unlikely miracle, and the response turned on the assumption that a single "piece" of matter could contain the blueprint for a body that included its full personhood—including memory. It was in further debating this very question that personal memories and bodies eventually became disentangled from one another in the Euro-American tradition, even as the doctrine of resurrection continued to find fertile ground in the imagination.

The relation between bodies and souls remained an ambivalent one, however—how could it not? Empiricism was such a strong cultural force that theological scholars had—as Vidal demonstrates—subjected Christianity's Judgment-Day resurrection claims to a logic that would conceptually wrench souls and bodies apart even as strange events continued to affirm their entanglement. Thus, even as scholars puzzled throughout the medieval and early modern periods over just how God would effect universal resurrection, the medieval economy of miracles was being slowly strangled as expanded "natural" explanations and "expert" testimony sometimes trumped lay experiential understandings. By the eighteenth century, proving miracles was becoming extremely difficult—though not by any means impossible, given that faith persisted in weaving itself uneasily through empiricist understandings. Moreover, the body's entanglement with personhood persisted in other subtle and insidious ways as well. Sometimes, however, the strength of faith could undermine rather than validate claims to the extraordinary, particularly when the extraordinary was perceived to have diabolic dimensions, as I will describe now as I turn to a fourth resurrection—the reanimation of the "unnatural" dead.

Resurrection Four: The Disturbing Lives of Vampires

The European concept of the vampire is attributed to late sixteenth- and early seventeenth-century Slavic and Greek cases of people who typically had died "bad" deaths and who returned to kill humans and animals. In order to remedy the situation, people had to behead or pierce the corpse (claimed to be resisting decay) or extract and burn its heart (which was claimed to have blood still in it) (Klaniczay 1990: 178). Alternatively, a corpse might be buried at a crossroads (as of a person dying from suicide, for example) and a stake driven through its heart to prevent it from wandering around at night (Copper 1974). Even in contemporary Inner Mani, the road continues to be a "place of death," and "revenants" (the "walking dead") are said to be met on the road (Seremetakis 1991).

As a widespread, popularized issue, vampire claims continued to surge throughout the seventeenth and into the mid-eighteenth century, spreading to Hungary and other European countries before acquiring their sexual overtones and becoming fodder for popular novels in the later eighteenth century and onward (Klaniczay 1990: 183). That transition from widespread horror to celebrated popular fiction is not coincidental and, indeed, brings me to precisely how this particular form of resurrection—the reanimation of putrifying corpses—relates to Christly and saintly miracles. As it happens, this connection is not my own but, rather, one made by Catholic clerics in the 1730s who were concerned that vampires were in diabolic competition with their saints and savior. "The vampire, like the Christian saint, was also a 'very special dead' . . . whose corpse resisted decay, whose grave radiated with a special light, whose fingernails and hair kept growing—like those of several medieval saints . . .—thus demonstrating the persistence of vital energy beyond death" (Klaniczay 1990: 181). Klaniczay goes on to remark that vampires were thus associated with "miracles" (such as the uncorrupted body), just as saints were, and, moreover, that their bloodsucking appeared as a horrifying reversal of Holy Communion. Thus, by the 1730s a debate about vampires raged that would see Catholic clerics seeking to deny vampires' existence and doctors seizing the opportunity to apply scientific reasoning to the problem.

Meanwhile, at the level of local experience, revenants continued to be a source of terror both before and well after the eighteenth century. In a well-documented work on the preindustrial European understandings of death and decay informing revenant accounts, Paul Barber (1988) tells the story of "The Shoemaker of Breslau." According to this piece of Prussian folklore, a prosperous shoemaker committed suicide in 1591 by cutting his own throat. In order to allow him a dignified burial and avoid disgrace, his widow and her sisters hired an old woman to wash and then bind the corpse so tightly that the suicide would not be apparent. Having told the community that the shoemaker had died of a stroke, the widow succeeded in seeing her husband buried in a "great ceremony." Nevertheless, rumors soon spread that the shoemaker had taken his own life (committing a murder against himself), and soon the shoemaker himself began to appear to people in the town. The ghost appeared both night and day, and at night he sometimes sat upon people in their beds with the effect that they felt he was smothering them. Finally, when enough witnesses had complained to the council and the issue had become too pressing to ignore, the authorities commanded that the grave be opened. Once opened, the corpse displayed a number of surprising features, including lack of both stiffness and decay, a bloated stomach, and new skin on his feet (Barber explains these various features as accurate and possible aspects of decay). Although the corpse was kept on display for twenty days so that all could see him, his ghost continued to rage, and thus the council ordered the shoemaker's corpse to be decapitated and dismembered, his heart (which appeared fresh) removed, and the whole burned on a pyre. Finally, according to the story, the ghost stopped appearing.

Barber's stories, which include both folklore and documented accounts, demonstrate that both commoners and authorities took revenant reports seriously enough to disinter and mutilate corpses. Likewise, they reveal that observers reported the appearance of exhumed corpses in enough detail that it is possible for Barber to surmise that these were real events, even if the explanation (that some of the dead became revenants) can be debated. Of course, the explanation was debated in the context of the eighteenth century's rising empiricism, the consequences of which were to explain these apparently unusual corpses as simply exhibiting normal signs of decay. (Another consequence was the transformation of vampires into the subjects of sexy fiction.) Nevertheless, the chasm of understandings between scholarly and folk, and even between various scholarly camps, continued to yawn. This was not least because the explanation offered did not address the root cause of the trouble—experiences and misfortunes that seemed to defy alternative explanation. Thus, the eighteenth century also saw the publication of "learned" books that explained vampires through occult arguments (Klaniczay 1990), and occasional vampire sightings continued to be reported into the twentieth century.

A fascinating example of the latter—and one that demonstrates that horrifying experiences rather than misrecognition of normal processes of decay is the primary issue—occurred in New England from the late seventeenth through the late nineteenth centuries. While New England families, like many Europeans, did not use the term "vampire," the practices that folklorist Michael E. Bell (2001) describes demonstrate similar fears of particular dead "returning" in some fashion to harm the living—not necessarily by wandering beyond the grave but by causing trouble from within it. In these New England cases, it was (quite aptly) "consumption" (the term used for tuberculosis and diseases with similar symptoms) that suggested an undecaying corpse feeding on the living from its grave. The last-chance, desperate cure involved exhuming the suspected corpse—usually a close relative who had already died of consumption—and removing and burning its heart or even burning the entire corpse while sick family members tried to waft the presumed inoculating effects of the smoke into themselves. Apparently in some cases, the corpse was decapitated and buried with its bones rearranged—Bell describes one excavated skeleton as having its bones arranged into a skull and crossbones pattern (166–71). In spite of these seemingly callous mutilations, however, Bell's accounts evoke the poignancy of the events as they transpired—as people watched their loved ones slip away before their eyes in numbers that defied the imagination. By the time several siblings in a family had died, grieving families exhumed their loved ones in a desperate act to hold onto those who still clung, however tenuously, to life.

To sum up, as vampires, corpses either walked around visibly while being simultaneously in their graves, or else remained in their graves feeding on the living from there. For anthropologists this fits a familiar cross-cultural pattern by which the dead actively engage with the living in negative as well as positive ways.[14] In the European tradition, there were a number of remedies for ending the antics of suspicious corpses, from burying the corpse upside down to outright "second" killing of the deceased by various means (Barber 1988). As Bell's careful work demonstrates, however, these revenants might not always have been understood to be the beloved dead persons themselves but could have been forms of postmortem "possession" of some kind, a possibility that confounds attempts to neatly define past understandings of death. Nevertheless, whatever might be the means, a belief that corpses could be reanimated surfaced with some frequency in medieval and modern Europe and in parts of eighteenth- and nineteenth-century New England as well. Moreover, the idea that such reanimations might be possible plagued some Catholic clerics, who were concerned that this belief competed dangerously with reanimations of the *miraculous* kind.

Transformations in Euro-American ontological understandings touching on the boundaries of life, death, and personhood took a strange and twisting path, then, as the incursions of empiricist logic proceeded unevenly. Thus, saints' bodies had an enduring agency—and indeed, the agency of other bodies persisted in a variety of ways as well. In this respect, recent attempts to overcome dualism restate in other terms what has long been the case, though the many different reincarnations of body/soul/mind/character are important to specify. Among the ŋoki like threads that bear mentioning in their relation to the subject matter here is that corpses continued to be subject to disarticulation, even if, by the eighteenth century, the reasons turned on an appreciation of the "wondrousness" of God's creation that intriguingly echoed Augustine's pragmatic sense of the miraculous. At the same time, the elusiveness of life's edges—at once palpably expressed in strange and unexpected events and in technologies with their own powers to haunt—have continued to demand explanation.

Contemporary Resurrections: The "Miracles" of Modern Medicine

The blunt contrast between proudly proclaiming the miraculous resurrection of a loved one and "exterminating a suspicious corpse" (Atwater 2000: 73) reveals twin sides of a moment in the very midst of a shift toward the dominance of Western biomedical definitions of, and explanations surrounding, death. Scholars of European vampire and burial traditions contend that violent actions against the deceased were responses to utter terror (during plagues and epidemics especially) and certainty that corpses could indeed return to steal blood from and kill the living. In turn, the transformation of vampire stories from horrified account to oral and literary legend coincided with eighteenth-century empiricist biomedical assertions that the blood found in the hearts and veins of certain corpses was part of normal processes of decay (Barber 1988), while miraculous resuscitations were simple cases of premature burial. Nevertheless, the acceptance of such assertions could only be possible if European definitions of what constitutes both death and personhood were changing in striking ways. Such changes were only gradual, however, and far from absolute, as I have previously indicated.

In fact, the rise of empiricism, and with it, the explaining away of miraculous resurrections and vampires did not end the matter. It is a continuing irony that theological and empirical dilemmas simultaneously affirm and destabilize each other's positions. Newly conceived, empirically derived biomedical revelations might conveniently explain away vampires while simultaneously discovering new and even troubling possibilities for reanimation long after the corpse decomposes. Thus, one nagging question replaces another as the boundaries between life and death are crossed in new ways to meet new technologies and the treatment of corpses has shifted in tandem. In the early nineteenth century, Mary Shelley (1984 [1818]) raised the issue of what constitutes personhood in ways that continue to be hauntingly compelling—as the enduring popularity of the Frankenstein myth attests. Through *Frankenstein*, she voiced the misgivings of many of her generation concerning the destruction of corpses in the name of science—and this in the context of flagrant violations and even murders committed in order to provide cadavers for experimentation as the corpse transformed from person awaiting rearticulation in resurrection to commodity through which humans could effect fantastic resurrections/resuscitations.[15] The ŋoki like, monstrous thread connecting medieval Christian resurrection wonders, disarticulated saints with amazing (and commodifiable) power condensed in a finger or a drop of blood, to the commodified miracles of "modern medicine" should not be lost on us, even as it is important to note their distinctions. The connections were not lost on Mary Shelley (see Butler 1996).

Let us pause to note that the medieval body (peasant or noble) could be revived through the intercession of mutilated saints whose parts could be exchanged as relics through gift, theft, or sale (Daston and Park 1998; Geary 1986; Pels 1998), even as nonsaintly bodies might be disarticulated for "good" reasons (Bynum 1991, 1995). By the eighteenth and nineteenth centuries, in contrast, elite corpses for the most part remained intact while the demand for dead experimental subjects put a premium on peasant and criminal bodies. Indeed, the demand became so great that transgressive acts of theft or sale could make even "respectable" citizens vulnerable in order that new forms of reanimation might be discovered through human medical means. Then, in the twentieth and twenty-first centuries the poor and the criminal have become freshly vulnerable in a new twist with the advent and then refinement of organ donation (Scheper-Hughes 2000).

In its present incarnation, the techniques of reanimation go against the grain of common sense in ways that medieval clergy could not have imagined—as the warm and the breathing are declared to be "dead." In her gripping and occasionally horrifying book, *Twice Dead*, Margaret Lock (2002) raises troubling questions surrounding the practice of organ donation and its accompanying brain-death criteria. Lock insightfully describes pertinent issues of belief surrounding the boundaries of life/death and raises important questions concerning consciousness and the distinction between mind and body that I will return to. Not surprisingly, given the subject matter, the most robust of her conclusions surround the shifting biomedical criteria for defining the end of life and the beginning of death. Thus, she charts the movement of criteria for diagnosing death from putrefaction or cardio-pulmonary criteria to brain death. In this regard, Lock demonstrates in my view that brain-death criteria—forged in the very crucible of organ donation and procurement in a capitalist form of bricolage—are problematic on empirical and ethical as well as metaphysical grounds. Not least among the objections are the claims that some people do recover from "brain death," possibly because the diagnosis of brain death itself is far from rigorous in many—particularly smaller—hospitals.

In the context of issues like these, as well as concerns that some practitioners might be (however unintentionally) rushing people to death for the sake of organ procurement, some doctors and scholars have objected to the very process by which the "new death," with its brain-death criteria, came to be defined. This process proceeded by way of an Ad Hoc Harvard Committee convened in 1968, which had the effect, as Lock suggests, of deflecting attention away from the "meaning of death to defining it in instrumentally measurable terms." She quotes Mita Giacomini's discussion of the Harvard Committee's report: " 'Redefining death was not simply a technical exercise, but an aesthetic act to fit the hopelessly comatose, the dead, and the organ donor into the same clinical picture' " (Giacomini quoted in Lock 2002: 91).

Besides the ethical issues implied by brain-death criteria being developed precisely to allow organ procurement, there are the vexing issues of what precisely constitutes death and whether it can be empirically measured, issues that turn on understandings of consciousness and personhood. Again, Margaret Lock clearly and precisely sums up the problems surrounding the defining of death as a discrete endpoint:

> The physician and ethicist Steven Miles claims that institutionalizing whole-brain death as the end of individual existence "was an act of reductionistic scientific hegemony." He celebrates the reopening of the discussion, arguing that a precise moment or technological criterion for determining death may be needed or feasible only in certain special circumstances, such as forensic medicine or organ donation. In most cases we do not know exactly when death takes place. I agree with this position and with that of Norman Frost when he states that not only do we not need to know, but we cannot know exactly when death takes place. If organs are going to be procured, then this activity must be justified on the basis of something other than complete biological death. (Lock 2002: 374)

Leslie Sharp (2001) has also explored several strands and implications of organ procurement and donation in a provocative article on practices and beliefs surrounding organ donation in the United States. Like Lock, Sharp notes the many differences of opinion surrounding organ donation, noting particularly the practice's implications for understandings of personhood and body-mind dualism:

Within this medicalized framework, a now dead donor's once personalized self is reframed not in reference to embodied forms of lived experience, but rather as seated solely within the mind. Here, brain death marks the death of the self and, therefore, of one's humanity, an understanding that renders possible the opportunity to remove viable organs from *a body that remains warm to the touch, has a pulse, and appears to breathe on its own* as long as it is attached to a ventilator and supported by a host of other complementary technologies that render the body relatively stable physiologically until and throughout procurement. (113; emphasis added)

Although Sharp suggests that the statements of organ procurement professionals and donor recipients at times contradict one another and themselves on this topic, the poignant statements of some "donor kin" especially challenge the hegemony of biomedical definitions that summarily define death as brain death:

Finally, they often insist that a donor's life essence persists after brain death is declared, throughout organ retrieval, and sometimes beyond by surviving in fragmented form as their organs (especially heart, lungs, and eyes) are placed in the bodies of strangers. More specifically, I have encountered numerous donor kin who only partially accept definitions of brain death (cf. Franz et al. 1997). Most often they assume that the person they knew is no longer a social being while rejecting the presumption that they were fully and completely dead at the time of donation. As one sixty-four-year-old man, speaking of his wife, stated, "She was never dead. She died when the organs were donated." (Sharp 2001: 124)

While this man's statement is somewhat cryptic—possibly asserting the discrepancy between "brain death" and "complete" or "cardiopulmonary death," the effect in any case is to challenge biomedical definitions that attempt to sharply differentiate life from death. The man's statement likewise points to the incompatibility between biomedical assumptions and lay beliefs—including "lay beliefs" held by many professionals in medical and related fields. This divide between an elite group and "common" people is not a new development—it is in evidence in the medieval period, through the eighteenth and nineteenth centuries, as well as into the twenty-first century present (Bell 2001; Klaniczay 1990; Seremetakis 1991). The entailments of this elite/"commoner" division are many and varied, crossing suppositions about what constitutes personhood, consciousness, death, and what, if anything, lies beyond.

With regard to folk ("commoner") understandings, the exchange and reanimation of body parts continues to provoke uneasiness, as explored for example in the recent film 21 Grams, in which the organ recipient takes the conjugal place of the organ donor, victims become predators, and the very weight of personhood is the topic of the film's extended meditation. A less familiar form of reanimation but one that likewise invites reflection on the soulless body as use value is the Visible Human Project (see Waldby 2000). Here, for the sake of medical knowledge, the cadavers of two people, a man and a woman—notably imprisoned criminals—were digitally reproduced slice by slice, so that all muscles, bones, and other tissues would be visible three-dimensionally. As Waldby points out, the very process by which these cadavers were transformed into "virtually immortal" specimens wondrously manipulable and even navigable three-dimensionally (the "user" can ride down the woman's spine as through a beautiful stony mountain cave) necessitates their complete annihilation as flesh, muscle, and bone. Each slice was followed by another finer one until only a powder remained. In the end, these criminals weighed even less than 21 grams, but they are ever-present and in motion through cyberspace. Immortal but never at rest, these two prisoners raise the bar on the ways in which the socially marginalized, the murderer, the suicide, the drug addict, and all those dying "bad deaths" continue to be vulnerable to transgressions of bodily (and according to some, spiritual) integrity. They point as well to the enduring problem of defining life when its boundaries are so disturbingly fluid. It is no wonder that ghosts, witches, and vampires continue to stir the imagination.

The Elusive Soul

Virtual cadavers and even organ donation are (so far) at most rumors for most Samburu. Yet here, the strange pair of missionized Christianity and "natural" science have been intervening in the lives of Samburu from the moment the first missionary entered the district in 1935; more to the point, Samburu understandings of personhood have been dynamic even if their transformations are nearly impossible to document. In the next chapter I will offer some tantalizing hints at the dynamism of the regional cultural context inflecting Samburu understandings. Meanwhile, here I note the more obvious transformations. That is, with the introduction of clinics, hospitals, and universal burial in Samburu District we are at a point at which the cultural, the Christian, and the scientific are hopelessly conflated in the dissemination of technologies and practices that colonial missionaries and administrators took for granted, even as such practices reveal ontological differences that can disturb some Samburu as they have and continue to do in the United States and Europe.

For the Samburu, the "wonders" of Europeans cut both ways. Most rural Samburu continue to associate missionaries of every denomination with miraculous medicines, but nothing can convince most Samburu that dying in a Catholic hospital with a priest on hand is a good death because any death so far away from home persists in being unpropitious. Thus, Samburu typically resist going to hospitals for fear of dying there, and many cadavers from clinic or hospital deaths go unclaimed because Samburu would rather see their loved ones put into "pits" than touch a hospital corpse. One Catholic missionary I know whose mission center includes a clinic referred to his church cemetery as the "cemetery of horrors" because every person buried there had died of tragic accidents or of illnesses treated too late. As the ability of lkiye ("death") to cling hazardously to the remains of the unpropitious dead continues to accord the latter a ghoulish agency, a "Christian" Samburu burial has become the monstrous reversal of its Euro-American counterpart.

The practice of universally burying the dead, then—seemingly inflected with Christian, hygienic, and linearly "modern" assumptions—is impinging upon the Samburu moral universe in contradictory ways. Wherever it is performed, universal burial typically follows Samburu rather than Christian mortuary practices, and indeed the exceptions provoke uneasiness and extended debates.[16] The recent (2004) death of a man related to an elite cosmopolitan Samburu family is one case in point. When he died of unknown causes in a town an hour's drive from his home, his wealthy and politically powerful relative ordered other family members to place his corpse into a waiting car, within which it was immediately and hastily transported to the deceased man's home for a burial that took place within three hours of death and without any biomedical intervention whatsoever. Bystanders expressed dismay and concern that the man had been buried at his home in spite of the unpropitiousness surrounding his death, and the haste with which it was accomplished merely added to the distress—the man's relatives clearly knew they were subverting crucial spatial practices.

Intriguingly, the growing practice of universal burial makes inappropriate burials like this one easier to accomplish because it literally allows their tracks to be covered. Since hyenas cannot uncover several feet of stone and soil, any lingering unpropitiousness will go undetected—for a time. Nevertheless, it is somewhat surprising that the man's family would take the risk of burying their relative at home in view of other similar burials that are supposed to have eventually led to misfortune. For example, the shocking murder of a prominent Samburu elite a few years ago led to widespread speculation that it had occurred because his father had been brought home to be buried after being killed by Turkana raiders, even as people likewise debated the practical matter of whether the elite son's murder was an assassination.

When performed appropriately, however, the perceived finality of universal burial has led some families to voice a preference for the practice, as they feel that burial enacts a more complete separation that eases grieving and prevents the occasional horror of dogs bringing corpse fragments home (Holtzman personal communication, 2004).[17] Moreover, and again affirming the dynamism of Samburu practices and ontological suppleness, many Samburu claim that in the past, Samburu *had* universally buried their dead. The practice of leaving the youthful and other unpropitious dead was initiated for two reasons: On the one hand, hyenas' disquieting abilities to detect unpropitiousness was recognized; on the other, Nkai's tendency to occasionally resurrect the dead made these tentative mortuary practices expedient. Although many Samburu, especially in the highlands, are letting go of their concerns about unpropitiousness remaining undetected and uncleansed for a dangerous period of time, some Samburu continue to find the resurrection issue disturbing. As one woman put it quite dramatically, if a person experiences apiu from beneath a mound of earth and several feet of piled stones, what good will it do? They will simply die again.

Nevertheless, Samburu apiu remains a robust miracle—not only in lowland rural areas where Samburu insist on following "tradition," but also in hospitals, where Samburu demonstrate that they have yet to unreflectingly acquiesce in biomedicine's arrogantly definitive ontology. The persistent miracle of resurrection makes biomedical intervention and universal burial enigmatic transformations, leading Samburu to continually reconsider their understandings of life's edges, the contours of personhood, and the cutting practices that preserve them.

Keeping the implications of these miraculous Samburu experiences in view, let me tie the fragments of this chapter somewhat tentatively and delicately together by ending where I ethnographically began—with the first narrative of apiu I ever heard, the one that stunned me in 2001 as I sat in the lowland house of a friend, calmly sipping my tea.

I saw one who *natipiuwa* ("resurrected/came back to life")[18] just recently—[he is] a Lmooli now. He died in Wamba Hospital. He died completely, completely, completely, completely, to the point that the doctors had chased me away. (Nompoi interview, 2001)

When Nompoi went in to see her son, the Italian doctor had already declared the child dead, and he was covered—including his face—with the green cloth that pronounced the biomedical death with more clarity than words (see also Sharp 2001). The nurses tried to send her away when they saw her, but she lingered in the ward anyway.

I was told to go away—and I was carrying the other [my other child] on my back. I said, I waited until they [hospital employees] had gone away for a moment [when they weren't looking]. And I went close to touch [him]. I said, "*Akita!*" [exclamation of disgust/uneasiness]. Let me hold/touch him. [She had to touch despite the hazards associated with handling the dead.] While I was touching him I touched a vein that was doing like this—tau, tau, tau.[19] It continued for awhile until a person from there, from that settlement of Lemasagari—Do you know that family? [What? Yes.] This settlement on the lower side. [Yes.] And the heart stopped. This one looked at me while I was judging, opening [the cloth], and touching—looked at me and kept quiet. (Nompoi interview, 2001)

Nompoi continued touching her son, watching again for signs of a beating heart, while the nurses persevered in trying to get her to leave the room. Finally, she managed to get them to look at just the right moment, and they exclaimed, "Hae! hae! hae! He is alive!" They called for the doctor, who came to see and then left again to get something to inject the boy with. According to Nompoi, he made several attempts to revive the child after that, then covered the little boy again and told Nompoi to leave. She said, "M-m-m, not until I see you throw him in those pits that you people [use].[20] I kept sitting. We sat until the enemies were impatient."[21] Having told her that it would take hours before they would know whether or not the injections had worked, the doctor allowed her to keep vigil near her son, and eventually he completely revived. Indeed, he was a young lmurran when his mother told me of the miracle.

What precisely transpired here? How should we treat this mother's claims? While it is possible to debate the terms of resurrection and resuscitation, to suggest that this or another mother's child was never "really" dead or to assert that brain death constitutes the death of the person—by whatever criteria it should be defined—is to acquiesce in the hegemony of a single biocultural model whose ontological assumptions remain insidiously submerged. Rather—in direct contradiction of the Harvard Committee's movement away from what death *means*—it is my contention that meaning is precisely what is at stake here. Thus, I disagree with Margaret Lock's choice of what appears to be an unequivocal Euro/biomedical definition of the "death of the person" (as "a diagnosis of an irreversible loss of consciousness together with a permanent loss of spontaneous breathing" 2002: 376).[22] Lock's presentation of the ethical, biomedical, and philosophical issues is impeccable; indeed, it is precisely because of the stunning excellence of her ethnography that I am disappointed with her conclusion. Lock's reluctance to fully enter into a consideration of the thorny issues of consciousness and personhood is consistent with anthropologists' reluctance in general to venture beyond what are supposed to be the limits of empiricism. In this respect, anthropology continues to hover uneasily between the Eurocentric empiricism in which it is rooted and the alternative ontologies and epistemologies of its human subjects.

Yet by considering resurrection over time and at a plurality of contact zones it becomes possible to reconsider the Enlightenment transition from bodies that are commodifiable and subject to disarticulation because they are irreducibly entwined with souls to bodies subject to disarticulation because of the very elusiveness of definitions of soul and personhood. Keeping this deeply philosophical transition in view is imperative if we are to make the effort to grapple with our own assumptions and understand not only the differences but also the veiled similarities between our slippery notions of personhood and the notions of our interlocutors. Empirical science has not only failed so far to offer satisfying answers to crucially important questions concerning the boundaries of life and personhood and the nature of experience;[23] it has continually succeeded in troubling these issues more—the "miracles of modern science" continue to astonish us. Thus, resurrection is an abiding reality, trope, and metaphor in the twenty-first century in the United States and Europe as among the Samburu—testament to a human desire and a recurring dilemma: *We have yet to account for experience,* even as we enduringly look at the shadowy notion of consciousness, at the elusive soul.

Chapter 8
Loip

Crossing the Boundary

Have you ever stood outside in a place so distant from roads and cities that the countryside surrounded you in a circle whose edges met the horizon at the place where the world falls into space? At dusk the colors curl down, sneaking slowly behind the curtain of the universe and letting the stars escape to fill the dome that holds us in. We can't touch the edges, but we can see them out there where the colors merge and the night comes up—the black membrane that Leropili once told me we cannot pass beyond. We cannot leave our universe. Even the dead are contained here.

When Turaso, the sister of my field assistant's grandfather, visited Nkai's home, her family ritually cleansed the site, as I related in Chapter 3. They were not entirely certain of what had transpired there, but they had an uneasy feeling that Turaso had successfully traversed a boundary they must struggle to maintain. In Samburu prescissive experience, lkiye ("death") already contains the exception, even if the majority of dead persons *do not return.* That is, while apiu ("resurrection") is the strangest, rarest, and most marvelous exception, there are other exceptions that happen more frequently, making the living and the dead both nomadic wanderers trespassing on one another's terrain. Even as Samburu continually strive to seal that transgressive wound, the form of this abjection itself is an aleph, an overdetermined point refracting a Samburu universe that is about both movement back and forth and, paradoxically, the cutting that would suspend that movement.

   Remember that all Samburu once walked freely along a leather strap connecting humans to Nkai until the first human cut was made. That first cut—a transgressive cut that initiated and required all subsequent cuts—created death and life simultaneously, a life apart from direct contact with Nkai made fragile by a death that continually threatens to overtake it. Thus, if humans made the first cut—a cut they must work hard to maintain—it is Nkai they beseech when their best efforts fail amid an avalanche of deaths that cause overwhelming grief. This is a subtle imaginary within visceral experience; this is the human intervention that is at once a reincarnation of experience and a playful artist pinching experience here and there as death both terrifies and coexists with many forms of crossing. There are many kinds of death and as many kinds of grief; hence a variety of travelers cross the wound, each an uncanny echo of a unique death and a unique set of relations between the living and the dead. The loss of a little girl (or a little boy) is bitter, unimaginable, inexplicable—demanding an erasure of every trace of her existence. She will not be remembered or commemorated—except in the silent long-ing of those who knew her. Her death forms the deepest contrast with the death of a sweet grandparent whose life will be remembered and who will continue to be fed for years to come. There is then, no single web of relations connecting the living and dead, nor a single kind of wanderer collapsing the cut, any more than grief is homogeneous and uncomplicated (see Bataille 1988; Rosaldo 1989; Seremetakis 1991).[1]

In this last ethnographic chapter I will maintain the conceptual fragil-ity of consciousness, personhood, and experience through descriptions of the in-between moments of life/death. I will weave in and out of many kinds of exception here, through a multitude of experiences by which the ordinary is constantly defied. As I suggested in Chapter 7, Samburu accept the extraordinary as possible—when so many have experienced the astonishing it becomes undeniable and worthy of explanation, even as explanation is already a part of experience. Stories of strange cross-ings between the living and the dead are shared and contemplated, rein-carnating within experience and transforming between persons, creating a dense imaginary that is always entangled within experience. The Samburu accounts I will relate here, then, are simultaneously singu-larly apart from and yet similar to the uncanny in a myriad of cultural contexts because they are narratives of *human* experiences—sharing a changeling thread always at the point of vanishing. But before I begin to describe many forms of Samburu wanderings in and out of life, a brief contextual tour of these transgressive movements is in order because I am going against the ethnographic grain for a pastoralist group known for its pragmatic eschewing of "life after death."

Mobile Concepts

While allusions to beliefs in an "afterlife," "souls," or "spirits" are com-mon in East Africa, particularly among agricultural groups, they are infrequent in the literature on Maasai and Samburu. In his classic eth-nography on the Samburu, Paul Spencer (1965) discusses a number of beliefs surrounding what he refers to as "supernatural forces" (185), including ldeket and ŋoki, but nothing concerning afterlife or "soul" beliefs or the absence thereof. Prefacing a discussion of *esakutore* (similar to Samburu l/nkairupok), theological scholar and Maasai specialist Jan Voshaar (1998) avers, "I do not know in Maasai of spirits, angels, or devils, if these are understood as being extra terrestrial and extra celestial beings, but there are devilish deeds and things between heaven and earth" (159). And in a footnote to her paper about Maasai medicine, Nina Johnsen (2002) proposes the following alternative to Dorothy Hodgson's (2001) gloss of *oltau* as "heart, soul, spirit." "In my experience this is only true in the sense of the living spirit, what animates the body of a person, as opposed to a dead body. To non-Christian Maasai there is no notion of a spirit having its own afterlife, or of a shadow world of ancestor spirits watching over the living" (29). While Hodgson's gloss undoubtedly reflects her work with Maasai Christians in the context of a spirit possession phenomenon that she argues is of foreign (external to Maasai) origin,[2] Johnsen's statement apparently rings very true for a key aspect of Maasai everyday understandings.[3] That is, while Maasai Christians may accept the extension of oltau to cover an introduced biblical concept, according to Johnsen it nevertheless would appear to simultaneously retain its more mundane features, particularly for non-Christians. For the Samburu, the mundane features of ltau do include some aspect of thought and strong feelings such as the bond between lovers as well as referring to the vigor of life,[4] and thus the gloss of "mind" is understandable. However, there is no sense in which it is a detachable life essence that carries on one's individual personality for an eternal period following "death."

Yet, even if Maasai oltau and Samburu ltau are less than "supernatural" signs, this does not rule out "more than natural" possibilities for other signs, as I have learned from extensive conversations with Samburu in relation to mortuary practices and what they refer to as loip ("shade," "shadow"), and likewise as Hodgson (1997, 2001) argues persuasively with respect to a phenomenon Maasai refer to as *orpeko*. In its negative aspects, Samburu loip comes up in conversations comparing North American and Samburu mortuary practices. Samburu typically find it surprising that Europeans bring flowers to all graves, even of people who died young. For Samburu, in contrast, it is only the old who are "sweet"—kerropil (they "smell good/sweet/righteous") or, in one woman's words, *kemelok ltunaŋani* (a person is/tastes "sweet"). People who die prematurely or in violent ways are not "sweet"—there is nothing good they have to offer the living. Indeed, Samburu say that loip, or *malika* (a Samburuized form of the Kiswahili *malaika*, angel/good spirit) of these unpropitious dead may wander among the living. If Swahili malaika, from which the Samburuized Kiswahili gloss for loip derives, refers to angels or good spirits, however, Samburu *milika* may be anything but good. Like Maasai orpeko, they can strangle the living, coming with chilling darkness—particularly to the very ill.

Some of the parallels between Samburu unpropitious, wandering loip and orpeko symptoms are intriguing, but a closer examination yields important distinctions. As I will elaborate, loip is a crucial, integrated feature of Samburu personhood, while in contrast Hodgson glosses Maasai orpeko as a foreign form of spirit possession: "Maasai have no long-term tradition of spirit possession; instead, spirit possession, or orpeko, is a recent phenomenon" (1997: 112). As Hodgson tells us, orpeko derives from the Kiswahili term *upepo* (spirit, strong wind). This, in turn, derives from a more general word, pepa ("sway, reel, stagger, totter"—Standard Swahili-English Dictionary 1939: 374–75). Hodgson dates orpeko to Maasai dispersion to Swahili areas following what Samburu refer to as *Mutai*—a series of wars, livestock diseases, and livestock epidemics in the 1870s to '90s that affected Maasai, Samburu, and other peoples in the region. The first case Hodgson mentions affected a Maasai woman (Nanoto) who was living on the coast when her symptoms occurred, which were diagnosed by a non-Maasai healer (on the coast) as "spirit possession."[5] Hodgson follows previous scholars and Christian pastors in describing a wide range of symptoms for orpeko, from back pain and apathy to nightmares and choking sensations. Most intriguing for my purposes are the two cases she quotes from an unpublished paper written by David Peterson in 1971. In both of these quotes, the young women concerned described "darkness" coming followed by a feeling of being strangled. The first quote clearly links the "darkness" with the strangling: "She would wake up at night with a start as 'darkness' would come and try to strangle her" (Peterson 1971 quoted in Hodgson 1997: 117).

Without the transcript, it is impossible to know what Maa term the young women used for "darkness," but for Samburu, the terms and the links with "darkness" and "shadow" would be very clear. Hodgson makes the compelling suggestion that orpeko is "an embodied expression of capitalist and modernist contradictions" that predominantly strikes Maasai women of childbearing age, enabling them to "resolve their structural crisis by strengthening their relationships among themselves and facilitating the formation of alternative female communities under the auspices of the Christian churches" (1997: 125).[6] Hodgson's analysis places orpeko in its specific cultural and temporal context, tracing its appearance and transformation in Maasai cultural space from the nineteenth century to the present. At the same time and toward a different aim, I am fascinated by the parallels between some of the symptoms of orpeko and phenomena described for other contexts.

Thus, if we look to the Mijikenda and related Kenyan coastal groups who are the source for the upepo, or orpeko Dorothy Hodgson discusses as affecting the Tanzanian Maasai[7]—we get a picture of grave offerings that I would like to highlight because of parallels with Samburu practices. In discussing the Mijikenda, David Sperling says that "the world of spirits, including the spirits of deceased persons (Swa. *koma*),[8] was of great importance to the Mijikenda, but it was a realm whose very being belonged to the material world" (1995: 86). Sperling quotes the mid-nineteenth-century missionary Johann Ludwig Krapf to suggest that for the Mijikenda, the "dead" lived in the sky, in the ground, or on their former land and that they "must be appeased with food" (Krapf 1847 quoted in Sperling 1995: 86), since they determined events affecting the living. In this regard, the Mijikenda are similar to many other Kenyan and Tanzanian peoples, including northern Kenyan groups in close proximity to the Samburu like the Turkana, Rendille, and Gabra,[9] although such practices have seldom been commented upon for the Maasai and Samburu. In addition, the Mijikenda share with the Maasai a phenomenon variously described as upepo or orpeko.

As I have already mentioned, upepo is a generic Kiswahili term for spirit, whether good, bad, or capricious. Of the nineteenth-century Mijikenda notion of upepo, David Sperling says that they contrasted greatly with koma (one's deceased relatives), with whom people had an active and continuing relationship through dreams, even if the appeasement strategies were sometimes similar. Mijikenda attributed an assortment of illnesses to various kinds of upepo, including headaches and ulcers, as well as misfortunes and even infertility (Sperling 1995: 87)—the remedy for which was to placate the "spirit" with offerings. The Swahili likewise attributed various ills to *jinn* and *shaitan* and, according to Krapf, similarly went to great lengths to appease them (Sperling 1995: 88). Although Sperling does not mention possession in connection with nineteenth-century upepo, for the contemporary context Linda Giles (1999) has elucidated with great precision the varieties of Swahili spirits that can possess people for good or ill—including again the jinn that can be cultivated for gain but that must be appeased to prevent misfortune.

And in this contemporary context, we can see that upepo is a reciprocal affair. That is, if upepo has infected the Tanzanian Maasai, Maasai "spirits" have likewise become part of the Swahili possession pantheon. Some of these are "regular Maasai spirits," while others "are perceived as Maasai spirits that have moved to the coast and adopted Islamic coastal attributes in a syncretic manner" (Giles 1999: 154). However, while Swahili cultivate spirit possession—even of the Maasai "spirits" they perceive to be "dirty," "uncivilized," and "polluting" (Giles 1999),

Maasai wish only to rid themselves of upepo (Hodgson 1997; Peterson 1971). And again, while Swahili and Mijikenda understandings of upepo strongly reflect Islamic influences in which jinn and shaitan may be capricious but not necessarily evil (see Sperling 1995), the preponderance of Christian influences has given both upepo and shaitan (or setan) clearly Christian (devilish) overtones when they enter Maasailand (see Hodgson 1997). What is common to upepo on the coast as well as in Maasailand, however, is the continuing need to appease them, particularly through dancing and drumming (but also through food and gifts on the coast), whether to foster an ongoing relationship or to dispel them.

Such methods of appeasement show continuity with nineteenth-century Swahili and Mijikenda upepo, even if the exact gifts offered and the singing styles and contexts have transformed over time. Moreover, while contemporary Swahili cultivate "spirit possession," some "spirits" (like jinn) are more dangerous than others (Giles 1999), and the evidence from Krapf suggests that nineteenth-century upepo may more often have had negative associations, as they have had for the Maasai (see Sperling 1995). Finally, and most crucially for my points here, upepo in all of these contexts have been either varied—being one term to encapsulate (and flatten) a pantheon of "spirits" that includes ritually "positive" ones—or have existed *alongside* some form of communication with deceased relatives. "Upepo," "orpeko," and "milika" are conceptual wanderers that, once they settle to inhabit a cultural space, morph and nestle themselves within and between dynamic understandings of troubling experiences.

The orpeko Hodgson describes for Tanzanian Maasai do not inhabit Kenya's Samburu District. However, as one approaches the Mukogodo Maasai region on the southern trail toward Nanyuki, the word upepo sometimes falls from the lips of the Samburu living there. And from Leroghi Plateau to Rumuruti, near Remeta's home, one hears milika used to describe similar phenomena. Rather than denoting spirit possession phenomena, however, Samburu assert that upepo and milika are borrowed terms to describe what I consider to be one of the most semantically dense of Samburu signs and one integrally related to personhood: loip.

Prescissing Loip

In Chapter 5 I described in detail dimensions of Samburu sesen ("body") necessary to mayian ("blessing") and ldeket ("curse"), including a diagram showing that ldeket forms in the nkosheke ("stomach"), moving from there through the ltau ("heart"), to be passed with

nkiyeŋet ("breath") and nkamilak ("saliva") into ltoilo ("voice")—
forming the words of the ldeket itself if it is indeed spoken. In prescissing Samburu lkiye ("death"), these terms become crucial again. When
Samburu are "taken away" from the living, a process unfolds that dis-
perses ltau, nkiyeŋet, nkamilak, and ltoilo in different ways. Two very different understandings of "life"—nkishui and nkishon—are dispersed
differently as well. Nkishui is the "life" that is "cut" when ltau is cut,
though not in a simple or straightforward way since some aspects of nkishui undergo transformation, as I will describe in a moment. Nkishon, in
contrast, is the "life" that is lived in actions that will be remembered. As
such, nkishon remains with the living, held in the memories and emu-
lated in the actions of one's descendants. To what extent nkishon may
also persist in other ways is a point of contention.

Ltau, the "heart" that is most closely associated with the passions of
living and some aspects of the personality, dissipates when it is "cut."
Nkiyeŋet is a more equivocal sign, which, for most Samburu I have
talked to, goes somewhere vague without disappearing or else goes back
to Nkai because it is Nkai who continually gives (or finally withholds)
nkiyeŋet.[10] The parallels between nkiyeŋet and Judeo-Christian understandings of the Divine Breath (in turn related to classical Greek understandings) have captivated some missionaries, who have tended to
reproduce their own ontological assumptions in their dictionary glosses.
Thus, missionaries typically gloss ltau as "heart, mind, and spirit," and
nkiyeŋet is used in the creation of a term for "Holy Spirit."[11] While most
Samburu have yet to adopt these missionary assumptions, members of a
growing Protestant minority have begun to hybridize Samburu and
Christian understandings in intriguing ways, creatively integrating the
Christian notion of soul with some of the ontological contours of both
Nkai and Samburu personhood—thus emphasizing Nkai's presence, the
notion of sacrifice, and the possibilities for intersubjective efficaciousness that the Old Testament likewise affirms (as in visiting the sins of the
fathers upon the sons).

The transformations that loip—the more overdetermined sign, in my
view—are undergoing here are doubly intriguing. When missionary
texts refer to it at all, loip is glossed as shadow, shade, and ghost—a sim-
plification that assumes a sacred soul (ltau or nkiyeŋet) in contradistinction to an unholy specter.[12] Samburu Protestants especially are
increasingly implying this dichotomy in their references to loip—with
some doubting the existence of loip altogether. In contrast, most Samburu discuss loip in more multivalent terms even as subtle shifts are
detectable, as highland Samburu tend to emphasize loip's more negative manifestations. Yet, for the most part, the integrated Samburu
semantic context continues to differ markedly from the dichotomous

Eurocentric configuration, and here, ltoilo ("voice") warrants attention as well. Like nkiyeŋet, ltoilo passes "somewhere" after ltau is "cut," this time most certainly *not* to Nkai. Rather, ltoilo lingers, ready to express itself in particular circumstances, as I will describe in due course.

Ltoilo and loip are closely connected metaphysically, but loip is the more open and complex in Samburu descriptions. Like many signs, it has a number of associations: At its most mundane, it is the shade cast by trees. Yet not all "shady places" are alike—there is loip generally, loip that women might gather under to engage in handicrafts and lively discussion, loip for playing *ntotoi* (a version of mbao),[13] loip for elders, loip for settling disputes. The latter can only be under "cool" trees, that is, trees without thorns because those with thorns might signal the flaring of tempers precisely when calm is needed. Loip is also the shadow of persons, animals, and things. Human loip sleep when people sleep or go somewhere unspecified. Many Samburu suggest that the loip that is one's shadow and the loip associated with some features of personhood are only metaphorically associated, while a few (the minority) are not so certain. In any case, when ltau is "cut," loip does not thoroughly disappear, drying and passing away with ltau. Some Samburu suggest that hyenas eat it with the corpse, more evidence of the close relationship between hyenas and the "dead," even as it suggests a certain "tangibility" associated with loip. Others suggest that somehow, although not in the mouths of hyenas, loip passes underground, which is where the "dead" carry on an existence that includes the slaughtering of animals. There is no simple "soul" here: again as with classical Greek notions, the many facets of the Samburu person each have their own destination, but Samburu are very open-ended in their understandings of what they are certain they cannot know entirely. As we will see, something like the nkishon that Samburu describe as a particular person's actions and behavior seems to linger, with memory, but how it does so is left unanswered.

While ltau's ("heart's") drying transformations after lkiye ("death") are readily observable, ltoilo ("voice") and loip ("shadow/shade") act more mysteriously even in life. Although historically they have too often been described in stereotypic and flattening terms, these are the Samburu signs that Western technologies have disturbed ever since Europeans started bringing cameras and tape recorders to Samburu settlements (see Behrend 2002). Yet the metaphysical resonances of audio and video recordings have merged with Samburu understandings—indeed, they have become uniquely *Samburu* metaphysical resonances, which Samburu seize upon as convenient placeholders for certain aural and visual elements that linger after ltau is cut (see also Ivy 1995). For example, when a person speaks, it is readily apparent to everyone that ltoilo has traveled with the words; where and how far is not precisely known. When a tape recorder records Samburu speaking or singing, it is as if ltoilo has been captured in that cassette—a fact that is familiar enough now that most people are ready to commit themselves to recordings. Many would not wish to hear the ltoilo of the "dead," however (at least not of the youthful dead),[14] even as they recognize that such tapes exist. Tape recordings already leave enough uncanny "echoes."

In the case of photography, there is more at stake—the capturing of loip typically creates more uneasiness, as it is linked to a spectral presence that should take shape only in death. Thus, the loip of the dead are like photographs—or rather, holograms, echoing former persons in ways that some Samburu still consider to be invariably unpropitious: While the loip of the sweet old dead are visible only to those who have wandered or are soon to go to the land of the dead, the loip that roam the countryside and appear visibly to healthy persons are eerily uncanny—like photographs. While many people have overcome this "metaphysical" uneasiness and enjoy having their photographs taken, I still know a number of Samburu, particularly women, who do not want themselves, their animals, *or their calabashes* to be photographed, lest I capture loip and, in so doing, separate what should be inseparable.[15] For Samburu who continue to be troubled in this way, photographs are dangerous duplications. In contrast, some old people (especially in the highlands) enjoy having their pictures taken, as if to spread their propitious sweetness and leave it for their descendants. The contemporary Samburu distinction between loip and latukuny is important here: When someone dies, the latukuny connection is intentionally severed, even if the newly dead person is very old, while photographs of old people can remain in their descendants' hands.

The entailments of ltoilo and loip specifically, and personhood generally, both undergo change in the process of dying, as loip and their ltoilo move off to inhabit a different space with other loip. Unlike the Christian soul, loip do not simply rest while awaiting resurrection, nor are they metonymic for the whole of one's existence—loip is one of many features of *ltuŋana* ("persons"), not all of which are encompassed by loip. That nkiyeŋet passes somewhere else, for example, is not inconsequential.[16] Moreover, the loip of the dead have "corporeal" dimensions, though not exactly in human shape. The loip of the sweet dead eat the food of the living, and they occasionally appear in a variety of shapes—as hyenas, for example, or as birds. Unpropitious loip may appear in white, misty form, accompanying ltoilo, or they may appear—in common with the Turkana "dead" (Broch-Due 1999a)—as little fires or twinkling lights. They might throw stones, and in some instances, they come in the shape of a heavy and suffocating darkness, like the orpeko that Hodgson (1997) describes.

The Propitious Dead

As I described in Chapter 6, the sweet old dead are fed milk, animal fat, and tobacco, establishing a powerful and propitious relationship of exchange between the living and the dead that recurs in anthropological scholarship surrounding death (Bloch and Parry 1982; Ivy 1995; Kan 1989; Strathern 1996). While milk and animal fat are strongly valued for their importance in sustaining life and thus are good gifts for dead who are valued, Samburu maintain that tobacco is quintessentially appropriate as an offering because it already belongs to the dead. Indeed, when old people demand a gift of tobacco they invariably incline their heads to show their white hair—in this way pointing to the close relationship they bear both to Nkai and to those who have already passed. Among the living, these old men and women are the most entitled to tobacco. As for the dead, it belongs to them because it was they who originally gave it to Samburu—a poignant gift from a dead mother to the son she wished to help.[17]

As the story goes, there was once a boy whose mother died, leaving him to be cared for by his mother's co-wife. Unfortunately, as is archetypically the case among the Samburu, she mistreated him, favoring her own son over him in every way. "She gave hers enough [food], and gave the other a small amount" (Letipo interview, 2001). The boy stayed this way for some time, until one day, he speared a hyena with his half-brother's spear—a hyena that, as it turned out, was his own "dead" mother. His mother the hyena ran to her hole, and the boy followed her tracks there, where his half-brother demanded that he go to retrieve the spear. The hyena, meanwhile, in appropriate Samburu fashion, had gone home to have a goat slaughtered for her so that she could heal from her wound. Knowing already the association between hyenas and the "dead," the boy feared to go down the hole "where the dead go," yet his half-brother was so insistent that he decided he must go even if it meant that he would die. So the boy "went through. He just went, you see, to where his mother was being treated. She said, 'Woii! Don't kill me,' then [recognizing her son] asked, 'What brought you here?'" (Leropili interview, 2001).

He said, "Mother, I was brought by problems." "What do they do to you?" "So and so's [his half-brother's] mother does this to me, punishing me. If my cows give birth, his mother cheats me. She doesn't even give me food. So I will leave those people—I will come here and stay with you." She said, "I tell you, my child, you don't know how to stay with the "dead." Go back. Go back and just stay there until the problems eat you, forcing you to go, or until you become big. Be strong also, because I don't know how to solve your problems while I am "dead" and you are "alive." Nkai doesn't want you, a living person, to come here." He said, "I can't go, my mother. I will stay [here] and if I die let me die." So she took some tobacco leaves and she told him, "Take this tobacco and go back to the people. Just give it to them because they will feel like chewing tobacco until she [his brother's mother] yawns, 'aee, I have a thirst for tobacco.' Then get this tobacco and put it underground to hide it. Go and bury it near the house—don't reveal where. And just bring a little [saying] 'Mother, take this thing' if she gets thirsty. She'll like you then—just stay and trick [her] and don't reveal [where it is] at all." (Letipo interview, 2001)

The mother's ploy worked, and from that time on, his half-brother's mother was kind and fair to him, giving him the same amount of food as her own son.

This story is a multivalent parable—legitimating the need to return the gift of tobacco to the dead from whence it came, but as well evoking the profound loss that a mother's death entails. This boy's mother did not survive to raise her child to adulthood as she should have, but rather left him motherless and vulnerable. Like the European story of Cinderella, the tobacco story points to a gap left in social relations when mothers die prematurely. In both cases, motherless children experience deprivation in the absence of their mothers, and subsequently their mothers manage to help them even in death. The Samburu trope of the motherless child suffering at the hands of his co-mothers recurs in Samburu stories, and its Maasai parallels are expressed in Saitoti's (1986) autobiography. By returning tobacco to the sweet old dead—the parents and grandparents from whom it came—Samburu likewise hope to receive blessings and help from those who have passed.[18] Nevertheless, the lamentations of motherless children in an otherwise upbeat story that establishes the character of right relations between the living and the dead are not to be missed.

Meanwhile, the importance of maintaining propitious relations with the sweet old Samburu dead is ubiquitously affirmed, beginning during the corpse's preparation for mortuary rites.

Don't you know that people cry because a person is sweet? [Mm.] No one will be there to remember. [Yes.] That one is just laid like that. [Yes.] An old person is the one to be smeared [with oil]. [Yes.] Yes, old people are smeared. What happens is that the fat is brought and poured on him or her, because for that one whose mouth could still open before s/he cut the heart, s/he is just given as much oil to drink as s/he can. But that one whose mouth is stuck [shut], like Loishopoko that day, wasn't the goat taken and slaughtered there? [Mm.] Were you there at that place? [No.] Wasn't it that the goat was taken to be killed there which it was said would smear the mouth or he was brought up this way? The deceased was brought and the goat was taken to be killed—what about him who had died awhile ago? They came and just poured that fat on him. There is nowhere it could pass. The mouth was forced open for the fat to get somewhere to pass. (Nolpesi interview, 2001)

In this way, Samburu establish—in the period immediately following death—that their obligations to grandparents continue even in death. Then, long after the corpse is "thrown" or buried, Samburu continue to bring offerings to their grandparents' mortuary site, usually on a monthly basis.

It is the usual practice when you go and meet the grave of your grandma whom you knew, or your grandpa, or even your mother. Don't you put some tobacco there? [You will put some if you chew it.] No! You will even put some if you don't chew it. You see, when you go near where she was laid to rest you will say that this is the tree she was lying under and you will put tobacco there. So isn't it for the "dead"? (Naismari Leurie interview, 2001)

Have you heard that? [What?] It is the Samburu tradition/practice because my own father died. You see now, the house of my mother, they went and slaughtered a ram [yes]. It is killed there [yes]. All the children of my mother poured oil and my mother poured, it was poured, milk was poured. Then they got up and put tobacco. And another time they came again and brought only milk and it was all poured, and tobacco [yes]. Then they went. [Because it is just every time?] (Every time?) [Yes] Mm, just once a month. Yes, just when they see another moon they go and put [it]. {Or if you are just on a journey and you pass that grave site of your people, whether it is your father's or grandfather's.} When you just realize (that you will pass near there) you take tobacco from home and you carry it. When you come to pass you just put this tobacco there, then you go. {Yes.} You put a leaf. You break a leaf, you place it on [the site]. (Mepukori Lenaibor interview, 2002)[19]

If their descendants forget them for awhile, or if they are hungry before a month has elapsed, grandparents can communicate their hunger by various means. One friend of mine explained this in the context of describing the variety of shapes the dead may take.

And you know for a person, once s/he has died, there is nothing that it is *not* going to be because some go and become birds, others go and become hyenas. So you see even now a bird, you know your grandmother can come and greet you and you could just say to yourself, "Woi, I am going to take this tobacco and go and put some on the grave of my grandmother." And someone else [a "dead person"] could say, "Bring it [tobacco] so I can eat"—s/he comes looking for it. [Others] become a snake. (Nolsintani Lemarei interview, 2001)

Because of their sweetness, the unexpected visits of birds do not frighten Samburu, but they do pose a warning that must be obeyed. In some instances, ancestors simply take what is their due. "He would just then come and ask you where food is: 'Are you going to give me food?'

And if now you bring a calabash as you milk and place it over there, it falls down. It just falls down, it would just fall down and milk is spilled on the ground . . . And those are just some of those aged people [taking the milk]" (Legol interview, 2003). Occasionally, the loip of the sweet dead may make their presence felt more uncannily, as in an incident Naismari Legol told me had occurred while she was still living with her parents. One day, when her family was living just a short distance from the site of where their settlement had been when her grandmother died, the cows spontaneously walked in single file toward the place where her corpse had been laid.

The cows filed home after she was not given food for some time. [And the cows came in a file, passing where she had been laid.] The cows came in a file—they usually came past that place when they had gone to the river but now as they came, the lead cow broke legs [bent down] to rest. [They rested?] The whole herd of cows lay down to rest and people tried to say "Haat! Haat!" but they were defeated. [Resting at that place?] Yes, [the cows] were resting there and people could not move them, and the people could not move them. But the herder was clever—he realized that it was because she had not been given food for some time. [Going to smear with fat.] So finally, he milked [a cow] onto the ground. He milked onto the ground, and when he had milked onto the ground, the leader moved and the entire herd filed home. (Legol interview, 2003)

When the herder reported what had happened, the family was immediately alarmed. All four of the woman's sons brought their wives and children and slaughtered goats on the site. Four goats, one for each son, were slaughtered, and the meat and fat were cooked and poured onto stones at the place she had been laid. According to Naismari Legol, the meat and fat dried and disappeared as soon as they were poured, and they could not see where the food had gone. "And so, a dead person, that person is not dead. They have not gone forever. S/he is just alive. [Yes, s/he is just alive.] S/he is just alive" (Legol interview, 2003).

Although Naismari Legol concludes by saying that her grandmother then "blessed her children, and then she blessed her children," her family's reason for rushing to make offerings to their deceased grandmother is evident in the tragic experiences of those said to fail in their obligations. Grandparents are "sweet"—they have blessings to offer the living so long as the living remember to feed them and give them tobacco just as their children were supposed to do while those parents and grandparents were living. Indeed, according to Naismari Legol, they are *still* alive, "taken from" the living and yet among them. As I elucidated in Chapter 5, while wrongs committed against one's parents and grandparents can result in immediate misfortune and in terrible ŋoki that will follow them and their descendants for generations, wrongs committed against the already "dead" can likewise have disastrous con-

Figure 11. Grandparents have a potent blessing during life and beyond. A grandmother at left is scraping a hide that will become my skirt in 1994. A grandfather at right is relaxing in the afternoon in 1993. Both were in the mood for storytelling.

sequences. Thus, "sweet" grandparents can confer sweet mayian ("blessings") or, alternatively, they can impart terrible ldeketa ("curses") in both life and death. Thus, appropriate relationships and sharing (exchange) practices must be maintained even after lkiye ("death"), or else lkiye of people and/or livestock is expected to follow. "And all your children just come and kill livestock there and pour oil, milk, and tobacco. Yes, and sometimes you say that maybe s/he [the dead person] is the one who is killing me" (Mepukori Lenaibor interview, 2002).

Obligations to one's old parents and grandparents should continue fluidly from life, through dying, and long after death. However, according to Samburu, failure is always possible—there are almost as many anecdotes of failure as there are of success. In the following case, for example, neighbors claim that a family failed to provide adequate offerings during the preparation of the corpse, and this resulted in the family's continual loss of its male elders.

{Which family?} Lekimariri's. {Of Lekimariri.} Yes. {Yes, I heard (you).} Another Lkileku. {I heard (you).} [[It is said that his mother was not properly prepared when she died.]] {Mm.} He went/died then and so all that family of Lekimariri? [[Always in all of that family there are no elders there.]] The people of that family are the ones who share the stomach/womb, they are how many? [Two?] [[Three.]] [Three.] [[They have all gone to follow those (dead) people.]] (Lenaisho interview, 2001)[20]

"They have all gone to follow those [dead] people." No one wants to "follow" the "dead"; no one wants the "dead" to come calling for them. Indeed, as one is placing the tobacco or other offering on the grave, one says, "*Tepero aapen yeyio ai. Nchoo iyioo nepo.*" (Sleep alone, my mother—or father, grandmother, or grandfather. Let us go.) In other words—don't bring me there with you. Let us go. The fear implied here is real—Samburu attribute many deaths to families' failure to feed their grandparents. And while it might seem that no one would forget to observe these rites, given the possible consequences, it is important to recognize that hunger is a recurring reality, especially in the dry season. Thus, parents are sometimes forced to choose between the needs of their living children and the demands of the deceased. In some accounts, though, there is no explanation given for the mistreatment of grandparents, even while they are living. And while this may result in an ldeketa ("curse") escaping from the lips or stomach of a dying old person, sometimes the loip of the sweet old dead follow their recalcitrant descendants, as in this account, narrated to me by a friend who knew the family it happened to.

There was a widow with two sons living near Baragoi. She was living with her younger son (a typical Samburu practice), who only had a few animals, while her older son—rich in livestock—lived in a nearby settlement. As it happened she became very ill, and decided to ask her older son to give her a goat to slaughter for soup that would speed her healing. Her son adamantly refused his mother, however, telling her that even if she died as a result, she was not going to get a goat from him. Some time passed, and she did indeed die. Meanwhile, to escape his mother's repeated request for a goat, the older son had moved near Maralal. After his mother's death he continued moving, eventually settling in Laikipia District. The younger son continued to live near Baragoi, where his mother had died, but continued hardship made him move in search of his brother's settlement. As he moved, staying in Maralal for awhile before finally reaching his brother's settlement in Laikipia, his mother's loip was accompanying him quietly. She had no quarrel with her younger son but intended to find the older one.

Not long after the younger son settled with his brother, one of the older brother's children became sick. After slaughtering a goat to speed the child's healing, the man's mother appeared to him in a dream telling him, "You thought I would not catch up to you, but I have. There is no reason to slaughter a goat for me now. I am going to take you." The man told the neighboring elders about his dream and they instructed him to slaughter a goat for his mother, which he did. Again his mother came to him, and again she told him not to slaughter: "You refused to slaughter a goat for me when I needed it, and I don't need it now. Leave your animals for your widows and their children because I am going to take you." The man died shortly after. (Nolsintani Lemarei interview, 2002)

The loip of the sweet old dead may take a number of shapes, asking to be fed, or they may simply take what is theirs—as when milk disappears from a calabash before people's eyes. Occasionally, when adult children have failed in their obligations, they may bring misfortune to the entire family or even, as in the previous story, follow a specific person and take them away before their time—an unpropitious death. While the many incidents of misfortune that Samburu attribute to angry grandparents are evidence that the social order is not always restored (Ivy 1995; Seremetakis 1991), the *potential* for blessings and good relations is always there in the case of these propitious deaths of the very old. The deaths of *young* people are neither propitious nor reparable, however. They cause lingering grief in the living and often disquiet in the dead because the loip of the young are never fed—they wander powerless and unsatisfied.

Poignant Erasures

My first experience of a Samburu death was the little girl whose death in my car I narrated in the opening chapter. Another time, while my husband and I were driving down the Wamba-Maralal road, we were stopped by an accident scene. A large open-bed truck had overturned, spilling its human occupants—many of them children—onto the dirt road. Their small forms were scattered about the scene, covered by their jackets. We transported some of the injured back to Wamba Hospital, where we saw a mother who had lost two of her children in the accident. She was already violently overcome with grief knowing about the accident, although at that point she only suspected her children's deaths.

Those who have seen it know that grief is horrific—it does not merely and abstractly disrupt the social fabric, it wracks the living, ripping them from the middle of their lives and into a terrifying hollow space. Yet, when old Samburu people die, grief can be calm even amid the sadness of parting. If an old person dies at night, the family typically lets them lie there peacefully until morning—there is no need to rush when all is as it should be. In contrast, when a young person dies the enormity of grief is unimaginable, and people scream, cry, shake, or vomit with the sudden horror of it. When a friend of ours lost a young nephew he had fostered for several years, he appeared at our house in the night, almost unrecognizable—he was so transformed by the death that had been reported to him. My husband went immediately to take him to the corpse—waiting was not an option—and as he walked from the car toward the site of the death (a drowning) he fell down repeatedly, crying uncontrollably and vomiting. Elders guarded the little corpse all night, and by morning, when we assisted with the mortuary rites, our friend was calm but visibly exhausted in his continuing grief. His wife did not leave the house or even her bed at all—women (especially young ones) are typically too grief-stricken to attend mortuary rites.

Immediately following the funeral we drove back home, but we had to stop the car when we approached the river that flows near Lodokejek. Here, a small bundle containing all of the possessions the child had owned, including clothes and ornaments, was thrown into the moving river. Even the calabash he drank milk from had to be utterly removed from human existence—thrown into the bush, unlike a no longer serviceable calabash of the yet living, which is put into the cow pen for the cattle to destroy. Photographs, clothing, toys—every little possible reminder of a child's existence is put into moving water or otherwise destroyed. Not even his name will remain, banished from the lips of those who loved him. This is the practice for young children as well as young adults because none of these are propitious deaths.[21] Grief remains, of course—I have talked to mothers who still have nightmares about their lost children. Yet for the sake of the living, every social trace must be annihilated.

Nevertheless, the loip of the youthful, childless, and in other ways unpropitious dead cannot be banished so easily. They are powerless to cause misfortune so long as their tangible traces have been erased, but they can unsettle the living (see also Ivy 1995). There is, for example, one known loip in the highland area I work in, who was known to be an unpleasant young woman. Now neighbors say that her loip appears as little fires or she throws stones at people as they pass her.[22] Throwing stones is a common thing for a "bad" loip to do. Other loip like these may even come into the house at night, bringing darkness with them and, at times, sitting on the living—particularly those who are ill, as I will discuss later.

The loip of those who died violently, such as lmurran in battles, also appear to the living, and these loip are those most closely and eerily associated with ltoilo. It is said that they invariably sing the last songs they sang while living, much as a tape recording of someone's voice will replay the same words or songs over and over again. Tapes and photographs can be destroyed, but Samburu view conversations as "alive" and able to linger uncontrollably. Thus, the loip of those who did not die "well" may call to the living, who see them as misty white shapes. Again, they may throw stones when someone approaches to see who is calling. Unlike European ghosts, stone-throwing loip seem mainly to disturb people they know, although the ltoilo, and sometimes the fires, of the "dead" may be heard by anyone: There is a little creek, Nkeŋok ("those who were taken"), we cross to get to our highland settlement after visiting Kisima or Maralal. On one of the first occasions we crossed it at night—before I knew its name or what the name means—I saw lights moving rapidly in the trees. My husband saw them too, and we followed them with our eyes, trying to see if they were an animal's eyes or flashlights. It seemed like the lights moved too rapidly—both across and up and down—for either possibility. When I mentioned this to Samburu friends, they noted that the creek is near the site of a large battle that killed many Lorokushu and Lpisikishu (clans) lmurran, and, moreover, that the creek specifically "took" some bulls long ago.[23] We continue to see those lights, and while we suppose they might be insects or animal eyes, we have yet to confirm the mystery and do find it just a bit unsettling.

The loip who walk abroad in these ways are eerie reminders that the rites performed to cut life apart from death are always temporary and tenuous because the dead surround us.

Travelers Back and Forth

When they cross the path of the living, the loip of the dead startle the persons who experience them—a jolt of the uncanny somewhat akin to the way lizards or snakes darting at the boundary of vision jar the senses with a movement that only slowly takes a definable shape. Sometimes the meaning of a strange experience shapes and reshapes itself very slowly, as in the case of child prophets like Remeta. Will this child return from wherever she has gone? Will Nkai want her so much so as to permanently claim her? When Turaso disappeared, her father and his neighbors searched everywhere for her, but she had utterly vanished without a trace and was drinking milk and honey at the beautiful home of Nkai. As it turned out, her father was right to offer sacrifices to "change the color" of that hill because his little girl was in some amount of danger. She was not sick or dying but had wandered into "Heaven," as it were, into the space that is somewhere else, the space of Nkai but also of death. While she sat there completely unafraid and enjoying the attention of a woman with plenty to feed her, two Nkai women argued back and forth about whether they would "take" little Turaso from her mother as punishment for her mother having taken a wooden post from the house of a dead woman. Because Turaso's mother did not realize her error, the Nkai woman who wanted to punish her relented, and Turaso was sent home.

Did Turaso care whether or not she was sent home? It is not possible to know, since this was not a question anyone remembers asking her. What those who knew her do claim is that she did not wish Nkai to take her father—when Nkai snatched him away Turaso refused to speak to Nkai for a very long time. In the most famous case currently remembered however, the child in question—the famous Samburu prophetess, Ɖoto Malapen—crossed into Nkai's home throughout her life and sometimes fervently wished she could remain there.[24] Ɖoto Malapen first began to talk to Nkai when she was a young girl, and her gifts for prophesying and healing started then. She visited Nkai's home on many occasions, and Nkai visited her as well, sometimes filling her calabash with milk.

Her daughter, Malapen, remembers some of these visits vividly because she experienced them as well even if she could not see Nkai herself. Thus, she often knew when Nkai visited her mother because darkness would suddenly fall all around them, a cool wind would blow, and thunder would be heard in the house.

And a thing thunders in the house, yes it thunders even where my father and I are seated, and we get sleepy. We just hear a thing that goes "tututu" but you don't see anything . . . When it comes to take my mother somewhere it is that thing that took her and it now gets dark and we don't see. Then it just goes and we don't see—it just goes. And she [her mother] is filled with water, having water all over her as if she were bathing, it's in her clothes, and wherever she is, water pours. (Malapen interview, 2002)

Nkai's visits to Ɖoto Malapen were not always of a benign character, however. Once, for example, when Nkai was angry because Ɖoto Malapen was afraid to prophesy and had begun to go to church instead, her daughter and other bystanders saw the blisters appearing on Ɖoto Malapen's flesh where Nkai was burning her.[25] She acquiesced in Nkai's demands, and the burning ceased. This is an interesting inversion of Maasai orpeko, for which Christian baptism is the cure rather than the cause of "spirit possession."[26] Yet I do not characterize these Samburu experiences as spirit possession phenomena because of their reciprocal and nomadic character: Samburu like Remeta, Turaso, and Ɖoto Malapen visit Nkai's home, where they are invariably fed and sometimes given messages, just as Nkai makes a variety of appearances "here"—as snakes, rain clouds shaped like elephant trunks, a simple voice inside an ailing child's head, or a force that can burn bodies, cause mudslides, or benignly fill calabashes.

In spite of their positive aspects, Nkai's personal relationships with

Samburu—particularly with children—are sources of uneasy wonder because the connection between the living and the dead remains palpable in these experiences. Indeed, Ɗoto Malapen once told her daughter, "I want this child [her daughter, the narrator] of mine to die, then we would go there" (Malapen interview, 2002). That is, Nkai's home was so beautiful that Ɗoto Malapen wished she could take her daughter with her, but while Nkai allowed Ɗoto Malapen to travel there and back while yet alive, she knew that her daughter would have to die to go there. Indeed, the only other Samburu to experience that beautiful place, and those who most commonly see the dead, are those who are very close to death themselves—an understanding that probably contributes to parents' uneasiness when their children visit Nkai. Here, the back-and-forth movement that prophets experience between Nkai's home and their own settlements parallels the reciprocal visits between the dead and the dying, visits that Samburu perceive to be neither dreams nor visions in any simple sense but, rather, literal crossings between twin sides of the same universe.

My Samburu acquaintance Nompoi—whose son's apiu I related in Chapter 7—offered a vivid example of this crossing experience. Thus, once when she was so close to death that her relatives had already begun to prepare her mortuary hide, Nompoi ventured to that beautiful place on "that side," which Ɗoto Malapen, Remeta, and other prophets have described. As she explained, "Even a dead person's ears are pierced [can hear]. I could hear all that was spoken. I could hear people chewing *miraa* [khat, a stimulant]: 'Man! Give me sticks, man! Give me *chaŋaa* [liquor]. Buy us some more chaŋaa, do you hear?'" After this conversation about miraa and chaŋaa, she ventured farther away, finding herself in a pasture full of cows with giant udders. She tried to run after them but was turned back by an unspecified person.

Some cows came with bells, "porou," "porou," "porou," "mbuu"! Bulls. And if I see these cows, the breast of one is this big [demonstrates with her hands]. And this one [another udder] was the size of that [twenty-liter] jug. When I tried to run, the cows came closer to me. It was like I was going, I was reviving. I thought the dead/corpses/ghosts [lmeneŋa] were talking to me. They said, "Hey! Mother, don't go and meet those cows because they are not yours. Do you see that dust that is coming from there—on that gap? It's those cows that are coming up [those are your cows]. It's your boys who are driving those cows— wait for your boys' cows to come because these aren't yours. I sat back down and I was dead, do you hear? I came back and sat, and these cows were white. And those cows were black and their udders white, and the cows' breasts were the size of my leg. When I saw them [cows] standing and the young calves lowing, "mpaaa," mpaaa," "odurr," "odurr," "mpooo," and the bulls scratching the ground fighting, "otutututu," I was laying and just dead. (Nompoi interview, 2001)

Not all experiences venturing beyond life are similar to visiting Nkai's home, however. An old neighbor of mine, Lembiyon, reported a more frightening experience that happened in the 1940s when he was a young man. Lembiyon became so sick that everyone thought he had died; they wanted him to be left in the bush (as appropriate for a warrior), but one of his brothers refused.

He took out his knife to fight with the people and said, "I will not let the beasts eat him when I can see a small life in him." Maybe there was a small life in me . . . You see where I was, was in another place. You see where I am lying there was a light surrounding me for a small distance . . . You see behind the light—it is dark [and he entered the darkness]. And there were small children, maybe these were *milikani* [pl. of *milika*, angel or spirit]. They were sitting there, small children with large stomachs. They are talking and I can also hear them singing and sometimes dancing, so it was like a party. "Hooo, moyiaaa, loiyaa, yooo," there in the dark. They continued and then they stopped, and some people came passing by, mm, mm, mm, and some looked at me like this, then went straight. Another comes and does the same and went away, and you see I can still remember very clearly how it was. [Yes, you remember. Do you know those people who were looking at you?] Oh! Knowing what? They just looked like beasts—maybe those things were sheitani ("devils"). And then something with a long mouth comes. You see, when it looks at me I run away. (Lembiyon interview, 2003)

Although he ran away, he remained in darkness for what seemed like several days, long enough for another person to appear, this time an old man, who sat on him so that he felt he was suffocating. At that point, however, he managed to speak to his brother, asking him to tell the old man to get off of him. When he said this, his brother "jumped and said, 'where is he?'" Lembiyon slowly regained strength after that, but he believes that the light that surrounded him was the little bit of life that remained in him that his brother recognized, and that when the light disappeared and he saw the dancing children, that small life had disappeared and he had died.

I do not think that the social status of the dying is insignificant to these Samburu experiences. Nompoi, a married woman with children, experienced a visit to a place as beautiful as Nkai's home, while in contrast, Lembiyon, a young unmarried warrior, had a frightening experience of children dancing in the dark and an old man who sat on him. Similarly, many Samburu report the unpropitious loip of the youthful dead coming to sit on them, bringing darkness into the house as they do so. In contrast, when old people are dying, they often announce that their friends are visiting them—and they show no fear, even if they refuse to go with them: "It's those milikani who have died long ago, they do come to request those very sick people to accompany them. And when your mouth says 'I can't go' or 'I am not going, go, I am not coming' [laughter], 'I am not going with you, leave me alone,' then they will go away" (Mesholo Lepurkel interview, 2003). Another old woman reported exchanging greetings with her dead friends, although she still refused to go with them: "They used to come [when she was sick] and say 'How are you? How are your children—are they okay? Can't you come and join us?' And I answered, 'I will not come [laughter]. You tell them I am not coming'" (Damaris Leŋwesi interview, 2003). Frequently when old people are visited like this, they not only exchange greetings but demand that milk be poured for their deceased friends. And occasionally, they *do* agree to go with them:

His friend came to him, one with whom he had exchanged cow gifts, he came to him and he told him, "let us go" . . . he told him, "get up, let us go," and he refused. So he [the dead friend] went back, but he returned to him again, and then before the third time he called his sons and he started to give them his final counsel . . . "You see what is going to be, you see my friend will not return alone again. He has visited me for two days now and on the third day he will not go back alone. I will go with him." He continued to advise them about everything he wanted to tell them, and then he died. I was told this by his sons. (Lembiyon interview, relating the experience of a friend, 2003)

Traces

I can smell my grandmother's perfume as I write in my little house in Samburu District. I remember my mother telling me that she smells it sometimes and finds it comforting. Now, suddenly and without warning, as I write about the "dead" of others, my grandmother's perfume has wafted toward me. Why? Is this my vivid imagination? There it is again. I wander in and out of the rooms, and she is not in the children's room but only in my room. I settle in again here to write these words, and she has come here too, but she is still not in my children's room. She loved roses above all things, and her perfume is floral. When I was a child she had linoleum with a pattern of very large roses. It was a simple three-room house with no bathroom, just a bedroom, living room, and kitchen with a big sink. That was the only running water in the house. The roses crept around the house, from the living room to the kitchen, and into the bedroom that still held many little treasures from my mother's childhood. In that bedroom, grandma gave me the first picture I ever had of my father—a black and white 8 x 10 in which he looked young, beautiful, and serious. I thought I recognized my eyes in his, and those eyes haunted me pleasantly as I grew. I never knew him, though. Yet I knew my grandmother very, very well. The roses on her floor went away when the house was pulled down and she went to live in town, but she always had roses in some form, like the glass block with the plastic rose inside—kept on the shelf below the ceramic squirrel.

I can still smell her perfume. If it is imagination, it is very active, with the power to send smell molecules into my nostrils, from or on to my olfactory bulb, conjuring feelings of my grandmother. I hear her calling me as a little girl—"Bilind-ee," the final syllable sung in high pitch, as if she were calling across the hollers. I remember so many things. How has she come all the way here, to Kenya, where I write these words? What would she have me write? What have I missed here in this attempt to understand Samburu prescissing of lkiye and loip? Have I missed the feelings, the emotional haunting that may be prescissed differently and yet shares something in the reality of knowing other persons to the point of crossing, exchanging latukuny, or as with my grandmother, sharing an appreciation for certain smells?

"Don't you know that people cry because a person is sweet?" Nolpesi asked that question in 2001. (I smell grandma's perfume again.) And of course sweetness is a different sign in Samburu, though sharing something in common with American sweetness, including the sweetness of some people. My grandmother was a sweet person, and I am remembering her. Yet, as Nolpesi said, "no one will be there to remember." Her memory will pass when her stories are no longer told, and even if her stories continue, she will not be remembered in time, in the way that those who loved her remember her now. It is no wonder that Samburu, as much as they fear the *contagion* of death, as much as they hate it and cherish living, yet welcome the old propitious "dead" into their homes as they lay, waiting to die. They welcome those they haven't seen in a long time, insist that the living around them—who are invariably too young to remember the people whose names they are hearing their parents or grandparents calling—pour good milk in a cup for these precious visitors.

Yet these are the sweetest crossings, the crossings between the sweet old dying and the propitious dead, crossings that resemble healthy mixes, cuts made at the right time. There are many terrifying deaths that contrast painfully with these, and personhood is always vulnerable—subject to madness, youthful or violent death, or a ŋoki that consumes entire families. Such hazards are all the more dangerous precisely because the boundaries of personhood are necessarily and propitiously permeable. Movement between, within, and across is constant, and vigilance is required to encourage healthy crossings and cut those that threaten health and life. It is not the division between life and death that is crucial then, but rather, recognition of the healthy cut—the proper boundary *and* the proper crossing. The old—living as well as deceased ancestors—are always proper, always sweet, and thus they are the ones to be fed long after their corpses decay, the ones who can even be buried within the settlement, and whose corpses can be touched without fear.

It is no wonder I can smell my grandmother's floral sweetness—having stayed long enough in Samburu that my prescissing has been hybridized, merging one sign with another in a place all about crossings. A deceased child however, can never be memorialized. All the things their small hands held, all that they were or cared about, will dissolve in the rushing water—as ephemeral as they were. Perhaps this is why children are the most frequent visitors to Nkai and the most common to resurrect—their hold here is a tenuous one, and they need careful protection.

Thus, Samburu personhood is enacted very slowly, long after a childhood marked by (too) easy movements between here and Nkai's home, between the land of the living and that of the dead, and between death and life itself. When children wake back up, dragging their mortuary skins behind them, it is indeed a tender miracle. Grief is held off once again for a time, and the path to personhood is resumed. Yet it is also a slender miracle, unexpected and wonderful because mortality is high—amid contaminated water, too many mosquitoes, not enough rain, dry cows, and empty stomachs. If food is a central organizing principle around which Samburu life depends (Holtzman 2001, 2002), this is because people are constantly on the edge of not having quite enough, contributing to life's fragility. There are many aspects of Samburu reality that contribute to experiences of permeability, then, but the primary one is undoubtedly that there are so many deaths to understand and, with them, so many chances for the extraordinary to happen, as the most jarring experiences magnify the dynamic contours of experience itself.

What I have described throughout this book are the ways in which Samburu prescissively experience a reality that is always more than imaginary—the multitudinous, roaming manifestations of loip are at once seen, felt, heard, and imagined. They are witness and witnessed; they are the thoughtful experiences that move in and out of life, as children wander into "Heaven," as grandparents take milk, take fat, take their own children before the eyes of many, as the dead wake up—blinking away a line that is uncanny *because* so strangely fluid. Ethnographically, I have examined loip as integrative of many kinds of experience—not merely ghostly echo or possessive spirit but divine occurrence, living projection, and ancestor with enduring carnal attributes. Theoretically, I have been persisting in telling stories with experiential trails, as experience happens within and through the imagination, merging the undeniable with the fantastic, the ordinary with the inexplicable, and forcing us to respect, re-see, revisit memory as not only elusive, illusory, and fictional but as a tangible, *effective* trace of a reality that haunts us because it is within, across, as well as beyond us.

Conclusion
Immediacies

Deceive me as much as he can, he will never bring it about that I am nothing so long as I think that I am something.
—*René Descartes*

I first went to work in northern Kenya with Samburu pastoralists in July 1992, with my eight-year-old son Jesse, and my six-year old son Jen. I settled in the Samburu lowlands to do a multisited project about gender, Christian missions, and development in three areas of varying accessibility to roads and social services. In a very short time my sons and I settled in to this beautiful but harsh countryside, where the bare needs of survival dictated the pace, activities, and texture of life. This was true throughout the lowlands but especially so in the site I chose as farthest from passable dirt roads and any kind of social services—the adjacent political subdivisions of Ngare Narok (Black Water) and Ndikir Nanyukie (Red Door/Opening).

Samburu, like their cultural and linguistic cousins, the Maasai, had been made famous in postcards and coffee-table books depicting "warriors" in long, red-ochred pigtails and young women decorated in large and colorful beaded collars. The rural Samburu I met in 1992 fit this description well, apparently matching the stereotypes of both Euro-Americans and their fellow Kenyan citizens down-country. True to more recent anthropological literature, however, the Samburu have been struggling in the aftermath of colonial policies that circumscribed their movements and curtailed their access to the best dry-season grazing lands, as well as by postcolonial policies that often exacerbated this situation, particularly in the context of periodic droughts.

As beautiful as the Samburu I met were, there was nothing romantic about the unfulfilled basic needs and sometimes outright hunger that I witnessed on a daily basis. Because of the modest resources I had—stretching a ten-month Fulbright into a two-year field stay—I frequently experienced a sample (just a sample) of this lack myself in ways that made a more lasting impression on me than the perhaps overly structured data I was collecting. As I read my journal entries now, I note with interest but not surprise how much I paid attention to the little details of living—details that are of the utmost significance to those, like Samburu, for whom necessary, and sometimes gravely urgent, travel is typically by foot; and food, water, and shelter are things that can never be taken for granted.

> *Journal Entry, May 1993. We left Lemon's settlement at 8:30 a.m. and arrived here at 12:30 p.m. I must not have kept good track of time on the way there because although we stopped a few times because things were falling off of the donkey, we were not delayed two hours. I suspect it took us three hours going. I kept close track of time while visiting settlements in order to see how far each group of them is. Musa and the children have gone to the river to bathe and fetch water. Nolowai is sitting here with me, playing with the mini Etch-a-Sketch Jen and Jesse got in the mail at Easter. She is about ten years old and quite pleased with it. She keeps showing me the figures she draws . . . Jen has been incredibly wonderful overall. I can't believe he walked six hours (with plenty of hills) and kept pace . . . I don't want to underestimate or forget how tortuous these walks can be though. I get used to the length and to the climbs, but the heat—I cannot get used to that. The sun is hotter here than anywhere I remember being. It is noticeably hotter than in Wamba and it makes you so very hot while walking. Then, most of the time, except on walks that cross the river, water is scarce.*
>
> *Journal Entry, August 1993, about the Lemons and my friend Meidimultim: That little settlement is the one I really liked before. They were very friendly and kind, and had given us fresh milk to drink. The husband was not home this time, but the younger wife (Meidimultim) was, and she was just as friendly. She gave us fresh milk almost right away again. We ended up staying until 2:45 p.m. talking and visiting. She was so friendly and open . . . In fact we don't want to stay at Lemons again. They are fairly hospitable, but not really. Each day we stay they give us less water than on the previous one. We gave them 1 ¹/₂ kg of sugar and a large bag of tea leaves. We also have already given the husband a flashlight and batteries twice. After two days, they wanted more sugar. Today we have run out of sugar completely—we gave more to Lemon (the husband) when they asked, also to an old mom, also to Meidimultim and then more tea leaves . . . Anyway the Lemon's are hospitable but not as much as they ought to be (by Samburu standards). The small amount of water they allow us—not enough this time to permit face washing in the morning—is not customary. At Meidimultim's, she wanted us to bathe. She told us to empty our container of dirty (well) water so she could put clean (river water) in. We said we didn't need to bathe then, thanks, but we took the water for our drinking container.*

I noted these little details (and my complaints) concerning hospitality because after a long, hot walk with just a little salty, medicine-flavored water to drink, being offered tea or fresh milk is highly meaningful, as any Samburu knows. The daily demands of existence—long walks taking cattle, camels, goats, and sheep for water and grazing, walking an hour or more for water to carry on one's back or on the backs of donkeys, lugging firewood from the nearest place it can be collected—these are some of the activities around which rural Samburu life is organized. And for those who are accustomed to it, all is well and good. If too many animals die, however, or if animals are not sufficient to start with, then the fact that the amount of water and grazing directly affects the amount of milk for adults and children to drink becomes even more meaningful. The health of animals and people is indeed interdependent. Likewise, it is pressing that those who have enough share with those who do not. To leave someone thirsty or hungry when you have water or food to give is more than unkindness—it is a calamitous wrongdoing.

> *Journal Entry, December 1992. I found a bottle cap under the car seat last night, so Lydia made a kerosene lamp with the beer bottle we had. Musa made dinner (Lydia made it the night before and my turn is coming). John told stories to the children (except Jen, who was talking to me).[1] It rained very hard, with thunder and lightning. I felt very vulnerable—up here in the mountains. Yesterday, after the lightning of the day before, we saw a milk calabash hanging at a settlement gate (two actually—one on each side). Lydia said that they were there so that Nkai would not kill them with the lightning. Then again today we saw beads hanging over a house doorway and Lydia said they were there for the same reason as the calabashes we saw yesterday. Also yesterday, while we were cooking our lunch, a man peeped through a hole beneath the window. Lydia and the others (all Samburu) got very angry and yelled at him. Just a few minutes later, Jen accidentally knocked the pot off the fire, spoiling a great deal of the food—we salvaged as much as possible from the floor. They said the food fell because the man peeped at it. They said that for Samburu, if someone peeks at others' food, that food will spoil somehow or will upset the stomachs of those eating it.*

Only a couple of months into my fieldwork, I did not realize that it was not the eyes of others that was the problem—it was the fact that we did not share our food with the man peeking at us that caused Jen's accident. Samburu herself, Lydia no doubt understood this, but her explanation highlights the tensions and ambivalence people can feel when they believe they have *just* enough. Angry with those who would remind them of social obligation—especially if they feel that need is not as great as curiosity—they blame another's eyes rather than their own failure to share. And indeed, as I discussed in Chapter 5, the eyes of a person do have efficacy. Nevertheless, that efficacy is only in response to what is seen—selfishness and other forms of wrongdoing. As fieldwork progressed, I would continue to witness the suffering brought by "eyes," a suffering that was invariably felt on both sides. Over a year after Jen overturned this soup pot, a cooking fire spread beyond the firestones to consume my friend Nolrafiki's belongings. As she related to me, everything I had ever given her was lost in that fire and her daughter's hand severely burned—all because of the eyes of others who had seen the gifts Nolrafiki had not shared. So many burns, so many deaths, in the midst of daily, unremarkable pleasures: How to think and write it? And what does the *movement to writing* mean?

Back to the (Theoretical) Beginning

As a doctoral student trained in the 1980s and '90s I was steeped in the theoretical texts of the "literary turn" and certain that memory transformed experience into fictions. Geertz had already told us that cultures were texts to be interpreted, while Derrida's "liberatory play" now meant that there was no single correct interpretation, no Truth. At the same time, Jacques Lacan's work was exciting feminists (and Julia Kristeva's related work alternately exciting and exasperating them) with new ways of understanding subjectivity—as relational, as defined against the other in ways that gave a foothold on how to write from the margins. In time, another current of Lacan's and Kristeva's work became important, a current that coupled with fresh readings of Husserl and Merleau-Ponty to define what I would call the "sensory turn" in anthropology. The Lacanian Real, the Kristevan *chora*, as well as new readings of phenomenology, have entered anthropology in interesting ways, making the literary turn bend the corner slightly as scholars in the humanities and social sciences struggle to reclaim the sensuous immediacy that they somehow lost in the play of signs and texts. Yet the fictions of memory remain—strengthened by readings of Pierre Bourdieu, Renato Rosaldo, Johannes Fabian, and theorists outside of anthropology. We can only claim partial Truths, fictionalized memories, sensuous immediacy mediated by the play of signs and memory, yet we are mesmerized by nostalgia and longing. We celebrate immediacy even within the *idea* of loss.

I did not experience the *idea* of loss in Samburu District, though. Increasingly, I had difficulty reconciling the literary turn (and, eventually, the persisting dichotomies of the sensuous turn) with my fieldwork. The problem became an ethical one for me—what are the implications, I asked myself, of imagining memory and its narratives to be fictional re-creations? What are the implications of suggesting that the gap between word and world (which Derrida theorized so powerfully)—between signifier and signified, name and thing, raw experience and memory—yawns widely enough to make immediacy "always already" an experience come too late? What are the implications, in other words, of conceding the loss of real experience and immediacy in their Truth, consoling ourselves with the celebration of the play of signs, of partial truths, of loss itself as the founding moment of subjectivity? My response has been that, while we must indeed resist totalizing narratives and the political hazards of naïve realism, we must do so while expanding our notion of what characterizes experience—claiming immediacy even if we cannot hold it. Yet how should we theorize immediacy?

Immediacy is not a new concern in the social sciences and humanities. Within psychoanalytic theory Jacques Lacan and, later, Julia Kristeva have reinterpreted Freud in ways that have led to a rethinking of unitary subjectivity, personhood, consciousness, and the relationship between oppositions like conscious/unconscious and mind/body. In the late 1980s and the 1990s, linguistic anthropologists drew upon Kristeva's as well as Bahktin's notions of intersubjectivity and intertextuality to understand how cultural meaning and forms are produced out of the dialogic encounter (see, for example Bauman and Briggs 1990; Mannheim and Tedlock 1995).[2] These approaches had their counterparts in phenomenological approaches to experience and the body (Csordas 1994b; Desjarlais 1992; Jackson 1996; Lambek and Strathern 1998; Kapferer 1997; Stoller 1989a, b, 1995, 1997; Stewart 1996; Strathern 1996).[3] What all of these approaches share, whether in linguistic or cultural anthropology, and whether based in phenomenology or the body generally, is an emphasis on experience, particularly sensuous or immediate experience. And, not coincidentally, this concern with sensuousness is visible in another strand of anthropology in the 1990s, in scholarship pertaining to "things" drawing variously upon Lacan, reinterpretations of Marx, and the Comaroffs' creative synthesis of global capitalism, textuality, and "occult" practices (Comaroff and Comaroff 1993; Masquelier 2000; Moore and Sanders et al. 2001; Spyer et al. 1998).

While this "sensory turn" has made a subtle shift in the first decade of the twenty-first century in recognition of immediacy's elusiveness (see Farquhar 2002), anthropology's fascination with embodiment, "materiality," and the critical play on substantive dualism has persisted. Thus, in a provocative essay Bill Brown (2001) attempts to destabilize materiality in alluding to reality while simultaneously maintaining materiality's philosophical utility by asserting that it is an intentional turning away from that same reality—perhaps in favor of the "Real." In this context he notes the "delight" that

has been taken in historicism's "desire to make contact with the 'real'," in the emergence of material culture studies and the vitality of material history, in accounts of everyday life and the material *habitus*, as in the "return of the real" in contemporary art, this is inseparable, surely, from the very pleasure taken in "objects of the external world," however problematic that external world may be—however phantasmatic the externality of that world may be theorized to be. (Brown 2001: 2)

The "real" here is not reality—Brown leaves reality out of quotes, referring to it as the external world—but rather the "mental" objects created in the process of humans' impressions of the world presumed to be composed of things. Indeed, the distinction between the Real—the discursive memories and entailments of human experience—and the external world of things is a crucial one. Brown's point is that it is only by leaving aside the question of the external world that scholars of material studies have been able to "grant them [things] their potency" (7), that is, to understand them at the horizon of human experience. Yet I am troubled by what I see as the far-reaching implications of setting reality (as some phantasmatic thing) aside. In doing so we may indeed open up exciting new possibilities, but what we at the same time foreclose may be other ways of experiencing reality, other ontologies, even other dualisms than that implied by starting from the position of materiality. Moreover, in treating reality as a phantasm, or fiction of the imagination, we take the ethical risk of consigning experience to the realm of fictional imagination at the precise moment when we should instead be asking how *both experience and the imagination are real.* In beginning to pursue this thought I would like to reexamine two crucial influences on sensuous anthropology—Kristeva's notion of chora, which has been inflected in approaches to embodiment, and Lacan's Real, which continues to surface in approaches to materiality. In doing so, I am tracing recent histories within anthropological thought as they pertain to the sensuous turn, hoping both to identify what anthropologists have recognized as phenomenology's elusory/illusory aspects at their source and to recuperate them—affirming the turn toward expansive experience that I have claimed throughout this book. At the same time, Kristeva's and Lacan's are powerful Grand Narratives whose efficacious entailments have been globally transposed. Thus, I will eventually and necessarily return to the problematics of the illusory—staking a claim not only for the ways in which the imagination is always real but for the hazards attending a real produced out of the imagined.

IMMEDIACY, CHORA, AND SENSUOUS EMBODIMENT

Julia Kristeva's theory has been controversial within feminist theory and anthropology (Butler 1990; Gross 1986, 1989; Spivak 1981; Straight 1991). Pertinent to my purposes here, Kristeva (1984 [1974]) has made a brilliant attempt to grasp sensuous immediacy in the process of describing the individuation of the subject—as it is understood by Euro-Americans. Kristeva names what she terms the chora as the body's non-expressive drives, which are ordered by the mother's own body (25, 27).[4] This is pure prelinguistic bodily being, the space of preverbal semiotic (as Kristeva uses the latter term). According to Kristeva, the chora never disappears; instead, it remains ever-present as a simultaneous disruption and partner to the symbolic "modality," which is socially and culturally ordered language. In this contested interplay between semiotic and symbolic, Kristeva identifies the primordial and eternal alienation and division within the subject (see also Kristeva 1991). The subject is always already divided within itself, and revolutionary poetic language takes advantage of this to liberate us from oppressive political hegemonies. It points to other possibilities always already within us in its refusal of particular symbolic orders. Of course, she does not answer the question of why prelinguistic chora is necessarily liberatory. Following Peirce, we might question what habits are produced by every instance of poetic language.

In any case, Kristeva suggests that the (Euro-American) ego is constantly formed anew out of the struggle between the semiotic and symbolic modalities. If, however, the ego is a Hegelian third (which simultaneously refuses synthesis in her thinking),[5] Kristeva follows Hegel farther, identifying negativity as a fourth. Negativity is not negation but an affirmative that she holds as "inseparable from Being": Negativity is "the *very movement of heterogeneous matter,* inseparable from its differentiation's symbolic function" (113). Defining negativity further and materially, Kristeva posits it as "the *separation of matter,* one of the preconditions of symbolicity" (117).

This sounds very much like Peirce's prescissive Ground (see Appendix 1)—a process of grasping and delimiting immediate experience prior to its mediation in cognition. Kristeva's elaboration of it places it before language, in the moment of rejection and separation from the maternal body, seeming to place it prior to the signifying practices Peirce would identify as *Thirdness.* The Kristevan "subject" forever bodily remembers and reenacts the Freudian moment when the mother's body became separate and objectified—a moment in developmental time at which the chora is met by the symbolic order, the semiotic becomes cognizable in antithesis, and the (Euro-American) subject is born. At this point in the subject's continually evolving present, the chora continues to have existence in the semiotic that erupts into the symbolic, and alternatives to the symbolic order become possible. Negativity is both the space and process at and during which this eruption of the semiotic into the symbolic occurs. Indeed, it is the material process of dividing that renders it—and the sign as well as the subject—possible. Negativity is a (Peircean) prescission, "cutting off," dividing, that makes the subject an identity separate from a (m)other and a member of a family and a society separate from others. In dividing, it locates and identifies as well.

As pathbreaking as Kristeva's notion of negativity is in many ways, it is problematic that even as she offers a theory of how signification occurs, a way out of Platonic dualisms, and an insertion of the body's importance to understanding the subject, her thought ends up offering instead a Western metaphor for signification, a reassertion of dualisms, and a body separate from mind. Even as Kristeva locates her chora in so-called material relations of the body, her theory reenunciates the western mythos of alienation and lack, which has appeared in various permutations from Marx and Freud to Lacan. Moreover, when she suggests that her notion of negativity designates "the process that exceeds the signifying subject, binding him to the laws of objective struggles in nature and society" (119), she exposes the division within her thinking between body and mind. For Kristeva, it seems, the process of prescissing Ground—of grasping immediate experience in sensory ways that go beyond Euro-American understandings of sensing[6]—is not an irreducible part of being human but rather is something outside of every human, like a Durkheimian social fact.

Importantly, these assumptions recur in phenomenological approaches. For example, Michael Jackson (1996), attempting to define an approach that can approximate the immediacy of people's experiences as lived in a real world, deftly argues that the "phenomenal world of human consciousness and activity is never reducible to that which allegedly determines the condition of its possibility" (22). Later, however, he concludes that "our gestures, acts and modes of comportment do not invariably depend on an *a priori* cognitive understanding . . . The meaning of practical knowledge lies in what is accomplished through it, not in what conceptual order may be said to underlie or precede it" (34).

While approaches to phenomenological anthropology like Jackson's,[7] and likewise Kristeva's description of chora and negativity, represent attempts to duplicate immediacy, their insistence on rupture, on a break between the so-called semiotic and symbolic functions—or for Jackson, between being and action—belies their claims. Indeed, both make similar moves. Kristeva's separation of language as a special level of cognition apart from, and in antagonism with, other levels of cognition and consciousness amounts to a conflation of language with mind so that symbolic/language/mind struggles in tension with the semiotic as cognitive experience of the body. Similarly, Jackson posits an acting, embodied subject for whom histories of being are unimportant, as if it were possible to separate *this* experience from the dynamic, intertwined, intersubjective histories of experience by which this subject moves from moment to moment.

In this context, I would note Jackson's approving nod to Michael Oakeshott's claim that "theoretical knowledge is more like a *post facto* rationalization of what is said and done than an explanation of it" (Jackson 1996: 35).[8] Yet *every* sign is mediated, whether linguistic, poetic, theoretical, or otherwise (a Third, in Peirce's terms). Humans do not enact conscious signs in tension with unconscious ones, theoretical ones in tension with glossolaliac ones. Thus, while I appreciate Jackson's desire to avoid simultaneously overintellectualizing experience and relegating it to overly deterministic "structures of the habitus," his claim that experience does not depend upon the understandings that "precede" it suggests an inaccurate approximation of experience itself. Experience as "practical knowledge" is already a signifying practice (in Peircean

Thirdness) that *must* bear on what experientially precedes it or risk an idealism that can treat experiences—human suffering, for example—in the abstract. Yet this sort of abstractness is precisely what Jackson wants to avoid.

Contra Oakeshott, all knowledge is a backward reflection, and to understand the raw experiences upon which it is based we need to have an adequate view of experience as expansive and reincarnating. It is only in this way that we can strenuously and repeatedly assert that truthful stories of pain follow real pain and as such are not merely attempts to make sense of suffering. *Rather, pain as a "story" in cognition, pain as a "story" in thought, is itself a form of suffering.* The sensory, immediate experience of pain (in Peircean Secondness) reincarnates into Pain in cognition (signifying Thirdness), and the latter undergoes nearly infinite cognitive processes before it becomes a narrative of conscious, enunciated experience. Insofar as that narrative is the culmination of these many real incarnations, a narrative of one's own suffering continues to *be* a form of suffering—a point I think most phenomenological anthropologists would agree with and that I want to push them a bit farther to make. The human is whole every single moment, living a constant process of sign relation. Where body becomes separate from mind, it does so at a metalevel of signification where humans meet in overlapping circles of community to reflect together upon their own being-in-the-world.

Yet human experience often belies the conceptual boundaries that contribute to its (re)enactment because the human is not only whole but constantly in movement—shifting with reality and simultaneously producing it. This is more than imaginary movement and is often dangerous in its elusiveness, a point I will return to.

Immediacy, the Lacanian Real, and the World of Things

Not surprisingly, given Kristeva's dependence upon Lacan, Lacan's and Kristeva's notions about the origin of the symbolic function out of the infant's separation from and rejection, by and of, the mother's body are nearly isomorphic. However, Kristeva's elaboration focuses on the semiotic as liberatory potential, while what I want to draw attention to is Lacan's interpretation of the unconscious and the "Real."

In Lacan's exemplary use of the famous fort-da game, the game of now you see it (her), now you don't as a means to pass the time, the child must learn to do without the mother (in a Western notion of caregiving) by some means. The game becomes the first "death of the thing" in the process whereby it surpasses the missing mother in pleasure and significance. The game, as diversion from what is actually desired, does more than substitute for the lack of the mother—it draws attention away from what is desired and produces pleasure from the lack rather than the presence. The game—or the fetish—is desired instead of what the game refers to, and whatever the lack refers to is buried in what Freud labeled the unconscious. In this process, death becomes the first fetish. That is, as the child pronounces the sounds that will command the plaything to appear or disappear, the child learns the language that signals absence, killing the "thing" in a move that both associates language with absence—of toys and mothers—and establishes the point of the meditation—the name and the thing are not one. Indeed, as Hegel also said, the name annihilates the thing in its existence:[9] "Thus the symbol manifests itself first of all as the murder of the thing, and this death constitutes in the subject the externalization of his desire. The first symbol in which we recognize humanity in its vestigial traces is the sepulture, and the intermediary of death can be recognized in every relation where man [*sic*] comes to the life of his history" (Lacan 1968: 84).

If, according to Lacan's famous interpretation of Freud, the "unconscious is structured like a language" (1968: 32), it is structured as a specific kind of language, a language characterized by substitution and exchange—and death in the process of the murder of the thing—based on what is again, as in Kristeva's thought, theorized as a universal developmental moment. For Lacan, the unconscious is the site of this repressed knowledge, and, as such, it is a collection of scenes of forgetting, of pleasurable diversions that represent many forgotten things but ultimately represent a lack that cannot be filled because it is the fact of dependence (on an/other or m/other) itself.

Again, as with Kristeva, there is a crucial moment when the Western subject is formed on the basis of separation from a bodily need. Yet Lacan's moment, as it remains in the adult unconscious, turns on a particular notion of what he refers to as the Real in relation to the death of things, of a (spiritual) symbolization in relation to (bodily/material) things. In a lucid discussion of the Lacanian fetish, Henry Krips (1999) defines the Lacanian Real: "The Real may take either of two forms: either an unsymbolizable point of excess, that which Freud associates with das Ding, or a residue, a leftover from the process of symbolization, a piece of white noise from which all categorizable sounds have been sifted" (41). The Real is not reality, then, nor immediate experience. Rather, for Lacan, the Real comprises an endless series of memories, ideas, and impressions that produce anxiety because in them, "the symbolic order breaks down" (Krips 1999: 37). The Real is not what is but is, on the contrary, a reminder that things are not as they appear, a reminder that something has been lost or "murdered." The Real is not "out there" but "within"—it is a site of disturbance from the excessive realm of the unconscious. The unconscious is the holder of the excess memories (not brute experiences) that cannot be named in the set of symbolic forms that constitutes the Lacanian unconsciousness. When this excess impinges upon consciousness, something like Freud's uncanny intervenes.

I think that Lacan's notion of the Real impinging on consciousness is an excellent metaphor for the process by which, in Peirce's terms, "man" becomes a sign. The Real is the metaphorical repository for what cannot be constantly held in conscious awareness, though it has been laid down in memory. This is what I find the most intriguing and useful about it, but, as with Kristeva's terms, I would simultaneously point up the Real as Lacan's peculiarly western notion of a sexual libidinal economy and further identify its usefulness in presenting just that—a Euro-American ontology denoting the signifying process whereby the *symbolic* excess that *Euro-Americans* cannot account for is rationalized.

In this way, a present crisis or anxiety is identified as a state of (Western) being, and an explanation offered for its origin. In so doing, a myth of human origins is created, a myth about where language and (individuated) subjectivity itself come from. It is a myth of primordial alienation, accounting for the selfish excess of Euro-American desire, of an exchange principle as much without end as it is without origin, insofar as its origins are a concealment of a lack that cannot be filled. While a number of scholars have raised caution concerning the tendency to assume that this ravenous process of globalization amounts to a global homogeneity (Appadurai 1996; see also Jameson and Miyoshi et al. 1998), the transposition of the ontology of loss and excess onto our interlocutors subtly reinsinuates that homogeneity in another guise.

In response to Derrida's "liberatory play," the imagination, and the fictions of the Real, I have moved to discursive embodiment, to materiality, to theorizations of the stuff we wish we could hold onto. In doing so I have critiqued Derrida, Kristeva, and Lacan while yet acquiescing in the gap, the duality, and the death of *being* they theorize. Like Salman Rushdie, I have admitted our loss, the underside of our imagination, and moved on:

It may be that exiles or emigrants or expatriates, are haunted by some sense of loss, some urge to reclaim, to look back, even at the risk of being mutated into pillars of salt. But if we do look back, we must also do so in the knowledge—which gives rise to profound uncertainties—that our physical alienation from India almost inevitably means that we will not be capable of reclaiming precisely the thing that was lost; that we will, in short create fictions, not actual cities or villages, but invisible ones, imaginary homelands, Indias of the mind. (Salman Rushdie 1992: 10)

Of course, that very imagination can be liberatory (see Straight 2005c). At the same time, even as we must agree with Rushdie about the transformation of that homeland in memory, it is simultaneously expedient to assert that (as is often the case) the fictionalized re-creation of former homes is based in the *reality* of them. Homes and lives were indeed lost, and however altered in memory they might be, there are real losses inscribed there too. This is not as obvious as it appears—the imagination has become such a powerful trope that we question every history, interrogate the claims of every memory,[10] and accept only partial truths. We are delightedly at play in the Real. Yet which of our interlocutors (or us) experiences partially, rather than as an absolute plenitude, an undeniable truth? The witness, too, experiences in plenitude, sensually provoked by her interlocutors, touched into speaking shared memory.

There is some irony in the fact that the Samburu take responsibility for the ontological cut—not doubting intersubjective crossings within experience—while Descartes' philosophical descendants affirm that only the cut is real, dividing one singular experience from another and precluding the affirmation of an/other. Yet, by way of my hybridized reading of a Samburu ontology, I want to give nothing up but, instead, enunciate as medium and witness, experiences that are always already extraordinary—[11]in their paradoxical intersubjectivity and inscrutability and in their continual unfolding within themselves.

Yet, remember I said that I would return to the problematics of the illusory. I will not acquiesce in the experiential gap—I will not, that is, conflate one dichotomy with another nor give up my claims to expansive experience—but I must recognize the ironies of the slide as one experience permutates into another, including within the imagination. The Samburu, of course, belong within the same historical space as that which Lacan's libidinal economy of the murdered thing encompasses so eloquently—and here the imaginings of dichotomy operate within the slide as well. This fact has consequences that are both troubling and forgettable. The Samburu are modernity's other—the sometime imaginary foil to an imaginary modernity (Latour 1993)—who are increasingly engaged in the self-assigned task of imagining themselves into the evaporating promise of a strange modernity that is losing its desire to imagine *them*. A Eurocentric philosophy cannot admit the Samburu, except as the rupture of an other that guarantees the "self" its subjectivity, a fact that makes it difficult if not impossible to suggest alternative ontologies as plausible—though I have done so here.

In more mundane terms, a Eurocentric geopolitics likewise has little time to imagine the Samburu, and neither does a Euro-American anthropology.[12] This is largely because the Eurocentric other has become a virtual reserve army, a cornucopia of commodifiable imaginaries ready to be invoked as convenient—as were the Japanese during World War II, the Vietnamese in the Vietnam era, and the recklessly conflated Arab and Muslim in this post-9/11 era. In turbulent times likes these, the Samburu become convenient exotics for the *leisurely* imagination, soothing interludes between one horror and another.

Where is reality here? Where is the gap when the imagination's real effects as witnessed in the "War on Terror" are so blatant? Let me consider in this vein Jean and John Comaroff's (2004) contemplation of how "illusion and fantasy have been implicated in the work of law enforcement in recent South African history" (805). The Comaroffs casually argue—quite reasonably take for granted, that is—that the imaginary is "grounded in the experience of the real" (807), going on to consider the productive possibilities of violent imaginaries. In other terms and with different aims, they demonstrate the facileness of a modernist ideology that would oppose imagination to experience. Indeed, it is more than facile; it is *strategically* false. The imagination, as I have said, can be—but is not currently—liberatory. Rather, it is a tactic whose power lies precisely in the belief in the modernist distinction between reality and fiction. Thus, for example, terrorism as an idea is both an incarnation of experiential terror and a tactical claim to terrors that *might be but are not (yet) real.*

Expansive experience is a way of theorizing this movement between the thoughtfully, imaginatively experienced and the experientially imagined, a movement that can be both wondrously and dangerously productive and that is not about the rupture and the gap but rather about a continuous sliding from one to the next incarnation. Indeed, to imagine the gap is to reimagine the facile logic of the imagination opposed to experience. The dream, the vision, and the nightmare are productive imaginings unfolding and folding into reality. Yet, even as the slide is inscrutable, the experiential witness must be heeded—we must relentlessly persevere in distinguishing between truth and lies. In the slide that is not a gap, in the movement that is not merely between one thing and another, immediacy must be granted its conceptual space even amid its own paradoxical impossibility. And so we come back again, recognizing the hazards of (particularly state-sponsored) imaginaries that monstrously deform experiences that do not belong to their authors—while simultaneously and crucially affirming the reality of the experiences of so many others, whose sufferings as well as joys undermine the claims of Official Memories, point toward alternative priorities, and open up a space for possibilities that some of us have not yet imagined how to imagine.

Traces of Nolsintani

This first photo appears on my web page. It is Nolsintani holding a calabash and smiling, looking away from the camera. She enjoys having her picture "taken," and this was a joyous occasion—there had been a lot of young people asking my husband and me to take their pictures and a lot of primping in the process. Were they concerned about their loip being captured? It would not appear so, though the response range is wide, from people in their thirties and older who still do not wish to be photographed to the light-hearted teasing of one of my friends that he wanted me to weaken him several times—by snapping his photo (he prefaced it with a specific reference to loip, but the sexual "play" was deliberate as well).

Nolsintani's joy is obvious in this photograph. This is a mechanical reproduction of a photograph that produces its own context from what enframes it—the camel in the background, the thorn branches, the dry ground. Like a mischievous, roaming loip, the photo—neither alive nor dead—cannot change even if it can trigger transformations in those who view it. (What associations does the image have for you?) It can only display a piece of what happened that day—and the rest is for me to tell you. We were talking, laughing, playing with several cameras. Yet it was an ordinary day. The children played, including ours, the young people took the livestock out to graze, animals were milked, water fetched, tea prepared. And the anthropologists were there, so everyone had enough sugar in their tea (except me—I can always take more sugar).

This second image (a film still) also shows Nolsintani, but she does not seem joyous here. Her eyes are huge—she stares into the camera as one astonished, as if to disenchant it or prevent it from enchanting her. I recognized that look as she was being filmed—she had it on the second day I knew her, on her wedding day in July 1994. My husband and I were filming her, and she stared into the camera like one transfixed. I wondered then if she was frightened, but when I saw that look again in 2004 I supposed she could not be, not precisely anyway. She has been filmed so many times, smiling, laughing, doing ordinary things. Yet, what is she trying to do with her eyes here? She says the camera fascinates her. And she wants to see every photo ever taken of her, back to the first ones we took in 1994. What can I do with these two looks—the one a look away from the camera toward the humans she was joking with, and the other a look directly at its lens, apparently mesmerized?[13]

For anthropologists, photographs are typically tools, simply representing their interlocutors to illustrate a point or for the sake of visual representation itself. Is the photo more immediate than these words? Where is the connection being made between you and photo, between you and

Figure 12. Nolsintani smiling while holding her calabash in 2002.

words? Now, if I send you to the store (can I send you?) to buy sour milk which I tell you to place near an outdoor fire, breathing all of it in, and then I tell you that this is like the smoky milk smell of a Samburu house—have we gotten closer? In *Sensuous Scholarship*, Paul Stoller (1997) contemplates the problem of how to write in the manner of the griot—poet-historians who pass on social knowledge not by "owning" history but by being "possessed by the forces of the past" (25). The griot's is a "historically conscientious and respectfully decentered conception and practice of depicting social life, a profoundly embodied

Figure 13. Nolsintani staring into the camera in 2004 (left), and staring into the video camera for the first time in 1994 (right). The images fail to capture time—the sustained moment during which she persisted in staring into the camera.

conception and practice of ethnography that reverberates with the tension between the political and the poetic" (26). Stoller acknowledges that simply to write in sensuously evocative ways is not enough, but that nevertheless the challenge of presenting the immediacy of life is a worthy one.

Evocatio is a conjuring act, a summoning forth of what transcends and surrounds the human—the Romans used it to usurp foreign divinities (Ando 2004). These words here, which you are reading now, are not all that I meant to write. I have conjured something, though, and you have experienced the "more" that only you can imagine. This thought, this feeling I have right now, looking at Nolsintani's smile and then at her huge eyes, is not in these words. And these images indeed are not Nolsintani, as the Surrealists cleverly pointed out in images meant to provoke and surprise.[14] Of course, loip is there—*something* of Samburu personhood is in the photo, in the recording, and also, I think, in the words. The photo, like my text, performs its own evocatio. To suggest a gap is to underestimate the intersubjectivity of experience, to suppose that imagination, whether of truth or of lies, has no connection with experience and no efficacy. Yet we know that it has. This is Nolsintani smiling. And it isn't. This is Nolsintani aware of the camera's possession of her. And it isn't. This is my ethnography of Samburu experience. And it isn't. I have been the medium, the silent transcript of the witness, the person in the text possessing you with the possibility of prescissing Samburu, of imaginatively experiencing the in-between of the in-between, the tracks with tears, the trace that is a tiny joy, a little suffering.

It's raining. A little more, a little more, and grass will fill the plains, fill the cows, fill the stomachs of the children. This is what I think of when I smell *ntalakwany,* that sweet Samburu grass. This is what Samburu fathers want their children to think of too.

From the Derridean Gap to Theorizations of Consciousness and Forgetting: Defending Expansive Experience Within the Play of Signs

> *We have no power of Intuition, but every cognition is determined logically by previous cognitions.*
>
> —*Charles Sanders Peirce*

Saussure's Sign and the Derridean Critique

Saussure's (1959) theory of the sign inspired a generation of structuralists committed to understanding both the mind and human societies as systems.[1] Although structuralism has been tremendously varied, neo-Cartesian, Kantian dualistic subjectivism underpins Saussure's theory of the sign and various forms of structuralism, as well as Derridean poststructuralism. Saussure suggested that linguistic signs comprised two parts, the sign-vehicle, or signifier, and the concept, or signified. Besides this two-part sign, Saussure proposed to separate the study of language into two domains, *langue* (the unchanging system of signs in relation to one another) and *parole* (language as it is put to use by communities of speakers). While suggesting the importance of the study of parole, Saussure devoted himself to the study of langue, of language as a system of signs comprising a structure that was autonomous from the community of language users and that could be "seen" apart from that community.

Saussure did not deny reality, but his double arbitrariness of signs effected a sort of Cartesian dualism. Saussure's model suggests two binary oppositions, one dividing mind in the form of concept from matter in the shape of sign-vehicles, while the other divides mind and concept from world. First, that is, he suggested an arbitrary, or unmotivated, relationship between sign-vehicles and concepts (an idea that has been challenged).[2] Besides this arbitrariness, Saussure also posited an unmotivated relationship between the concept, or signified, and the world. Saussure understood language to organize and categorize the potentially infinite matter popularly known as reality.

Derrida (1976) based his critique of structuralism largely on Saussure's two-part notion of the sign. If, in developing his method, Saussure did not address himself to ontological questions, Derrida set himself the task of making Saussure's ontological assumptions explicit. However, even if some of Derrida's points are philosophically cogent, they are largely based on a (creative) misreading of Saussure (Ellis 1989) and in many instances could be seen as inspired by Saussure rather than critical of him. Derrida reads Saussure by way of Plato, repeating the mantra of centuries of philosophy when he draws attention to the idea that Saussure's signs are defined in relation to what they are not. In that negative space of not-this, Derrida carves his indeterminacy of meaning, his infinite "play." According to Derrida, if there is no determinate relationship between concept and thing, understanding and world, then there is no single "Truth," no positive Being, no transcendental signified— that is, no positive concept that can stand alone and define itself by merely being what it is. The result is a liberatory "play," the license to entertain an infinite number of interpretations of texts, to effect a sort of Nietzschean mythic creation that constantly shifts, thereby eluding the authority of would-be Grand Narratives that give power to particular groups over others.[3] At least, that is the socially responsible interpretation of Derrida's accomplishment. A more skeptical interpretation might be that an infinite "play" of meaning can preclude ethics as well, forgetting the inevitable (even if shifting) group of powerful "players" ever lurking in the shadows, making their playful interpretations heard loudest.[4]

Derrida takes the idea of an unmotivated relationship between signifier and signified in the development of a language and transforms it into a Platonic gap between eternal Ideas and mutable Copies. "The difference between signified and signifier belongs in a profound and implicit way to the totality of the great epoch covered by the history of metaphysics, and in a more explicit and more systematically articulated way to the narrower epoch of Christian creationism and infinitism when these appropriate the resources of Greek conceptuality" (1976: 13). He uses his (no doubt intentional as well as creative) (mis)reading of Saussure to critique the notion that there are any eternal Ideas or Forms at all. Instead, copies are all we have, all we can have access to, perhaps all there is. If there is no transcendental Being, no god, no originary Truth, then meaning is shifting, indeterminate, radically relative.

Yet, I thought, how many ways can Truth be revised around a little girl's death? Sometimes it is the most terrible signs that force us to ask our questions differently. I cannot take even Saussure's sign and Derrida's gap for granted. Samburu experience word and world differently. I need more than the usual attention to signs. My vignettes of a little girl's death in Chapter 1 are my texts, my expressions of the Real. I can pretty them up, dress them down, I can change what happened if I want to. I can even excise them entirely. Nevertheless, there is also the writing in thought, in memory. Whatever I do, she is there, however transubstantiated. Some reincarnation of that reality is there—an assemblage of positionings in the car, a useless bellows, a little death.

Admittedly, the death is one thing and my memory of it another. And her father's and mother's memories of it yet quite another. Derrida seems to have me trapped in his (as well as Lacan's) prisonhouse of language. For her father and mother she did not merely die, she died for a reason. She died *because*. It may have been another death before hers that they failed to chase away completely. It may have been some other fault they failed to remedy. It may even have been the fault of the little girl's grandfather or great-grandfather. Whatever the reason, it would eventually be known, and that knowledge cannot be disentangled from the experience of death itself. These are signs, not reality. These are the Lacanian Real. And yet, I am not willing to surrender reality—I am claiming that it is *there*, reincarnated, transubstantiated in memory, in every kind of text. I want to suggest that reality is radically implicated in human imagination and experience, even there, within the Real. That is in the elusive land of universals. In the land of difference, I want to consider the idea that within the Real, the indeterminacy of Being makes it necessary to consider ontologies strikingly different from our own.

The Peircean Triadic Sign

Peirce's theory of the sign would appear at fundamental odds with Saussure's, and insofar as it resolves much of Derrida's critique of the latter, it would also appear as a challenge to Derrida, although Derrida does engage with Peirce—on which, more later. Notably, two triads are related integrally to one another in Peirce's thought, an irreducibly triadic sign and a triadic ontology.[5] I would suggest that, in his exposition of a triadic ontology, Peirce places his sign as triadic process at the horizon of human experience and consciousness, referencing reality (somewhat obliquely) under the term of Ground. As we shall see, it is possible to read an indeterminate Being in Peirce, at this intriguingly messy nexus of human, world, and sign. However, and crucially, an indetermi-

nate Being does not mean indeterminate Truth, as in Derrida's thinking. Through Peirce I suggest that reality constantly shifts between the
determinate and indeterminate, with Being as a process of engaging
with and *be-ing* it. In its determinate moments (or events), reality
becomes something (like substance) we might be able to agree upon.

I will begin with Peirce's triadic sign sharply contrasted with Saussure's dyadic one. However, keep in mind that Peirce's triadic sign is one
process within a more encompassing process of Being. His sign, that is,
can be taken as a metaphor for cognition and thought—processes that
are part of experience and reality without being the sum total of them.
One way to conceive of this is to consider Peirce's triadic sign as describing processes in the Real (as in Lacan), while his triadic ontology offers
a way of understanding reality as it pertains to what I am calling *expansive
experience* (which eventually transubstantiates *into* the Real). I will attend
to Peirce's triadic ontology after I elucidate his sign as it relates to cognition.

Peirce's sign comprises a representamen, an object, and an interpretant. While Saussure's signifier is a sound- or word-shape, even if imagined in thought, Peirce's representamen is not confined to the
linguistic. For Peirce particularly, the representamen is the tool (not
necessarily linguistic) by way of which an object is known, while the
interpretant is the illumination that *exceeds* the representamen's mode
of knowing the object:[6]

Now a sign has, as such, three references: first, it is a sign [representamen] *to*
some thought which interprets it [interpretant]; second, it is a sign [representa-
men] *for* some object to which in that thought it is equivalent; third, it is a sign,
in some respect or quality [ground], which brings it into connection with its
object. (Peirce 1958: 51–52; bracketed portions mine)

A sign, or *representamen*, is something which stands to somebody for something
in some respect or capacity. It addresses somebody, that is creates in the mind
of that person an equivalent sign, or perhaps a more developed sign. That sign
which it creates I call the *interpretant* of the first sign. The sign stands for something, its *object*. It stands for that object, not in all respects, but in reference to a
sort of idea, which I have sometimes called the *ground* of the representamen.
(Peirce 1931–35: 2.228)

A representamen can be a word- or sound-shape as in Saussure's signifier, but it can also be a gesture or even a cloud—as in the semiotic
approaches that have developed out of interpretations of Saussure as
well as of Peirce. Moreover, Peirce clearly states that signs develop into
other signs ad infinitum, so that the interpretant of one sign becomes
the representamen of another and the representamen of one sign is the
interpretant of a previous one.

While Saussure's signifier is *one part of a dyadic sign*, for Peirce, the representamen is *already a triadic sign*, relating in turn to another sign (the object of the representamen as word-shape) and to a more fully developed sign (the interpretant). Saussure's signifier is a sound- or word-shape that always denotes the same concept, while in Peirce's terminology that sound- or word-shape is a particular kind of triadic sign (a legisign)[7] taking up the position of representamen for an object (the static and impossible component of Saussure's signified here) to an interpretant.[8] Thus, Saussure's signified must carry the additional burden of the interpretant's specification of meaning, and this it is not equipped to do (see also Sheriff 1989). For this reason, it is not adequate to the task of elucidating communication, thought, and even Being, whether living in texts or in everyday action. Peirce's sign, though, does precisely that.

I take Peirce's triadic sign relation as a metaphoric description of the processes of cognition (including all neural activity) and thought. Peirce's triadic sign describes cognition as a living, continually metamorphosing generator and product of perception and intersubjective understanding.[9] According to Peirce, every representamen has been the interpretant of a previous sign, and every interpretant can form the representamen of a future sign—although it does not have to. The terms representamen, object, and interpretant mark ephemeral positions in an ongoing process of cognition with both linear and nonlinear aspects. There is no closed system of signifiers chained to signifieds (as Derrida would accuse Saussure of) here. Grammar and language as such are not Peirce's primary concern. Rather, meaning, understanding, and belief (as a collection of habits) are.

Yet this ongoing process of signing, this ad infinitum, is precisely the object of Derrida's critique—a critique he manipulates Saussure to make but in which he likewise skillfully engages Peirce. Indeed, Derrida appreciates Peirce's movement "from sign to sign" (Derrida 1976: 48). He praises Peirce's acuity in recognizing that understanding is through signs: "Peirce goes very far in the direction that I have called the deconstruction of the transcendental signified, which, at one time or another, would place a reassuring end to the reference from sign to sign" (49). He continues, following Peirce to one possible conclusion, eliding reality by positing the entire world as sign(s): "The so-called 'thing itself' is always already a *representamen* shielded from the simplicity of intuitive evidence. The *representamen* functions only by giving rise to an *interpretant* that itself becomes a sign and so to infinity" (49).

Derrida is so far right: By the time I recognize the word 'tree' written on a page, for example, I have already processed all of the components of Saussurean linguistics, mostly below the level of conscious awareness. Peirce would argue that triadic relations are involved in this process of *prescissing* (focusing selectively) morphemes, phonemes, and so on, and the newest generation of cognitive scientists would no doubt agree with that assertion.[10] As I work my way up to varying degrees of conscious awareness, I arrive at 'tree' as a recognizable word-shape, a representamen. In an instant, I relate it to a hypothetical object (a concept of tree in some respect—Ground), to a thought (interpretant) that is immediately a grasping of something more about tree. The 'tree' on the page, then, is a representamen for me, though one that is itself already a triadic sign.[11] Thus, 'tree' is the representamen of a sign of possibility (Rheme), which I can develop into further signs. What I am calling attention to is the obvious—we share the same tree in reality, not in any simple way, not in a correspondence theory of truth sort of way. And the simultaneity of different modes of Being means that we presciss trees differently, even if we partake of the same tree in the same instant. It is never the same tree, yet it is.

I think Derrida is wrong in conflating ontology and sign relations, creating a system closed to reality instead of positing the relation between signing and Being in the midst of reality. In a rigorous reading of Peirce a text cannot stand alone as a sign, any more than a tree outside my door or in a Samburu settlement can stand alone as a sign. This is because it cannot *be* a sign, unless a third—cognizing interpretant—mediates its relation to something else. This is why, as John Deely notes, Descartes' contemporary John Poinsot held the position that "an object *as* object is never a sign" (Deely 1994: 139; emphasis added). Yet, trying to position himself under a certain kind of paradox of Copies without Forms—or rather, Copies that *are* Forms, Derrida argues precisely the opposite in his peculiar reading of Peirce: "*The thing itself is a sign*" (Derrida 1976: 49; emphasis in original). In contrast, for Peirce, signs must belong to the triadic relation Jakobson has termed *renvoi* (Deely 153),[12] *not* to the fullness of reality (what is typically referred to as unmediated reality). Yet it is indeterminate reality that Derrida's work effectively eschews.

Having said that, it is time I elucidated Peirce's triadic ontology and its notions of Firstness, Secondness, and Thirdness, because death is not merely a sign in the Real. What I have so far elaborated is sufficient for understanding the benefit of the semiotic approach, sufficient for describing every single death as its own multivalent sign, as a sign of signs, intersubjectively experienced, crossing between me and you if we share text and context. We could say I have written a little girl's dying moments upon my memory, suffering a gap in the process of inscription. Her death is merely a sign, transformable, manipulable, open to the play of interpretation. That much is already transparent in the exposition of the Peircean triadic sign. Yet this is where I say, not enough, not true. I have not written Samburu girls, their fathers, or death itself upon my memory. I have *expansively experienced* that girl, that father, and that singular death. You can only nod your head or shake it negatively, but you cannot utterly affirm or refute me. Experience is as real as divinity. Descartes gave us that—one of his finest and most complex assertions. It is not only the subjectivity to keep one's eye on, it is the undeniability of experience. It is important to understand Peirce's triadic sign first and to keep it in view, but it is especially crucial to continue onward, to examine his ontological triad. This is the triad I will use to suggest that I expansively experienced an unbearable tragedy that I am not willing to trivialize in the play of signs. It happened. It happened to me, in me, and through me, as it did to everyone who shared that terrible context with me. Where it became inscription, it did so in a process of reincarnation. Death transubstantiated within me and all of us, it touched us in a way that my text will never touch you. Yet my own memory of it is not merely an approximation, it is another incarnation of that death. That is what makes it terrible. And that is why I am not content with imagining playful texts. I want to distinguish reality from the Real, but I want to do so in ways that suggest that the Real is not opposed to reality but is rather a series of incarnations of it.

Three Modes of Being: Peirce's Ontological Triad

Firstness is perhaps Peirce's most elusive concept (followed closely by Ground). By it, Peirce meant the qualities of immediate feeling before being seized fully by conscious awareness. Secondness is the brute reaction that occurs when a new feeling impinges on another. Thirdness brings the first two into synthetic relation in such a way as to establish a habit, law, or developed idea. In Peirce's most concise description of these three modes of being he states that "First is the conception of being or existing independent of anything else. Second is the conception of being relative to, the conception of reaction with, something else. Third is the conception of mediation, whereby a first and second are brought into relation" (Peirce 1958: 158). Feelings of Firstness are immediately present and cease utterly to be instances of Firstness when any other state of mind intervenes. Firstness, then, is pure immediacy and potentiality. Secondness, in turn, is reaction, "as when a person blindfold suddenly runs against a post" (151). Firstness is the ephemeral moment when something may come into awareness or communion (or not) but prior to the moment of communion. That communion happens in Secondness, and actual realization of that awareness does not happen until mediating Thirdness.

Peirce attempts to capture the present's ephemerality in a way that we could relate to Heidegger's being-in-the-world. As Peirce says, "all that is immediately present to a man is what is in his mind in the present instant. His whole life is in the present. But when he asks what is the content of the present instant, his question always comes too late. The present is gone by, and what remains of it is greatly metamorphosized" (Peirce 1931–35 I.310).

E. Valentine Daniel (1996) elaborates eloquently Peirce's extended concern with the elusiveness and ephemerality of the present as ontological mode: "The present qua present is like a tiny bubble in the tide of continuity that, howsoever fleetingly, is an isolated monad, imprisoned in itself, lodged in the heart of time and yet not part of time" (126). For Heidegger, Being is fundamentally about a present that (like a Peircean object) can only be known by the past and the future rather than by itself. Thus, Heideggerean Being cannot be realized for what it is, but only in relation to what it is not. It reveals itself only fleetingly and recedes continually (Heidegger 1962). We can detect what captured Derrida here, but, as I will argue, *the Being that appears to recede in conscious thought is yet a part of thought, and thought includes contact with reality, a reality that is not transformed in the expansive experience that begets thought, but reincarnated.* Before supporting and explaining that assertion, let me consider other readings.

Derrida has critiqued Heidegger's search for Being as falling prey to a search for Originals when there are none. Similarly, Umberto Eco (1999) has grappled with Peirce's notion of Firstness, considering it in the context of the triad of ontological Firstness, Secondness, and Thirdness. Given Peirce's triadic orientation and the fact that his sign consists of an irreducible triad linking representamen, object, and interpretant, Eco seems to feel obligated to ask how an ephemeral feeling that simply *is* but that ceases to be as soon as another feeling presents itself can also belong to a triad.

Eco elucidates a notion of correspondence ("primary iconicism")— distinct from the one-to-one correspondence often found in naïve realism—as when a "stimulus is *adequately* 'represented' by that [a particular] sensation and not by another" (106; bracketed portion mine). Using his notion of primary iconicism, Eco suggests that Firstness might be understood as pure potential, with primary iconicism in the state of not yet finding the impresser (a Firstness) that adequately represents itself (as impression) but as ready to find it. We infer Firstness backward in other words. From here, Eco suggests that we can now describe examples that fall in-between, examples of dyadic "stimulus-response." This is a brilliant visual illumination, but even so, I have a methodological disagreement with Eco. Recall the assertion that "an object as object is never a sign" (Deely 1994: 139). In order to be a sign, an object must refer beyond itself (as in Jakobson's renvoi) in a *triadic* relation, rather than simply existing as itself. That is, there must be a connection real-ized in experience—it is through experience that something more is known about the object than can be known by the representamen alone. Thus, even if Firstness is pure potential, to infer its shape from the impression it makes is to re-create it as a representamen in a triadic *sign* relation. Rather, Peirce's description suggests that Firstness is its *own ontological mode.* Just as Derrida leaves reality out of the process of Being, Eco's primary iconicism fails to specify the precise relation between Peirce's ontological triad and his phenomenological one (the sign).

I suspect that in his extended discussion of how Firstness and Ground can be thought—even as the triadic relation to which Firstness belongs would seem to make the latter's existence impossible—Eco conflates ontology and sign relations. This may be in part because Eco—and Peirce also, I suspect—is ambivalent about Being, wanting to keep pre-linguistic experience in view yet concluding that "being manifests itself to us right from the outset as *an effect of language*" (Eco 1999: 22). Thus, he begins with promising statements like "Being is the horizon, or the amniotic fluid, in which our thought naturally moves" (17–18); and "The first opening to being is a sort of ecstatic experience" (20). Yet he concludes that "being is something that is said," even though it might be "the horizon of every other evidence" (22). Now, I do not think that Being is an effect of language even if we use language to enunciate it. As I will soon elaborate, I think that Being as a simultaneous movement between the modes of Firstness, Secondness, and Thirdness is probably more of what Peirce had—or should have had—in mind, and that we probably already grasp Being in Secondness (and possibly in Firstness) prior to its enunciation in either thought or language in just the sort of ecstatic experience Eco mentions. That is getting ahead, however.

Eco's ambivalence is a product of his decision to keep Being language-bound (as Derrida does also), even as he deftly and exhaustively elabo-rates cognition—a process of which language is perhaps the "highest," but not only, level (it is the level he mainly focuses on).[13] As such, his consignment of Being to an effect of language is not surprising. He attempts to locate in Peircean ontological Firstness a triadic sign relation that simply isn't there, and he uses the notion of a cast impression look-ing backward toward the object that pressed itself into it as a metaphor for understanding that Firstness. While there are firsts (representamen), seconds (objects), and thirds (interpretants) in the Thirdness of signs, my suggestion is that *ontological* Firstness, Secondness, and Thirdness are related to each other heuristically but not necessarily organically. Although he is making different points, Richard Parmentier's (1994) discussion of "Thirdness as Mediation" makes this relationship between Peircean semiotic and ontology clear.

But the common element tying together Peirce's various views is the fundamental idea that anything that either comes between two things in order to link them together, transfers a characteristic feature from one thing over to another, or synthesizes elements from disparate realms of reality *must exist at a higher logical and ontological level than the initial two things* . . . In fact, the *genuine* reality of Thirds or triads, including prototypically fully symbolic representations with their three references, implies that they are *not reducible to either Seconds or Firsts,* although they require these lower-ranking categories as much as they determine them. (Parmentier 1994: 33; emphases added)

Many years of contemplation led Peirce to believe that genuine triadic relations characterized consciousness as well as the universe more broadly, relations that were ontologically different from "lower-ranking categories." I would go farther and emphasize that Firstness and Secondness, as *ontological* processes, have certain habits that make them *tend* to go toward Thirdness, though we cannot determine (at this time anyway) whether they always reach it. Whether or not they do, Peirce's Firstness, Secondness, and Thirdness are apt metaphors for describing simultaneous modes of Being.

Eco's treatment of Firstness, then, as if it *must* relate to an experience in Secondness and Thirdness, leads him to describe perception as beginning somewhere "in a vague and swampy region between Firstness, Secondness, and Thirdness" (113), rather than in the Thirdness of signs, where it belongs.[14] Peirce was abundantly clear about the relationship between ontological Thirdness and signs in one of his letters to Lady Welby. Following a detailed exposition of Thirdness, he said unequivocally, "A sign is a sort of Third" (Peirce 1958: 389; letter to Lady Welby dated October 12, 1904). Ontological Thirdness, by its very nature, requires a triadic sign relation. Conversely, a sign, because it is a triadic relation involving a mediating thought or something like it, must be an ontological third. In contrast, of ontological Firstness Peirce says: "The idea of the present instant, which, whether it exists or not, is naturally thought as a *point of time in which no thought can take place or any detail be separated,* is an idea of Firstness" (Peirce 1958: 384; emphasis added).[15] As I will elaborate momentarily, the process of separation that Peirce refers to here belongs to Ground and comes after Firstness, in the midst of Secondness.

Now we can suggest that whatever Firstness, and even Secondness, are, they are not signs. Firstness is so primordial as to be pure presence prior to phenomenological experience, and Secondness is likewise pure presence that does not yet take the character of what we properly consider to be thought. Suffice it to say that Eco needn't look for how Firstness can exist logically without already being its own negation but should look instead to how it can exist logically at all. That is, we are not dealing here, as Eco seems to suggest, with the paradox of Being known by not-being or that-which-shall-not-be-named, because Firstness is not a triadic relation, nor even a dyadic one. It is pure presence, and if it cannot logically exist, that is *not* because it owes its existence to what it opposes. Nor is it because we must use language to reflect back on what it might have been—any more than we would say that tasting food is an effect of language because we describe it via that medium after the fact.

If Firstness cannot exist, it is because we have difficulty imagining anything that is not always already in the world, although I will suggest a possibility for imagining it—as a quantum potential *inside* of Secondness—farther on in this discussion. For now, I will suggest that, by its mere dynamic existence as presenc-ing in the world, everything would *appear* to already be Secondness—the coming together of two "presences" (two continually changing presenc-ings). As two presenc-ings in touch with one another, they need not be the opposites so popular in binary code and philosophical expositions of being/not-being.[16] They are two positive "things" partaking of each other before being brought into corresponding relation by a third that relates them.[17] I suggest that Derrida holds us in Thirdness, transforming all *things* into signs by his own divine utterance and banishing the possibility of both Being and reality because of their refusal to limit themselves to language. Moreover, Derrida's arguments both point to and refuse the sort of mystical suppositions that Heidegger offered because they long—even demand—to break free of, while remaining deeply rooted in, metaphysical and ontological dualism.

Derrida's is the gap between word and world, between spirit and matter, between the points of an ontology those of us trained in Euro-American academies cannot imagine ourselves away from even as we destabilize it in practice—as in the miracles I discuss in Chapter 7. For the Samburu the world is dynamic and interanimated, and people radically intersubjective. This suggests an ontology for which the Derridean gap is an intruder on the terrain of sense making, a foreign deity declaring truth in the form of an end to truth, a noisy philosopher ignoring what is most transparent in experience. Rather than claiming Samburu ways of being-in-the-world as only another instantiation of the Real, I want to rigorously specify the relationship between reality and what we understand as the Real. I want to consider that Samburu ontological understandings may be excellent approximations of that relationship and to find what is common between some Samburu understandings and our own. First, however, I will continue the work of remystifying the ontology that those in the Euro-American traditions count as ours.

Indeterminate Being: Peirce and Contemporary Cognitive
Science

Lacoff and Johnson's (1999) exposition of the notion of embodied
mind (a continuation of the work they began in their popular *Metaphors
We Live By*, 1980) and embodied realism corresponds in many ways to
Peirce's earlier conceptualization of sign relations, broadly defined.
Peirce related human physiology to sense perception, pointing out the
inconceivably complex nature of the process of relating activity in the
nervous system with the activity of sense impressions (Peirce 1958: 21–
24). Thus, one way of reading Peirce on this point is that humans meet
world by way of their unique physiology.[18]

Like cognitive and neuroscientists generally, Lacoff and Johnson
maintain that most of human thought is "unconscious" (about 95 per-
cent—1999: 13), located in the most basic levels of cognition involving
an enormously complex "circuitry." That circuitry is composed of axons
and dendrites (connections); neural cell bodies ("units"); synapses connecting axons, dendrites, and neural cell bodies; and neural firing,
which occurs when there is sufficient chemical action at the synapses.
According to neuroscientists, this process characterizes both thought
and language (Lacoff and Johnson 1999: 571; see also, for example Carter 2002; Damasio 1994, 1999; Feldman 1985; LeDoux 2002; Shastri
1996). Moreover, humans' neural networks perform the steps of this
process as a result of human action and being in the world (yes, think
of Heidegger and Merleau-Ponty here).[19]

I would argue that the recent work of many neuroscientists supports
Peirce's notion that humans move in and perceive the world at the intersection of the peculiarities of their physiology and the world, generating
conceptual categories (metaphors) based on that confluence. Stated
another way we might say that humans meet world by way of their own
structure in order to reduce a possibly infinite world (and, indeed, the
seeming infinity of their own *being*) to a manageable understanding of
that world and themselves.[20] Peirce's declaration that "man is a sign"
(1958: 71) can be understood in this respect—though again, Peirce
implicitly limits that particular sign ("man") to language, which I would
avoid doing, since his own thought opens us outward toward the sign
relations in pre- and nonlinguistic levels of cognition. In bringing their
own structure to the world, humans generate metaphors for both themselves and world, and it is these very basic, largely unreflectingly used
metaphors that Lacoff and Johnson examine and elucidate.

Mark Turner (1996) examines cognition similarly, but in terms of
"story" rather than metaphor. (Nevertheless, keep in mind that his use
of "story" is itself metaphorical.) Turner asserts that human thought is

"literary" at its core, such that the most basic concepts (of container and of motion along a path, for example) are "stories" that we project as parables onto further, more complex "stories." For example, he explains that we "have a neurobiological pattern for throwing a small object . . . [that] underlies the individual event of throwing a rock and helps us create the category throwing" (16). Lacoff and Johnson would probably say that the conceptual category of throwing becomes a metaphor for other concepts, like Heidegger's "thrownness" and "being-in-the-world." Lacoff and Johnson do not mention Heidegger, but in their multitudinous array of examples they suggest that the concept of Being as "Being Located" ("here" as opposed to "elsewhere") is a metaphor based on the orientation that is necessary for us to move and function (1999: 205). More pointed for present purposes, Lacoff and Johnson likewise identify language as a common metaphor for thought: Thus, thinking is *metaphorically* construed as linguistic activity, with every thought corresponding to "a linguistic expression; and hence, every thought . . . [being] expressible in language" (246).

Nevertheless, cognition (or thought) is not only a linguistic activity.[21] It is a predominantly unconscious process involving neuronal firings based on sensorimotor experiences in the real world at cognition's "lowest" levels. Indeed, one concern I have about Lacoff and Johnson's emphasis on metaphor (similar to Turner's use of "story") is that—in spite of their own assertions—it implies a linguistic basis for cognition *and* a cognitive basis for all experience. *Yet both cognition and language are reductionistic processes that transform unwieldy information into something we can function with.* In their discussion of mapping verbs (language) to sensorimotor functions they are illuminating how we understand and describe those functions—and use them metaphorically elsewhere in thought. They are not, however, explaining how we tell ourselves to do those functions, or how we *experience* those functions. In fact, the difference between cognitive mapping programs that do try to account for how we tell ourselves to do those functions and our own functioning and experience is that our movement and being in the world *exceed* linguistic description.[22] To replicate the motion of raising an arm through a complicated series of computer commands is to describe an aspect of something. No language presently available describes all aspects of it. We experience *more*, both consciously and unconsciously, and this is what poetry, glossolalia, ecstatic experience, and Peircean ontological Firstness/Secondness try to recapture or re-create. (Experience as phenomenologists following Husserl and Merleau-Ponty tend to apply it, however, is already in Peircean ontological Thirdness, as I discussed in the Conclusion.)[23] Perception (also a process of Thirdness) reduces an infinite amount of information in a set of simultaneously linear (incremental) and weblike neurochemical processes.

I would suggest that we are in touch with that seemingly infinite amount of world in ontological Secondness.[24] *Reality touches us somewhere, somehow as it gets reduced, modified in neuronal firings and synaptic weight changes.* Thus, I think that Peirce's ontological Secondness describes our contact with world, while Thirdness as a triadic sign relation describes cognition from the first steps of processing world to the metaphorical connections of language experienced in moments of focused attention. Consciousness (a broader term here than conscious awareness), in this conceptualization, includes Firstness (on which, more soon), expansive experience in Secondness[25] and cognition in Thirdness (taking Secondness as the portal to the Thirdness of cognition):

> At no *one* instant in my state of mind is there cognition or representation, but in the *relation* of my states of mind at different instants there is. In short, the Immediate (and therefore in itself unsusceptible of mediation—the Unanalyzable, the Inexplicable, the Unintellectual) runs in a continuous stream through our lives; it is the sum total of consciousness, whose mediation, which is the continuity of it, is brought about by a real effective force behind consciousness. (Peirce 1958: 56; emphases added)[26]

By the time an adult thinks a single conscious thought, utters or writes a single word, Thirdness is already involved. A lifetime of experience is taken into account, as synapses become "heavy" enough with the weight of previous and present connections to "act" through neural firing. Thought is an accomplishment of something; it is an action with effects that establish themselves in habits—with a habitus more pervasive than Bourdieu or anyone else could contemplate. Moreover, in habitus (a collection of habits for Peirce), beliefs are formed on the basis of which further thought and action occur: "The essence of belief is the establishment of a habit, and different beliefs are distinguished by the different modes of action to which they give rise" (Peirce 121). We have reached the point where we need to take up Bourdieu's insights afresh—we need to (re)theorize forgetting.

Peirce, Bourdieu, Memory, and Forgetting: Grounding Expansive Experience

What is reality? Suppose we say it is that which is independently of our belief and which could be properly inferred (by the most thorough discussion) from the sum of all impressions of sense whatever. (Peirce 1958: 140)

Notice that there is nothing in this definition to either preclude or require reality to be "material"—the sum of all sense impressions may include impressions of nonhumans, and those impressions may include more than matter. Peirce's definition was framed quite broadly, to include possibilities he might not yet have imagined. Moreover, his theory included objects of imagination as belonging to reality, and his notion of ontological Firstness embraced potentiality. The difficulty I have, and that Eco has also had and addressed in different terms than I am here, is in contemplating Firstness as mere possibility in experiential terms—though experience is central to Peirce's thought. Yet Firstness would seem to belong to reality and experience at their most fundamental levels (where reality typically becomes conceptualized as some kind of essence). I have not been content with ontological Firstness as a mere feeling, or qualia, as Peirce would have it, because I am skeptical that humans experience qualia at all—as feelings not already in Thirdness— and I am fairly certain that they do not within conscious awareness. Moreover, I am not satisfied with Eco's solution because of his apparent conflation of ontology and sign relations and also because he seems to offer a method for contemplating Peircean Firstness rather than suggesting how it can exist (or be defined). A part of the quandary is that, as ontological categories, Peirce's Firstness, Secondness, and Thirdness seem logically correct and even necessary, and yet, recent work in cognitive neuroscience and physics has shrunk the elements of experience and reality. It is to physics in this case that I will look for a possible solution that radically joins reality and experience—offering a Euro-American scientific conceptualization of ideas typically reserved for mystics and our anthropological "others."[27]

Quantum physics has become increasingly popular in recent years, and most people are familiar with the claim that whether light behaves as a wave or as a particle is determined by the very process of observing it. According to a growing number of physicists, the quirky phenomena of quantum physics may join forces with cosmic phenomena if a unified theory can be devised and shown mathematically to account for it all. As it may apply to consciousness (and eventually to cosmic "stuff"), some physicists have proposed that human (and nonhuman) neurons contain quanta, which, like other quanta, are in a yes-no state—a state of potentiality. As with quantum phenomena generally, we cannot know what would happen if the theoretical quanta in neurons did not "collapse," that is, go one way or the other through interaction with the environment. Perhaps they would remain in an indefinite, pensive sort of "yes-no" state. Physicists like Sir Roger Penrose and Stuart Hameroff have suggested the possibility that microtubules ("tiny filaments of protein in neuronal cell walls"—Carter 2002: 306) are microinformation-processing systems that, shielded from the environment, may be able to contain quantum yes-no states for up to half a second. During that time, these undetermined little sub-units might be interacting with others in that or other neurons, firing off as little "blips of consciousness" with every collapse (computational "answer" to a yes-no state).[28] Put another way, these physicists seem to be suggesting that we are in reality and reality is in us, a reality that is constantly moving between the indeterminate and the determinate, between the decided and what may or may not become decided.

All of this suggests that reality itself may not be energy or matter per se but something we have not yet guessed or "sensed"—to which matter, as Euro-Americans understand it, belongs. For those who argue that this movement between undecided and decided—and the power of "observers" in that process—suggests that reality is fiction after all, I would strenuously counter that once light becomes either wave or particle it has become so in reality (and it is therefore determined, as in our usual Euro-American notion of substance). Reality need not be "tangible"—it might be characterized better in terms of *movement* between the undecided and the decided; and all that is decided become events, many of which have far-reaching implications for humans. (We might say that humans themselves are macro events.) With regard to Peircean ontological Firstness, all of this suggests that some "things" *may* remain undecided if let alone, and that there may be dimensions of experience that are, indeed, mere—though real—potentialities, momentary flickers on the multitudinous horizons of simultaneous and ongoing experiences. What or whether the micro undecided states have to do with macro human realities is not yet known, but one thing seems plausible: The quanta of us may be part of what makes us real, and if so, they may impinge on our choices in ways we have not yet guessed. Let us suppose they are part of the Ground we share, and that Ground in turn describes the twin-sided moment of memory and forgetting.

Recall that Peirce suggested that Ground is a "sort of idea" that brings the sign in relation to its object.[29] Eco (1999) expounds at length on Ground in relation to Firstness, reaching the same obstacles as with the latter, partly because he tries to identify what kind of substance it is. (Icon? No—that would already be Thirdness. See Eco 102–3.) I suggest that Ground is a *process of ontological prescission*.[30] Just as Firstness and Secondness can be ontological modes but can also be positions in Thirdness, so too can Ground be an aspect of prescission in the triadic sign but also in the modes of Being, which are Firstness and Secondness. In Thirdness, Ground has been equated with cultural context and Wittgenstein's language games (Sheriff 1989). It is the semantic basis upon which two people sharing a common cultural context can immediately "cut off" potential aspects of a representamen's object that would otherwise render their communication meaningless. In this sense, prescissive Grounding is never singular but instead is a plural aspect of expansive experience by which the habitus is enacted in every thought and utterance, eliminating the "noise" that members of another culture might take as meaningful "sound" and arriving at the particular aspect of an object that the representamen should be referring to its object by way of.

As I see it, this precission, or cutting, offers us a rigorous refinement of the *how* of Bourdieu's habitus. I want to include not only the bodily habitus Bourdieu elaborates but also the previously hypothesized quantum phenomena held taut in their undecided states for up to half a second before collapsing in "decision," in cutting, in precluding other possibilities. I want to include the perceptual "screening" by which humans sensually focus quite differently from other creatures. I want to include processes of forgetting that have so far been too monumental for neuroscience (particularly as basic processes in cognition proceed to more consciously aware ones involving unique biographical, cultural memories). And note, such processes are not brain-bound—"forgetting" begins everywhere.[31] So I want also to include, for example, the processes invoked in recent studies of the retina that suggest that a significant amount of image processing occurs *locally* in the retina, the place where images are created *before* proceeding to the brain for more perceptual processing and interpretation.[32] I want to include such processes by way of suggesting that there are aspects of reality that we "take in" even without realizing it, and we do so in ways that profoundly affect us. (And remember that we ourselves are part of reality, however indeterminate the latter seems.) Amid the process whereby some elements of human experience are selected out, others selected in, there are unconsciously aware aspects of our experience of reality that become connected to consciously aware ones—as when a particular smell in the background of a joyful or terrifying experience becomes associated for us with joy or terror itself. Again, this signals the profoundness of the habitus.

It signals as well the need to continue challenging ourselves over the issue of agency—that last bastion of unique selfhood and free will. With so much "undecided" at the level of quantum phenomena, so much unanswered about consciousness, and, further, given that—whether "routine" or unconscious or conscious—"we" make decisions ("we" being an intersubjective pronoun here), I think we are ripe for a more supple understanding of agency, self, and consciousness. It would appear that the concept of "agency" allows Euro-American unitary selfhood to sneak in again, in contrast to other sorts of consciousness and will—including so-called collective ones. I am reminded of Bourdieu's words, written some time ago, which already called for more nuanced understandings in my opinion than critiques of his determinism allowed: "The construction of the world of objects is clearly not the sovereign operation of consciousness which the neo-Kantian tradition conceives of; the mental structures which construct the world of objects are constructed in the practice of a world of objects constructed according to the same structures . . . The mind is a metaphor of the world of objects which is itself but an endless circle of mutually reflecting metaphors" (Bourdieu 1977: 91). As I also do here, Bourdieu refutes the Kantian notion of a subject imposing order on a chaotic world apart from and substantially different from itself. At the same time, however "unconscious" our decisions may be—all the way down to the level of individual neurons or even subunits of quanta—it is somehow "we" who "choose," we who forget, we who remember. So long as we abstract body from brain, our own being from reality, we can imagine that choices are made for us even within ourselves. If we refuse those particular abstractions, other imaginings become possible. That decisions of millennia are encoded in our genes gives us something to ponder but does not disempower us. It does call for a reconsideration of what or who "we" are and how "we" are connected to each other and world.

Peirce's ontological Secondness is the mode of Being in a sensed *real* world (and Firstness may be that world in movement between undetermined and determined, which includes us), and it precedes language by uncountable "steps" in consciousness. The beginning of Secondness may be the moment at, or just before, the process of prescission I have been describing here—a process I think Peirce would equate with Ground and that is shaped by our unique physiology and features of memory and forgetting we may never fully understand. We could say that we are signs at the level of Thirdness but Ground in Secondness—or between the Secondness of expansive experience and phenomenological Thirdness.

We are ourselves a brute (expansive) contact with some things—and some ones—with respect to the Ground of our own physiology. We are alternately Secondness and Ground. Pure Secondness happens every moment. As Ground, we move through the world, enacting a "cutting," "categorizing" prescission within it vis-à-vis our physiology. And because the world around us is itself a continually reincarnating movement comprising Firstness, Secondness, and Thirdness in the presence of other beings and things, our own being in the world is not only intersubjective but Originary (contra Derrida). Every moment of "being-in-the-world" is being in a *new* world by way of an ontological Secondness by which we change the world moment by moment. Moreover, that Secondness is double. It is a secondness by way of contact, but also, within that continually occurring Originary contact with the world, there is an immeasurable moment when we have inescapably prescinded the world as it was just then *for us*, by virtue of our own physiology (and a little something more), but have not yet prescinded the world in thought.

What I would want Peirce to say is that Firstness may be the point at which we and *infinite* reality have not yet diverged (to *create* us as things—momentarily defined answers—abstracted from that possibly infinite reality of taut potentiality and ephemeral affirmation), while Secondness is that moment when we *have*, through a (mystical seeming) process of selecting out/cutting/prescissing (Ground) that simultaneously "imagines" and therefore accomplishes divergence and contact (through its very possibility). Secondness, then, is the moment that marks a divergence from the infiniteness of Being in the world *and* a contact with and within it.

Firstness, then, may exist *within* as well as outside of Peirce's notion of Secondness. And Secondness may be the moment prior to Forgetting.[33] These experiences of Firstness, Secondness, and Thirdness occurring constantly and all over us involve "screening," memory, and forgetting every step of the way (and they are inseparably cultural, historical, and so on). Both forgetting and memory are profoundly a part of Being and consciousness at all levels. Consider this: Pondering the relationship between memory and consciousness at a fairly familiar level of cognition, Rita Carter (2002) conjectures that we may be consciously aware even when we "get lost" in daydreams during which we forget how we drove a certain distance, or when in dreamless sleep or even under anesthesia, but that perhaps we do not "lay down any memory of it" (31). What Carter does not note is the other side of forgetting—the conscious intrusion on habit that accords us the power Bourdieu has been accused of losing in the maw of systems of the habitus. We take in a seemingly infinite amount of world that we then reduce, or presciss for thought (ontological Secondness) and then *in* thought (in Thirdness). *Choosing* to remember is one crucial way we presciss: Changing from "automatic pilot" to a decision to take an alternative route suggests that we are not slaves of the habitus in any simple sense. Yet, the forgetting that is an entailment of that remembering is every bit as crucial as what we do remember. Consciousness is forged through both memory and forgetting. We may forget, but that does not mean we did not experience, and it does not mean that some forgotten expansive experience of reality did not affect the shape of those things we did choose to remember. Somewhere within experience we continually cross the gap we ourselves have imagined, and we imagine again.

Appendix 2
The "I" Verb Stem

Terms deriving from the 'i' life stem:

Aisho	giving birth right now; to give birth
Ishoi	birth (general category)
Keisho	she's giving birth (now)
Ketiishe	she has given birth
Inoto	time when someone was born (in Maasai, can also mean, "Have you found it?")
	Here, 'i' is the life stem; noto refers to time.
Keino	s/he was born
Meino	s/he was not born
Meiuu	he has not sired him/her
Keiuu	he has sired him/her
Aishu	to be alive
Nkishui	life
Keishu	s/he is living
Meishu	s/he is not living
Naishu	a living female thing
Loishu	a living male thing
Nkishu	cattle (Can it be something bringing life, keeping life going? *Meye loreito moidiei*: "A person stepping on cow dung can't die"; *Ltau oishiwe likae*: "The heart lives with another one." Samburu say the latter proverb during drought, to say that the lives of the people depend on the lives of the cows.)
Nkiteŋ	one cow: living thing breathing: ayeŋ is to breathe (nkiyeŋet is breath)
Nkishon	often glossed as life; it is the life of behavior and actions
Kerisho	s/he, or it who/that takes away life (metaphorically, can refer to that category of persons who kill through "mysterious" or seemingly "remote" means)
Nkai	"God"
Inia Ai	that "God"

Nkaitok   "Gods"
Nkaiisho   someone with exaggerated sense of importance, making
him/herself like Nkai

Frans Mol 1981 has argued that the Nkai derives from an "I" stem
seen in words referring to birth. My remarks here are an elaboration of
and comment on Mol 1981, as well as Stoks 1989 and Voshaar 1998—all
works by scholars of the Maasai. I want particularly to continue from
Stoks's suggestion that "life" and "giving" can be examined together in
Maa linguistics, although I travel a somewhat different path than he
does. In Maa linguistic usage, "u" indicates return or motion toward the
speaker. My suggestion is that with its "u" suffix (preceding the "i" suffix, which indicates the word as a general category), nkishui (life) indicates life that clings to a person, life that is coming toward or staying
with the person—it keeps returning to, remains with, the person. So we
say, "Ikiponu," We are coming back, as opposed to "Ikipo," We are
going away, where 'o' indicates action away from the speaker. Mol suggests that "sho" indicates general or continuous meaning, but I think
that "sh" by itself indicates the continuous action—as in nkishui, while
the "o" performs its usual function of indicating movement away from
the speaker. Similarly, as the life of one's behavior or actions, nkishon
indicates action away from the speaker, and indeed for Samburu it is
the life that is visible to others and is passed to one's children through
inheritance and example.

Turning from nkishui to ishoi (birth), then, I would suggest that
rather than limiting "sho" here to "usually" or "continuous," it is possible to specify the usual action involved more precisely as "I usually give
out" or "I am in the act of giving out life." I would then suggest that
nkishui is the general category of life that stays with the person, while
ishoi is the general category of the kind of life given to another. In this
way, rather than treating "i" as the stem for birth and giving birth (as
Mol does), I am bringing Stoks's observation that "giving" and "life"
share a linguistic root to bear on Mol's arguments concerning the derivation of Nkai.

However, Voshaar counters Stoks's argument on precisely this point
of putting "giving" and "life" together. Voshaar (1998: 134) argues that
the "i" in 'giving' (aisho) is open, while the "i" in 'life' (nkishui) is
closed. As I hear it, and as the Samburu whom I know also hear it, the
'i' is closed in both. Furthermore, Kaisho (with the same pronunciation)
means both "I will give [something to someone]" and "I will give
birth." This supports what I contend here—that the verb for "birth" is
not only related to "life" (all forms of both sharing the "i" stem) but
that there is not a separate word for birth apart from life at all. Rather,

what we translate as birth, giving birth, etc., should be translated as giving-life, life-that-is-given (*out* or *away*)—as opposed to nkishui, which should be understood linguistically as life that *stays* or belongs (to someone or something). When paired with its opposite (lkiye, death), this makes sense in the larger, cultural web of meaning. Lkiye derives from the verb aya, to take. While birth is life that is given as a gift to someone or something and life is that which stays, death is that which is taken away—from others and from the scene of sociality itself.

Notes

Author's Note

1. These stories and others are compiled in Jorge Luis Borges, *Collected Fictions* (New York: Penguin, 1999).

Chapter 1. Experience

1. I came across my original field notes after writing the reflective narrative. Traumatic memories are fairly accurate, I think, even if incomplete (see the Conclusion). I didn't write the smell into my notes, but that is what lingered most in memory.

2. For an excellent exegesis of the rationality debates see Ulin 2001. See also Kapferer 2003.

3. See Tambiah 1990 and Douglas 1999 for arguments concerning the European intellectual tradition and its import for anthropology. See Turner 1992 for a discussion of radical ethnographic alternatives to Evans-Pritchard's largely accepted norm for analyzing experience and belief.

4. For a moving personal account of suffering as he moved into the "village of the sick," see Stoller 2004.

5. See Appendix 1, where I offer an elaborated thesis supporting my points here. For those who prefer to avoid that technical discussion, I summarize my essential conclusions here.

6. This technology has allowed some researchers to suggest that it may be possible to tell lies apart from narrations of experience because one is tied to the physiological correlates of memory, while the other (lying) is imagination constructed from various experiences without being tied to one in particular.

Chapter 2. Signs

1. Loibonok (masculine plural) and nkoibonok (feminine plural) are healers, prophets, dreamers—men and women known to communicate with Nkai.

2. Lkileku were young men circa the 1930s, while Lterito were young men circa the late nineteenth and early twentieth centuries.

3. If I may switch from a philosophical to a cognitive heuristic domain, Stephen Reyna's (2002) cogent discussion of individual variations in people's understandings of the "same" sign bears on the history of individual and collective signs. Reyna distinguishes between individual and locational contingents. "The latter are meanings associated with signs due to a person's placement within a population. The former are meanings that get associated with signs

because the hippocampus and the amygdala 'clicked' and stored some idiosyncratic perceptual and emotional happenings in a person's life with the basics of the sign" (132–33). In Lemeteki's case, the basics pertaining to goats as sign would include the notion that goats can communicate with certain people, while the locational contingent involves actually being able to understand those communications. Finally, Lemeteki's particular communicative events and experiences with goats would belong to the individual contingent shaping his understanding of goats. This is one way to bring Peirce's ontological principles, cognitive science, and anthropology into conversation with one another. However, Reyna's identification of these different contingents does not mean that we have different places or ways of storing information depending on how many people we share it with, but rather is a heuristic way of accounting for the degree of similarity and variation between understandings of signs. Ultimately, my approach differs from Reyna's in that his is based in Kantian assumptions whereas I begin with world and with humans as part of world. I focus on prescissing as a process of "cutting off," or forgetting, seemingly infinite information we cannot handle but which we do have contact with. This is a forgetting consistent with Bourdieu's habitus while allowing for more openness—see Appendix 1 and Straight 2005b.

4. See particularly—both within and outside phenomenological approaches —Abu-Lughod 1993; Csordas 1994b; Daniel 1996; Desjarlais 1992; Geurts 2002; Jackson 1989, 1996; Stewart 1996; Stoller 1989, 2004; and Turner 1992.

5. There is an additional issue to consider, of course—Truth. Lemeteki's claim that he understands the language of goats, cows, gazelles, crickets, and other creatures invites a particular Euro-American or Western academic interpretation. How do we understand communicating goats, divine occurrences, and miracles? If we look to context-specific truth, we have shaped ethnographic experience in notable ways. For an extended critical discussion of the rationality debates as they impinge on these issues, see Robert Ulin 2001. See also Winch 1964. More recently, Renato Rosaldo (1989) has dealt with this vexing issue, taking a Derridean approach to truth in context. Edith Turner (1992) offers a more radical reading of the Truths of other interlocutors, and I appraise these various approaches and offer possibilities elsewhere (Straight 2006; on the problem of Truth, see also Straight 2002b). In this book I make declarative statements based on Samburu claims without implying that they are pure works of the imagination, because ultimately we often cannot know. I thus substitute agnosticism and openness for "contextual truth" which I read as either an undertheorized approach or else a respectful, side-stepping euphemism for the nonrational. Of course, a corollary to the issue of Truth is that of lies. While I would suggest that lies also involve some form of contact with world, there is a troubling and obvious difference between a lie that untruthfully claims suffering for example, and a true account of suffering. We cannot always know for certain whether the stories we hear are true, imagined, or downright lies. Yet the fact of the difference between these possibilities is crucial in my view if we are to avoid slipping into a postmodern idealism akin to (born of the same history as) capitalist flexible accumulation in which anything goes, anything can be justified. However problematic the issues of Truth, lies of various sorts, and totalizing narratives become, the solution is not to hide in the "play of signs."

6. On similar notions of sacrifice among the Dinka, see Lienhardt 1961: 238–39. I will discuss this notion of sacrifice again in Chapter 7.

7. On loibonok and their counterpart practitioners, see also Fratkin 1979, 1991, and Anderson and Johnson 1995.

8. I use the term "purity" advisedly. "Pure Samburu" is the term educated Samburu use, while Samburu who do not speak English say "Samburu pii"—completely Samburu.

9. See also Günter Schlee 1989 on the regional distribution of shared practices in northern Kenya and southern Ethiopia. His work is ground breaking in attending to permeable yet fixed cultural boundaries. See also Tablino 1999.

10. The reciprocal character of my arguments, tacking between my readings of Samburu and Euro-American understandings, runs throughout this book implicitly and explicitly. In discussing Samburu aduŋ, besides the neuronal arguments I invoke, I am also aware that I come very near to retracing Geertz's webs of signification or, even more aptly, Ortner's key symbols. In its intentional aspect, mine is a gesture of appreciation for a fertile history of anthropological approaches and an attempt to push them in new directions—wedding them to Peirce, cognitive theories, and historical approaches, as well as a version of structuralism (and poststructuralism).

11. See Straight 2005a, b.

12. See Shanafelt 2004 on how anthropologists have historically maintained "a gap between magic and miracle" (319), as well as Favret-Saada 1980 and Stoller and Olkes 1987 for anthropologists' personal accounts of engaging with the extraordinary. Shanafelt supports a distinction between miracle as wonder to our interlocutors and occurrences strange to (particularly Euro-American) outsiders but not to our interlocutors. In this way, she is subverting traditional anthropological assumptions by which anything inexplicable to anthropologists is examined as "magic." For anthropological accounts of the miraculous and marvelous, see Geertz 1968; Grindal 1983. See Shanafelt 2004 for a fairly exhaustive critical summary. Grindal (1983) writes reflexively about seeing a resurrection; however, it is more accurately the witnessing of a corpse's temporary reanimation.

13. See Godfrey Lienhardt's (1961) classic work on divinity and experience among the Dinka where he also describes the ways in which Dinka experience through divinity's actions in the world (e.g., 280–81), although in different terms and to somewhat different ends than I do here. Lienhardt describes Dinka philosophical understandings as being inseparably connected to mundane and extraordinary experience. He also notes the sharedness of Dinka experience, and in doing so importantly opens up the possibility of considering the grounds of human experience as always already cultural and yet partaking of a sharedness that crosses cultural boundaries in ways I alluded to in Chapter 1 and will describe in bits and pieces throughout.

14. It is always problematic to suggest that interpretations can be chosen as if selecting among commodities. That trope wants continual scrutiny when it becomes an insidious metaphor transposed to the cultural logic of everyday lives and sufferings.

15. On the entanglement of seeming opposites like West/rest, see Van der Veer 2001. See also Comaroff and Comaroff 1991, 1997.

16. Kiswahili is one of Kenya's two official languages—the other is English.

17. The terms "junior elder" and "senior elder" are Spencer's. See Spencer 1965, where he uses these terms to differentiate elders based upon their relationship to (and generational distance from) the current lmurran ageset. Spencer's creation of these terms is based on subtle distinctions the Samburu describe, although there are no formal terms designating them.

18. The Samburu and the Pokot have an alliance that forbids overt warfare, so the hostilities with the Pokot had to be addressed somewhat more delicately.

19. Girlhood can be further subdivided into young girlhood and older girl-hood (*nkarkun*, plural; *nkarkuni*, singular)—when girls take lmurran as boyfriends and dance and sing with them. (Maasai refer to these girls as esiankiki, in contrast to Samburu nkarkuni.) Married women are variously referred to as *mparatut* (used to address a woman, often used where specific relationships are indicated), *ngorio* (general term for wives or married women), *nkitok* (a term which literally means big or great in importance), and *ntomononi* (married women, especially mothers, and particularly used to refer to a woman who has just given birth).

20. Although there is no specific term used to denote mothers of lmurran, their status is marked visually by the blue and white beads strung on a leather string (at first, at least—stronger string can be used later) with cowrie shells at the bottom that they wear hanging from their earrings. (These are called *siririmin*, and mothers receive them in the context of their sons' circumcision ceremony, once the *Lmuget Lenkarna* (Ceremony of the Name) has been performed). Once a woman's son is married, she removes the siririmin from her ears and puts them under her neck ornaments. Once her son has a child, she strings the sirirmin around her grandchild's waist. An old woman (past child-bearing) is referred to as an *ntasat.*

21. The usual and preferred practice is for a young woman to be initiated as part of her marriage ceremony, but spending time as a *surmolei* is becoming increasingly common as more girls get upper elementary, and occasionally, secondary education.

22. On development ideologies and Samburu local knowledge, see Straight 2000.

23. See Aud Talle 1988 on the gendered implications of novel housing forms for the Maasai.

24. Without a careful and balanced study, it is impossible to say what the levels of alcoholism are, but anecdotally it is clear that drinking has been a growing problem since the colonial government introduced beer halls in the 1950s (see Holtzman 2001). As it would be expected, drinking is more devastating to poorer families because of a tendency to buy liquor with whatever cash one might have. The incidence of alcohol-related violence, however, probably has little to do with wealth, except insofar as poverty provides additional reasons to be frustrated.

Chapter 3. Nkai

1. Lienhardt 1961 also discusses the immanence of Dinka divinity, including noting claims of women seeing Divinity (see 46).

2. As I explained in Chapter 2, naibon is the suite of skills possessed by Samburu loibonok, a ritual office that runs in specific Samburu families. In direct contrast, children and young people like Remeta who visit or talk to Nkai do not belong to loibonok lineages. This can be a point of difficulty for Samburu themselves, as in the case of the most famous Samburu nkoiboni. While a number of claims have been made, trying to link her to the Lemeteki or Leaduma families through an illegitimate union, Doto Malapen herself denied that she was illegitimate, asserting with a twinkle in her eye and her thumb and forefinger squeezed together demonstrably, that her family had ticks and that is all. In other words, as described in Chapter 2, the only special skill her family possessed

was to control ticks. Yet she became one of the most sought-after prophetess/ diviners in Samburu District.

3. This is *barleria proxima* (Acanthaceae), according to Heine, Heine, and Konig 1988. See also Fratkin 1975.

4. This might be *Ficus wakefieldii*, *Ficus glumulosa* (Moraceae), *Ficus thonningii*, or *Measa lanceoloata* (Myrtaceae)—Heine, Heine, and Konig 1988 (the authors list all three without specifying). See also Fratkin 1975.

5. Lodo and mporo are both words for blood. Lodo is more general, while mporo is often associated with birth. The plant may be *Commicarpus plumbaginous* (Nyctaginaceae), *Erlangia* (Compositae), or *Gutenbergia* (Compositae)—Heine, Heine, and Konig 1988. See also Fratkin 1975; Kokwaro and Herlocker 1982. Although I seemed to like the smell of this plant, my favorite smell in Samburu District is ntalakwani. Ntalakwani is a grass Samburu use in many ceremonies—it has a green smell and grows well after rains—a blessing of Nkai. Heine, Heine, and Konig (1988) variously identify it as *Tetrapogon tenellus*, *Tetrapogon cenchriformis*, and *Aristida adscensionsis* (Gramineae).

6. In fact, Pokot were also involved in these clashes, which, in this case, were largely over land. Smaller groups like the Samburu, Pokot, Maasai, and Okiek have been reacting, both peacefully and sometimes violently, to increasing land pressure as larger (and politically powerful) groups claim land formerly occupied by the smaller ones—either through squatting or the granting of title through often dubious legal means.

7. For other stories of vanishing, see for example Stoller 1989: 85–87, 92–93, concerning Sorko—a patrilineage of Songhay praise singers to the spirits who disappear under water in the Niger River for extended periods of time. They visit the home of Harakoy Dikko, the spirit queen of the Niger River, and are known to perform a variety of superhuman feats. The difference here is that Samburu children and adults visiting Nkai's home do not represent any particular lineage of ritual practitioner and indeed, typically prophesy only briefly and then resume life as usual. It is as if Nkai inexplicably and suddenly snatched them, fed them, and returned them.

8. There may be other forms of whiteness that speak to indigenous concerns. For example, Harakoy Dikko, Songhay spirit queen of the Niger River, is described as having long white hair (see Stoller 1989a: 85) and is associated with the color white (a color of Islamic purity) in contrast to other spirits that are red or black.

9. A few of the many excellent reviews of the issues can be found in Bray and Colebrook 1998; Broch-Due, Rudie, and Bleie 1993; Fuss 1991; Grosz 1994; Oyewumi 1998.

10. The arguments put forth by brilliant thinkers such as Butler, Kristeva, Grosz, and Irigaray are anything but facile (and a number of scholars have problematized gender, the body, or both as rooted in Western epistemologies and ontologies—e.g., Strathern 1988, 1993; Oyewumi 1998), yet the peculiar Western problem of "gender" and the "body" continues to trouble scholarly discourses. Elizabeth Grosz's (1994) arguments demonstrate the ease with which one side or the other falls prey to the accusation of essentialism. Grosz outlines three categories: egalitarian, constructionist, and sexual difference (the overcoming third). In this way she can imply a form of essentialism for earlier feminists like Simone de Beauvoir and Mary Wollstonecraft because their arguments depended upon a clearly delineated *sexual* difference, while simultaneously implying that contemporary feminist theorists like Julia Kristeva are essentialist

and constructionist because for them gender is constituted based on an under-theorized biological determinism (Grosz 1994: 15–16). Grosz chooses instead to celebrate the works of theorists like Judith Butler, Luce Irigaray, Gayatri Spivak, and Moira Gatens for their ability to refuse mind/body dualism.

11. Grosz discusses Mary Douglas's work at length in the context of Julia Kristeva's theory, but her training in Western psychoanalytic theories seems to prevent her from considering the farther-reaching implications for ontologies of Douglas's work.

12. I hesitate to insert myself into this well-marked and subtle terrain, and insofar as I will, it is not in order to thoroughly undo the works of my predecessors whose works I suggest, following Peirce, must be judged by the habits they entail. It is not so difficult to dismantle a theory by the simplifying process of translating and representing it for another, if related, purpose. The value I see in the theories of Kristeva, Butler, and Grosz among others is in their different ways of daring to form a language for the liberatory struggles of marginalized human beings. What I would like to do is to offer a solution to what I see as a weakness they all share in different ways—a solution meant to strengthen rather than refute their models, models that I see as each suited well to different tasks. That weakness, as I will clarify further in this book's Conclusion, is a failure to take adequate *theoretical* account of experience and, in so doing, to risk an idealism that fictionalizes suffering. I am working out for myself and for you, the reader, scholarly grapplings with gender, in order to suggest that experience is so miraculous in its enormity that parts of it must be foreclosed and forgotten in order to arrive at something understandable and recognizable for particular communities.

13. On the embeddedness and assumptions of sex-gender, see especially Oyewumi 1998.

14. Note that this first point is in the realm of Peircean Thirdness. A second and related problem turns on Peircean Firstness and Secondness. See Appendix 1.

15. Indeed, it cannot be the same, since reality is continually dynamic and changing—and of course differs temporally, spatially, culturally, and so on—and reality includes our own intersubjectivity. For humans, reality is intersubjective and interworlded.

16. Though the Holy Breath is feminine—see Gelpi 2001; Johnson 1993.

17. I am saying "come to be" because it is no more accurate to assume that the authors of the Bible shared with the twenty-first century West the twinned notions of sex and gender than it is to assume that our cross-cultural contemporaries do. Moreover, even taking contemporary Western gendered understandings as a basis, feminist biblical scholars have pointed out God's gendered complexity, destabilizing the notion of a masculine Judeo-Christian God. See, for example, Johnson 1993; Sered 1996.

18. Some of these stories are occasionally attributed to older generations than the Leisa. There is widespread agreement about the Leisa as the cause of the 1870s to 1890s disaster, but how they met or did not meet their end is more debatable. I draw on stories told by a number of different people, though my best information comes from the living grandson of a Leisa girl.

19. I discuss the implications of illicit forms of sexuality in Straight 2005b.

20. Nouns have feminine and masculine prefixes, but, as Oyewumi (1998) has pointed out for the Yoruba, there are no words for man or woman. Instead,

there are social categories that foreground key social distinctions like whether a person has undergone initiation or not, marriage, and so on. Small children are *nkera*—a feminine noun—regardless whether they are male or female. To be a girl or boy in English likewise implies an age category with social implications. However, to be a so-called gendered adult in Samburu is to always be a particular kind—married, childbearing, past childbearing, and so on. Thus, we might say that there is a "sex"-initiation-marriage-childbearing-retired system but not a sex-gender one.

21. Samburu do not use the longer feminine article 'en' that Maasai use. Instead, a feminine noun begins simply with 'n', a masculine one with 'l', except in cases where the article is too difficult to pronounce, in which case it is dropped.

22. Mol also has some inaccuracies, not all of which relate to gender. He translates *Enkai magilani* as deriving from the verb *agil*, to break, thus suggesting that it means " 'He Whose robes has many folds' or 'He, which is unbreakable' " (1978: 75). Besides the problem of translating a feminine noun as 'He' that appears in many of his glosses, magilani does not refer to many folds or being unbreakable, even if it might be a metaphor based on agil. It means a person who knows everything and knows how to do everything. It can be used for humans only if they are magilani in one specific domain or skill. Only Nkai is magilani in an unqualified sense. Thus, for one searching for Christian comparisons, Mol would do better with omniscient and omnipotent.

23. See Burton 1991. See also Lienhardt 1961 on feminine divinities among the Dinka.

24. Spencer devoted more attention to women and gender relations in his work on the Maasai (e.g., 1988) but did not revisit his ontological or gendered classification of Nkai.

25. See also Rigby 1992 on Christianity among the Maasai.

26. I am grateful to Dorothy Hodgson for alerting me to this article and sending it to me while I was in the field.

27. Godfrey Lienhardt describes a similar story for the Dinka as well, but with a clearly male divinity. See Lienhardt 1961: 33–35.

28. Four is a common number in Samburu ceremony, so this may be more coincidental than it appears.

29. If the mother lives but the child dies before its umbilical cord falls off, the mother buries it beneath her cooking fire—the fire in this case metonymically represents the mother.

30. Voshaar cites Mol's work on the derivation of the noun Enkai as supporting a feminine hypothesis for the deity. See Appendix 2 for my extended discussion of this work, particularly in reference to Samburu.

31. The noun Voshaar translates as womb in these references, *nkosheke*, is the term used for stomach as well as womb. Although it can be understood as womb from its context in many cases, it may be circumspect to allow for simultaneous meanings, since nkosheke is a very important sign for Samburu, one that extends to men as well as to women.

32. This is not to suggest that they have been absent in every story performance over time, but rather to suggest that even if there has been a loss of detail in some stories, lost features were probably so taken for granted or inessential that they could be left out.

33. Women in some Samburu families let their hair grow long either while pregnant or until their baby is weaned. Some do it only when they have pre-

viously lost a child, while others do it for every child. Since the person who visited Nkai did not note that Nkai was pregnant, it is likely that Nkai was nursing a child.

34. When ceremonial houses are prepared, the door must face either Mount Diro or Mount Kenya.

35. The old women we interviewed in Timothy's family—who had known Turaso—noted that the community was afraid. Although Turaso claimed she had visited Nkai's home, this did not necessarily give them comfort. On the one hand they knew that something more powerful than humans was at work here, but they were not certain it was Nkai. On the other hand, even if it were Nkai, Nkai is known to wreak devastation as well as bring good things.

36. He meant to suggest that airplanes could not penetrate space itself—as powerful as Europeans seem to be, in other words, even they cannot go beyond the universe. They cannot escape Nkai or Nkai's womb.

37. Or the strength of Euro-American insistence upon mapping two and only two genders onto two and only two kinds of genitalia in spite of "intersex" traits appearing in 1 of every 1,000 or 2,000 births depending on definition (Blackless et al. 2000).

38. Naado is an old Samburu woman related to Turaso; she knew and talked to Turaso firsthand about her experience being taken to Nkai's home in her childhood, during the late 1880s/early 1890s. Whether or not Turaso indeed told her that Nkai was a certain red is impossible to know, but her claim gives continuity to the idea that redness is a common color to attribute to Nkai, one that old people do not see as implausible for old stories. Turaso, like all Samburu who went all the way to Nkai's home, reported the presence of calabashes there.

39. Such terms for Europeans are common cross-culturally. See for example Jackson 1995 on "whitefellas" and Stoller 1989a, Stoller and Olkes 1987 on *anasara*.

40. See also Jackson 1995: 11–14 for a poignant discussion of the implications of European racial constructions for Australian Aborigines.

41. The colorful "Samburu" cloth I was wearing was the latest fashion for Samburu, imported from Indonesia and worn as well both by other Kenyans and by tourists. When I returned from the field (after a year) I noted that cloth wraps like these had become ubiquitous in the United States as well—continuing the trend of "ethnic" or "exotic" fashions that I noted in the mid-1990s (see Straight 2002a). For Remeta, my cloth and beads were consistent with "modern" Samburu fashions.

42. An association between divinity and snakes is common elsewhere in East Africa (indeed, it is occasionally the topic of local news stories) and in other parts of Africa as well. For example, Stoller reports that in West Africa, "the snake is called Sajara, who lives in grottos, but will sometimes appear in the sky" (Stoller, personal communication, July 2005).

43. For similar prophecies among the Maasai, see Hodgson 2005.

44. Ntomonok, plural of ntomononi. This is a respectful term used to address women who have newly given birth or those generally of an age and marital status to be capable of giving birth. Mparatut also refers to married women, but it expressly means wife and is not polite in some contexts. Ntasat is a past-child-bearing woman; *nkokon* is a grandmother. All can be translated into English as "woman." See n. 20 on lack of "woman" in Samburu.

45. This is not to suggest that Eurocentric Otherness is simple. If race is any

indication, it is far from simple—see for example Stoler 1989a. However, it is based on an ontology distinct from Samburu, as tempting as it is to frame Samburu separations in terms of Otherness. I suggest that Samburu separations are more subtle than West/rest because to examine them in the terms of European ontologies is to unduly flatten them, to lose the contours that make them meaningful. At the same time, there is undoubtedly something shared here, which allows this translation to work.

Chapter 4. Latukuny

1. Mporoi is the clotted blood associated with childbirth. It is closely connected to the child and to the woman's fertility.
2. See Blystad 2000 for an ethnographically rich comparative example in East Africa. Blystad discusses fertility and infertility among the Tanzanian Datoga in broad terms, aiming to understand fertility as experienced by Datoga women themselves—as part of a set of bodily and ritual practices over which women can take some measure of control even in the midst of sources of vulnerability that encompass divine and human action in the world.
3. I discuss this with respect to Kristeva and Lacan in the Conclusion.
4. This is regardless of whether receivers' desires for the objects turn on remembering or forgetting that previous ownership.
5. Following Gregory 1997 I employ here the terms "inalienable keepsakes" (for objects that do not circulate) and "inalienable detachables" (for objects that do circulate while still retaining some "thing" or "essence" of their previous possessor). On inalienable possessions, also see especially Weiner 1992. For classic treatments, see Marx 1977: 116; and Mauss 1967 [1925].
6. Most people suggest that Nkai makes exceptions for those who are attending school or work. Yet it is assumed that they will still wear their beads while at home.
7. As a noun, ntoome is related to ntomononi—a woman of child-bearing age, quintessentially one who has recently given birth.
8. A woman cannot generate fire without a man any more than she can conceive a child without a man. Similarly, though a man may kindle a fire and stimulate a woman to conceive, only a woman can sustain and bring forth fire and life.
9. This also bears on what are considered to be incestuous relationships—regardless of chronological age.
10. For comparison, see Broch-Due 2000 for a fascinating discussion of Turkana gender and fertility, including the significance of milk and calabashes in understanding the importance of women in bringing forth and sustaining life.
11. Lorien is olea africana (oleaceae). Lorien should not be confused with *lorrian*, swamp.
12. The lgweita tree (*Cordia sinensis*—Heine, Heine, and Konig 1998) is usually green, dries slowly, and "has fire"—ntoome and lpiroi are made from it. Its sticks are also straight and lightweight so that they don't harm animals beaten with them in herding.
13. Thus we could say that sobua and lorien—in all their complexity as objects referring elsewhere—are dicent indexical legisigns. They are signs of a general type (replicas) whose connection to their objects is complexly metonymic and whose interpretants are actual existents (fecundity or lack thereof).
14. This notion of identity and difference appears paradoxical insofar as

there is constant intermarriage and mixing, and insofar as Samburu "identity" contains both people and ritual practices of others. See Gottlieb 1996 for a beautiful elaboration of these seeming paradoxes for the Beng of Côte d'Ivoire.

15. See Lienhardt 1961, particularly 21–23, concerning the relationship between cattle, persons, and divinity among the Dinka.

16. Heine, Heine, and Konig 1988 identify serishoi as *Boscia coriacea Pax* (Capparaceae).

17. Heine, Heine, and Konig identify silalei as *Boswellia hildebrandtii* (Burseraceae). When burned, the gum smells like frankincense.

18. Lmurran at *loikar*, those who are spending long periods in the bush away from social life, also fit into this category. They are liminal—outside the bounds of sociality—and they smear fat on themselves but don't wash their bodies during their stay in the bush. They do, however, wash their hands before eating meat so as to avoid ingesting their *kereet*.

19. See Stoller 1989a for an interesting comparison to Songhay in West Africa, where fragrance is likewise important for health (e.g., 115–17), and not taking care of oneself—and the filth that results—is associated with illness and death (e.g., 61).

20. Indeed, Samburu sesen is not a "body" awaiting its opposite—it is not opposed to "mind" or "spirit." Certainly, some shared aspect of sesen and body partake of reality and our prescissing of it. That is, there is a moment of being-in-contact by way of something we might call our unique and shared human physiology, and in the reductive prescissing moment that inevitably occurs, we must suppose that something (and therefore something shared) remains. *A body opposed to mind is not part of that sharedness*, and thus we do not begin nor do we end with it. We take up sesen, a sign for which sweat, smell, fertility, and luck are all treated by the Samburu in ways Europeans would regard as "tangible" (see also Strathern 1996).

21. See Johnsen 2002 on the Maasai.

22. It is necessary to steal it several times.

23. The fat used to fill the lboliboli is derived from the bull the groom brings to be slaughtered for the marriage ceremony (*rikoret*). (Lboliboli as calabash should not be confused with *mboliboli*, eggs.)

24. While in the strictest sense lorien is women's general fecundity and sobua is men's, the fertility and well-being of an entire family are typically referred to as lorien. Thus, lorien is the more general term.

25. Lienhardt (1961: 45) similarly mentions that Dinka eldest sons are closely associated with their fathers and youngest sons with their mothers.

26. The choice of terminologies touches on a continuing debate concerning the use of broad terms for translation and the risk of flattening cross-cultural concepts. See Kapferer 1997 as well as Henrietta Moore and Sanders 2001. However, while the latter attempt to do justice to this dilemma and indeed offer nuance and subtlety to these issues, the title of their edited volume (*Magical Interpretations, Material Realities*) weakens their points somewhat. On the one hand, they ask whether "Western teleological beliefs about progress, development, rationality and modernity—those ready-made explanations for social change that provide answers to the Big Questions in life—[are] really so different from the idea that occult forces move the world" (19). On the other hand, the title of the book suggests that "matter" is "real" while "magic" is an "interpretation." Moreover, they do not interrogate belief or reality itself but seem

instead to merely repeat Evans-Pritchard's supposition of multiple logics interpreting the "same" (Euro-American understanding of) "reality." (See also Kapferer 2003 on the unexamined assumptions of some recent approaches to "magic" or "occult" phenomena.) Many of Moore and Sanders's contributors seem to do likewise, although the arguments of a couple of them—most notably Isak Niehaus and Susan Rasmussen—are more supple. With specific regard to the terms "magic" and "witchcraft" it is important to note their own rich and intriguing history in the so-called West. See Luhrmann 1991, for example, for a rich elucidation of the importance of belief and/in magic for the London neopagans she worked with. For Euro-Americans, "magic" is tied to a notion of belief as that apart from the scientifically empirical, which, as I note here, is quite different from Samburu understandings of practices anthropologists would typically label as "witchcraft." See also Tambiah 1990 for the Euro-American philosophical underpinnings of "magic," "witchcraft," and "science" as these relate to the history of anthropological thought (and, more recently, Shanafelt 2004). While Evans-Pritchard's (1937) view of cultural logic ultimately won out, Lévy-Bruhl's (1926) discussion of "primitive" understandings that transcend Euro-American dualism and Radin's (1937) equivocal retort to it are worth reexamining.

27. Among those implications, I would point out that people do suddenly become sick or poor for no reason and women are sometimes inexplicably barren. We share these things, and we cannot always remedy these situations any more than the Samburu always can. The Samburu can sometimes cure illness and infertility, however, in ways that those who invoke the term "stress" could consider.

28. The practices I am describing here could be placed in the traditional anthropological conceptual framework of "sympathetic magic," although I do not choose to do so for my present purposes. Comparative examples are too pervasive to cite (beginning at least with Frazier's *Golden Bough*). See Kapferer 2003 and Tambiah 1990 for a nuanced discussion of magic as conceptual concept.

29. In response to the broader cultural politics of a cosmopolitan Kenya self-consciously attempting to reclaim a "cultural heritage," Samburu Christians have placed renewed value on the practices of their unconverted, "backward" Samburu fellows—"we still have our culture," they say proudly—and have begun to assert the possibility of separating "religion" and "culture." That is outside the scope of my argument and aims in this book, however, so I will leave it for another time.

30. I put "legitimate" in quotes because it is never legitimate to put latukuny into circulation outside the family (or beyond the hands of very trusted friends)—that is the very crux of the dilemma.

31. Some women rationalized the selling by suggesting that it would be okay, so long as they did not purchase food with the proceeds. Many others were not so sure.

32. For excellent critical discussions examining the usefulness of anthropological concepts like witchcraft and sorcery, see Jackson 1989 (especially 88–96) and Kapferer 2003.

33. See Weiss's (1996, 1998) provocative ethnography of the Haya, for example.

Chapter 5. Doki

1. In *Strangers to Ourselves* (1991), Kristeva extended this logic to an under-standing of the concept of foreigners, a particular kind of otherness she tracked across time and space, beginning with classical Greece and Rome. Again, how-ever, she exercised a great deal of poetic license as she made general pronounce-ments across cultural and temporal differences.

2. See particularly Braidotti 1997; Butler 1990; Cixous 1976; Irigaray 1977, 1985.

3. See, for example, Amos and Parmar 1984; Minh-ha 1987.

4. See, for example, Kapchan 1996; Ong 1988; Tsing 1993.

5. See for example, Bauman and Briggs 1990; Mannheim and Tedlock 1995.

6. Examples include Csordas 1994a, b; Desjarlais 1992; Howes 1987; Jackson 1989b, 1996; and Stoller 1989.

7. I am of course borrowing Marilyn Strathern's (1988) terminology here.

8. I have already alluded to some of the propitious sharing and illicit exchanges that also comprise Samburu intersubjectivity. See Bercovitch 1998 for an illuminating comparison of "shared personhood" framed in terms of exchange. Of the Atbalmin of Papua New Guinea, Bercovitch writes, for exam-ple, "People could add to or diminish another's flesh or vital force, and they could influence his or her heart or thinking in a manner that could be likewise either helpful or harmful" (214).

9. This power to harm one's relatives and neighbors is common cross-culturally, although typically expressed in the idiom of witchcraft and sorcery. See, for example, Jackson 1989; Stoller and Olkes 1987.

10. Spencer (1965: 186) mentions the relationship between a person's eyes and unpropitious consequences, but he does so in arguing that this is a form of "witchcraft" practiced by neighboring Turkana, not Samburu. Samburu in both the *lpurkel* (lowlands) and *ldonyio* (highlands) mentioned this Turkana attribute but also attributed it to some Samburu unrelated to Turkana. Moreover, in con-trast to Spencer, they described ldeket to me as beginning with any hungry per-son's eyes, and this bears no relationship to people who deliberately cause misfortune to others through mysterious means. See also Johnsen 1997: 271; Voshaar 1998: 155–56 on the Maasai.

11. I continue to put glosses in quotation marks to remind you that these do not correspond, but merely approximate. Even the senses, even hearts, stom-achs, and saliva, can be radically different signs.

12. This is reminiscent of the American metaphor in which a mischievous or mean person is referred to as a stinker. Yet the Samburu term is not metaphori-cal in any straightforward sense, as I will elucidate more fully in Chapter 6.

13. Ltau is also the site where strong affective attachments, as between lovers, are stored. Since *nkwe* (head) is associated with *mparnot*—a complex of memory and thought—Samburu seem to share in common with Euro-Americans a notion of emotions as generated from the heart or gut, while thought is in the head. Yet nkosheke is much more than emotion—it is disposition and personal-ity, and it has motivational force. While the nkwe may have memory/thought, the nkosheke likewise "thinks." More crucially, nkwe belongs to sesen ("body") as surely as nkosheke does. I will discuss these issues in more detail in subse-quent chapters.

14. *Keata nkamilak*—they have saliva. This includes all laisi, families known for their blessing and cursing abilities, as I discussed in Chapter 2. Most laisi are said to originate from Rendille families.

15. Laŋeni are men or women from Masula and Loŋeli clans mostly, who specialize in diagnosing unpropitious conditions, especially based on their knowledge of similar past unpropitious conditions. They are "knowing," or "wise" people.

16. Of course, the snake was unlucky, since we killed it for our own safety.

17. For earlier comparisons of the evocative efficacy of ritual speech see Favret-Saada 1980; Irvine 1972.

18. See for example Csordas 1994b. The continuing popularity of charismatic forms of Christianity, as well as New Age and neopagan forms of worship and belief forcefully indicates Euro-American ambivalence concerning personhood and agency.

19. It is about 125 years, but according to Samburu generational reckoning—in which fathers should be two ageset generations older than their oldest sons—it is approximately four birth generations.

20. On Samburu prohibited foods, see also Holtzman 2003. One Lmasula subclan can eat rhino. With lions, Samburu can kill them and cut their skin into strips for *mungen* (lion ornaments men must wear for a number of rituals)—the mungen can be sold and the money used for food or anything. To eat the lion, though, brings the same misfortune as other itadee. Eating hyenas and dogs is so terrible that people don't know even how to categorize or cleanse it. It seems to be almost as bad as eating a person; moreover, in the case of eating a hyena, it is like eating death.

21. Lkileku were young men circa the 1930s. See Table 1.

22. I do not mean, nor do I intend, to minimize actions like infant neglect and infanticide. Yet it is difficult to fully translate the motivations underlying it unless we have ourselves spent a lifetime prescissing a reality that is recurringly painful and harsh. As Jean Jackson (1994) has illuminated, "all pain has cultural meaning" (210). Yet Jackson's challenge is to understand precisely what that means, because, as she explains, pain challenges the limits of subject/object and preobjective/objective dualisms. My suggestion is that how we experience birth defects has to do with a lifetime of prescissing reality, and for the Samburu, real trauma happens so frequently as to beg for explanation and response—even if the response is to push away painful manifestations of life.

23. The word for what we call "cannibal" is *nkampit*, for which there is no adequate translation. *Nkampito* (pl.) vary, some eating people as this one does, and some just being wild, ravenous meat eaters. They do not all have two mouths, as in this tale.

24. I have not exhausted Samburu forms of wongdoing and their unpropitious consequences. There is, for example, a category for minor violations—*ntolo*. Samburu can say someone is *kotolo*, s/he is ntolo or doing ntolo. Ntolo is acquired by doing small wrongs. For example, eating certain tabooed foods (like birds perhaps) is ntolo. Killing animal kids is ntolo. Touching one's own face is ntolo because it is as if one is mourning and thus it becomes like a prediction of something bad—for a girl to put her arm over her head is a similar ntolo to grabbing the face. A more serious ntolo is for children to repeatedly beat a woman's firestones—that might even bring about the woman's death (which would then bring ŋoki). If a person does repeated ntolo, it can pass to their children, children's children, and so on, like ŋoki. It can take the form of a birthmark, discoloration on the face, and so on, in subsequent children. It can also take the form of temperament in a child, seen for example in someone who gets angry easily. Sometimes the differences in actions or consequences between ntolo and

ŋoki are difficult to discern, and I strongly suspect that the rules are somewhat fluid rather than absolute.

25. The name "kiarabu" itself betrays these spirits' origins—it is Kiswahili for an Arab method, language, or in this case, thing.

26. At the same time, through ritual action ŋoki can sometimes be *forced* to withdraw, a process that is too radical for the terms of departure, and yet it may be that an unbecoming is too strong.

27. On the constraints of interpretation, see especially Ahearn 2001; Eco 1999.

28. See also Gupta 2002 for an article with a similar subtext but with a more extensive discussion of reincarnation accounts.

29. Here, the common thread between reincarnation and ŋoki is the thread itself, even as the two are in many ways one another's inverse, as I earlier suggested.

Chapter 6. Death

1. See also Ivy 1995.

2. As I described in Chapter 5, marar is an unpropitious condition acquired from beating weaker persons or from a wrongdoing of similar gravity, which takes control of the wrongdoer, causing him or her to commit additional, more serious wrongs—to the point of killing another human being. Lmogiro is the unpropitious condition a person acquires from killing—both will eventually transform into ŋoki.

3. For a West African example of illness and death being associated with enduring filth, see Stoller 1989a.

4. The Maasai term is *enkeeya*. The Samburu form of enkeeya, in contrast— (nkeeye)—means a terminal or potentially terminal illness. It appears as if enkeeya likewise derives from aya, to take.

5. Anaŋ means to throw down with force, such that the object is not going to move again. Besides referring to death, it can also be used metaphorically to refer to something that one loves very, very much.

6. Throughout the discussion of the dead that follows, the terms in parentheses refer to corpses in these various age and gender categories. That corpses have their own names corresponding to the names of living age-gender groups reinforces the notion that the living become something else at death. The literal meaning of nkiyo is something one has heard about without yet seeing. In death, bigger boys are referred to as *laimouwarani*—wild things/things with horns.

7. The literal meaning is one who has fire (married elders got complete fire when they married).

8. The literal meaning is the blood and other secretions a woman has in the days after giving birth. All married women are called in death as if they were mothers.

9. Concerning the centrality of cutting, mixing, and purity in relation to Nkai, recall Kratz and Pido's discussion of Maasai beadwork, which I noted in Chapter 2: "Maasai deliberately 'cut' beadwork patterns and activities such as pouring, because to create pure color fields or a continuous milk flow would seem to claim the purity and power attributed only to God" (2000: 53).

10. The word derives its literal meaning from the verb *atem*, trying but failing.

11. The word derives its literal meaning from the verb *arrorro*, almost falling.

12. See also Broch-Due 2000 for an excellent discussion of the multiple significance of gender and parenthood in relation to Turkana mortuary practices.

13. The literal meaning is something that has no place. It can also refer to lone buffalo.

14. Which home one dies in can also be meaningful. If a married woman dies in her natal home, her corpse will be carried through a hole made in the settlement's fence for that purpose rather than through the gate because she already has her own gate (at her married home).

15. With all deaths, an animal is slaughtered for the elders who "throw" the dead, not only for them to eat but also for fat to cleanse the burial implements and the hands of those assisting afterward. Besides this cleansing slaughter, there are also various other animals normally given in the course of the funeral, or their equivalent monetary value paid. It is unpropitious in these circumstances (any death) to haggle over the monetary value—the person entitled to the compensation simply states the amount (invariably a fair amount). Additionally, when it is in unpropitious circumstances (death and also adultery fines), the largest possible denomination of bills is given. Some of the animals given in the context of funerals include *Nkerr* (sheep), given to the person who drew the outline for the gravesite; *lashe* (male calf), given to the person who broke the legs of a married person for burial (a married person's legs are broken for putting them into the proper fetal position); and a heifer given to the person who shaves the dead person if there are inauspicious circumstances surrounding the death so that it cannot be a family member. On animal exchange in the context of Turkana burial practices, see Broch-Due 1999b.

16. Much that is both bad and good about a person is stored in their stomach—both ldeket and mayian form there, for example. A goat's innocent stomach is an appropriate substitution for the part of the corpse that smells most of wrongdoing.

17. Another disadvantage pertains to apiu ("resurrection"), as I will discuss in the next chapter.

18. Moreover, there is some indication that very bad cases of wrongdoing will not go unnoticed even if a person is buried. Thus, there is one story in which a hyena actually disinterred the deceased and brought his head back to his settlement—an extremely unpropitious (and no doubt traumatic) occurrence. That family knew they had cleansing to do.

19. See Lienhardt 1961: 289–90 for an important comparison with Dinka mortuary practices.

20. In the case of a dead married elder with children, it will also be necessary to give away a goat or sheep (known as *lkine looŋkeenita*—sheep of the straps) to neighboring elders about a month after the death. They will slaughter and eat it far from the mourning family's home—the mourning family should not touch it in any way after they give it. Indeed, it is also referred to as *sigiria* (donkey)—an animal whose consumption is highly tabooed.

21. Though outside the scope of this book, the implications of this for understanding gender relations in Samburu are important, and I will examine them another time.

22. Lacan 1988: 223 and 249 quoted in Borch-Jacobsen 1991: 49.

23. This of course also points up the continuing and troubling implications of blame-the-victim explanations, the discursive underbelly likewise of neoliberal flexible accumulation, which blames the impoverished for their condition. While the Samburu moral universe is based on an ethic of sharing, the deferral

of punishment (as ŋoki can be in cases in which it is perceived to take a genera-tion or more to appear) can weaken the consequences of transgressions. Never-theless, the practice of continual introspection, as Samburu ask themselves what wrongs they might have committed against others, brings the importance of right action into every conversation in ways not true in an overly simplified ego-bound universe.

Chapter 7. Resurrection

1. Apiu is the root form of a verb meaning to come back to life after being dead—in other words, to revive, resurrect, spontaneously resuscitate.

2. Since Samburu in the highlands have been burying people for some time rather than placing them in the bush for the hyenas, it is not surprising that some people in the highlands have not heard of it happening. Nevertheless, I seldom came across a Samburu family either in the highlands or the lowlands in which at least one person had not heard of apiu.

3. On the haunting in-betweenness of death, see also Rosaldo 1989.

4. Loikar typically refers to the time and place when/where lmurran eat a lot of meat in the soro for an extended period. Here, the girl was taken to loikar for the purpose of healing. See Johnsen 1997 on Maasai *olpul.*

5. Lenaura and his wife were both talking. Curved brackets indicate Lenaura; square brackets indicate my notes or my research assistant, Musa, and me; and no brackets indicate Lenaura's wife, the main storyteller here.

6. The leaves used to cover the corpse are an intensely meaningful sign relat-ing to the mortuary process. When the dead return to life, their metonymic ico-nography becomes a captivating summation of resurrection itself. In one story of a person who had been dead for three days, children ventured near and found the person moving the leaves away: "When children just moved around there they found the person just raising their hands moving the leaves like this [gestures with his hands]" (Lenaura interview, 2001).

7. There is another difference worth noting as well—Jesus' corporeality. In the Matthew text we are told that Mary Magdalene and Mary actually held Jesus' feet, while in John we are told that Jesus cautioned them against touching Him because He had not yet ascended to His "Father." It is only later (presumably after journeying to God and back) that He allows people to touch Him and His crucifixion wounds.

8. Ronald Finucane is a medievalist whose work on medieval miracles has been of enormous benefit to me. I have also benefited from Finucane's personal communications concerning medieval scholarship and the intriguing question of how and when the transformation from resurrection as miracle to resurrec-tion as empirically explainable natural event might have occurred. He surmises that it may have taken place in the seventeenth-century at the higher levels of the Catholic Church hierarchy and is currently examining sixteenth- and seven-teenth-century papal canonization records to investigate this more precisely. However, he also notes that it may have occurred much later in other societal domains. On related issues see Daston and Park 1998.

9. Saints were celebrated in their tendency to save victims of hanging, guilty or innocent. One genre of medieval painting depicts saints holding up persons being hanged (Bartlett 2004).

10. Once resurrections had become natural, spontaneous resuscitations, means needed to be devised for dealing with them. Thus, in the eighteenth cen-

tury statutes were passed to try to remedy the problem; moreover, bodies were sometimes buried with various devices meant to alert the living to the spontaneous resuscitation of the dead (Lock 2002: 66–69). See also Tebb and Vollum 1905 for a fascinating turn-of-the-twentieth-century ensemble of stories of "premature burial" and discussion of what should be done to prevent it. Given the evidence of exhumed corpses showing disturbing signs of having awakened in the grave, fears of being buried too soon had some foundation.

11. See also Daston and Park 1998 concerning the storage and display of relics and natural wonders. An interesting accompaniment to miraculous healings was the practice of fashioning objects in the shape of healed body parts and hanging them in churches. These were often hung among natural objects (such as ostrich eggshells) believed to be wondrous and to possess healing properties. Natural wonders, like saints' body parts, were agentive objects.

12. Bodies were also linked to dispositional character traits and behavior by which states of ill health could be diagnosed and cured. In the thirteenth and fourteenth centuries for example, *complexio* embraced the notion that "a person's behavior, appearance, aptitude, and moral stature were perceived to be intricately connected to his or her physical, humoral, natural condition" (Groebner 2004: 365). In this formulation, every individual had a unique complexio. Ironically for the development of the individual ego, the individual uniqueness implied in this iteration of complexio would, by the eighteenth century, be replaced by one that privileged group identity. Thus, while in the medieval period the body was read medically for "internal" states linked to both health and character and associated with a "complexio" unique for every individual, by the eighteenth century complexio was understood to distinguish entire ethnic groups or races from one another and defined "who" could be used as what kind of experimental medical subject (Groebner 2004; Schiebinger 2004).

13. We must be cautious about carrying these parallels too far, as will be seen below—the earlier notions Vidal discusses turned on the assumption of the soul and body being jointly replicable.

14. For the classic work, see Hertz 1960 [1907]; Turner 1969; Van Gennep 1960. See also Bloch and Parry 1982; Bloch 1996; Chambert-Loir and Reid 2002; Comaroff 1984; Kan 1989; Parkin 1992; Strathern 1996.

15. Margaret Lock (2002: 298–306) provides a thorough history of human vivisection, including the gruesome theft and careless destruction of corpses in the late eighteenth and early nineteenth centuries, the period in which Mary Shelley wrote *Frankenstein*.

16. See Hodgson 2005 for a Maasai view of Christian burial.

17. In an area in which Jon Holtzman was working in the early 1990s, a dog brought part of an infant's corpse back to the settlement of its parents not long after it was "thrown." The utter horror and anguish this provoked were further and inevitably exacerbated by the need to understand why it had happened.

18. This is the past tense of the verb apiu conjugated.

19. The Samburu term for heart is ltau. Tau would appear to be onomatopoeia.

20. See Stoller 1989a, pp. 53–54 concerning Songhay ambivalence about hospitals: "When they arrived at the hospital, Mariama trembled. She knew that the hospital village housed the dying and the dead. People went to the hospital village and did not return to their homes" (53).

21. Nompoi referred to the doctor and nurses here as elephants. Elephants

can and do kill people, and thus the term is metaphorically associated with war enemies or implicit enemies. Foreigners to Samburu society, and Europeans particularly, are frequently put into this category.

22. With regard to the issue of defining death's onset specifically, Lock has given us plenty of empirical cause for concern: The criteria for and conceptual agreement with "brain death" continue to provoke debate; smaller, tertiary hospitals continue to make mistakes in diagnosing it; a number of respected medical professionals and scholars offer convincing arguments that a focus on organ donation has resulted in less strenuous efforts to preserve the lives of individuals suffering head trauma or to develop technologies to improve results; and, finally, one medical researcher in Japan has had some success in actually slowing the damage after head trauma and thus preventing brain death itself.

23. See, for example, Carter 2002; Damasio 1999; Dennett 1984; LeDoux 2002; Pinker 1997.

Chapter 8. Loip

1. On the dead as constituting social relations see Comaroff 1984. On death's power to dangerously upset social relations and the role of rituals in controlling the potential hazards, see the classic works by Hertz (1960 [1907]); Turner (1969); Van Gennep (1960). See also Bloch and Parry 1982. In contrast, see Rosaldo 1989 concerning the importance of taking emotion into account in understanding death, and Seremetakis 1991 concerning society's inability to completely restore the social order after death.

2. That Hodgson's gloss reflects Maasai Christian understandings in particular is indicated by the consistency between her gloss and Frans Mol's (1978). Hodgson glosses 'oltau' as 'heart, soul, spirit', while Mol glosses it as 'soul, heart, spirit' under 'soul' and as 'heart, mind, soul, spirit' under 'heart'. My suspicion is that many of Mol's glosses reflect his attempts to find Maasai terms for the translation of biblical concepts. Moreover, the choices are in flux. Thus he notes, for example, that the Holy Spirit was increasingly being translated as Enkiyaŋet Sinyati (something like 'pure/upright/unblemished breath' rather than Oltau Sinyati (something like 'pure/upright/unblemished heart' (35).

3. I am basing my Maasai impression on fieldwork for my master's degree that I conducted in the summer of 1989 and on informal discussions with Maasai acquaintances and specialists since then.

4. For example, when girls praise their lmurran boyfriends or when the latter eat a lot of meat, they "get ltau."

5. Nanoto told the interviewer that she was first afflicted between 1900 and 1910, although this seems a little inconsistent with the claim that she was "healed" in 1930 after requesting permission from her father to linger to hear the words of a Lutheran evangelist. Hodgson includes Nanoto as typical of the Maasai afflicted because she was a woman of childbearing age, but I wonder about Nanoto's circumstances. Could she have been both of childbearing age *and living with her father* throughout the period from 1900 to 1930?

6. See Susan Rasmussen 1995: 40 and Mario Aguilar 2000: 258 for an alternative view.

7. I am attending to regional practices here with due attention to the historic relationships Samburu have had with their neighbors (see James 1998 on Mauss's pathbreaking notion of regional systems of societies sharing a connected history). Through their close link to the Maasai and a migration history

that includes movement as far south as Mount Kenya (by their own oral accounts) and as far north as southern Ethiopia and the Lake Turkana region (see Sobania 1991), various Samburu families in the new millennium claim descent from Kamba, Meru, Pokot, Turkana, and Rendille, as well as Maasai, the now-extinct Laikipiak, Nchemps, and various Maa-speaking groups the Laikipiak are said to have decimated. With regard to loibonok, the net may be cast even wider. In the aftermath of the Laikipiak wars, Laikipiak were decimated and dispersed among an assortment of Maa- (including Samburu) and non-Maa-speakers, and a number of other Maa-speakers also sought refuge with various groups. This scattering included loibonok, of course (although it was not limited to them) and thus some contemporary Samburu loibonok trace their descent to both Maasai and Laikipiak, while some (Uas Nkishu) Maasai loibonok even settled with the Nandi (Anderson 1995). Not all Samburu loibonok trace their descent from "outside," however. Thus, although they are not currently practicing naibon, the Lolmiŋani family is said to be "pure" Samburu (from Lmasula clan), and indeed the "original" Samburu loibonok family. Moreover, while some Maasai loibonok clearly benefited from British colonization (Waller 1995), others, including some Samburu loibonok, were detained or intentionally dispersed to reduce their influence. See also Fratkin 1979, 1991 on Maasai and Samburu loibonok.

8. Sperling's footnote bears repeating here: "Krapf explains the meaning of the word koma as 'a man who died and who is believed to exist in the grave'" (Sperling 1995: 98 n. 20).

9. See Broch-Due 2000 on the Turkana; Tablino 1999 [1980] on the Gabra; Voshaar 1998 on the Maasai; Schlee 1989 on regional continuities in northern Kenya; and Anderson and Johnson 1995 on ritual and belief in East Africa more broadly, including the Meru and Kikuyu.

10. For a comprehensive discussion of life force and breath among the Dinka, see Lienhardt 1961: 206–7.

11. See, for example, Mol 1978: 35; Wagner 1998: 215.

12. See Wagner 1998: 208.

13. See Straight 2005b for a description of ntotoi in relation to transgressive sexuality.

14. Whether the dead were young and thus unpropitious or old and "sweet" is important here. Photographs and tape recordings of the youthful dead should be destroyed, while those of the sweet old dead can be kept.

15. Recall my description in Chapter 4 of filming my friend's wife cleaning her calabashes—it is as if latukuny is being captured in its most potent form yet. However, what is at stake is more than latukuny, but personhood tout *corps.* Having shared milk and friendship, she was not concerned about what I might be getting in the transaction.

16. Indeed, some Samburu Christians that I know suggest that loip is not a good equivalent for the Christian soul; rather, nkiyeŋet is closest to their understanding of the soul because it is known to move away somewhere after death, possibly going to Nkai. This is even though loip is said to possess some of a person's memory and shape and to move with one's ltoilo ("voice").

17. See Holtzman 2003 where he relates another version of this story—a more ambivalent version that emphasizes both tobacco's sacred aspects and its possibilities for weakening Samburu nkanyit ("shame").

18. See also Voshaar 1998 concerning the Maasai practice of putting tobacco in the hearth as an offering to the dead.

19. Since my research assistant, Musa, and I were both talking frequently in this conversation, I have put my words in square brackets and his in curved brackets.

20. Lenaisho's words have no brackets; his wife's are in double square brackets; Musa's are in curved brackets; and mine are in single square brackets.

21. While memorializing practices seem more familiar in cross-cultural accounts, the erasure of the dead—whether of all dead or certain categories of the dead—happens as well. See, for example, Conklin 2001 on mortuary cannibalism; and Jackson 1995: 61 on erasure of the dead through their objects (and see 94 on the haunting presence of the dead).

22. In his classic study of the Azande, Evans-Pritchard (1976 [1937]) describes ghosts with some behavior similar to that of Samburu "bad" loip. He also differentiates the Azande soul in ways that bear comparing with Samburu understandings.

23. That is, elephant bulls are said to have drowned. Moreover, some Samburu say it also "took" some Laikipiak in the late nineteenth century.

24. She was alive as of 2002 when I last visited her, although she was becoming confused. It is important to note that Samburu like Doto Malapen often do not come from loibonok families. Thus, Doto Malapen had no legitimate connection to loibonok lineages, yet Nkai chose her, communicating with her throughout her life.

25. Doto Malapen related this incident to me in the 1990s, and her daughter independently related it in 2002. It has become a famous event, and thus a number of Samburu have likewise alluded to it when discussing her as a prophetess.

26. See Hodgson 2005 for a description of two Maasai prophets' (a woman and a man) experiences with Maasai divinity (Engai). Although Hodgson does not mention the similarities between these experiences and the orpeko experiences she describes in her earlier work, I find the parallels notable. While the Samburu do not characterize any of these experiences as spirit possession, all are different aspects of "otherworldly" experience, of reciprocal movements between "here" and "there" (*inia bata*—that side, as Samburu gloss it). In this way, they reflect Samburu simultaneous awareness of and uneasiness with the tenuousness of our footing here. Perhaps this is what Hodgson invokes when she mentions Maasai continued uneasiness about corpses and death in spite of Christian teachings about the afterlife.

Conclusion. Immediacies

Epigraph: Descartes 1904, vol. 7: 25.

1. Lydia, Musa, and John were my research assistants for my quantitative study. Musa also assisted me with the open-ended interviews.

2. Mannheim and Tedlock (1995) examine fieldwork as dialogic encounter. On putting fieldwork "in relation," see Michael Herzfeld 1987; Anna Tsing 1993, 1994; and Tanya Luhrmann 1996, where each brings ethnographic experience to bear on a consideration of anthropology as a discipline in different ways. Herzfeld compares aspects of modern Greek identity to anthropology's discursive understandings. Tsing creates a critical dialogue with anthropological ideas of the "local" and with ethnographic genres more generally that privilege a West/rest opposition over the lived particularities of an anthropologist's interlocutors—including their own negotiation with global structures of power. Luhrmann examines the fate of postcolonial Parsis and the fraught position that anthropology has come to occupy since the literary turn—a literary turn I am

likewise concerned with. See chapter 7 in Luhrmann 1996 on an extended discussion of the straitjacketing implications of the literary turn and a review of deliberately dialogic ethnographies.

3. See Ricoeur 1973 for an early, pathbreaking example.

4. Like Derrida, Kristeva is invoking and engaging with Plato's notion of chora in *The Timaeus.*

5. Her third is not Peirce's interpretant insofar as the representamen and object would lose their individual identity within it rather than being something more known about the object through the relation.

6. On the limits of Euro-American understandings of sensing and other cultural possibilities, see Geurts 2002.

7. See also Csordas 1994b, where he discusses Kristeva's influence on phenomenological anthropology. Additionally, Michael Jackson identifies Husserl's Lebenswelt (life-world), Merleau-Ponty's praktognosia (practical knowledge), Heidegger's Being-in-the-World, and a critical view of Bourdieu's habitus as crucial. With regard to Bourdieu however, and Jackson's (1996) assertion (echoed by many anthropologists) that he vascillates between a determined and a determining "subject," I do not think that Bourdieu is so much vacillating as he is trying to heuristically freeze the motion that does not actually freeze, account for what seems ever to remain elusive, imagine insides turning out and outsides turning in—in the Western ontologies of his thought. For Bourdieu, humans move through the world, the products of modes of the habitus that are the possibly irreducible conjoining of cognition and sociality. Commenting on Bourdieu, I would suggest that it was a theory of consciousness he was after—one that requires of us something more profound than the impossible paradoxical assemblage of structure and agency.

8. Jackson cited Oakeshott 1962 here. I certainly agree that we should avoid generalizing fieldwork observations as rules that govern behavior, the "unconscious," or culture. My point here is that separating theoretical knowledge in the way that Jackson, following Oakeshott, suggests is to impose an unwarranted dualism. Our interlocutors' narratives are immediate in the telling, to be sure. Likewise however, our own narratives of field experiences—even if approximations of our interlocutors' experiences—are immediate for us, just as reading someone else's narrative is an immediate experience for the reader.

9. See Schwenger 2001.

10. A theoretical hold on suffering—or its obverse—has important entailments. Thus, in the "Random Samples" section of a recent (2000) issue of *Science*—a journal for science professionals and those with some proficiency in the technical jargons of various "hard science" fields—the authors cite a longitudinal study of memory to make what I see as unwarranted interpretive leaps. In the study they cite, psychiatrist Daniel Offer asked a group of fourteen-year-old youths a series of opinion questions in 1962 and then returned to ask them the same questions many years later, when they were forty-eight. Based on variations in their answers over time, the author of this brief piece cites a psychologist's response that this study indicates that "even healthy people can't be relied on to give accurate accounts of their childhood, she says, and it bears on the heated controversy over people's memories of child sexual abuse. Clinicians taking a patient's history, she warns, 'should be very wary'" (Random Samples, 2000: 1961). To make such a switch from nontraumatic, trivial memories to memories of trauma that probably get laid down in notably different ways—owing to the physiological correlates of trauma itself—is startling. And it is in just this way,

under the cloak of "science," on the one hand and the fictionalizing, literary turn on the other, that we risk *implying* (not saying) that the narratives—and traumas themselves—of sexual abuse survivors, exiles, refugees, and the variously exploited and marginalized are fictions. Yet to do so is to normativize collective memory forms that conceal and submerge the nonnormative and the in-between.

11. Let me compare this positing of experience as extraordinary with Slavoj Žižek's (2004) allusion to the "univocity of Being" (55). Discussing Bataille's pure expenditure and Lacan's chain of signifiers, Žižek remarks that "a miracle is no longer the irrational exception that disturbs the rational order, since everything becomes a miracle; there is no longer the need to assert excess against normality, since everything becomes an excess—excess is everywhere, in an unbearable intensity. Therein lies resides the true transgression. It occurs when the tension between the ordinary phenomenal reality and the transgressive Excess of the Real Thing is abolished" (55). Yet, in his engagement with Deleuze via Lacan, Žižek maintains the force of the opposition; indeed, I suspect that the excess of the Real Thing appears and reappears in his monologue not because the tension between reality and the Real is abolished but because Žižek continues himself to reify the Real. My suggestion is not to abolish tension but to posit alternative ontological possibilies that include an expansive experience that does not simply dissolve oppositions nor does it locate the Thing in its difference, in the gap between perceptions (Žižek 62). The gap belongs to the excessive signifying of a Real that is posited to be experientially inseparable from a reality it thinks and is imagined through. This is not an abolishment of tension—the tension and the dialectic belong to one geopolitically hegemonic cultural imaginary. My argument of experience as extraordinary is rather more humble and mundane—an affirmation simultaneously of our inscrutability and our intersubjective crossings. Phenomenal reality never exists apart from the Real; it *is* the Real in one incarnation.

12. For example, to sell a book one has to convince a lot of (predominantly Euro-American privileged) readers that its matter matters—an increasingly difficult task if the subject is a community still at the margins of the margins, only barely troubling itself with the West.

13. Jean Rouch comments that for "the Songhay-Zarma, who are now quite accustomed to film, my 'self' is altered in front of their eyes in the same way as is the 'self' of the possession dancers: it is the 'film-trance' (ciné-transe) of the one filming the 'real trance' of the other" (Rouch 2003: 99).

14. I would like to thank Paul Stoller for pointing out to me the similarities between evocation as I employ it here and the evocative methods that Jean Rouch developed in his films. See Rouch 2003; Stoller 1992 for an elaboration of Rouch's methods.

Appendix 1

Epigraph: Peirce 1958: 41.

1. Chomsky's (1965, 1975) theory of grammar fits squarely here, as do Lévi-Strauss's (e.g., 1969a, b, 1973) analyses of myth, kinship, and exchange. More recently, Foucault's (e.g., 1979, 1990) theory of power and discourse is predicated on structuralist notions, as is Bourdieu's (1977) idea of the habitus (although the inspiration for Bourdieu's habitus also comes from Mauss's (1979) work pertaining to the body and Heidegger's dwelling, or being-in-the-world).

2. In other words, following Saussure, there would be no reason that 'ffitter' might not have been chosen rather than 'centipede' to convey the concept known as centipede. Once chosen, however, the sign-vehicle 'centipede' would become irreducibly connected (experientially) to the psychological concept centipede. To be fair to Saussure, he was attempting to create a method of studying and comparing the world's languages in relation to the human mind, not a method of understanding the relationship between concept and world (Ellis 1989).

3. See Eco 1999; Ahearn 2001 for critiques of infinite play suggesting that interpretations should be evaluated.

4. More than this, Derrida has, as I have already mentioned, misread Saussure and has repeated rather than remedied the problems created by Saussure's dualistic thinking. First, Derrida has substituted an ontology for a method. Even if Saussure's two-part sign contains hidden ontological assumptions, the method itself is not a theory of ontology. True, in positing a langue versus a parole and a concept arbitrarily connected to the world, Saussure did seem to assume the possibility of separating mind from body, perception from world. Derrida has not addressed these issues, however. Rather, he has used Saussure merely to negate the duality of Being/nonbeing. As John M. Ellis (1989) has shrewdly pointed out, Derrida suggests, incorrectly, that Saussure's langue is a system of signifiers (rather than signs composed of signifier and signified) in need of a transcendental signified that would refer to nothing beyond itself. Very early in *Of Grammatology*, for example, Derrida states: " 'Signifier of the signifier' describes on the contrary the movement of language: in its origin to be sure, but one can already suspect that an origin whose structure can be expressed as 'signifier of the signifier' conceals and erases itself in its own production. There the signifier always already functions as a signifier" (1976: 7). Later, he quotes Saussure's contention that although there is an unmotivated relationship, that does not mean that the "choice of the signifier is left entirely to the speaker" (Saussure quoted in Derrida 1976: 46). Yet Derrida seems to presume, particularly in his later writing (1979, for example) that the speaker/reader/writer can indeed choose what Derrida mistakenly calls the "signifier." What Derrida means to say and later makes explicit, as I will describe below, is that the process of signing can be compared to the "becoming unmotivated" of the trace. For excellent critical commentaries on Derrida, see Gashé 1986; Megill 1985; and Zuckert 1996. In contrast to Derrida's use of Saussure's sign, according to Saussure, a signifier is simply a sign-vehicle, a sound- or word-shape that denotes a concept. Sign-vehicles are only understood in a system in which each is understood in relation to all of the others in that system. Thus, a transcendental (or any) signified could not be a signifier; that is, a concept cannot be a sound- or word-shape. In English, the concept of tree cannot refer to the word-shape 'horse'—the word-shape 'tree' conjures *some aspect of* the concept of tree, and it does so in relationship to 'horse', 'grass', and every other sound-shape. To suggest that 'tree' brings the concept of car to mind is complete nonsense. There is no play of signifiers in that respect. Similarly, the concept of tree is understood in relation to other concepts such as dog, flower, and house. That the concept that tree conjures for a language user is not isomorphic with the concept that dog evokes is a basic requirement of making sense in communicating.

5. The relationship between Peirce's triadic ontology and triadic sign is apparent from his ten classes of signs. His own diagram showing these classes, and a great many diagrams meant to simplify his, remain difficult to decipher.

For somewhat exhaustive elucidations, see Daniel 1984; Parmentier 1994. Parmentier's diagram of the trichotomies (17) is the clearest I have seen.

6. As Peirce states very clearly, "a sign is something by knowing which we know something more" (Peirce 1958: 390).

7. A word on a page can be either legisign or sinsign, actually, depending on use. If a word is referenced abstractly, one of many of the same type—as when we count how many times 'the' appears on a page (what Peirce calls a "replica"), 'the' is a sinsign. If, in contrast, we read the word in its textual context, it is a legisign (Peirce 1958: 391). In other words, it is a sinsign if in the Secondness of referring, and a legisign if in the Thirdness of interpreting in context.

8. The word as legisign is a third. As I will point out later, all signs are already thirds, even if they are also firsts, seconds, or thirds in subsequent sign relations.

9. Metamorphosizing is not the most precise term here, though. Each sign relation opens onto another and is the result of a previous one. *It is an endless chain, a series of incarnations based on others rather than the transformation of those others.*

10. See Peirce 1958: 212. Peirce suggests the terms prescind, presciss, prescission, and prescissive, which he says correspond to a Latin term meaning "to cut off at the end," to refer to the process of selecting one element from a collection of elements.

11. On words on a page as representamens, see also Sheriff 1989.

12. See Jakobson 1980 [1974]).

13. I say "highest" because humans can experience focused attention (what we *might* loosely gloss as conscious awareness) in language while not being able to do so in, say, all aspects of cognition associated with experiencing a particular smell.

14. I am treating perception here as cognitive scientists treat it, as a process within cognition, whether it is perceptions based on stimuli from reality or the imagination. (See, for example, Carter 2002 and Pinker 1997, although Pinker's view of cognition repeats and reifies mind-body dualism too much for my purposes.) Cognitive scientists do not tend to worry themselves over the fantastic problem of what to call the evanescent moments prior to neural processing, and I would prefer to let perception remain the rigorous term they use it as, leaving Being and consciousness to describe the so-far unexplainable.

15. Peirce calls what I am discussing as an ontological triad his "cenopythagorean categories," comparing them to Hegel's three stages of thought and the three categories in Kant's table of four triads (Peirce 1958: 384, letter to Lady Welby dated October 12, 1904). Elsewhere, he identifies his three categories as replicated in logic, biology, and cosmology—hoping to at last elucidate a "Grand Vision," though he was never sure he had (see Deely 1994: 194).

16. Peirce relates his cenopythagorean categories as all things that are, as positives rather than negatives: "Firstness is the mode of being of that which is such as it is, positively and without reference to anything else. Secondness is the mode of being of that which is such as it is, with respect to a second but regardless of any third. Thirdness is the mode of being of that which is such as it is, in bringing a second and third into relation to each other" (Peirce 1958: 383, letter to Lady Welby dated October 12, 1904). When the triadic sign relation comes into the equation, each representamen exists, "such as it is," but that being is already the culmination of a multitude of past triadic relations. I am suggesting the thought problem/possibility that there is an originary moment of ontological Firstness that is not also a representamen.

17. In order to further clarify ontological Secondness (and the theoretical possibility of Firstness), we need to think through Peirce's desired Grand Vision, which would unite cosmology, logic, biology, and so on. We need to consider signs as Thirds that not only do not have to be linguistic but that also do not need to be in the mode of thought (or cognition). We need to think of signs that are only cognized by a Third in the most metaphorical sense of a Third thing bringing two other things into relation with that Third thing itself and with each other. Peirce's triad has long been said to have application to mathematics and physics, as well as biology (e.g., Hoffmeyer 1996; Sebeok 1968, 1975, 2001; Sowa 1997, 2000). Sebeok (1968), for example, specifies the genetic code as a Peircean triadic relation. In chemistry and physics, Peirce's triad has been used in understanding the actions of matter as they impinge upon one another as processes involving triadic thirdness (see Hoffmeyer 1996; Bhushan and Rosenfield 2000). These examples do not involve a cognizing being, but they do involve a Third mediating two others. Of course, it is a matter of debate whether this is an admissible use of Peirce's triad. The Third should not be a Hegelian synthesis, for example, but rather a Third mediating a First and a Second in such a way as to produce something more that is yet related to the Second as the First also is. Nevertheless, a case might be made for Peircean triadic relations in contexts that do not involve cognizing beings, with one advantage of considering the possibility being that teleology as such is removed from the equation, as it might also be in human cognition (depending upon one's position on determinism). In any case, human cognition—in its broadest sense, beginning at the most basic levels of nerve endings and neuronal firings—is the quintessential case for understanding the relationship between Peirce's ontological triad and his triadic sign.

18. It is a pity that Lacoff and Johnson do not cite Peirce, because they expand metaphor beyond its usually linguistic confines to describe cognition as a process in a way that Peirce's triadic sign would do well to capture. (And if Peirce's triadic sign is itself a metaphor, so are Lacoff and Johnson's metaphors—taken as a set—a metaphor of the process they describe.)

19. I am thinking of Heidegger's *Being and Time* (1962) and of Merleau-Ponty's *Phenomenology of Perception* (1962).

20. This brings Descartes' dispositions and Kant's schema to mind, but here it is not forms in the mind. Rather, it is human physiology and the entirety of human being in the world, now and through time, which meets world by way of comprehending some part of it. Humans meeting world by way of their own structure can also be thought at the level of Thirdness with regard to new versions of materiality that attempt to transcend the mind-body or spirit-matter dichotomy by suggesting that an object and the context of its use cannot be separated. See, for example Pels 1998; Ferme 2001; although I am not sure that they go far enough.

21. For an excellent and readable exposition of cognition by moving through an exploration of the Western human infant's development of a sense of "self," see Daniel N. Stern 1985, 1990. His *Diary of a Baby* (1990) is a popular book that parents are meant to enjoy even as it elucidates the self-creating aspect of the cognitive process. His *Interpersonal World of the Infant* (1985) is more scholarly but still highly readable.

22. Eco 1999 similarly alludes to excess, but it is important to clarify the distinctions between his point and mine here. Succinctly, Eco suggests that "being can be nothing other than what is said in many ways" (42), again reinforcing

the language-boundedness of Eco's thought on being in relation to perception. Eco goes on to say that we have an "excess of real knowledge," by which he means that our knowledge is always perspectival and infinitely so. Thus, we need to "prune away the excess of being that can be stated by language" (43). I largely agree with Eco with regard to human knowledge being perspectival and in "excess," as it were. My thoughts on Being, however, are quite different, as I am suggesting that Being is prior to language even if our reflections on it are often through language. Thus there is the "excess" that is reality as we partake of it in expansive experience and there is the "excess" of human knowledge, to which Eco refers, that we create in the linguistic and extralinguistic signifying characterizing phenomenological experience. And these are not separate—one continually reincarnates into the other.

23. See especially Michael Jackson 1996 for a cogent and engaging application of the phenomenology of experience for anthropology. I do part company with him, as I elucidated in the Conclusion, because I think that experience in the terms of phenomenology is not complete enough. At the same time, I agree with his methodology in many respects.

24. I realize that I am going out on a philosophical and certainly Euro-American scientific limb here, even if I am doing it with precision.

25. We need a different term to distinguish the phenomenological experience of Thirdness and the "pure contact" with world that occurs in Secondness. I will refer to the latter simply as "pure contact" or "pure experience."

26. This still does not exhaust consciousness, insofar as it can be collective as well—a heuristic reading—and this is crucial if we are to prevent assumptions of Western-style unique selfhood as a universal model. This is where neuroscientific attempts to view, touch, and measure can become discordant with metaphorical attempts at cross-cultural understanding, although some approaches in neuroscience are so fluid and rich that they allow for intersubjectivity and expanded notions of consciousness. See Carter 2002. For two very different and interesting dimensions of intersubjectivity in neuroscience and neurobiology, see Barinaga 2002; Frith and Frith 1999.

27. I am immensely grateful to Johannes Fabian for conversations and articles that inspired me to link forgetting in anthropology to the processes I was reading about in neuroscience. See Fabian 1996, 1999, 2001, 2002. See also Ricoeur 2004 on the link between memory and forgetting in the practices of anthropology and history.

28. See Carter 2002: 304–6; also Penrose 2000.

29. Referring to ground with a lower-case "g"—as in semiotic ground, Parmentier shorthands it as "some respect, character, reason, or quality that brings the sign into connection with its object (1994: 28). While Eco and I are discussing Ground ontologically, it is useful to bear in mind that there is conceptual continuity between semiotic and ontological varieties of ground.

30. I think that semiotic ground could be usefully thought of in these processual terms as well.

31. Yet forgetting is not yet well understood. There is a lot of work on sensory coding that goes far in describing the process, yet it has not advanced far enough to account with precision for all of the ways that humans differ from nonhumans, much less describing possible cross-cultural variation. See Laurent 1999 on olfaction, for example, where the author entertains the possibility of specific pathways for different species niches. Sensory perceptual systems are not, of course, referred to in the metaphoric terms of remembering and forget-

ting. With respect to what is referred to in these terms (verbal memory, for example), once again the specifics of forgetting are not yet understood very well. Proximate causes (such as areas of brain activation for items subsequently remembered) may be identified, but why these areas are activated in some cases and not in others is a matter of some speculation, though some broad factors are currently being identified in recent and ongoing studies. See, for example, Brewer et al. 1998; Wagner et al. 1998.

32. This is even truer, say, of the turtle brain, but it also happens in the human retina. See Kolb 2003. How are "unnecessary" elements of a visual experience—"noise"—tagged for elimination in this process? (What makes yes-no questions get answered one way rather than another?) What are the processes and features of conditioning in the retina and the visual cortex that lead to "forgetting"? Can human forgetting differ cross-culturally even in the retina? I do not intend to focus only on one component of sense. Perceptual processes involving "forgetting" for the creation of meaning happen for all components of sense, of which the visual is merely the most studied. Recent evidence suggests that olfactory processing may differ in significant ways from visual and aural, for example. Indeed, the olfactory system may be the more complex—"designed to accommodate the unpredictability of the olfactory world" (Laurent 1999: 727).

33. To put this in other terms, recent work in neuroscience has accomplished much for both cognition and consciousness with regard to the mind-body conundrum—sufficiently refuting, for example, understandings of cognition that locate it precisely and centrally within the brain. Perception and cognition are more diffuse than a brain-focused theory can allow, with cognition at any moment involving simultaneous and seemingly infinite modes and activities of perception. I have already intimated this in my earlier discussion of research on the retina. There is growing evidence in cognitive neuroscience and neurobiology to suggest that cognition happens through processes occurring throughout our entire beings—through every neuron—from neurons in the retina, two olfactory areas in the nose (see end of note), the intricate architecture of the ear, every nerve ending, and so on. In short, processing affecting perception (part of the process of perception itself) is constantly taking place throughout us as we monitor what surrounds us and what is within us, and biochemical and electrochemical signals pass back and forth between all of these areas and our brains. Even the brain itself is not centralized—memory (and meaning as well) are stored and gleaned from all over the brain, in the neocortex and the hippocampus, as well as in other areas (see Carter 2002; Damasio 1995, 1999; LeDoux 2002). (With regard to two olfactory areas, I am referring to the usually recognized olfactory organ, as well as the VNO—Vomeronasal Organ. The latter is a source of some debate. See Keverne 1999 for evidence against, and his bibliography for evidence for.)

Glossary

Aduŋ	to cut; to make a cut, a division
Aisho	giving birth (giving life). Pregnancy and childbirth are usually referred to metaphorically rather than directly. A woman who appears ready to deliver can be called a frog (ntuaa). It may be that her stomach resembles a frog's throat. A pregnant woman might also be referred to as being outside the house (boo). A newly delivered woman is a limping cow. And there are others.
Aidetidet	to dream
Apiu	to resurrect, come back to life from the dead; related words: natipiuwa (came back to life)
Atua	to have died
'i' life stem	see Appendix 2
Itadee	wrongdoing related to eating prohibited foods
Keitipiu	make to come alive
Koŋu	stinky; can be associated with persons who either simply stink or have committed antisocial or immoral acts
Laiŋoni	bull, but it has various metaphorical uses, such as referring to an lmurrani who has died. It also refers to "charms" used for killing people.
Laibartak	shaved ones; refers to newly circumcised boys; feminine form (for newly circumcised girls) is nkaibartak
Lairuponi	singular. Lairupok is plural. Feminine forms are nkairuponi (s.) and nkairupok (pl.). This is a person who can kill at a distance, someone who uses "charms" (various plant products and other substances) to kill people or animals. Typical gloss might be witch.
Laisi	families known to have particularly potent nkamilak and thus particularly powerful ability to bless and curse
Latukuny	personal substance that contains things belonging to the person, including fertility and generative luck; latukuny is in hair, blood, sweat, etc.
Lbene	bag; particularly women's bag of special objects
Lboliboli	fat-containing calabash; brides must carry one

Ldeket	curse (ldeketa, pl.). related words: ketedekishe (s/he cursed [someone]); adekisho (action of cursing); kedekisho (s/he/they is/are cursing [someone])
Lkiye	death; derived from verb "aya"—to throw down. In other words, people who die are taken away from the living, and they are 'thrown' in the bush. Death is not usually spoken of directly (and neither are pregnancy and childbirth) but metaphorically. People can "sleep" or they can have been "thrown" (verb is anaŋ, from which lmenaŋa derives), for example. Death is enkeeya in Maasai (also apparently from the verb "aya").
Lmartewin	statues, particularly those on Mt. Ɖiro
Lmeneŋai	dead, living dead, from verb anaŋ, to throw (lmeneŋa, pl.)
Llpil	instant or sudden shock, as from getting bad news. This is also the first form of shock one gets at hearing of death, and then it takes shape in the stomach, becoming lputukuny.
Lmasi	long hair, as of lmurran and also of women in families that observe the practice of letting their hair (and the child's) grow long until weaning
Lmurran	Samburu of the warrior age-grade
Lŋonchoi	unpropitiousness (something like a substance) a person acquires as a result of being "cursed" that eventually becomes ŋoki if not remedied
Lpapit	hair (don't say "hair" at night—associated with death)
Lpayian	married Samburu elder
Lodo	general term for blood (including birth-related blood in animals), including a woman's menstrual blood; see *sotoony*, *mporoi*, and *mporo*
Loibonok	(pl.) ritual practitioners who variously heal, divine, and prophesy; feminine form is nkoibonok (pl.)
Loik	bones (*loito*, s.)
Loikar	a place where lmurran eat meat for many days
Loip	shade—especially used for gathering and relaxing; special loip (certain trees) used for dispute resolution; shadow—general shadows and person's, said to detach from the person and move around after death
Lomon	derived from the verb "amon," to beseech. Lomon are words, particularly news. They are also guests. It is supposed that guests come to ask for things, and it is likewise supposed that they will bring news.

Lorien	species of tree (*olea Africana/oleaceae*) used for cleaning calabashes; also fecundity and luck
Lputukuny	grief and shock associated with grief that is stored in the stomach. A person still carrying this grief is referred to as having a bad stomach. Vomiting at the shaving ceremony rids the person of this.
Lshata	wood, as in firewood
Ltau	heart—can also refer to personality, strength of will (of the living only)
Ltim	gate of one household (ltimito, pl.). The marriage ceremony is referred to as ltim, and remore can also be referred to that way.
Ltoilo	voice; can survive in some fashion after death
Ltuŋana ŋeni	wise people (ltuŋani ŋen—wise person); ŋeni shares a root with nkwe
Mayian	blessing
Mparnot	thought and memory, including both generational and life memories—life memories may get transferred somehow to one's loip after death, although there is no unanimity on this.
Mporoi	a single clot of blood (human or animal); also used to refer to newborn child's umbilical cord before it falls off and to the newborn child itself—that is only for people; also a single red marriage bead
Mporo	lots of blood clots (animals or people); afterbirth blood (people only)—can be stolen to steal fertility; red marriage beads
Nkai	Samburu divinity
Nkaji	house (nkajijik, pl.), owned and built by one woman (each wife in a polygynous home has her own house); the usual spatial arrangement is for the first wife to build her house to the right of the ltim (gate) of her husband, the second wife to the left, third wife to the right after the first wife's, and so on
Nkamilak	saliva; people's ability to bless and curse is in their saliva, and laisi are supposed to have particularly potent saliva in this regard—keata nkamilak
Nkaŋ	settlement (nkaŋitie, pl.), may be composed of more than one family (more than one ltim/gate)
Nkeene	rope, often leather
Nkima	fire, used also to refer to fertility and other forms of fecund productivity
Nkishon	life, specifically in reference to behaviors, actions, and

	personality; nkishon is inherited and also transmitted through example
Nkishui	life, specifically the life that provides locomotion and speech
Nkiyeŋet	breath; has "spirit" associations for Christian converts or those exposed to Christian ideas
Nkomom	face; also luck and wealth-generating potential associated with a particular man
Nkosheke	stomach—emotions originate here, and so do blessings (mayian) and curses (ldeket)
Nkuaama	smell (n.)
Nkwe	head; metaphorical for intelligence and knowledge (including special)
Ɖoki	unpropitious consequences of serious wrongdoing; a state/thing that is inherited across nine ageset generations
Ntaleŋoi	Ntaleŋo is plural. This is the word for ritual practices and the objects used in them. See also *ntasim.*
Ntasim	This is singular. Ntasimi is plural. This is the word for ritual practices and the objects used in them. See also *ntaleŋoi.*
Ntolo	minor wrongdoing
Ntomononi	Singular. Ntomonok is plural. Women, mothers in particular—has strong birthgiver connotations. The word is related to the verb "amon," to beseech. It is supposed that women who have given birth have beseeched Nkai to give them children. Lomon—words, guests—also has a relationship with the verb amon. Women are not guests, though, they are supplicants. And girls, who are "guests" in a way, are never ntomonok.
Rerei	words, speech
Reteti	tree associated with Nkai; name derived from "aret," to help
Ropili	"sweet" smelling; associated with morally upright persons; kerropil—s/he smells good/virtuous/sweet
Sakut	another word for lairuponi
Sanyon	wrongdoing related to wealth and property
Sesen	Samburu "body"
Sieri	seerr, seerii; customary way of doing things, habits
Sitan	charms used for causing harm, as those bought from laibonok or those loibonok themselves buy from other ethnic groups. It is probably from Kiswahili shetani but this cannot necessarily be confirmed.

Sobua	man's walking stick; associated with his luck, blessing, and wealth-generating potential
Soro	the bush (well beyond settlements, it is the true "bush"—opposed to the social spaces of nkaŋitie)
Sotoony	people only—the dried clotted blood that can stick to a person
Sotua	a thing coming from inside; it refers to the umbilical cord; can also refer to a very close friendship (a friendship that is "deep inside"), a friendship that will continue with the children of those who formed it—it is so close that the children cannot marry one another
Ushe	lairuponi ntasimi that do not kill (as laiŋoni do) but that "divert" someone from the "path of life"—bump them off the road a bit

Bibliography

Abu-Lughod, Lila. 1993. *Writing Women's Worlds: Bedouin Stories.* Berkeley: University of California Press.

Aguilar, Mario I. 2000. "Pastoral Disruption and Cultural Continuity in a Pastoral Town." Pp. 249–64 in Dorothy L. Hodgson, ed., *Rethinking Pastoralism in Africa: Gender, Culture, and the Myth of the Patriarchal Pastoralist.* Oxford: James Currey.

Ahearn, Laura. 2001. *Invitations to Love: Literacy, Love Letters, and Social Change in Nepal.* Ann Arbor: University of Michigan Press.

Alvarez, Robert R., Jr. 1995. "The Mexican-U.S. Border: The Making of an Anthropology of Borderlands." *Annual Review of Anthropology* 24: 447–70.

Amariglio, Jack and Antonio Callari. 1993. "Marxian Value Theory and the Problem of the Subject." Pp. 186–216 in Emily Apter and William Pietz, eds., *Fetishism as Cultural Discourse.* Ithaca, N.Y.: Cornell University Press.

Amos, Valerie and Pratibha Parmar. 1984. "Challenging Imperial Feminism." *Feminist Review* 17: 3–19.

Anderson, David M. 1995. "Visions of the Vanquished: Prophets and Colonialism in Kenya's Western Highlands." Pp. 164–94 in David M. Anderson and Douglas H. Johnson, eds., *Revealing Prophets: Prophecy in Eastern African History.* London: James Currey.

Anderson, David M. and Douglas H. Johnson, eds. 1995. *Revealing Prophets: Prophecy in East African History.* London: James Currey.

Ando, Clifford. 2004. *Roman Religion.* Edinburgh: Edinburgh University Press.

Antze, Paul and Michael Lambek, eds. 1996. *Tense Past: Cultural Essays in Trauma and Memory.* New York: Routledge.

Appadurai, Arjun. 1986. "Introduction: Commodities and the Politics of Value." Pp. 3–63 in Arujun Appadurai, ed., *The Social Life of Things: Commodities in Cultural Perspective.* Cambridge: Cambridge University Press.

———. 1996. *Modernity at Large: Cultural Dimensions of Globalization.* Minneapolis: University of Minnesota Press.

Atwater, Cheryl. 2000 "Living in Death: The Evolution of Modern Vampirism." *Anthropology of Consciousness* 11 (2–3): 70–77.

Bacigalupo, Luis E. 2006. "Talking About Religion in Philosophy: From a Catholic Point of View." In James B. White, ed., *Talking About Religion.* South Bend, Ind.: University of Notre Dame Press.

Barber, Paul. 1988. *Vampires, Burial, and Death: Folklore and Reality.* New Haven, Conn.: Yale University Press.

Barinaga, Marcia. 2002. "Cells Exchanged During Pregnancy Live On." *Science* 296, 5576 (June): 2169–72.

Bartlett, Robert. 2004 *The Hanged Man: A Story of Miracle, Memory, and Colonialism in the Middle Ages.* Princeton, N.J.: Princeton University Press.

Basso, Keith H. 1996. "Wisdom Sits in Places: Notes on a Western Apache Land-scape," Pp. 53–90 in Steven Feld and Keith H. Basso, eds., *Senses of Place*. Santa Fe, N.M.: School of American Research Press.

Bataille, George. 1988. *Inner Experience*. Albany: State University of New York Press.

Bauman, Richard and Charles L. Briggs. 1990. "Poetics and Performance as Critical Perspectives on Language and Social Life." *Annual Review of Anthropology* 19: 59–88.

Behar, Ruth. 1997. *The Vulnerable Observer: Anthropology That Breaks Your Heart*. Boston: Beacon Press.

Behrend, Heike. 2002. "Spirit Mediumship and the Media of Spirits." Paper Presented at the panel "Technology, Modernity and the Promise of Transformation," at the 45th Annual Meeting of the African Studies Association. Washington, D.C., December 5–8.

Bell, Michael E. 2001. *Food for the Dead: On the Trail of New England's Vampires*. New York: Carroll and Graf.

Bercovitch, Eytan. 1998. "Dis-Embodiment and Concealment Among the Atbalmin of Papua New Guinea." Pp. 210–31 in Michael Lambek and Andrew Strathern, eds., *Bodies and Persons: Comparative Perspectives from Africa and Melanesia*. Cambridge: Cambridge University Press.

Beyssade, Michelle. 1993. "Privileged Truth or Exemplary Truth?" In Stephen Voss, ed., *Essays on the Philosophy and Science of René Descartes*. Oxford: Oxford University Press.

Bhushan, Nalini and Stuart Rosenfeld, eds. 2000. *Of Minds and Molecules*. Oxford: Oxford University Press.

Blackless, Melanie, Anthony Charuvastra, Amanda Derryck, Anne Fausto-Sterling, Karl Lauzanne, and Ellen Lee. 2000. "How Sexually Dimorphic Are We? Review and Synthesis. *American Journal of Human Biology* 12: 151–66.

Bloch, Maurice. 1996. "Internal and External Memory." Pp. 215–231 in Paul Antze and Michael Lambek, eds., *Tense Past: Cultural Essays in Trauma and Memory*. London: Routledge.

Bloch, Maurice and Jonathan Parry, eds. 1982. *Death and the Regeneration of Life*. Cambridge: Cambridge University Press.

Blystad, Astrid. 2000. "Precarious Procreation: Datoga Pastoralists at the Late 20th Century." Ph.D. dissertation, Department of Social Anthropology, University of Bergen.

Borch-Jacobsen, Mikkel. 1991. *Lacan: The Absolute Master*. Trans. Douglas Brick. Stanford, Calif.: Stanford University Press.

Borofsky, Robert. 2000. *Remembrance of Pacific Pasts: An Invitation to Remake History*. Honolulu: University of Hawai'i Press.

Bourdieu, Pierre. 1977. *Outline of a Theory of Practice*. Trans. Richard Nice. Cambridge: Cambridge University Press.

Braidotti, Rosi. 1997. "Comments on Felski's 'The Doxa of Difference': Working Through Sexual Difference." *SIGNS* 23, 1: 24–40.

Bray, Abigail and Claire Colebrook. 1998. "The Haunted Flesh: Corporeal Feminism and the Politics of (Dis)Embodiment." *SIGNS* 24, 1: 35–67.

Brewer, James, Zuo Zhao, et al. 1998. "Making Memories: Brain Activity That Predicts How Well Visual Experience Will Be Remembered." *Science* 281, 5380 (August): 1185–87.

Broch-Due, Vigdis. 1993. "Making Meaning Out of Matter: Perception of Sex, Gender, and Bodies Among the Turkana." Pp. 53–82 in Vigdis Broch-Due,

Ingrid Rudie, and Tone Bleie, eds., *Carved Flesh/Cast Selves: Gender as Social and Symbolic Practices*. Oxford: Berg.

————. 1999a "Creation and the Multiple Female Body: Turkana Perspectives on Gender and Cosmos." Pp. 153–85 in Henrietta L. Moore, Todd Sanders, and Bwire Kaare, eds., *Those Who Play with Fire: Gender, Fertility and Transformation in East and Southern Africa*. London: Athlone.

————. 1999b. "A Proper Cultivation of Peoples: The Colonial Re-Configuration of Pastoral Tribes and Places in Kenya." Pp. 53–93 in Vigdis Broch-Due and Richard A. Schroeder, eds., *Producing Nature and Poverty in Africa*. Uppsala: Nordic Africa Institute & Transaction Publishers.

————. 2000. 'The Fertility of Houses and Herds: Producing Kinship and Gender Among Turkana Pastoralists." Pp. 165–85 in Dorothy L. Hodgson, ed., *Rethinking Pastoralism in Africa*. London: James Currey.

Broch-Due, Vigdis and Ingrid Rudie. 1993a. "Carved Flesh—Cast Selves: An Introduction." Pp. 1–39 in Vidgis Broch-Due, Ingrid Rudie, and Tone Bleie eds., *Carved Flesh, Cast Selves: Gendered Symbols and Social Practices*. Oxford: Berg.

Broch-Due, Vigdis, Ingrid Rudie, and Tone Bleie, eds.. 1993b. *Carved Flesh, Cast Selves: Gendered Symbols and Social Practices*. Oxford: Berg.

Brown, Bill. 2001. "Thing Theory." *Critical Inquiry* 28, 1: 1–21.

Brown, J. W. 1991. *Self and Process: Brain States of the Conscious Present*. New York: Springer.

Burke, Timothy. 1996. *Lifebuoy Men, Lux Women: Commodification, Consumption, and Cleanliness in Modern Zimbabwe*. Durham, N.C.: Duke University Press

Burton, John W. 1991. "Representations of the Feminine in Nilotic Cosmologies." Pp. 81–98 in Anita Jacobson-Widding, ed., *Body and Space: Symbolic Models of Unity and Division in African Cosmology and Experience*. Stockholm: Widding, Almqvist & Wiksell.

Butler, Judith. 1990. *Gender Trouble: Feminism and the Subversion of Identity*. New York: Routledge.

Butler, Marilyn. 1996. "*Frankenstein* and Radical Science." Pp. 302–313 in Mary Shelley, *Frankenstein: Norton Critical Edition*, ed. J. Paul Hunter. New York: Norton.

Bynum, Caroline Walker. 1991. "Material Continuity, Personal Survival, and the Resurrection of the Body: A Scholastic Discussion in Its Medieval and Modern Contexts." Pp. 239–97 in Bynum, *Fragmentation and Redemption: Essays on Gender and the Human Body in Medieval Religion*. New York: Zone Books.

————. 1995. *The Resurrection of the Body in Western Christianity, 200–1336*. New York: Columbia University Press.

Carrier, James G. 1995. *Gifts and Commodities: Exchange and Western Capitalism Since 1700*. New York: Routledge.

Carter, Rita. 2002. *Exploring Consciousness*. Berkeley: University of California Press.

Chambert-Loir, Henri and Anthony Reid. 2002. "Introduction." Pp. xv–xxvi in Henri Chambert-Loir and Anthony Reid, eds., *The Potent Dead: Ancestors, Saints, and Heroes in Contemporary Indonesia*. Honolulu: Asian Studies of Australia with Allen & Unwin and University of Hawai'i Press.

Chomsky, Noam. 1965. *Aspects of the Theory of Syntax*. Cambridge, Mass.: MIT Press.

————. 1975. *Reflections on Language*. New York: Pantheon.

Cixous, Hélène. 1976. "The Laugh of the Medusa." Trans. Keith Cohen and Paula Cohen. *SIGNS* 1, 4: 875–94.

Clark, Leon E. 1970. *Through African Eyes*, vol. 5, *The Rise of Nationalism: Freedom Regained.* New York: Praeger.

Cohen, Anthony. 1994. *Self-Consciousness: An Alternative Anthropology of Identity.* London: Routledge.

Colville, Elizabeth. 2002. "Rembembering Our Dead: The Care of the Ancestors in Tana Toraja." Pp. 69–87 in Henri Chambert-Loir and Anthony Reid, eds., *The Potent Dead: Ancestors, Saints and Heroes in Contemporary Indonesia.* Honolulu: Asian Studies of Australia with Allen & Unwin and University of Hawai'i Press.

Comaroff, Jean. 1984. "Medicine, Time, and the Perception of Death: Listening." *Journal of Religion and Culture* 19: 155–69.

Comaroff, John and Jean Comaroff. 1991. *Of Revelation and Revolution*, vol. 1, *Christianity, Colonialism, and Consciousness in South Africa.* Chicago: University of Chicago Press.

———. 1993. Introduction. Pp. xi–xxxi in Jean Comaroff and John Comaroff, eds., *Modernity and Its Malcontents: Ritual and Power in Postcolonial Africa.* Chicago: University of Chicago Press.

———. 1997. *Of Revelation and Revolution*, vol. 2, *The Dialectics of Modernity on a South African Frontier.* Chicago: University of Chicago Press.

———. 2000. "Millenial Capitalism: First Thoughts on a Second Coming." *Public Culture* 12, 2: 291–343.

Conklin, Beth. 2001. *Consuming Grief: Compassionate Cannibalism in an Amazonian Society.* Austin: University of Texas Press.

Connerton, Paul. 1989. *How Societies Remember.* Cambridge: Cambridge University Press.

Copper, Basil. 1974. *The Vampire in Legend, Fact and Art.* Secaucus, N.J.: Citadel.

Csordas, Thomas. 1994a "Introduction: The Body as Representation and Being-in-the-World." Pp. 1–23 in Thomas Csordas, ed., *Embodiment and Experience: The Existential Ground of Culture and Self.* Cambridge: Cambridge University Press.

———. 1994b. *The Sacred Self: A Cultural Phenomenology of Charismatic Healing.* Berkeley: University of California Press.

Damasio, Antonio R. 1994. *Descartes' Error.* New York: Putnam.

———. 1999. *The Feeling of What Happens.* San Diego: Harvest, Harcourt.

———. 2000. "Body and Consciousness: A Conversation with Antonio Damasio." Grant Jewell Rich, interviewer. *Anthropology of Consciousness* 11, 3–4: 54–61.

Daniel, E. Valentine. 1984. *Fluid Signs: Being a Person the Tamil Way.* Berkeley: University of California Press.

———. 1996. *Charred Lullabies: Chapters in an Anthropology of Violence.* Princeton, N.J.: Princeton University Press.

Daston, Lorraine and Katharine Park. 1998. *Wonders and the Order of Nature, 1150–1750.* New York: Zone Books.

De Biran, Maine. 1929 [1804]. *The Influence of Habit on the Faculty of Thinking.* Baltimore: Williams and Wilkins.

Deely, John. 1994. *New Beginnings: Early Modern Philosophy and Postmodern Thought.* Toronto: University of Toronto Press.

Dennett, Daniel C. 1984. *Elbow Room: The Varieties of Free Will Worth Wanting.* Cambridge, Mass.: MIT Press.

Derrida, Jacques. 1976. *Of Grammatology.* Trans. Gayatri Chakravorty Spivak. Baltimore: Johns Hopkins University Press.

————. 1979. *Spurs: Nietzsche's Styles/Eperons: les styles de Nietzsche.* Trans. Barbara Harlow. Chicago: University of Chicago Press.

Descartes, René. 1985 [1641]. "Meditations on First Philosophy." Trans. John Cottingham. In *The Philosophical Writings of Descartes,* trans. John Cottingham, Robert Stoothoff, and Dugald Murdoch, 2: 3–62. Cambridge: Cambridge University Press.

————. 1904. *Oeuvres de Descartes.* Ed. Charles Adam and Paul Tannery. Paris: J. Vrin.

Desjarlais, Robert R. 1992. *Body and Emotion: The Aesthetics of Illness and Healing in the Nepal Himalayas.* Philadelphia: University of Pennsylvania Press.

Douglas, Mary. 1999. *Implicit Meanings: Selected Essays in Anthropology.* London: Routledge.

Eakin, Paul John. 2000. "Autobiography, Identity, and the Fictions of Memory." Pp. 290–306 in Daniel L. Schacter and Elaine Scarry, eds., *Memory, Brain, and Belief.* Cambridge, Mass.: Harvard University Press.

Eco, Umberto. 1995. *The Search for the Perfect Language.* Trans. James Fentress. Oxford: Blackwell.

————. 1999. *Kant and the Platypus: Essays on Language and Cognition.* Trans. Alastair McEwen. New York: Harcourt.

Eichenbaum, Howard and J. Alexander Bodkin. 2000. "Belief and Knowledge as Distinct Forms of Memory." Pp. 176–207 in Daniel L. Schacter and Elaine Scarry, eds., *Memory, Brain, and Belief.* Cambridge, Mass.: Harvard University Press.

Ellis, John M. 1989. *Against Deconstruction.* Princeton, N.J.: Princeton University Press.

Ensminger, Jean. 1987. "Economic and Political Differentiation Among Galole Orma Women." *Ethnos* 52, 1/2: 28–49.

Evans-Pritchard, E. E. 1976 [1937]. *Witchcraft, Oracles and Magic Among the Azande.* Oxford: Clarendon Press.

————. 1940. *The Nuer.* Oxford: Oxford University Press.

————. 1951. *Kinship and Marriage Among the Nuer.* Oxford: Oxford University Press.

————. 1956. *Nuer Religion.* Oxford: Clarendon Press.

Fabian, Johannes. 1996 *Remembering the Present: Painting and Popular History in Zaire.* Berkeley: University of California Press.

————. 1999 "Remembering the Other: Knowledge and Recognition in the Exploration of Central Africa." *Critical Inquiry* 26: 49–69.

————. 2001. "Forgetting Africa." *Journal of Romance Studies* 3: 9–20.

————. 2002. "Forgetting Africa." Paper presented at the Annual Meeting for Association of Social Anthropologists of the United Kingdom and the Commonwealth, April 8–12, Arusha, Tanzania.

Farquhar, Judith. 2002. *Appetites: Food and Sex in Postsocialist China.* Durham, N.C.: Duke University Press.

Favret-Saada, Jeanne. 1980. *Deadly Words: Witchcraft in Bocage.* Cambridge: Cambridge University Press.

Feldman, Jerome. 1985. "Four Frames Suffice: A Provisional Model of Vision and Space." *Behavioral and Brain Sciences* 8: 265–89.

Ferme, Mariane. 2001. *The Underneath of Things: Violence, History, and the Everyday in Sierra Leone.* Berkeley: University of California Press.

Finucane, Ronald. 1977 *Miracles and Pilgrims: Popular Beliefs in Medieval England.* Totowa, N.J.: Rowman and Littlefield.

————. 1982. *Ghosts: Appearances of the Dead and Cultural Transformation*. London: Junction Books.

————. 1997. *The Rescue of the Innocents: Endangered Children in Medieval Miracles*. New York: St. Martin's.

Foucault, Michel. 1979. *Discipline and Punish: The Birth of the Prison*. New York: Vintage Books.

————. 1990. *The History of Sexuality*. Vol. 1, *An Introduction*. New York: Vintage.

Fratkin, Elliot. 1975. "Herbal Medicine and Concepts of Disease in Samburu." Institute of African Studies, Seminar Paper 65, University of Nairobi.

————. 1979 "A Comparison of the Role of Prophets in Samburu and Maasai Warfare." *Senri Ethnological Studies* 3: 53–67.

————. 1989. "Household Variation and Gender Inequality in Ariaal Pastoral Production: Results of a Stratified Time Survey." *American Anthropologist* 91: 430–40.

————. 1991. *Surviving Drought and Development: Ariaal Pastoralists of Northern Kenya*. Boulder, Colo.: Westview Press.

Friedman, Jonathan. 1994. *Consumption and Identity*. Studies in Anthropology and History 15. Chur, Switzerland: Harwood.

Frith, Chris D. and Uta Frith. 1999. "Interacting Minds—A Biological Basis." *Science* 286, 5445 (November): 1692–95.

Fuss, Diana. 1991. *Essentially Speaking: Feminism, Nature, and Difference*. New York: Routledge.

Galaty, John. 1982. "Being 'Maasai': Being 'People of Cattle'"; Ethnic Shifters in East Africa." *American Ethnologist* 9: 1–20.

————. 1986. "East African Hunters and Pastoralists in Regional Perspective: An Ethnoanthropological Approach. *SUGIA, Sprache und Geschichte in Afrika* 7, 1: 105–31.

Gashé, Rodolphe. 1986. *The Tain of the Mirror: Derrida and the Philosophy of Reflection*. Cambridge, Mass.: Harvard University Press.

Geary, Patrick. 1986. "Sacred Commodities: The Circulation of Medieval Relics." Pp. 169–91 in Arjun Appadurai, ed., *The Social Life of Things: Commodities in Cultural Perspective*. Cambridge: Cambridge University Press.

Geertz, Clifford. 1968. *Islam Observed: Religious Development in Morocco and Indonesia*. New Haven, Conn.: Yale University Press.

Gelpi, Donald I. 2001. *The Gracing of Human Experience: Rethinking the Relationship Between Nature and Grace*. Collegeville, Minn.: Liturgical Press.

Geurts, Kathryn Linn. 2002. *Culture and the Senses: Bodily Ways of Knowing in an African Community*. Berkeley: University of California Press.

Giles, Linda L. 1999. "Spirit Possession and the Symbolic Construction of Swahili Society." Pp. 142–64 in Heike Behrend and Ute Luig, eds., *Spirit Possession: Modernity and Power and Africa*. Madison: University of Wisconsin Press.

Gordon, Avery and Christopher Newfield. 1995. "White Philosophy." Pp. 380–400 in Kwame Anthony Appiah and Henry Louis Gates, Jr., eds., *Identities*. Chicago: University of Chicago Press.

Gottlieb, Alma. 1996. *Under the Kapok Tree: Identity and Difference in Beng Thought*. Chicago: University of Chicago Press.

Gregory, Chris A. 1997. *Savage Money: The Anthropology and Politics of Commodity Exchange*. Amsterdam: Harwood.

Grindal, Bruce. 1983. "Into the Heart of Sisala Experience: Witnessing Death Divination." *Journal of Anthropological Research* 39, 1: 60–80.

Groebner, Valentin. 2004. "Complexio/Complexion: Categorizing Individual

Natures, 1250–1600." Pp. 361–83 in Lorraine Daston and Fernando Vidal, eds., *The Moral Authority of Nature.* Chicago: University of Chicago Press.

Gross, Elizabeth. 1986. "Philosophy, Subjectivity and the Body: Kristeva and Irigaray." Pp. 125–44 in Carole Pateman and Elizabeth Gross, eds., *Feminist Challenges: Social and Political Theory.* Sydney: Allen and Unwin.

Grosz, Elizabeth A. 1989. *Sexual Subversions: Three French Feminists.* Sydney: Allen and Unwin.

———. 1994. *Volatile Bodies: Toward a Corporeal Feminism.* Bloomington: Indiana University Press.

Gupta, Akhil. 1992. "The Reincarnation of Souls and the Rebirth of Commodities: Representations of Time in 'East' and 'West.' *Cultural Critique* (Fall): 187–212.

———. 2002. "Reliving Childhood? The Temporality of Childhood and Narratives of Reincarnation." *Ethnos* 67, 1: 33–56.

Gupta, Akhil and James Ferguson. 1992. "Beyond 'Culture': Space, Identity, and the Politics of Difference." *Cultural Anthropology* 7: 6–23.

Hardwick, A. Arkell. 1903. *An Ivory Trader in North Kenia: The Record of an Expedition Through Kikuyu to Galla-Land in East Equatorial Africa, With an Account of the Rendili and Burkeneji Tribes.* London: Longmans, Green.

Heidegger, Martin. 1962. *Being and Time.* New York: Harper and Row.

Heine, Bernd, Ingo Heine, and Christa König. 1988. *Plant Concepts and Plant Use: An Ethnobotanical Survey of Semi-Arid and Arid Lands of East Africa.* Vol. 5, *Plants of the Samburu.* Saarbrücken: Breitenbach.

Herren, Urs. 1991. "Socioeconomic Strategies of Pastoral Maasai Households in Mukogodo, Kenya." Ph.D. dissertation, University of Bern.

Herzfeld, Michael. 1987. *Anthropology Through the Looking Glass: Critical Ethnography in the Margins of Europe.* Cambridge: Cambridge University Press.

Hertz, Robert. 1960 [1907]. *Death and the Right Hand.* New York: Free Press.

Hillman, Eugene. 1989. *Many Paths: A Catholic Approach to Religious Pluralism.* New York: Orbis Books.

Hodgson, Dorothy. 1997. "Embodying the Contradictions of Modernity: Gender and Spirit Possession Among Maasai in Tanzania." Pp. 111–29 in Maria Grosz-Ngate and Omari H. Kokole, eds., *Gendered Encounters: Challenging Cultural Boundaries and Social Hierarchies in Africa.* New York: Routledge.

———. 2001. *Once Intrepid Warriors: Gender, Ethnicity, and the Cultural Politics of Maasai Development.* Bloomington: Indiana University Press.

———. 2005. *The Church of Women: Gendered Encounters Between Maasai and Missionaries.* Bloomington: Indiana University Press.

Hoffmeyer, Jesper. 1996. *Signs of Meaning in the Universe.* Trans. Barbara J. Haveland. Bloomington: Indiana University Press.

Holtzman, Jon. 1996. "The Transformation of Samburu Domestic Economy." Ph.D dissertation, University of Michigan, Ann Arbor.

———. 2001. "The Food of Elders, the 'Ration' of Women: Brewing, Gender, and Domestic Processes Among the Samburu of Northern Kenya." *American Anthropologist* 103, 4: 1041–58.

———. 2002. "Politics and Gastropolitics: Gender and the Power of Food in Two African Pastoralist Societies." *Journal of the Royal Anthropological Institute* 8, 2: 259–78.

———. 2003. "In a Cup of Tea: Commodities and History Among Samburu Pastoralists in Northern Kenya." *American Ethnologist* 30: 136–59.

———. 2004. "The Local in the Local: Models of Time and Space in Samburu District, Northern Kenya." *Current Anthropology* 45, 1: 61–84.

Hoskins, Janet. 1998. *Biographical Objects: How Things Tell the Stories of People's Lives*. New York: Routledge.

Howes, David. 1987. "Olfaction and Transition: An Essay on the Ritual Uses of Smell." *Canadian Review of Sociology and Anthropology* 24: 390–416.

———. , ed. 1996. *Cross-Cultural Consumption: Global Markets, Local Realities*. New York: Routledge.

Ichikawa, M. 1978. "Ethnobotany of the Suiei Dorobo." Discussion Paper 95, University of Nairobi Institute of African Studies.

Irigaray, Luce. 1977. "Women on the Market." Pp. 170–91 in Irigaray, *This Sex Which Is Not One*. Trans. Catherine Porter with Carolyn Burke. Ithaca, N.Y.: Cornell University Press.

1985. *Speculum of the Other Woman*. Ithaca, N.Y.: Cornell University Press.

Irvine, Judith. 1972. *Public Performance and the Wolof Griot: Verbal and Structural Sources of Power*. New Brunswick, N.J.: African Studies Association.

Ivy, Marilyn. 1995. *Discourses of the Vanishing: Modernity, Phantasm, Japan*. Chicago: University of Chicago Press.

Jackson, Jean. 1994. "Chronic Pain and the Tension Between the Body as Subject and Object." Pp. 201–28 in Thomas J. Csordas, ed., *Embodiment and Experience: The Existential Ground of Culture and Self*. Cambridge: Cambridge University Press.

Jackson, Michael. 1989. *Paths Toward a Clearing: Radical Empiricism and Ethnographical Inquiry*. Bloomington: Indiana University Press.

———. 1995. *At Home in the World*. Durham, N.C.: Duke University Press.

———. 1996. "Introduction: Phenomenology, Radical Empiricism, and Anthropological Critique." Pp. 1–50 in Michael Jackson, ed., *Things as They Are: New Directions in Phenomenological Anthropology*. Bloomington: Indiana University Press.

Jakobson, Roman. 1980 [1974]. "A Glance at the Development of Semiotics." Pp. 1–30 in *The Framework of Language*. Trans. Patricia Baudoin. Ann Arbor: Michigan Studies in the Humanities, Horace R. Rackham School of Graduate Studies.

James, Wendy. 1998. "Mauss in Africa: On Time, History, and Politics." Pp. 226–48 in Wendy James and N. J. Allen eds., *Marcel Mauss: A Centenary Tribute*. New York: Berghahn.

Jameson, Fredric and Masao Miyoshi, eds. 1998. *The Cultures of Globalization*. Durham, N.C.: Duke University Press.

Johnsen, Nina. 1997. "Maasai Medicine: Practicing Health and Therapy in Ngorongoro Conservation Area, Tanzania." Ph.D. dissertation. Institute of Anthropology, University of Copenhagen.

———. 2002. "Maasai Marketing Medicine: Ethnic Identity, Modernization and the Trade of Ideas for Substances." Paper presented at Association of Social Anthropologists of the Commonwealth of Great Britain Annual Meetings, Arusha, Tanzania, April, 2002.

Johnson, Elizabeth A. 1993. *She Who Is: The Mystery of God in Feminist Theological Discourse*. New York: Crossroad.

Johnson, Mark. 1998. "At Home and Abroad: Inalienable Wealth, Personal Consumption and the Formulations of Femininity in the Southern Philippines." Pp. 215–40 in Daniel Miller, ed., *Material Cultures: Why Some Things Matter*. Chicago: University of Chicago Press.

Kahn, Miriam 1996. "Your Place or Mine: Sharing Emotional Landscapes in Wamira, Papua New Guinea," Pp. 167–96 in Steven Feld and Keith H. Basso eds., *Senses of Place*. Santa Fe, N.M.: School of American Research Press.

Kan, Sergei. 1989. *Symbolic Immortality: The Tlingit Potlatch of the Nineteenth Century.* Washington, D.C.: Smithsonian Institution Press.

Kapchan, Deborah. 1996. *Gender on the Market: Moroccan Women and the Revoicing of Tradition.* Philadelphia: University of Pennsylvania Press.

Kapferer, Bruce. 1997. *The Feast of the Sorcerer: Practices of Consciousness and Power.* Chicago: University of Chicago Press.

———. 2003. "Introduction: Outside All Reason—Magic, Sorcery, and Epistemology in Anthropology." Pp. 1–30 in Bruce Kapferer, ed., *Beyond Rationalism: Rethinking Magic, Witchcraft, and Sorcery.* Oxford: Berghahn.

Keane, Webb. 1997. *Signs of Recognition: Powers and Hazards of Representation in an Indonesian Society.* Berkeley: University of California Press.

Keverne, Eric B. 1999. "The Vomeronasal Organ." *Science* 286, 5440 (October): 716–20.

Kipury, Naomi Ole. 1983. *Oral Literature of the Maasai.* Nairobi: Heinemann.

Klaniczay, Gabor. 1990. *The Uses of Supernatural Power: The Transformation of Popular Religion in Medieval and Early-Modern Europe.* Trans. Susan Singerman. Princeton, N.J.: Princeton University Press.

Knauft, Bruce. 1989. "Bodily Images in Melanesia: Cultural Substances and Natural Metaphors." Pp. 198–279 in Michel Feher, Ramona Naddaff, and Nadia Tazi, eds., *Fragments for a History of the Human Body*, vol. 3. New York: Urzone.

Kokwaro, John O. and Dennis J. Herlocker. 1982. "A Check-List of Botanical, Samburu and Rendille Names of Plants of the 'IPAL' Study Area, Marsabit District, Kenya." IPAL (Integrated Project in Arid Lands). Technical Report D-4. Nairobi.

Kolb, Helga. 2003. "How the Retina Works." *American Scientist* (January/February): 28–35.

Kratz, Corinne A. 1990. "Sexual Solidarity and the Secrets of Sight and Sound: Shifting Gender Relations and Their Ceremonial Constitution." *American Ethnologist* 17, 3: 31–51.

1994. *Affecting Performance: Meaning, Movement, and Experience in Okiek Women's Initiation.* Washington, D.C.: Smithsonian Institution Press.

Kratz, Corinne A. and Donna Klumpp. 1993. "Aesthetics, Expertise, and Ethnicity: Okiek and Maasai Perspectives on Personal Ornament." Pp. 195–221 in Thomas Spear and Richard Waller, eds., *Being Maasai: Ethnicity and Identity in East Africa.* London: James Currey.

Kratz, Corinne A. and Donna (Klumpp) Pido. 2000. "Gender, Ethnicity, and Social Aesthetics in Maasai and Okiek Beadwork." Pp. 43–71 in Dorothy L. Hodgson, ed., *Rethinking Pastoralism in Africa: Gender, Culture, and the Myth of the Patriarchal Pastoralist.* Oxford: James Currey.

Krips, Henry. 1999. *Fetish: An Erotics of Culture.* Ithaca, N.Y.: Cornell University Press.

Kristeva, Julia. 1982. *Powers of Horror: An Essay on Abjection.* Trans. Leon S. Roudiez. New York : Columbia University Press.

———. 1984 [1974]. *Revolution in Poetic Language.* New York: Columbia University Press.

———. 1989. *Black Sun: Depression and Melancholia.* Trans. Leon S. Roudiez. New York: Columbia University Press.

———. 1991. *Strangers to Ourselves.* New York: Columbia University Press.

Lacan, Jacques. 1968. *The Language of the Self: The Function of Language in Psychoanalysis.* Trans. with commentary Anthony Wilden. Baltimore: Johns Hopkins University Press.

————. 1977 *Écrits: A Selection.* Trans. Alan Sheridan. New York: Tavistock.

————. 1981. *The Four Fundamental Concepts of Psychoanalysis.* Ed. Jacques-Alain Miller, trans, Alan Sheridan. New York: Norton.

Lacoff, George and Mark Johnson. 1980 *Metaphors We Live By.* Chicago: University of Chicago Press.

————. 1999 *Philosophy in the Flesh: The Embodied Mind and Its Challenge to Western Thought.* New York: Basic Books.

Lambek, Michael and Andrew Strathern, eds. 1998. *Bodies and Persons: Comparative Perspectives from Africa and Melanesia.* Cambridge: Cambridge University Press.

Latour, Bruno. 1993. *We Have Never Been Modern.* Trans. Catherine Porter. Cambridge, Mass.: Harvard University Press.

Laurent, Gilles. 1999. "A Systems Perspective on Early Olfactory Coding." *Science* 286, 5440 (October): 723–28.

LeDoux, Joseph. 1996. *The Emotional Brain.* New York: Simon and Schuster.

————. 2002 *Synaptic Self: How Our Brains Become Who We Are.* New York: Viking.

Lesorogol, Carolyn Kornfeld. 1991. "Pastoral Production and Transformations Among the Samburu of Northern Kenya." Master's Thesis, University of California, Los Angeles.

————. 2002. "Cutting Up the Commons: The Political Economy of Land Privatization Among the Samburu of Northern Kenya." Ph.D. dissertation, Washington University, St. Louis.

————. 2003. "Transforming Institutions Among Pastoralists: Inequality and Land Privatization." *American Anthropologist* 105, 3: 531–42.

Lévi-Bruhl, Lucien. 1926. *How Natives Think.* London: Allen & Unwin.

Lévi-Strauss, Claude. 1969a [1949]. *The Elementary Structures of Kinship.* Trans. James H. Bell, John R. Von Sturmer, and Rodney Needham. Boston: Beacon Press.

————. 1969b. *The Raw and the Cooked.* Trans. John Weightman and Dorren Weightman. New York: Harper and Row.

————. 1973 *From Honey to Ashes.* Trans. John Weightman and Dorren Weightman. New York: Harper and Row.

Lienhardt, Godfrey. 1961. *Divinity and Experience: The Religion of the Dinka.* Oxford: Clarendon Press.

Lock, Margaret. 2002. *Twice Dead: Organ Transplants and the Reinvention of Death.* Berkeley: University of California Press.

Lock, Margaret and Nancy Scheper-Hughes. 1987. "The Mindful Body." *Medical Anthropological Quarterly* 1, 1: 6–41.

Luhrmann, Tanya M. 1991. *Persuasions of the Witch's Craft: Ritual Magic in Contemporary England.* Cambridge, Mass.: Harvard University Press.

————. 1996. *The Good Parsi: The Fate of a Colonial Elite in a Postcolonial Society.* Cambridge, Mass.: Harvard University Press.

Lutz, Catherine. 1988. *Unnatural Emotions: Everyday Sentiments on a Micronesian Atoll and Their Challenge to Western Theory.* Chicago: University of Chicago Press.

Malkki, Liisa. 1995. *Purity and Exile: Violence, Memory and National Cosmology Among Hutu Refugees in Tanzania.* Chicago: Chicago University Press.

Mannheim, Bruce and Dennis Tedlock. 1995. "Introduction." Pp. 1–32 in Dennis Tedlock and Bruce Mannheim, eds., *The Dialogic Emergence of Culture.* Urbana: University of Illinois Press.

Marcus, George E. and Michael M. J. Fischer. 1986. *Anthropology as Cultural Critique: An Experimental Moment in the Human Sciences.* Chicago: University of Chicago Press.

Masquelier, Adeline. 2000. "Of Headhunters and Cannibals: Migrancy, Labor, and Consumption in the Mawri Imagination." *Cultural Anthropology* 15, 1: 1–45.

————. 2001. *Prayer Has Spoiled Everything: Possession, Power, and Identity in an Islamic Town of Niger.* Durham, N.C.: Duke University Press.

Martin, Emily. 1987. *The Woman in the Body: A Cultural Analysis of Reproduction.* Boston: Beacon Press.

Marx, Karl. 1977. *Karl Marx, Selected Writings.* Ed. David McLellan. Oxford: Oxford University Press.

Mauss, Marcel. 1967 [1925]. *The Gift: Forms and Functions of Exchange in Archaic Societies.* Trans. Ian Cunnison. New York: Norton.

————. 1979. *Sociology and Psychology: Essays.* Trans. Ben Brewster. London: Routledge.

Mead, Margaret. 1928. *Coming of Age in Samoa: A Psychological Study of Primitive Youth for Western Civilization.* New York: Morrow.

Megill, Allan. 1985. *Prophets of Extremity: Nietzsche, Heidegger, Foucault, Derrida.* Berkeley: University of California Press.

Merleau-Ponty, Maurice. 1962. *Phenomenology of Perception.* Trans. Colin Smith. London: Routledge.

Miller, Daniel. 1994. *Modernity: An Ethnographic Approach.* Oxford: Berg.

————. 1995. "Introduction: Anthropology, Modernity and Consumption." Pp. 1–22 in Daniel Miller, ed., *Worlds Apart: Modernity Through the Prism of the Local.* London: Routledge.

Minh-ha, Trinh. 1987. "Difference: A Special Third World Women Issue." *Feminist Review* 25: 5–22.

Mol, Frans. 1978. *Maa: A Dictionary of the Maasai Language and Folklore.* Nairobi: Marketing and Publishing.

————. 1981. "The Meaning and Concept in Maa of 'Enkai' (God)." AMECEA Apostolate to the Nomads 50. Nairobi.

Moore, Henrietta L. and Todd Sanders, eds. 2001a. *Magical Interpretations, Material Realities: Modernity, Witchcraft and the Occult in Postcolonial Africa.* London: Routledge.

————. 2001b. Magical Interpretations and Material Realities: An Introduction. Pp. 1–27 in Henrietta L. Moore and Todd Sanders eds., *Magical Interpretation, Material Realities: Modernity, Witchcraft and the Occult in Postcolonial Africa.* London: Routledge.

Morris, Rosalind. 2000. *In the Place of Origins: Modernity and Its Mediums in Northern Thailand.* Durham, N.C.: Duke University Press.

Oakeshott, Michael. 1962. *Rationalism in Politics and Other Essays.* London: Methuen.

Obeyesekere, Gananath. 2002. *Imagining Karma: Ethical Transformation in Amerindian, Buddhist, and Greek Rebirth.* Berkeley: University of California Press.

Ole Saibull, Solomon and Rachel Carr. 1981. *Herd and Spear: The Maasai of East Africa.* London: Collins and Harvill.

Ong, Aihwa. 1988. "Colonialism and Modernity: Feminist Re-presentations of Women in Non-Western Societies." *Inscriptions* 3 and 4: 79–93.

Oyewumi, Oyeronke. 1998. "De-Confounding Gender: Feminist Theorizing and Western Culture, a Comment on Hawkesworth's 'Confounding Gender'." *SIGNS* 23, 4: 1049–62.

Parkin, David.1992. "Ritual as Spatial Direction and Bodily Division." Pp. 11–25 in Daniel de Coppet, ed., *Understanding Rituals.* London: Routledge.

Parmentier, Richard J. 1994. *Signs in Society: Studies in Semiotic Anthropology.* Bloomington: Indiana University Press.

Peirce, Charles Sanders. 1931–35. *The Collected Papers of Charles Sanders Peirce.* Vols. 1–6. Ed. Charles Hartshorne and Paul Weiss. Cambridge, Mass.: Harvard University Press.

———. 1958 *Charles S. Peirce: Selected Writings.* Ed. Philip P. Wiener. New York: Dover.

Pels, Peter. 1998. "The Spirit of Matter: On Fetish, Rarity, Fact, and Fancy." Pp. 91–121 in Patricia Spyer, ed., *Border Fetishisms: Material Objects in Unstable Spaces.* New York: Routledge.

Penrose, Roger. 2000. *The Large, the Small and the Human Mind.* Cambridge: Cambridge University Press.

Peterson, David. 1971. "Demon Possession Among the Maasai." Unpublished paper.

Pinker, Steven. 1997. *How the Mind Works.* New York: Norton.

Priest, Doug, Jr. 1990. *Doing Theology with the Maasai.* Pasadena, Calif.: William Carey Library.

Radin, Paul. 1937. *Primitive Religion: Its Nature and Origin.* New York: Dover.

Random Samples. 2000. "Memories Are Made of This and That." *Science* 288, 5473 (June): 1961.

Rappaport, Roy. 1979. "The Obvious Aspects of Ritual" Pp. 173–221 in Roy Rappaport *Ecology, Meaning, and Religion.* Richmond: North Atlantic Books.

Rasmussen, Susan J. 1995. *Spirit Possession and Personhood Among the Kel Ewey Tuareg.* Cambridge: Cambridge University Press.

Republic of Kenya Ministry of Livestock Development (MOLD). 1992. *Range Management Handbook of Kenya*, vol. 2.2, *Samburu District.* Nairobi: Republic of Kenya Ministry of Agriculture.

Reyna, Stephen P. 2002. *Connections: Brain, Mind, and Culture in a Social Anthropology.* London: Routledge.

Rich, Adrienne. 1978. *The Dream of a Common Language: Poems, 1974–1977.* New York: Norton.

Ricoeur, Paul. 1973 *Phenomenology, Language, and the Social Sciences.* London: Routledge.

———. 1991. *From Text to Action: Essays in Hermeneutics II.* Trans. Kathleen Blamey and John B. Thompson. Evanston: Northwestern University Press.

———. 2004. *Memory, History, Forgetting.* Trans. Kathleen Blamey and David Pellauer. Chicago: University of Chicago Press.

Riesman, Paul. 1977. *Freedom in Fulani Social Life: An Introspective Ethnography.* Chicago: University of Chicago Press.

Rigby, Peter. 1992. *Cattle, Capitalism, and Class: Ilparakuyo Maasai Transformations.* Philadelphia: Temple University Press.

Rosaldo, Michelle Zimbalist. 1980. *Knowledge and Passion: Ilongot Notions of Self and Social Life.* Cambridge: Cambridge University Press.

Rosaldo, Renato. 1989. "Introduction: Grief and a Headhunter's Rage." Pp. 1–21 in Rosaldo, *Culture and Truth: The Remaking of Social Analysis.* Boston: Beacon Press.

Rouch, Jean. 2003. *Ciné-Ethnography.* Ed. and trans. Steven Feld. Visible Evidence 13. Minneapolis: University of Minnesota Press.

Rushdie, Salman. 1992. *Imaginary Homelands: Essays and Criticism, 1981–1991.* New York: Granta with Viking Penguin.

Russell, Tom. 2000. *Brain Death: Philosophical Concepts and Problems.* Aldershot: Ashgate.

Saitoti, Tepilit Ole (1986). *The Worlds of a Maasai Warrior: An Autobiography.* Berkeley: University of California Press.

Sallis, John. 1991. *Crossings: Nietzsche and the Space of Tragedy.* Chicago: University of Chicago Press.

Saussure, Ferdinand de. 1959. *Course in General Linguistics.* Ed. Charles Bally and Albert Sechehaye, trans. Wade Baskin. New York: McGraw-Hill.

Schacter, Daniel L. and Elaine Scarry, eds. 2000. *Memory, Brain, and Belief.* Cambridge, Mass.: Harvard University Press.

Schattschneider, Ellen. 2001. "Buy Me a Bride: Death and Exchange in Northern Japanese Bride-Doll Marriage." *American Ethnologist* 28, 4: 854–80.

Scheper-Hughes, Nancy. 1993. *Death Without Weeping: The Violence of Everyday Life in Brazil.* Berkeley: University of California Press.

———. 2000. "The Global Traffic in Human Organs." *Current Anthropology* 41, 2: 191–224.

Schiebinger, Londa. 2004. "Human Experimentation in the Eighteenth Century: Natural Boundaries and Valid Testing." Pp. 384–83 in Lorraine Daston and Fernando Vidal, eds., *The Moral Authority of Nature.* Chicago: University of Chicago Press.

Schlee, Günther. 1989. *Identities on the Move: Clanship and Pastoralism in Northern Kenya.* Manchester: Manchester University Press.

Schwenger, Peter. 2001. "Words and the Murder of the Thing." *Critical Inquiry* 28, 1: 99–113.

Sebeok, Thomas A. 1968. "Is a Comparative Semiotics Possible?" Pp. 614–27 in Jean Pouillon and Pierre Maranda, eds., *Échanges et communications: mélanges offerts à Claude Lévi-Strauss à l'occasion de son 60ème anniversaire.* The Hague: Mouton.

———. 1975. "Zoosemiotics: At the Intersection of Nature and Culture." Pp. 85–95 in Thomas Sebeok, *The Tell-Tale-Sign.* Lisse, Netherlands: Peter de Ridder.

———. 2001. *Global Semiotics.* Bloomington: Indiana University Press.

Sered, Susan Starr. 1996. *Priestess, Mother, Sacred Sister: Religions Dominated by Women.* Oxford: Oxford University Press.

Seremetakis, C. Nadia. 1991. *The Last Word: Women, Death, and Divination in Inner Mani.* Chicago: University of Chicago Press.

———. 1994. *The Senses Still: Perception and Memory as Material Culture in Modernity.* Boulder, Colo.: Westview Press.

Shanafelt, Robert. 2004. "Magic, Miracle, and Marvels in Anthropology." *Ethnos* 69, 3: 317–40.

Sharp, Lesley A. 2001. "Commodified Kin: Death, Mourning, and Competing Claims on Organ Donors in the United States." *American Anthropologist* 103, 1: 112–33.

Shastri, Lokendra. 1996. "Temporal Synchrony, Dynamic Bindings, and SHRUTI: A Representational But Non-Classical Model of Reflexive Reasoning." *Behavioral and Brain Sciences* 19, 2: 331–37.

Shelley, Mary. 1984 [1818]. *Frankenstein.* New York: Bantam Classics.

Sheriff, John K. 1989. *The Fate of Meaning: Charles Peirce, Structuralism, and Literature.* Princeton, N.J.: Princeton University Press.

Sobania, Neal. 1991. "Feasts, Famines and Friends: Nineteenth Century Exchange and Ethnicity in the Eastern Lake Turkana Region," Pp. 118–42 in John G. Galaty and Pierre Bonte, eds., *Herders, Warriors, and Traders: Pastoralism in East Africa.* Boulder, Colo.: Westview Press

————. 1993. "Defeat and Dispersal: The Laikipiak and Their Neighbors in the Nineteenth Century." Pp. 105–19 in Thomas Spear and Richard Waller, eds., *Being Maasai: Ethnicity and Identity in East Africa.* London: James Currey.

Sowa, John F. 1997. "Matching logical structure to linguistic structure," Pp. 418–44 in Nathan Houser, Don D. Roberts, and James Van Evra, eds., *Studies in the Logic of Charles Sanders Peirce.* Bloomington: Indiana University Press.

————. 2000. "Ontology, Metadata, and Semiotics." Pp. 55–81 in Bernhard Ganter and Guy W. Mineau, eds., *Conceptual Structures: Logical, Linguistic, and Computational Issues.* Lecture Notes in Artificial Intelligence: Subseries of Lecture Notes in Computer Science 1867. Berlin: Springer.

Spear, Thomas. 1993a. "Being 'Maasai', But Not 'People of Cattle': Arusha Agricultural Maasai in the Nineteenth Century." Pp. 120–36 in Thomas Spear and Richard Waller, eds., *Being Maasai: Ethnicity and Identity in East Africa.* London: James Currey.

1993b. "Introduction." Pp. 1–18 in Thomas Spear and Richard Waller, eds., *Being Maasai: Ethnicity and Identity in East Africa.* London: James Currey.

Spear, Thomas and Richard Waller, eds.. 1993. *Being Maasai: Ethnicity and Identity in East Africa.* London: James Currey.

Spencer, Paul. 1965. *Samburu: A Study of Gerontocracy in a Nomadic Tribe.* Berkeley: University of California Press.

————. 1988 *The Maasai of Matapato: A Study of Rituals of Rebellion.* Bloomington: Indiana University Press.

Sperling, David. 1995. "The Frontiers of Prophecy: Healing, the Cosmos and Islam on the East African Coast in the Nineteenth Century." Pp. 83–101 in David M. Anderson and Douglas H. Johnson, eds., *Revealing Prophets: Prophecy in Eastern African History.* London: James Currey.

Spivak, Gayatri. 1981. "French Feminism in an International Frame." *Yale French Studies* 62: 159–64.

Spyer, Patricia. 1998a. "Introduction." Pp. 1–11 in Patricia Spyer, ed., *Border Fetishisms: Material Objects in Unstable Spaces.* New York: Routledge

Spyer, Patricia, ed. 1998b. *Border Fetishisms: Material Objects in Unstable Spaces.* New York: Routledge.

Stallybrass, Peter. 1998. "Marx's Coat." Pp. 183–207 in Patricia Spyer, ed., *Border Fetishisms: Material Objects in Unstable Spaces.* New York: Routledge.

Stern, Daniel N. 1985. *The Interpersonal World of the Infant: A View from Psychoanalysis and Developmental Psychology.* New York: Basic Books.

————. 1990 *Diary of a Baby.* New York: Basic Books.

Stewart, Kathleen. 1996. *A Space on the Side of the Road.* Princeton, N.J.: Princeton University Press.

————. 2005. "Still Life" Pp. 27–44 in Bilinda Straight, ed., *Women on the Verge of Home.* Albany: State University of New York Press.

Stewart, Pamela J. and Andrew Strathern. 2000. "Body and Mind in Mount Hagen, Highlands Papua New Guinea." *Anthropology of Consciousness* 11, 3–4: 25–39.

Stewart, Susan. 1993. *On Longing: Narratives of the Miniature, the Gigantic, the Souvenir, the Collection.* Durham, N.C.: Duke University Press.

Stoks, Hans. 1989. "A Perception of Reality with an East-Nilotic People." Paper presented at First Joint Symposium of Philosophers from Africa and from the Netherlands, Rotterdam, March 10, 1989.

Stoler, Ann. 1989. "Making Empire Respectable: Race and Sexual Morality in Early 20th Century Colonial Cultures." *American Ethnologist* 16, 4: 634–60.

Stoller, Paul. 1989a. *Fusion of the Worlds: An Ethnography of Possession Among the Songhay of Niger.* Chicago: University of Chicago Press.

————. 1989b. *The Taste of Ethnographic Things: The Senses in Anthropology.* Philadelphia: University of Pennsylvania Press.

————. 1992. *The Cinematic Griot: The Ethnography of Jean Rouch.* Chicago: University of Chicago Press.

1994. *Embodying Colonial Memories: Spirit Possession, Power, and the Hauka in West Africa.* New York: Routledge.

————. 1997. *Sensuous Scholarship.* Philadelphia: University of Pennsylvania Press.

————. 2004. *Stranger in the Village of the Sick: A Memoir of Cancer, Sorcery, and Healing.* Boston: Beacon Press.

Stoller, Paul and Cheryl Olkes. 1987. *In Sorcery's Shadow: A Memoir of Apprenticeship Among the Songhay of Niger.* Chicago: University of Chicago Press.

Straight, Bilinda. 1997a. "Gender, Work, and Change Among Samburu Pastoralists of Northern Kenya." *Research in Economic Anthropology* 18: 65–91.

————. 1997b. "Altered Landscapes, Shifting Strategies: The Politics of Location in the Constitution of Gender, Belief, and Identity Among Samburu Pastoralists in Northern Kenya." Ph.D. dissertation, University of Michigan, Ann Arbor.

————. 1999. "Gendering God: Sacred Spaces and Mundane Objects Among the Samburu of Northern Kenya." Paper presented in session "Gendering Objects," 98th Annual Meeting of the American Anthropological Association, Chicago, November.

————. 2000. "Development Ideologies and Local Knowledge Among Samburu Women in Northern Kenya." Pp. 227–48 in Dorothy Hodgson, ed., *Rethinking Pastoralism in Africa: Gender, Culture, and the Myth of the Patriarchal Pastoralist.* Oxford: James Currey.

————. 2002a. "From Samburu Heirloom to New Age Artifact: The Cross-Cultural Consumption of Mporo Marriage Beads." *American Anthropologist* 104, 1: 1–15.

————. 2002b. "Introduction." Special Issue, *Conflict at the Center of Ethnography. Anthropology and Humanism* 27, 1: 3–9.

————. 2005a. "Cutting Time: Beads, Sex, and Songs in the Making of Samburu Memory." Pp. 267–83 in Wendy James and David Mills, eds., *The Qualities of Time: Temporal Dimensions of Social Form and Human Experience.* ASA Monograph Series. Oxford: Berg.

————. 2005b. "In the Belly of History: Memory, Forgetting, and the Hazards of Reproduction." *Africa* 75, 1: 83–104.

————. 2005c. "Introduction." Pp. 1–25 in Bilinda Straight, ed., *Women on the Verge of Home.* Albany: State University of New York Press.

————. 2006. "A World-Creating Approach to Belief." In James B. White, ed., *How Should We Talk About Religion: Perspectives, Contexts, Particularities.* South Bend, Ind.: University of Notre Dame Press.

————. Unpublished. "Hegemonic Pens, Subaltern Voices: Constructions of Kenyan and Maasai Identity in the Colonial and Post-Independence Periods." University of Michigan, Ann Arbor, 1991.

Strathern, Andrew. 1982. "Witchcraft, Greed, Cannibalism and Death. Pp. 111–33 in Maurice Bloch and Jonathan Parry, eds., *Death and the Regeneration of Life.* Cambridge: Cambridge University Press.

————. 1996 *Body Thoughts.* Ann Arbor: University of Michigan Press.

Strathern, Andrew and Michael Lambek. 1998. "Introduction: Embodying Sociality: Africanist-Melanesianist Comparisons." Pp. 1–25 in Michael Lambek
and Andrew Strathern, eds., *Bodies and Persons: Comparative Perspectives From
Africa and Melanesia.* Cambridge: Cambridge University Press.
Strathern, Marilyn. 1988. *The Gender of the Gift: Problems with Women and Problems
with Society in Melanesia.* Berkeley: University of California Press.
————. 1993. "Making Incomplete." Pp. 41–51 in Vigdis Broch-Due, Ingrid
Rudie, and Tone Bleie, eds., *Carved Flesh/Cast Selves: Gendered Symbols and Social
Practices.* Oxford: Berg.
Tablino, Paul. 1999. *The Gabra: Camel Nomads of Northern Kenya.* Limuru, Kenya:
Paulines Publications.
Talle, Aud. 1988. *Women at a Loss: Changes in Maasai Pastoralism and Their Effects
on Gender Relations.* Stockholm Studies in Social Anthropology. Department of
Social Anthropology, University of Stockholm.
Tambiah, Stanley Jeyaraja. 1990. *Magic, Science, Religion, and the Scope of Rational-
ity.* Cambridge: Cambridge University Press.
Taussig, Michael. 1993. *Mimesis and Alterity: A Particular History of the Senses.* Lon-
don: Routledge.
Tebb, William and Perry. Vollum. 1905. *Premature Burial and How It May be Pre-
vented.* 2nd ed. London: Swan Sonnenschein.
Thomas, Nicholas. 1991. *Entangled Objects: Exchange, Material Culture, and Colo-
nialism in the Pacific.* Cambridge, Mass.: Harvard University Press.
Time Magazine. 1967. "Dressing Up the Maasai." 90, 21, November 24.
Tsing, Anna Lowenhaupt. 1993. *In the Realm of the Diamond Queen: Marginality in
an Out-of-the-Way Place.* Princeton, N.J.: Princeton University Press.
————. 1994. "From the Margins." *Cultural Anthropology* 9, 3: 279–97.
Turner, Edith with William Blodgett. 1992. *Experiencing Ritual: A New Interpreta-
tion of African Healing.* Philadelphia: University of Pennsylvania Press.
Turner, Mark. 1996. *The Literary Mind.* Oxford: Oxford University Press.
Turner, Victor. 1969. *The Ritual Process: Structure and Anti-Structure.* Chicago:
Aldine.
Ulin, Robert. 2001. *Understanding Cultures: Perspectives in Anthropology and Social
Theory.* 2nd ed. Oxford: Blackwell.
Van Gennep, Arnold. 1960. *The Rites of Passage.* Chicago: University of Chicago
Press.
Van Der Veer, Peter. 2001. *Imperial Encounters: Religion and Modernity in India and
Britain.* Princeton, N.J.: Princeton University Press.
Vidal, Fernando. 2002. Brains, Bodies, Selves, and Science: Anthropologies of
Identity and the Resurrection of the Body. *Critical Inquiry* 28 (Summer):
930–71.
Voshaar, Jan. 1998. *Maasai: Between the Oreteti-Tree and the Tree of the Cross.* Kam-
pen, The Netherlends: Kok.
Wagner, Anthony D., Daniel L. Schacter, et al. 1998. "Building Memories:
Remembering and Forgetting of Verbal Experiences as Predicted by Brain
Activity." *Science* 281, 5380 (August): 1188–91.
Wagner, Stephen. 1998. *A Short Grammar and Lexicon of the Samburu Language.*
Nairobi: Evangelical Lutheran Church in Kenya.
Waldby, Catherine. 2000. *The Visible Human Project: Informatic Bodies and Posthu-
man Medicine.* New York: Routledge.
Waller, Richard. 1985. "Economic and Social Relations in the Central Rift Val-
ley: The Maa-Speakers and Their Neighbors in the Nineteenth Century," Pp.

83–151 in Bethel A. Ogot, ed., *Kenya in the Nineteenth Century*. Nairobi: Book-wise.

———. 1995. "Kidongoi's Kin: Prophecy and Power in Masailand." Pp. 28–64 in David M. Anderson and Douglas H. Johnson, eds., *Revealing Prophets: Prophecy in Eastern African History*. London: James Currey.

Waller, Richard and Neal W. Sobania. 1994. "Pastoralism in Historical Perspective," Pp. 45–68 in Elliot Fratkin, Kathleen A. Galvin, and Eric Abella Roth, eds., *African Pastoralist Systems: An Integrated Approach*. Boulder, Colo.: Lynne Rienner.

Ward, Benedicta. 1987. *Miracles and the Medieval Mind: Theory, Record and Event 1000–1215*. Philadelphia: University of Pennsylvania Press.

Weiner, Annette. 1992. *Inalienable Possessions: The Paradox of Keeping-While-Giving*. Berkeley: University of California Press.

Weiss, Brad. 1996. *The Making and Unmaking of the Haya Lived World: Consumption, Commoditization, and Everyday Practice*. Durham, N.C.: Duke University Press.

———. 1998. "Electric Vampires: Haya Rumors of the Commodified Body." Pp. 172–94 in Michael Lambek and Andrew Strathern, eds., *Bodies and Persons: Comparative Perspectives from Africa and Melanesia*. Cambridge: Cambridge University Press.

Winch, Peter. 1964. "Understanding a Primitive Society." Pp. 78–112 in Bryan R. Wilson, ed., *Rationality*. Oxford: Blackwell.

Žižek, Slavoj. 2004. *Organs Without Bodies: Deleuze and Consequences*. New York: Routledge.

Zuckert, Catherine H. 1996. *Postmodern Platos: Nietzsche, Heidegger, Gadamer, Strauss, Derrida*. Chicago: University of Chicago Press.

Index

adornment, 19, 21, 31, 39, 41, 51, 54, 58, 61–66, 70–71, 74, 84–85, 87, 90, 122–24, 222 n. 20, 226 n. 41, 227 n. 6, 232 n. 9. *See* also cloth, clothing

adultery, 60–61, 116, 127, 227 n. 9

aduŋ. *See* cutting

afterlife, 154–55, 160–61, 172–73. *See* also ghost; soul; supernatural; vampire

agency, 100–102, 139, 211, 235 n. 11

ageset system, 19, 29–31, 75, 96

alienability, alienation, 71, *See also* inalienability

ancestor veneration, 100–102, 162–66. *See* also mortuary practices

Anderson, David, 220 n. 7, 237 nn. 7, 9

angel, 155–56. *See* also soul; supernatural

Appadurai, Arjun, 72, 92, 187

Aquinas, Thomas, 139–40

Ariaal, 35

atonement. *See* sacrifice

Augustine, Saint, 23, 144

Bahktin, Mikhail, 95, 180

BCMS. *See* Christianity, Anglican

Beauvoir, Simone de, 95, 223 n. 10

Being, 6, 110–12, 115, 183, 187, 196, 198–200, 202–5, 212–13, 239 n. 7, 240 nn.11, 1, 243 n. 22

Bible Churchmen's Missionary Society (BCMS). *See* Christianity, Anglican

biomedicine, Western, 81, 144–48, 150, 235 nn. 12, 15, 236 n.22. *See also* hospitals

birthing, 50–51, 76, 80, 86–87, 94, 118, 227 nn. 1, .7, 232 n. 8

blacksmiths. *See* Lkunono

"blessings" (mayian), 96–97, 99, 103–4, 116, 158, 165–66, 168, 233 n. 16

body, 24, 41–44, 54, 81, 86, 94, 112–13, 133–34, 138–40, 144–45, 158, 160, 180, 182–85, 212–13, 223 n. 10, 228 n. 20,

230 n. 13, 234 n. 7, 235 nn. 12, 13, 240 n.1, 241 n. 4, 242 n. 14, 243 n. 20

Bourdieu, Pierre, 42, 180, 208, 211–12, 220 n. 3, 239 n. 7, 240 n. 1

boys (and sons), 22, 28–29, 35–36, 39, 49, 85–87, 102–3, 105, 107, 115–17, 162–63, 167–68, 228 n. 25

brain death, 145–48, 151, 236 n. 22

"breath," 97–98, 100, 159, 237 nn. 10, 16

Broch-Due, Vigdis, 43, 161, 223 n. 9, 227 n. 10, 233 nn. 12, 15, 237 n. 9

Brown, Bill, 181–82

burial, 120, 122–23, 148–51, 233 n. 18, 234 n. 2, 235 n. 16; premature, 137, 144, 234 n. 10, *See also* mortuary practices

Butler, Judith, 42–43, 182, 223 n. 10, 224 n.12, 230 n. 2

calabash, 11, 41, 58, 63–66, 76, 84, 88, 119, 124, 165, 168, 171, 226 n. 38, 228 n. 23, 237 n. 15

cameras. *See* photography

cannibalism, 11, 81, 89, 91, 228 n. 18, 231 n. 23, 238 n. 21

capitalism, 7, 63, 65, 72–73, 92–93, 108–9, 139, 181, 189, 233 n. 23. *See also* commodities

Carter, Rita, 206, 209, 213, 236 n. 23, 242 n. 14, 244 nn. 26, 28, 245 n. 33

Christianity, 7, 20, 23, 29, 41, 45–53, 62–63, 90, 106, 130, 133–40, 143–44, 148–49, 155, 159, 171, 224 nn. 16, 17, 225 nn. 22, 25, 229 n. 29, 231 n. 18, 234 n. 7, 236 n. 2, 237 n.16; Anglican, 45; Catholic, 45, 63, 141; medieval, 135–41, 234 nn. 8, 9

Cinderella, Samburu parallel to, 162–63

cloth, clothing, 41, 58, 62–63, 66, 70. *See also* adornment

cognition, 184–85, 199, 203, 206–8, 242 nn. 13, 14, 243 nn. 18, 21, 245 n. 33

cognitive science. *See* neuroscience

colonialism, 7, 26, 41, 57–59, 61, 70–71, 73
Comaroff, Jean and John, 6, 23, 80, 189,
    221 n. 15, 235 n. 14, 236 n. 8.1
commodities, 11, 59, 63–64, 72–73, 89–92,
    113, 128, 139, 145. See also capitalism
consciousness, 145, 180, 184–87, 197, 199,
    208, 210–13, 242 n. 13, 244 n. 26
consumption. See tuberculosis
corpse, treatment of, 118, 122–23, 134–35,
    139, 145, 163–64, 166, 169, 233 n. 16,
    234 n. 6, 235 n. 15
creation stories, 50–51
Csordas, Thomas, 220 n. 4, 230 n. 6, 231 n.
    18, 239 n. 7
"curses," 96–100, 102–6, 109, 116, 158,
    165–68, 230 n. 10, 233 n. 16
cuts, logic of. See cutting
cutting, 8, 10, 21–22, 25, 70, 81, 113, 118–
    20, 126, 153–54, 175–76, 183, 211–13,
    220 n. 3, 221 n. 10, 232 n. 9

Daniel, E. Valentine, 17, 127, 220 n. 4, 242
    n. 5
daughters. See girls
death: of children, 1–2, 120, 123, 130–31,
    135–37, 154, 168–69, 175–76, 197, 225
    nn. 29, 31, 237 n. 14; of old people, 120,
    123–24, 161–68, 174–76; of youth, 121,
    169–70, 173, 175–76, 237 n. 14. See also
    brain death; burial; corpse; mortuary
    practices
debts, 105–6
Derrida, Jacques, 16, 42, 95, 100–102, 112,
    128, 180, 187, 195–200, 202–3, 205, 239
    n. 4, 241 n. 4
Descartes, René, 12, 177, 188, 195, 201, 243
    n. 20
development, 59, 222 n. 22, 228 n. 26
Dinka, 50–51, 220 n. 6, 221 n.13, 222 n. 1,
    225 nn 3.23, 27, 228 n. 25, 233 n. 19
Divine Breath. See Holy Spirit
divinity, abstract, 7, 10, 14–15, 23, 37–41,
    44, 46, 48, 50, 102; Christian (God), 45–
    48, 53, 222 n. 1, 226 n. 42, 232 n. 9
division, logic of. See cutting
Douglas, Mary, 43, 219 n. 3, 224 n. 11
dreams, 110–12, 157, 167–68, 172
dualism, 12, 24, 41–42, 44, 93–94, 112–13,
    118, 128, 138–40, 144, 180, 182–85, 195,
    205, 223 n. 10, 228 n. 20, 229 n. 26, 231

n. 22, 239 n. 8, 241 n. 4, 242 n. 14, 243
    n. 20

Eco, Umberto, 25, 202–5, 210, 232 n. 27,
    241 n. 3, 243 n. 22, 244 n. 29
education, 27–28, 35–36, 222 n. 21
embodiment. See body
emotion. See "stomach"
Evans-Pritchard, Edward Evan, 49, 166, 219
    n. 3, 229 n. 26, 238 n. 22
exchange, 72, 83–86, 91, 230 n. 8
experience: expansive, 8, 10, 15, 24, 113,
    115, 185, 201, 213, 240 n. 11; extraordi-
    nary, 7, 10, 130, 142, 154, 221 nn. 12, 13,
    238 n. 22

Fabian, Johannes, 180, 244 n. 27
famine, 47, 60–61
fathers, 85, 102, 105, 107, 228 n. 25
fecundity. See fertility
fertility, 74–80, 82, 87–88, 95, 124, 227 nn.
    7, 8, 232 n. 7. See also fire
fire (house), 74–76, 79, 83–84
food practices, 19, 29, 35, 80, 86, 89, 97,
    104–7, 116, 157, 162, 164–66, 168, 170,
    178–79, 228 n. 18, 231 nn. 20, 24, 233 n.
    6.20
foragers. See Ltorrobo
forgetting, 21, 208, 211–13, 220 n. 3, 244
    nn. 27, 31, 245 nn. 32, 33. See also
    memory
Frankenstein (Shelley), 145, 235 n. 7.15
Fratkin, Elliot, 27, 35, 220 n. 7, 223 nn. 3,
    4, 237 n. 7

Gabra, 157, 237 n..9
Geertz, Clifford, 220 n. 10, 221 n. 12
gender, 35, 41–45, 48–54, 74, 83, 95, 107,
    118–19, 223 n. 10, 224 nn. 12, 13, 17, 20,
    225 nn. 22, 23, 24, 30, 226 nn. 37, 44,
    227 n. 10, 233 nn. 12, 21
ghost, 159, 167–70, 173–74, 238 n. 8.22
Giles, Linda, 110, 157–58
girls (and daughters), 21–22, 28, 31, 35–36,
    39, 49, 54–55, 60–61, 80, 84, 86–87, 97,
    107, 130–31, 222 n. 19, 224 n. 18, 228 n.
    25, 236 n. 4
globalization, 7, 59, 92, 187
"God." See divinity
grandparents, 102–3, 119–22, 164–68,
    174–76, 220 n. 20, 226 n. 44

grief. *See* mourning

Grosz, Elizabeth, 43, 182, 223 nn. 9, 10, 224 n. 12

ground (Peircean), 197, 210–13, 244 nn. 29, 30

Gupta, Akhil, 113, 232 n. 5.28

habitus, 41, 184, 208, 211, 213, 220 n. 3, 239 n. 7, 240 n. 1

Hameroff, Stuart, 209–10

"hau," 72–73

healers. *See* loibonok

"heart," 97–98, 100, 151, 155, 158–60, 230 n. 13, 235 n. 19, 236 nn. 2, 4

"heaven," 55, 59, 69, 170, 172

Heidegger, Martin, 6, 95, 202, 205–6, 240 n. 1, 243 n. 19

Hodgson, Dorothy, 35, 50, 110, 155–58, 225 n. 26, 226 n. 43, 235 n.16, 236 nn. 2, 5, 238 n. 26

Holtzman, Jon, 7, 19, 27, 30, 32, 35, 92, 107, 126, 176, 222 n. 24, 231 n. 20, 235 n. 17, 237 n. 17

Holy Spirit (Divine Breath), 159, 224 n. 16, 236 n. 2

hospitals, 148–51, 168, 235 nn. 20, 21. *See also* biomedicine

house: Samburu, 33–34, 39, 74, 226 n. 34; "modern" (mabati), 33, 39, 41, 59, 65

hyena(s), 14, 121–22, 131–32, 160–61, 231 n. 20, 233 n. 18, 234 n. 2

identity, 20, 57, 65, 70, 235 n. 12. *See also* subjectivity

imagination, imaginary, 13, 73, 128, 154, 181–82, 187–89, 219 n. 6

immediacy, 180–82, 184, 186, 189, 200–202, 208, 211–13

inalienability, 71–73, 83–86, 89, 227 n. 5; fictitious, 71

incest, 60–61, 116, 127, 227 n. 9

intersubjectivity, 11, 81, 86, 92, 95–96, 101–2, 106–7, 109, 112–13, 115, 128, 159, 181, 184, 188, 205, 211–12, 224 n.15, 230 n. 8. *See* identity; subjectivity

Islam, 12, 157–58

Jackson, Michael, 95, 184, 220 n. 4, 226 nn. 39, 40, 229 n. 32, 230 nn. 6, 9, 239 nn. 7, 8, 244 n. 23

Jakobson, Roman, 202, 242 n. 12

jinn, 157–58. *See also* soul

Johnson, Douglas, 220 n. 7, 237 n. 9

Johnson, Mark, 206–7, 243 n. 18

Kant, Immanuel, 15, 220 n. 3, 243 n. 20

Kapferer, Bruce, 219 n. 2, 228 n. 26, 229 nn. 28, 32

karma, 112–13

Keane, Webb, 15–17, 72, 100–102

Kratz, Corinne, 20–22, 232 n. 9

Kristeva, Julia, 52, 94, 96, 180–87, 223 n. 10, 224 nn. 11, 12, 227 n. 3, 230 n. 1, 239 nn. 4, 7

Lacan, Jacques, 5, 13, 94–95, 128, 180–81, 185–88, 197–98, 227 n. 3, 233 n. 22, 240 n. 11

Lacoff, George, 206–7, 243 n. 18

language, 42, 48–49, 51, 113, 118, 158, 184, 186, 195–200, 203–7, 215–17, 222 n. 19, 223 n. 5, 224 n. 20, 225 nn. 21, 22, 227 n. 7, 232 nn. 4, 5, 6, 8, 10, 11, 234 n. 1, 235 nn. 18, 19, 21, 236 n. 2, 240 n. 1, 241 nn. 2, 4, 242 n. 7, 244 n. 22

ldeket. *See* "curses"

Lienhardt, Godfrey, 51, 220 n. 6, 221 n. 13, 222 n. 1, 225 nn. 23, 27, 228 nn. 15, 25, 233 n. 19, 237 n. 10

Lkunono (blacksmiths), 20

Lmurran, 29–32, 39, 60–62, 80, 116, 121, 124–27, 169, 173, 234 n. 4, 236 n. 4

Lock, Margaret, 145–46, 151, 234 n. 10, 235 n. 15, 236 n. 22

loibonok, nkoibonok, 5, 14–15, 18–19, 41, 56, 69, 87, 104, 107, 127, 133, 170–72, 219 n. 1, 220 n. 7, 222 n. 2, 226 nn. 35, 38, 237 n. 7, 238 nn. 24, 25, 26

ltau. *See* "heart"

ltoilo. *See* "voice"

Ltorrobo (foragers), 20, 50

Maasai, 21–22, 49–52, 62–63, 106, 154–58, 171, 177, 216, 223 n. 6, 225 nn. 21, 22, 24, 25, 226 n. 43, 228 n. 21, 230 n. 10, 232 nn. 4, 9, 235 n. 16, 236 nn. 2, 3, 5, 7, 237 n. 18, 238 nn. 25, 26

"magic," 85, 221 n. 12, 228 n. 26, 229 n. 28

Mannheim, Bruce, 17, 230 n. 5, 238 n. 2

marginality, 42, 239 n. 10, 240 n. 12

marriage, 19, 21, 28, 31–32, 60, 74–76, 82–83, 90, 97, 107, 120

Marx, Karl, 70–72, 181, 227 n. 5
materiality, 16, 71–73, 169, 181–82, 227 n.
    5, 235 n..11, 238 n. 21
Mauss, Marcel, 71–72, 227 n. 5, 236 n. 7,
    240 n. 1
mayian. *See* "blessings"
medicine. *See* biomedicine
memory, remembering, 73, 176, 186, 189,
    197, 208, 211–13, 219 n. 6, 230 n. 13,
    239 n. 10, 244 nn. 27, 31, 245 nn. 32, 33.
    See also forgetting
men. *See* boys; fathers; gender; grand-
    parents; lmurran; marriage
Merleau-Ponty, Maurice, 95, 206, 239 n. 7,
    243 n. 19
Mijikenda, 157–58
mind, 41–42, 44, 112–13, 138–40, 144, 155,
    180, 182–85, 195, 228 n. 20, 230 n. 13,
    241 n. 2, 242 n. 14, 243 n. 20
missions, missionaries. *See* Christianity
modernity, 59, 66, 188–89, 228 n. 26
Mol, Frans, 49, 216, 225 nn. 22, 30, 237 n.
    11
Moore, Henrietta, 180, 228 n. 26
mortuary practices, 119–24, 149–50, 155,
    163–64, 233 nn. 15, 19, 20, 234 n. 6, 235
    n. 17, 238 n. 21. *See also* burial; corpse
mothers, 39–40, 84–85, 102, 105, 107, 118,
    150–51, 162–63, 167–68, 182–83, 185,
    222 nn. 19, 20, 225 nn. 29, 31, 33, 226 n.
    44, 227 n. 1, 228 n. 25
mourning, and grief, 124–25, 127, 143,
    154, 168–69, 176
murder, 115–17, 126–27, 233 n. 2

negativity (Kristevan), 94, 183
neurobiology. *See* neuroscience
neuroscience, 140, 206–8, 220 n. 3, 221 n.
    10, 242 n. 14, 244 nn. 26, 27, 245 nn. 31,
    32, 33
New England, 143
nkiyeŋet. *See* "breath"
nkosheke. *See* "stomach"
Nuer, 49–50

Obeyesekere, Gananath, 112
objects. *See* materiality
ontology, 43–44, 58, 112–13, 130–31, 138–
    40, 144, 148, 150, 159, 197–213, 224 n.
    11, 225 n. 24, 239 n. 7, 240 n. 11, 241 nn.
    4, 5, 242 n. 16, 243 n. 17

organ donation, 145–48, 236 n. 22
other, otherness, 26, 66, 113, 221 n. 15, 226
    n. 45, 230 n. 1, 240 n. 12
Oyewumi, 223 n. 10, 224 n. 20

Parmentier, Richard, 203–4, 242 n. 5
Peirce, Charles Sanders, 8, 16–17, 183–84,
    197–213, 220 n. 3, 221 n. 10, 224 nn. 12,
    14, 239 n. 5, 241 n. 5, 242 nn. 6, 7, 8, 8,
    10, 15, 16, 243 nn. 17, 18, 244 n. 29
Pels, Peter, 110, 243 n. 20
Penrose, Sir Roger, 209–11, 244 n. 28
person, personhood, 60, 66, 81, 86, 88, 92–
    93, 95–96, 113–15, 119, 123, 138–40,
    144, 151–52, 158–61, 168–69, 175–76,
    180, 230 n. 8, 233 n. 12, 237 n. 15
phenomenology, phenomenological turn
    in anthropology, 8, 95, 185, 239 nn. 7, 8,
    240 n. 11, 244 nn. 22, 23, 25
photography, 160–61, 169–70, 190–92, 237
    nn. 14, 15, 240 nn. 13, 14
physics, quantum, 209–11
Pido, Donna (Klumpp), 21–22, 232 n. 9
Plato, 196, 239 n. 4
Pokot, 30, 221 n. 18, 223 n. 6, 237 n. 7
postcolonialism, 7, 11, 41, 95
prescissing, 8, 15, 25, 44, 60, 70, 91, 96, 113,
    118, 133, 159, 176, 183, 193, 200, 210,
    212–13, 231 n. 22, 242 n. 10
prophets, prophetesses. *See* loibonok

race, 57–60, 223 n. 8, 226 nn. 38, 39, 40, 45
Real (Lacanian), 5, 185–88, 197–98, 201,
    205, 240 n. 11
reality, 44, 112–13, 115, 176, 181–82, 200,
    205, 209–13, 224 n. 15, 228 n. 26, 231 n.
    22
reanimation, 138–45, 221 n. 12. *See also*
    organ donation; vampires
reincarnation, 112–13, 232 n. 29
relics (medieval), 139, 145
Rendille, 21, 90, 157, 230 n. 14
revenants. *See* vampires
Rosaldo, Renato, 220 n. 5, 234 n. 3, 236 n. 1
Rouch, Jean, 240 nn. 13, 14

sacrifice: animal, 55, 86, 104, 108, 116–17,
    120, 122, 160, 163, 165, 167–68, 228 n.
    23, 233 nn. 15, 16, 20; human, 18–19,
    127, 133, 220 n. 6
Sanders, Todd, 180, 228 n. 26

Saussure, Ferdinand de, 195–99, 241 nn. 2, 4

Schlee, Gunter, 221 n. 9, 237 n. 9

school. *See* education

selfishness, 60–61, 97, 178–99

Seremetakis, Nadia, 130, 141, 147, 154, 168, 236 n. 1

sex, sexuality, 42–44, 54, 187, 223 n. 10, 224 nn. 13, 17, 19, 226 n. 37, 237 n. 13

sharing, 65, 97, 233 n. 23

Sharp, Lesley, 146–47

shaving, 124–26

Shelley, Mary, 145, 235 n. 7.15

signs, 9, 15–7, 24, 94, 100–102, 158–59, 180, 182–85, 195–208, 219 n. 3, 220 n. 5, 227 n. 13, 230 n. 11, 234 n. 6, 239 n. 5, 241 n. 4, 242 nn. 6, 7, 8, 9, 11

smell, 37–38, 79–82, 85, 116–17, 119–22, 129, 155, 174–75, 211, 223 n. 5, 228 n. 19, 242 n. 13, 245 n. 33

Sobania, Neil, 20, 237 n. 7

sons. *See* boys

soul, spirit, 138–40, 151–52, 154–59, 235 n. 13, 236 n. 2, 237 n. 16. *See also* afterlife; ghos; loip; supernatural; vampire

Spencer, Paul, 30, 50, 96, 106, 125, 154–55, 221 n. 17, 225 n. 24, 230 n. 10

Sperling, David, 157–58, 237 n. 8

spirit. *See* soul

spirit possession, 109–10, 155–58, 171, 236 n. 5, 238 n. 26

Stoller, Paul, 191–92, 219 n. 4, 220 n. 4, 221 n. 12, 223 nn. 7, 8, 226 nn. 39, 42, 228 n. 19, 230 nn. 6, 9, 232 n. 3, 235 n. 20, 240 n. 14

"stomach," 96–100, 102–3, 109, 116, 158, 225 n. 31, 233 n. 16; emotion generally, 236 n. 1

Strathern, Andrew, 162, 235 n. 14

Strathern, Marilyn, 72, 223 n. 10, 230 n. 7

structuralism, 118, 240 n.1

subjectivity, 86, 93–94, 180, 182–88, 211–12, 239 n. 9.7. *See* also identity; intersubjectivity; personhood

supernatural, 138, 141–44, 154–55. *See* also afterlife; angel; ghost; soul; vampire

Talle, Aud, 35, 63, 222 n. 23

tape recorders, 160–61, 169–70, 237 n. 14

Tedlock, Dennis, 17, 230 n. 5, 238 n. 2

theft, and unpropitiousness, 72, 86–90

tobacco, 120–21, 162–64, 166–67, 237 nn. 17, 18

tuberculosis, 143

Turkana, 21, 107, 157, 161, 227 n. 10, 230 n. 10, 233 nn. 12, 15, 237 nn. 7, 9

Turner, Mark, 206–7

vampires, 11, 141–44. *See also* reanimation

Vidal, Fernando, 138, 140, 235 n. 13

violence, domestic. *See* murder

Visible Human Project, 148

"voice," 97–98, 100, 159–61, 169–70, 237 n. 16

Voshaar, Jan, 49–52, 106, 216, 225 nn. 30, 31, 230 n. 10, 237 nn. 9, 18

wage labor, 27, 32, 35, 65–66

Waldby, Catherine, 148

Waller, Richard, 20

warriors. *See* lmurran

Weiner, Annette, 72, 85, 227 n. 5

Weiss, Brad, 92, 229 n.33

"witchcraft," 22, 85, 229 n. 26, 32, 230 nn. 9, 10

witness, philosophical implications of, 6, 24, 128, 176, 189, 192

women. *See* birthing; gender; girls; marriage; mothers; grandparents